SHERRY EHRHARDT
"THE WATCH LADY"

WANTS TO BUY
YOUR OLD
WRISTWATCHES

NAWCC # 081357

PATEK
VACHERON
ROLEX
CARTIER
MOVADO
UNIVERSAL GENEVE
LE COULTRE
GRUEN
ILLINOIS

ANY COMIC CHARACTER
ANY MOONPHASE
ANY CHRONOGRAPH

CALL OR WRITE
404-664-8271
8825 Roswell Road
Suite 496
Atlanta, Georgia 30350

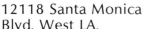

Roy Ehrhardt

Is Buying

Patek Philippe

Prince - Movado

Concord - Piaget

Bubble Backs

Le Coultre

Cartier

Rolex

Repeaters

Accutron 214

Chronograph's

Vacheron Constantin

Unusual Gold Cases

Moon Phase Calendar

To Reach Roy on his 24 hour <u>Nationwide Satellite</u>
<u>Pager Simply Do This</u>

1. Dial 1-800-443-7243 wait, then dial 009943, wait, then dial your area code and phone number and "#" then hang up your phone.
2. Roy will return your call immediately if close to a phone or as soon as he can get to one.
3. <u>Call when you have a GOOD watch for sale!</u>

Roy Ehrhardt
P.O. Box 9808
Kansas City, MO 64134
1-800-458-8525
904-343-3316 - 669-4791
FAX 904-669-4791

VINTAGE®
AMERICAN &
EUROPEAN
BOOK 4
WRIST
WATCH
PRICE GUIDE

SHERRY & ROY EHRHARDT
JOE DEMESY

Roy Ehrhardt - Editor
Larry Ehrhardt - Assistant Editor
Sherry Ehrhardt - Advertising Sales
Bethany Mousadi - Typesetting
Tracy & Rose Vanderhoof - Graphic Artist
Janet VanSelus - Research
Johanna Caperoon - Book Sales
David A. Mycko - Character Values

First Edition
Heart Of America Press, Umatilla, Florida 32784

ACKNOWLEDGEMENTS

The illustrations shown in this book have been supplied by fellow collectors who have generously allowed us to use material from their libraries, helped us in other ways, or dealers who have advertised in this book. We would like to take this opportunity to "thank" each for the help they have given us:

Annette's, Stockton, CA
Antiquorum, Geneve, Switzerland
Robert "Bob" Arnold, Atlas, MI
Don & Sharon Bass, Sandusky, OH
Sherril Bloom, Miami, FL
Annette L. Born, Brookline, MA
Burley Bullock, Houston, TX
Jim Burns, Kansas City, MO
Steve Campbell, Mississauga, CA
Johanna Caparoon, KC, MO
Alfredo Castro, Miami, FL
James Chandler, Parrish, AL
Charlotte Jewelry, Charlotte, NC
Christie's, NY, NY
Mike Clark, Richardson, TX
Richard Cohen, Philadelphia, PA
John Cole, London, England
Joseph Conway, Newton, MA
Fred Cooper, Cardiff, CA
Helmut Crott, Aachen, W Ger.
Pete Davis, Kansas City, MO
Joe Demesy, Fort Worth, TX
Sam DiMartino, Chalmette, LA
Steve Dubinsky, Tarrytown, NY
Paul Duggan, Chelmsford, MA
Paul & Linda Dunn, KC, MO
John Dryden, Mississauga, CA
Bernie Edwards, Northbrook, IL
Alpha Ehrhardt, Tavares, FL
Larry Ehrhardt, Leesburg, FL
Ray Ellis, Escondido, CA
Aaron Faber, NY, NY
Burt Finger, Denton, Tx
Peter Fossner, NY, NY
J. Michael Fultz, Chicago, IL

Richard Gilbert, Sarasota, CA
Good Old Days, Singapore
Brad Gold, Los Angeles, CA
Keith Gray, Coral Gables, FL
Jon Hanson, Beverly Hills, CA
Pete Harvey, San Marcos, CA
Jack Hendlmyer, Houston, TX
Jeff Hess, St. Petersburg, FL
Spencer Hodgson, Arlington, IL
Ken Jacobs, Los Angeles, CA
Eric & Rae Jorgensen, Assonet,MA
Jack Karamikian, NY, NY
Tom & Claire LaRose,
    Greensboro, NC
Don & Linda Levison, SF, CA
Erick Lorenz, NY, NY
Bill Marin, Los Angeles, CA
Harvey Marcus, NY, NY
Frederick Mayer, Pittsburg, PA
Jessie Medlock, Vandalia, OH
Bill Meggers Jr., Ridgecrest, CA
Warren Messing, Miami, FL
Don Meyer, Carrolton, TX
Denzil L. Miller, Dayton, OH
Rod Minter, Lombard IL
Muller & Joseph, West Germany
David A. Mycko, Miami, FL
Pat & Paul Morgan, Decatur, IN
Jeff Morris, NY, NY
Dennis & Linda Nichinson, NY, NY
Steven Oltuski, Toronto, Canada
Otis Page, Buttonwillow, CA
Osvaldo Patrizzi, Geneve, Swiss
Charles Perosa, NY, NY
David Resnick, Denver, CO

Rolex Watch Co., NY, NY
Patrick Ryan, Rockport, MA
Miles Sandler, Overland Park, KS
Loren Scanlon, Modesto, CA
Daryn Schnipper, NY, NY
Sig Schonholtz, Los Angeles, CA
David Searles, Ogunquit, ME
"Bill" Selover, St. Augustine,FL
Marc Shaffman, Miami, FL
Sheldon, Bradenton, FL
Mike Simons, Richardson, TX
Jonathan Snellenburg, NY, NY
Sotheby's, NY, NY & London
Ken Specht, Miami, FL
Ron Starnes, Tulsa, OK
Dave Steger, St. Louis, MO
Tami Steiner, S. Miami, FL
Ralph Sturgeon, Dallas, TX
Donald Summar, Columbia, PA
Lance Thomas, Los Angeles, CA
Kevin L. Tierney, NY, NY
Jules Velan, Germany
George Waluk, Houston, TX
P.J. Waslien, Beverly Hills, CA
Bob, Jean & Jennifer Webb,
    St. Charles, MO
Bob Wingate, Dallas, TX
Paul Zuercher, Denver, CO

A special thanks to the various AUCTION HOUSES for use of illustrations from their catalogs. A complete list is presented on page 562.

A copy of this book may be obtained by sending
$27.00 Pre-paid UPS to:

Published & Distributed By

Heart Of America Press
P.O. Box 9808
10101 Blue Ridge Blvd.
Kansas City, Missouri 64134
Phone (816) 761-0080
Book Orders
(800) 458-8525

We Sell Reliable Information

ISBN: 0-913902 58-6 / Paperback

JOE DEMESY
Dealer in Fine Watches
1-800-635-9006
Fort Worth, TX 76137

ROY EHRHARDT, JR.
Fine Watches
Umatilla, FL 32784
904-669-4791

Roy Ehrhardt, Jr., is well known for his publishing company, Heart of America Press, where he has published and/or authored many of the finest price guides and information books on Horology today.

Roy is a respected Fellow of the NAWCC. He has long been admired for his no nonsense approach in publications and special speaking programs on Vintage Watches at Regionals of the NAWCC. To provide an authoritative basis for these books and lectures, he maintains one of the largest private Horological libraries in the world, including thousands of slides and photographs of actual watches.

Roy and his wife Alpha, live in Tavares, Florida.

Joe has been involved in the business of antique Vintage watches since 1979 and is well-known by dealers and collectors worldwide.

He has specialized in the buying and selling of Vintage wrist watches for the last five years. As one of the world's largest dealers in high-grade timepieces, Joe travels extensively throughout Europe and North America and attends all the major auctions in Germany, England, Switzerland, Italy and New York. He also attends many of the watch shows and trade fairs in Italy as well as most of the NAWCC regionals in the United States.

Joe's worldwide travels enables him to stay in constant touch with the latest market prices in antique wrist watches of all kinds.

Joe resides in Arlington, Texas.

SHERRY EHRHARDT
The Watch Lady
Atlanta, GA - 404-664-8271

The author is a member of the NAWCC, and attends many of their regional shows and chapter meetings. She has also attended Sotheby's & Christie's auctions in New York and hundreds of antique shows, flea markets, and jewelry stores in nearly all parts of the United States.

Sherry has been associated with and active in the Vintage jewelry wrist watch market for the past ten years. She is currently working on the next edition of the Vintage Wrist Watch Price Guide and actively buying and selling watches.

Sherry and her husband, Lynn La Noue, live in Atlanta, Georgia.

Joe has been in close touch with the wrist watch market for the past five years. He is a member of the AWI and the NAWCC, Inc., attending most of the regional and national shows and many of the chapter meetings that have a trading session or mart. During the last three years he has attended all of the major wrist watch auctions held in the United States, Switzerland, England and Germany as an active buyer and an observer of price trends.

Sherry has been associated with and active in the Vintage jewelry wrist watch market for the past ten years. She has attended many of the larger NAWCC marts, and hundreds of antique shows and flea markets in nearly all parts of the United States, with emphasis on the East and Midwest.

The prices in this book are based on what a wrist watch will sell for at the NAWCC marts and the top auctions, without the added buyer's premium. Recorded here are actual recent sales of rare or expensive watches, and averaged top values for the more common types which never make the auctions but which are usually bought and sold on a one-on-one basis.

Common commercial grade gold wrist watches that have nothing going for them other than the gold case were figured at gold spot of $400.00 per ounce.

No attempt has been made to predict the future prices but only to report the recent happenings in the market place among knowledge-ablve collectors and dealers.

This book does not indicate the high prices asked and many times received by Madison Avenue, New York, or Main Street, U.S.A. jewelry stores, antique dealers at a major show, or, for that matter, any sale that would have to help support high overhead, travel, and marketing expense such as fancy showrooms, wages, and expensive advertising. Perhaps the value given in this book could be considered **high wholesale** or **low retail.**

This book is not a price list but an indication of value. It does not tell the buyer what he or she should pay but what they might expect to buy or sell for at the "top price" level outside of retail jewelry stores. Values in this book are based on the following concept of retail value: **THE PRICE A KNOWLEDGEABLE COLLECTOR OR INVESTOR WHO WANTS THE WRIST WATCH AND HAS THE MONEY, WILL PAY ANOTHER COLLECTOR OR DEALER WHO KNOWS THE VALUE.** Consequently, no watch sales have been used that occur among individuals and dealers who have no market information or the perception of actual supply and demand.

Use the values given in this book as a guide but, more importantly, use your own judgment based on your knowledge or desires of your particular collecting area and circumstances.

Remember, THE PRICE YOU PAY MUST ULTIMATELY BE YOUR OWN, and is the value of the wrist watch to you at that particular moment.

Despite the fact that the values shown are based on sales between knowledgeable persons, there are still many wrist watches for sale at bargain prices". In other words, many wrist watches have not yet been "discovered" by collectors, and, consequently, are available at prices far below those they will warrant when their real importance becomes generally known. It is our hope that this book will be of real value to you by helping you build your collection for the least possible cost and with a good chance for future value appreciation.

THINGS THAT DETERMINE THE VALUE OF A WRIST WATCH

TOP BRAND NAMES: The most popular and sought after wrist watch is one by Patek Philippe of Geneva, Switzerland, with all other things being equal; that is, case style, metal, features, type, etc. Other important top names, but not necessarily in the order of their importance, are Audemars Piguet, Baume & Mercier, Breguet, Cartier, Concord, Corum, Gubelin, Piaget, Rolex, Tiffany, Universal Geneve, Vacheron & Constantin.

These are followed by Agassiz, Buche-Girod, Chopard, Ditisheim, Girard-Perregaux, International, LeCoultre, Longines, Lucien Piccard, Matthey-Tissot, Mido, Movado, Ollendorff, Omega, Tissot, Touchon, Ulysse Nardin, Wittnauer, Zenith and Zodiac; again, not necessarily in that order. There are others but this is enough to give you a good idea of the better makes.

The most popular United States makers are Hamilton, Illinois, Hampden, Elgin and Waltham.

STYLE: Public popularity, fads, or fashion determines which style is preferred at any given time. Before a Vintage wrist watch is bought (to wear) at retail, the customer will always first put it on his arm to see how it looks or how someone else thinks it looks. Style is in the eye and mind of the buyer, and some styles are more popular than others.

UTILITY: A wrist watch has the advantage over most all other things to collect——**It is useful.** This single factor puts the wrist watch at the top of the list of Vintage items to collect, both for enjoyment to wear and for future long-term investment. An originally expensive wrist watch will always be in demand. Commercial grade "junk" will always be junk.

CASE METAL: The intrinsic value of the case metal is the only value some Vintage wrist watches have. Many metals and materials have been used for cases over the years. Some of them (in descending order of importance) are:

platinum, 22-18-14-10-9 karat gold, silver (both sterling and coin), gold-filled, gold plated, nickel, stainless steel, and plastic. Watches made by the top makers and cased in platinum and gold, are worth much more than the weight of the metal.

CASE MARKINGS: Many Vintage wrist watches by makers and jewelers such as Patek, Cartier, Rolex, LeCoultre, Tiffany, Hamilton, etc. were cased, boxed and timed at the factory. These watches in their original, marked cases are worth much more than watches in unmarked cases. All wrist watch companies making movements, at one time or another (and some for the entire life of the company), sold movements ONLY, with dials marked according to the specifications of the buyer, which were then cased in custom made or standard cases supplied by many American and European casemakers. These cases are sometimes described as "Contract Cases".

PRECIOUS AND SEMI-PRECIOUS STONES: Many different stones were used to decorate the dials, cases and bracelets of men's and ladies wrist watches. Several factors are involved in valuing watches with these stones. The size, color and quality of the stone are the most important factors in determining their value. The top name makers used only the finest stones available. Others used whatever the public would bear. It is very difficult to give a value for a watch containing stones without an actual examination of the watch and each stone. This was not possible for watches illustrated in this book, therefore, the actual value may be more or less than the value shown.

CONDITION: Here are some things to look for when buying a Vintage wrist watch. The condition of the dial, crown, case, movement, and bracelet (if permanently attached) must be considered.

Dial: Most wrist watches have metal dials. If it is a metal dial, has it been refinished or does it need to be? Refinishing costs from $15 to $75, and sometimes much time and effort on your part. On applied figure dials, are there any missing or damaged figures? Is the dial original? Are there scratches that cannot be removed, feet missing, dial bent or damaged? The more valuable the watch, the more valuable the dial.

Case: Notice the amount of wear. On a gold case, is it bent or dented from rough use; is the gold worn through; does it have bent or damaged or replaced lugs? Look at the spring bar holes. Are they worn, etc.? Initials or dedications hurt the desirability and therefore the value. On gold-filled cases, look closely at the corners and high edges of the case for wear (brass showing).

Bracelet: Be careful about buying a watch with a permanently attached bracelet that does not fit your wrist. Some types, such as mesh, costs a lot to shorten and even more to lengthen.

Movement: It should be original (this is more important in some watches than others). "Running" condition and complete without botched repairs is important. The finish should be good; the nickel or rhodium plating should not be worn off; no corrosion or rust; no scratches or non-original parts.

Crown: The original crown is important when they were marked, such as Patek or Rolex.

RECASING: There is an ever-growing problem in recasing the most expensive, top name wrist watches such as Patek, Cartier, LeCoultre, etc. The real value of these recased watches is the value of the movement, plus the value of the gold content of the case. There is some very good recasing being done that is difficult to tell from the original. If a recase is done well enough to be accepted by everyone, then it assumes the value of an original. When it is discovered that the watch is a recase, the apparent value will drop dramatically.

CASE STYLES PREFERRED ON PATEK PHILIPPE WRIST WATCHES: At this time, in the order of their importance, is the rectangular curved case, the rectangular; the square, and last, the round. Unusual lugs can increase the value tremendously.

CASE VARIATIONS THAT ADD VALUE: Hinged lugs, curved case, enamel case, tu-tone color, numerals on bezel, numerals on enamel bezel, large "Art Deco" style numerals on dial.

MOVEMENTS: Unlike pocket watches, movements play a small part in the value of the wrist watch, except for complicated watches. We look for some of the high grade Hamiltons and the more scarce Illinois, Hampden, and Rockford to get more attention in the near future, with a resulting rise in value.

WATCH BANDS OR BRACELETS: Most gold wrist watch bands and bracelets are not important and usually are worth a small premium (10% to 20%) over the precious metal content, if in mint condition. The exception is the marked ones made for or by the high-grade European watch companies such as Patek, Rolex, Cartier, etc. Exotic skin bands such as lizard, crocodile or alligator, enhance the look and value of the watch. Signed, original straps and buckles are sought after and have value, with a gold Patek bringing about $75.

ORIGINAL COST VERSUS VALUE TODAY: Expensive wrist watches are mostly hand-finished and the parts were hand-fitted. Very few of these expensive watches were made when compared to the millions of inexpensive commercial grade, machine-made watches. Therefore, these hand-finished watches are scarce to rare, and will still last a lifetime or more if properly cared for. They represent a status symbol that many people desire. Usually only the educated, moneyed, or people associated with the wrist watch trade are aware of top makers such as Patek, Cartier, Audemars or

Rolex. These companies only advertised to customers who could afford to buy expensive watches, therefore, the common folk would not be aware of these watches. Comparatively speaking, expensive high quality is still expensive high quality in a Vintage wrist watch, and junk is still junk.

COMIC CHARACTER: The comic character Vintage wrist watches are the exception to the above statement. Most of them are of low quality (pin pallet construction), but they have a wide appeal to collectors outside the watch market because of the collectibility associated with comic characters. They were offered for sale in beautiful and interesting boxes (sometimes worth as much as the watch), which appealed to the children then——and the child in us now.

JEWELRY WATCHES: Before World War I, wrist watches were considered to be ornamental jewelry and were not necessarily used as timepieces only. Until the soldiers started wearing them, it was considered "sissy" or "unmanly" to wear one. Expensive wrist watches that combined diamonds and other precious stones with platinum or gold (sometimes with enamel) in a decorative style have always been produced, even in the beginning.

Heavy markup, sometimes three, four or five times cost, was used as the sticker or retail price to cover fancy showrooms and expensive (usually national) advertising.

Collector value of a majority of these pieces is usually no more than the salvage value of the stones and the platinum or gold content of the case and bracelet.

Some designs that are considered popular now will bring a premium but it is usually limited to 10% to 20% above salvage value, except for the very special pieces or pieces by top name makers that command attention as status symbols.

COMPLICATIONS, ALARMS, CHRONOGRAPHS, CALENDARS, REPEATERS: Any feature added to the original time only wrist watch raises the value of a Vintage wrist watch. Complications increased the initial cost because of the added expense to the manufacturer, and the comparatively few people who wanted or needed one makes them scarce when compared to time only wrist watches. The value of each of these added features depend on many things; among them being the maker, the case metal and the case style.

MILESTONES OR FIRSTS: Many inventions either did not work well or, for one reason or another, did not find public acceptance and were not mass produced. Because of the enormous market for wrist watches, there has always been ample money available for research and development. Changes and improvements have been many and often, bringing us up to the electronic age. Of this work, the early varieties of "Self-winding" (being a good example) are being collected by a few. In the past, information on wrist watches has been hard to find. Now with an occasional wrist watch book becoming available, I am sure that collectors for these will increase, and, because of short supply of collectible Vintage wrist watches, this will tend to push up the price.

ORIGINAL BOX — TIMING CERTIFICATES — GUARANTEES: All of these help the value of any wrist watch but the papers must have matching serial numbers. The more valuable the watch the more valuable the box and papers become.

COLOR OF THE CASE: At this time, solid gold watches are the most desirable (and worth more), in yellow gold, followed by green gold and then white gold. A rich yellow color is preferred in gold, gold-filled, or gold plated.

MULTI—COLOR OR TU—TONE CASES: Two or more colors in the case is popular now with Vintage wrist watch collectors. The separation between the value of a single color and a multi-color case increases as the value of the watch increases.

ALL PRICES IN THIS BOOK ARE FOR MINT CONDITION WATCHES.

OTHER USEFUL INFORMATION

AMERICAN & EUROPEAN WRIST WATCH MARKET: At this time, it appears that generally the European market is about twenty percent stronger than the American market.

AUCTIONS: There are four major auction houses in Europe, each holding about two auctions per year. Probably 800 to 1200 wrist watches are auctioned each year. There are two major and three minor auction houses in the U.S., which will probably auction about 400 to 500 wrist watches this year.

DEALERS: There are about six major Vintage wrist watch dealers that buy and sell full time in America. The other major buyers and sellers are mostly retail jewelry stores; for instance, stores on Madison Avenue in New York that cater to the public with Vintage watches. There are probably about ten major European wrist watch buyers. Most of them come to the auctions and the larger National Association of Watch & Clock Collector's regional marts. And, there are hundreds of "hip pocket" dealers everywhere that offer wrist watches to the public or collectors when supply permits.

COLLECTORS —— EUROPEAN VS AMERICAN: The Europeans began collecting wrist watches before the Americans. However, collectors are now springing up all over the U.S. They are beginning their collections with the companies who made railroad watches, such as Hamilton, Illinois, etc.

RARIETIES: Wrist watch collecting is in its early stages now, and rare and valuable wrist watches will be found by collectors who are able to identify them. Many will be bought for very little money compared to their real value. We have tried to give you help in your search with this book.

PRIVATE LABEL OR JEWELER'S CONTRACT WRIST WATCHES: Watch manufacturers, importers and distributors make use of names that are found on either the dial, movement, or the case. There are various reasons for this: advertising, identification, etc. Some of these names were used for many years (example Tiffany and Cyma), others maybe only on one small batch of watches. A book issued in 1943 by The Jeweler's Circular Keystone called **Trade Marks of the Jewelry and Kindred Trades**, listed 148 company names and addresses of U.S. companies who were at that time using over 2500 names, many of which appear only on the dials. This book could not cover all of even this one year, much less 70 years of serious wrist watch production from around the world. We have instead selected from the material available to us the examples that we believe best represent the wirst watches that are available today.

The number of watches shown for each company in no way indicates its importance to collectors. We did, however, show as many as was practical for some companies that are important to collectors, such as Patek, Rolex, Cartier, Vacheron, Universal, Audemars, Hamilton and Illinois. Large numbers of other companies, such as Bulova, Gruen, Elgin and Waltham, were used because lots of these watches can be found. Others, such as Cyma, Tavannes, Longines and Marshall Field, were given because we had good pictures that represented many different styles or a large line for one year.

In future editions we will continue to give you the best information we have available. **CURRENT TOP NAME PRODUCT LINE CATALOGS:** All companies issue periodic product line catalogs to regular customers and sometimes make them available to the public at a small charge. There are two ways to get these catalogs: (1) Go by your local jewelry store and get one if they have them available; (2) Order them directly from the company by paying the required fee. The companies with wrist watches for sale run advertising campaigns in selected over-the-counter magazines and how to order instructions are usually included in the advertisement. Also, Vogue Magazine does one or two special Holiday Preview issues about mid-Summer, in which they present their "Catalog Collection", with instruction on how to order them. The 1983 September issue included Cartier, Rolex, Baume & Mercier, Concord, Omega, Piaget and Corum. Prices for the individual catalogs run from $2 to $5. These catalogs sometimes include a retail price list which can give you an idea of what current styles are being offered, and, with your knowledge of markups, will help you decide how much to pay for a used one.

1983 STYLES. For the past few years, top name companies such as Patek Philippe, Rolex, Cartier, Baume & Mercier, Concord, Piaget and Corum have been offering as their **top of the line**, wrist watches that are **identifiable from any angle,** which includes a bracelet just as distinctive as the watch. These companies are also the most heavily copied by the Far East companies who make fakes.

RAILROAD U.S. APPROVED WRIST WATCHES: The first wrist watch approved for railroad use was an Elgin B.W. Raymond on the Pittsburg and Lake Erie Railroad in early 1960. Here is a list of some of the railroad approved wrist watches, some of which are new and still available.

1. Ball, 13''' Size, 21 Jewel, Official RR Standard Model 1604B.
2. Ball 11½''' Size, 25 Jewel, Official RR Standard Trainmaster Model 2821.
3. Ball 11½''' Size, 25 Jewel, Official RR Standard Trainmaster Model 2620B.
4. Bulova Accutron Railroad Model 214.
5. Bulova Accutron Railroad Calendar Model 218.
6. Bulova Accutron Quartz Day-Day Model 92843 & 91818.
7. Bulova Accutron Quartz Ladies Model 92278.
8. Croton Railroad Timer.
9. Elgin 13''' Size, 23 Jewel, B.W. Raymond Chronometer.
10. Elgin 13''' Size, 21 Jewel, B.W. Raymond Chronometer.
11. Elgin 13''' Size, 21 Jewel, B.W. Raymond 1604-B.
12. Elgin 13''' Size, 21 Jewel, B.W. Raymond AS 10041.
13. Eterna-Sonic Model 133T–RA1550.
14. Hamilton Electric Model 505, 50, 51, and 52 Railroad Special.
15. Hamilton Electronic Product No. 910917.
16. Longines Ultronic Model 6312.
17. Pulsar Model JG041 and JG0385.
18. Rodania Quartz Model 09361, Ref. 3488.1.
19. Seiko Quartz Models FJ055M, FJ056M, HA163M, HA164M, and UX015M.
20. Universal Geneve Models 1205-0 and Unisonic RR52-0.
21. Wyler Models 1370RA, 4125RA, 3425RA, 1324, 1337-RA1550, 433T-RA1550 and 4176.

Collectors of Vintage railroad approved wrist watches prefer the Elgin, Ball and Hamilton Railroad Models but not much attention has been paid to the others.

GLOSSARY

Adjusted: Term applied to watch movements and some small clock movements to indicate that they have been corrected for various errors, such as isochronism, temperature, and positions.

Agate: A stone which is a variety of chalcedony, usually containing a pattern such as banding, eyes, etc.

Alarm: An attachment to a watch whereby, at a predetermined time, a bell is sounded.

Alloy: The mixing of more than one metal in order to produce one of greater hardness, malleability and/or durability.

Animated: Imitating or giving life-like movement to a watch dial. (Usually Comic Character)

Applied Figures: Figures which have been attached to the dial, usually with screws or small bolts with nuts.

Arabic Figures: Figures on a dial, such as 1, 2, 3, as opposed to Roman Numerals, such as I, II, V, IX.

Art Deco: A style of design between 1910–1935, most importantly influenced by cubist geometry.

Automatic Winding: See Self-winding.

Baugette: A step cut used for rectangular stones, of a small size.

Balance: The oscillating wheel of a watch, which in conjunction with the hairspring (balance spring) regulates the speed of a clock or watch. May be made bi-metallic to compensate for temperature changes and may be studded with screws for regulation.

Bearing: The support for a pivot or arbor. Jeweled bearings are used where there is danger of rapid wear on the pivots of fast moving parts such as the balance staff and also train wheel pivots.

Beat: The sound of the ticking of a watch, caused by the teeth of the escape wheel striking the pallets or arms of the escapement.

Beveled: Inclining from a right line to form a slant.

Bezel: The groove in which the glass (crystal) of a watch is set.

Breguet: A horological genius of the late 18th and early 19th century. The name applied to the type of hairspring which has its last outer coil raised above the body of the spring and curved inwards.

Bridge: Upper plates in a ¾ plate watch for the support of the wheels,. or pallet. Always has at least two feet or supports.

Brilliant Cut: The most beautiful form of cutting a diamond. It is also used for other clear stones. The standard brilliant has 58 facets, 33 in the crown and 25 in the base.

Bubbleback: Slang term for the early Rolex Oyster Perpetual (ca 1930 to 1950's).

Calendar, Moonphase: A disk, usually with a blue background, containing the moon phases and further decoration of stars which rotates one complete turn per month. Located at the 6th or 12th hour position. In reality, the moon rotates around the earth in 29 days, 12 hours, 44 minutes and 2-4/5 seconds.

Calendar, Perpetual: A perpetual calendar mechanism is self-adjusting, that is to stay it automatically indicates the months of varying length and is self-correcting for leap years.

Calendar, Perpetual Retrograde: The date hand moves through an arc on the dial and returns to 1 after reaching the proper date 28, 29, 30 or 31.

Calendar, Simple: Automatically registers one or all of the following: day, date, month and moonphase, and must be manually adjusted for months having total days other than 31.

Calibre: The size or factory number of a watch movement.

Cap Jewel: The flat solid jewel upon which rests the pivot end. Also called the "endstone".

Center-seconds hand: Sometimes called sweep-seconds hand. Mounted on the center post of watches.

Champferred: A beveled or sloped edge.

Champleve: Enameling done by cutting grooves in the metal into which the ground enamel is melted. The surface is then ground and polished.

Chapter Ring: The circle on the dial that contains the numbers for the hours and minutes. So called because in early clocks it was a separate ring attached to the dial.

Chromium: Very hard crystalline metallic chemical element with a high resistance to corrosion, used as plating on wrist watch cases.

Chronograph: A mechanical watch with hour and minute hand and a center sweep-second hand which can be controlled by one or more special buttons, in the side of the case or through the crown. The sweep-second hand may be started, stopped, and made to return to zero without interfering with the timekeeping of the watch.

Chronograph, Double Button: Stop and start on one button without returning to zero. One button to return to zero (flyback).

Chronograph, Simplified (One Button): Sweep-second hand runs continuously on this single button chronograph when at rest. Press completely down to return to zero, hold down until timing begins upon release, push down halfway to stop, release to start again, or all the way down to flyback. Usually of cheaper construction.

Chronograph, Split Seconds: Same as chronograph but is fitted with an additional center sweep-second hand (total of 2) with separate controls (buttons) to permit the timing of two events simultaneously. Example: The split-second chronograph with two chronograph hands permits ascertaining, in races of all kinds, the times of arrival of competitors following closely upon each others heels. The chronograph is set in motion by pressing a button whereupon both hands begin to move. At the arrival of the first competitor the one hand is stopped by pressing this button again and the time is read off. When the button is pressed a third time this hand catches up with the other in one jump, whereafter both move on together. At the arrival of the second competitor the first hand is again stopped and the time noted down. In this way, any desired number of time recordings can be made. A button fitted in the winder serves to return both hands to zero.

Click: A spring-tensioned pawl holding the ratchet wheel against the tension of the main-spring, enabling the spring to be wound, usually making the clicking noise as the watch is wound.

Cloisonne Enamel: A type of enamel work in which thin strips of metal are soldered to the base to form the outlines of the design. Colored enamel is then placed in each section.

Cock: An overhanging support for a bearing such as the balance cock; a cock has a support at one end only.

Compensating Balance: A balance with a bi-metallic rim made of brass and steel. The diameter increases or decreases with changes in temperature to compensate for these changes.

Conical Pivot: A pivot which curves back into the main body of its arbor, such as those used with cap jewels. (Balance staff pivots.)

Convertible Case: Watch case built into a sliding frame allowing the dial side to be turned over facing the wrist to protect it.

Convex: A domed surface.

Crown: A grooved circular piece fastened to the stem for winding the watch. (Slang term "Winding Knob or Button)

Curb Pins: The two regulator pins almost pinching the hairspring.

Curvex: Case with a slightly curved back to fit the wrist better. (Patented by Gruen)

Cushion: Square form with rounded edges.

Detent: The setting lever. A detainer or pawl.

Dial Train: The train of wheels under the dial which moves the hands. The cannon pinion hour wheel, minute wheel and pinion.

Diamond Dial: Dial set with diamonds for markers, numerals, etc.

Digital: See Jump Hour.

Doctor's Watch: See Duo-Dial.

Dollar Watch: A practical timepiece with a non-jeweled movement. The case and movement an integral unit with a dial of paper on brass or other inexpensive material. Ingersoll sold his first Dollar watch for $1.00 in 1892. (Taken from "The Watch That Made the Dollar Famous" by George E. Townsend.)

Double-Roller Escapement: A form of lever escapement in which a separate roller is used for the safety action.

Duo-Dial: Separate hour and seconds dials. (Slang term "Doctor's Watch")

Duplex Escapement: A watch escapement in which the escape wheel has two sets of teeth. One set locks the wheel by pressing on the balance staff. The other set gives impulse to the balance. The balance receives impulse at every other vibration.

Ebauche: A term used by Swiss watch manufacturers to denote the raw movement without jewels, escapement, plating, engraving. The manufacturers supply their ebauches to trade name importers in the U.S.A. and other countries who have them finished, jeweled, dialed, cased, etc., and engraved with their own (advertised) name brands.

Elinvar: A nonrusting, nonmagnetizing alloy containing iron, nickel, chromium, tungsten, silicon and carbon. Used for balance and balance spring. (Hamilton)

Elongated: The state of being stretched out or lengthened.

Embossed: To carve, raise or print so that it is raised above the surface.

Emerald Cut: A style of rectangular or square cut, featuring steps of elongated facets.

Enamel: (Soft) A soluble paint used in dials. (Hard) A porcelain-like paint used as an ornamental coating, acid-resisting and durable.

Engine-Turned: A form of machine engraving similar to etching.

Engraved: To cut into, to form a pattern or design either by hand or machine.

Filigree: Ornamental open work executed in fine gold or silver wire.

Flat Hairspring: A hairspring whose spirals develop on a flat surface. As opposed to the overcoil (Breguet) hairspring.

Fourth Wheel: Usually the wheel which carries the second hand and drives the escape wheel; it is the fourth wheel from the great wheel in the going train of a watch.

German Silver: A silver-white alloy composed mainly of copper, zinc, and nickel, called silver but containing none.

Gilded: To give a golden hue; gold plating.

Gilding: The process of coating the surface of metal with gold by painting on a mixture of mercury and gold and then heating to evaporate the mercury.

Gold: Pure 24K gold is yellow in color. It is very soft and not acceptable for use in articles subject to wear, unless alloyed with harder metal. The choice of alloy metals determines the color of the gold.

Gold-Filled: Another name for rolled gold.

Gold Plated: Electro-plated a few thousandths of an inch thick with pure or alloyed gold.

Grande Sonnerie: A quarter hour repeater; a type of striking in which the last hour struck is repeated at each quarter. Present day usage sometimes applies the term to a quarter hour which can be made to strike at will.

Green Gold: True green gold cannot be made of less fineness than 17 karat: usually made of 10 to 14 karat gold, alloyed with silver to make it as pale as possible and then the finished piece is electroplated with 18 karat green gold. True green gold is 17 parts pure gold and 7 parts pure silver.

Greenwich Civil Time: Also called Universal Time (UT). It is Local mean time as measured at Greenwich, England. (G.C.T.)

Hairspring: The spiraled spring attached to the balance to govern the speed of the balance oscillations.

Hexagonal: Six sided.

Hour Recorder: Small offset hour recorder dial has an indicator hand that advances one hour marker each time the minute recorder counts off 60 minutes. Usually placed over the 6th hour marker.

Hunting Case: Spring-loaded lid or cover over the face of the watch. (Example: See Hamilton Flintridge)

Independent Seconds-Beating: Fitted with a special center sweep seconds hand that advances by one jump every second. Sometimes called "Jump Second".

Index: The regulator scale. Used to help in adjusting the regulation. Most balance wheel clocks and watches had indexes.

Integral: A part that is permanently attached to another part, thus becoming one. As in a bracelet permanently attached to the head of a wrist watch.

Invar: A steel alloy containing about 36 percent nickel that remains the same length at different temperatures. Used in the making of balance wheels. Also used for pendulum rods in clocks for temperature compensation. Similar to Elinvar.

Isochronism: Quality of keeping equal time during the normal run of the mainspring, usually the qualities of a well-formed overcoil hairspring.

Jewel: Synthetic or semi-precious stones used for bearings in watches and precision clocks.

Jump Hour (or Digital): The hour indicator advances instantaneously at the beginning of the hour.

Jump Second: See Independent Seconds-Beating.

Lapis Lazuli: Synonym for lazurite, or ultra marine. An azure-blue stone with vitreous lustre, sometimes with gold specks used in jewelry and an occasional wrist watch dial.

Ligne (‴): A Swiss watch size, 2.2558mm. or 0.0888 in.

Luminous: Giving off light; glows in the dark. (See Radium)

Mainspring: The flat, ribbon-like tempered steel spring wound inside the barrel and used to drive the train wheels. Most American clocks eliminated the barrel.

Marquise Cut: A cut for diamonds in which the stone is brilliantly faceted and then shaped like an elongated almond or tear-drop with pointed ends.

Matte: A dull or flat finish.

Mean Time: When all days and hours are of equal length. This is oppsed to Solar Time where all days are not of equal length.

Meantime Screws: The adjustable screws in a better grade balance used to bring the watch to close time without the use of the regulator. Sometimes called "timing screws".

Middle-Temperature Error: The temperature error between the extremes of heat and cold characteristic of a compensating balance and steel balance spring.

Milled: Having the edge transversely grooved.

Minute Recording: Small offset minute recorder dial that advances 1 minute with each revolution made by the second hand. Usually one of three types: 1) Continuous; 2) semi-instantaneous; 3) Instantaneous. Usually placed by the 3rd hour marker.

Minute Repeater: A striking watch that will ring the time to the minute by a series of gongs activated by a plunger or push piece. A watch striking the hours, quarter hours, and additional minutes.

Nickel Silver: An alloy of nickel, copper, and zinc; usually 65 percent copper, 5-25 percent nickel, and 10-30 percent zinc, containing no silver.

Non-Magnetic: A balance and spring composed of alloys that will not retain magnetism after being put through a magnetic field.

Octagonal: Eight sided.

Open Face: A watch dial with the figure "12" at the winding stem.

Oval: Elongated circle.

Palladium: One of the platinum group of metals and much lighter. Will not tarnish and can be deposited on other metal by electroplating. Value is less than gold or platinum.

Pavé: A style of setting stones where a number of small stones are set as close together as possible; to completely cover.

Pennyweight (DWT): A unit in troy weight equal to twenty-four grains or one-twentieth of an ounce.

Perpetual Winding: See Self-winding.

Phillips' Spring: A balance spring with terminal curves formed on lines laid down by M. Phillips. The term "Phillips' curve" is rarely used.

Pin Pallet: The lever escapement wherein the pallet has upright pins instead of horizontally set jewels. Used in alarm clocks and nonjeweled watches.

Poising: An operation to adjust the balance so that all weights are counterpoised. In other words, statically balancing a wheel or balance in a watch.

Position Timing: Adjusting a watch so that it keeps precise time when the watch is placed in a given position. Adjusted to three, four, five or six positions.

Power Reserve Indicator: See Up & Down Indicator.

Purse Watch: Folding, covered, or otherwise protected watch for carrying in the purse or pocket. (Example: Movado Ermeto)

Quick Train: A watch movement beating five times per second, or 18,000 per hour.

Radium: A radioactive metallic element that gives off light. Used on luminous dials.

Regulator: Part of the balance bridge which resembles a racquette (racket) and contains vertical pins which straddle the hairspring. When the regulator moves towards the stud, the effective length of the hairspring is made longer and the balance slows in speed; when the pins are moved farther from the stud, the hairspring is made shorter and the watch goes faster.

Repeating Watches: Usually one of six types: 1) Quarter repeaters—striking a deep note for the last hour (as shown on the dial) and two shrill notes, ting-tang for each quarter; 2) Half-Quarter Repeaters—striking the last hour, the quarters, and a single blow for the nearest half-quarter; 3) Five-Minute Repeaters—striking a deep note for the last hour (as shown on the dial) and one shrill note for each five minutes after the hour; 4) Minute Repeater—striking a deep note for the last hour (as shown on the dial), two shrill notes, ting-tang for each quarter, and one shrill note for each minute past the last quarter. The most complicated and popular today; 5) Clock Watches—the hours and quarters are struck automatically as the watch goes but the hours, quarters and minutes can be repeated at will by a slide in the case band; 6) Carillon—the quarters are struck on two, three, or four different notes. Sometimes known as "Cathedrals".

Repoussé: Decorating metal by hammering out a design behind or on the reverse side in order to create a design in relief.

Reverso: See Convertible Case.

Rolled Gold: A metal plate formed by bonding a thin sheet of gold to one or both sides of a backing metal. Made by rolling the sandwich until the gold is at the desired thinness.

Rose Cut: Method of faceting stones with many small and usually not precision cuts.

Rose Gold: karat gold alloyed with copper.

Sapphire Crystal (Synthetic Sapphire Crystal): Extremely hard material used for watch crystals.

Self-winding: Wrist watch that will wind itself by use of a rotor or other mechanical means by swinging movement of the arm. If worn by a normally active person for four hours, it will remain running for 30 hours.

Setting Lever: The detent which fits into the slot of the stem and pushes down the clutch lever.

Silvered: Silver in color, not necessarily in metal content.

Sizes of Watches: The American sizes are based on 30ths of an inch. The Europeans use the ligne which is equal to .089 inches or 2.255 millimeters. In every case, the diameter is measured across the outside or largest part of the lower plate of the watch, right under the dial. In oval or other odd shaped movements, the size is measured across the smaller axis.

Staff: A pivoted arbor or axle usually referred to the axle of the balance; as the "balance staff".

Sterling: The minimum standard of purity of fineness of English silver; 925 parts pure silver to 1000 parts.

Stopwatch: A simple form of chronograph with controlled starting and stopping of the hands; sometimes also stopping the balance wheel. A timer in pocket watch form.

Stopwork: The mechanism on a barrel of a watch that permits only the central portion of the mainspring to be wound, thus utilizing that portion of the spring whose power is less erratic.

Subsidiary Seconds: Small dial, usually opposite the winding crown on a chronograph and at the 6th hour position on a time only watch, that indicates the seconds and makes one revolution per minute.

Sunk Seconds: The small second dial which is depressed to avoid the second hand from interfering with the progress of the hour and minute hand.

Sweep Seconds: See Center Seconds.

Tank Case: Flat, square, conservatively tailored case. (Introduced by Cartier, Patented by Gruen).

Tiger Eye: Silicified fibrous variety of "Riebeckite". A stone that when cut properly displays an eye-like effect.

Timepiece: Any watch that does not strike or chime.

Timing Screws: Screws used to bring a watch to time, sometimes called the mean-time screws.

Tonneau: Shape of case with its widest point across the center and tapering towards square ends.

Tourbillion: A watch in which the escapement, mounted on a cage attached to the fourth pinion, revolves around the mounted and stationary fourth wheel.

Train: A combination of two or more wheels and pinions, geared together and transmitting power from one part of a mechanism to another, usually from the power source (weight or spring) to the escapement.

Troy Weight: The system of weights commonly used in England and the United States for gold and silver. One pound equals 12 ounces, 1 ounce equals 20 pennyweights (dwt.) and 1 pennyweight equals 24 grains (gr.).

Tu-tone: Two colors of metal in the case or dial finish.

Up and Down Indicator: The semi-circular indicator hand or window indicator that tells how much the mainspring has been unwound and thus indicates when the spring should be wound. On wrist watches usually indicates how many hours are left. (Same as Power-Reserve Indicator).

Vermeil: Gilded silver.

Vibrating Tool: A master balance of certified accuracy as to vibrations per hour which is mounted in a box with glass top. The box may be swiveled to set the balance into its vibratory arcs. The balance to be compared or vibrated is suspended by its hairspring attached to a scaffold and when the box is twisted on its platform both balances will start vibrating. Thus the suspended balance may be compared (in speed) with the master balance and its hairspring lengthened or shortened until both balances swing in unison.

Waterproof: Airtight so that no water can enter.

White Gold: 24 karat yellow gold alloyed with nickel to make 14 or 18 karat white gold.

OBSERVATIONS OF THE WRIST WATCH MARKET
by
Roy & Sherry Ehrhardt - Joe Demesy

September 1, 1989 was the cutoff date for revising prices in this issue of VINTAGE WRIST WATCH PRICE GUIDE BOOK 4. The lower of the two prices given for each watch in this book are what we believe dealers and collectors have been paying at the NAWCC marts in the United States. On high dollar watches many times dealer & collector prices may be equal.

A new record price for a Vintage wrist watch sold in the U.S. was obtained this year for a Patek world time with a cloisonne dial for $275,000. Other record prices were a Patek split at $280,000, and a rectangular Patek minute repeater at $345,000. The current major emphasis is on complicated pieces.

The Hong Kong market is expanding, and has continued support from the Orient with new interest developing in France.

A price leveling has occurred on many high-grade pieces, such as Patek chronographs, Rolex bubble backs, diamond dials and bezels & round gold. Interest is still strong in the Orient for Rolex. Recently it is cheaper to buy in Europe such things as Rolex Oyster Moonphase, Vacheron & Constantin and Patek chronographs & 18K gold rectangles.

A major part of the market in the U.S. is now made up of the private sector being influenced by articles in magazines such as Forbes, U.S.A. Today, and Connoisseurs, and even a Bill Cosby T.V. show was based on a Patek Philippe world time wrist watch. Many celebrities have recently began to get interested and are collecting high-grade pieces.

A softening or leveling off of the low-end gold and gold-filled, silver and stainless steel Vintage market has occurred, primarily, it seems because the collectors of those pieces have moved on to the more expensive. The causes for this are many, but the primary one is, we believe, the loss of interest by the magazine and news paper writers looking for the sensational.

The U.S. Made Illinois, Hamilton, Elgin & Waltham in unusual or interesting cases are still finding good buyers, but at lower prices. Illinois and Hamilton seem to be the most popular.

We have a good section on military pieces which are now very much sought after by collectors.

Many collectors are now becoming aware of character watches and look for some rising of prices in this area as soon as all of the sleepers are gone.

VINTAGE WRIST WATCHES have been rapidly gaining in popularity during the last 8 years. Definite evidence is seen worldwide by the number of wrist watches appearing in the Horological Auctions and the increase in shops, dealers and new auction houses, exclusively trading in them.

We attribute the increase in the price buyers are willing to pay to five major reasons: (1) United States of North America's dollar value compared to other world currency, giving the major markets --Italy, Germany, France, Switzerland and Asia--more buying power; (2) more disposable income among younger buyers; (3) the nostalgia movement which express consumer's increasing disenchantment with our modern throw-away world; (4) spread of knowledge about the desirability and availability of VINTAGE WRIST WATCHES through many good books and the major United States news media; and (5) this is the first time in our memory that a collectible is also useful and the end is, if at all, we believe a long time in the future.

The dealer or collector must like, want and have the money to buy the vintage wrist watch or it has less value at that point in time. Some of the things that make a VINTAGE WRIST WATCH worth money are ORIGINAL COST, MAKER, COMPLICATIONS, ORIGINALITY, CONDITION and, last but not least, how the buyer likes the way it looks on his or her wrist!

Pickers for the European & Asian market have a very marked effect on the market at the United States NAWCC Regionals. A good example is when a foreign market "discovers" a new desirable piece, such as the "Hamilton Ventura", to name one, and then buys up all in sight, but after a few months the fascination seems to wear off, and the market gets soft. Some cycling of the market is bound to happen; prices do not necessarily continue to go up on everything.

We are glad to see more and more Americans entering the market to help provide stability and slow growth with values based on a good concept of supply and demand. Remember **the only substitute for knowledge is money. Happy and successful hunting.** We hope you find a way to use this book as a tool to help you make some extra money or build a collection with knowledge.

14K $800-900   14K $800-900   14K $600-700

A73 — 14k yellow solid gold; square fancy end; 17 j. $220

A75 — 14k yellow solid gold; square CC, fancy end, R.F.D.; 17 j. $215

A77 — 14k yellow solid gold; two tone, square R.F.D.; 17 j. $200

14K $500-560

14K $700-770   14K $600-670

A83 — 14k yellow solid gold; square bar end, R.F.D.; 17 j. $210

A79 — 14k yellow solid gold; round fancy end ring; 17 j. $200

A81 — 14k yellow solid gold; fancy round index dial; 17 j. $185

Platinum $900-1000

A85 — 10% irid. plat.; square roll end, black figure index dial; 17 j. $350

14K $400-450   14K $800-900   14K $700-780

A87 — 14k
yellow solid
gold; round
scallop cone
shape, raised
figure dial;
17 j. $250

A89 — 14k
yellow solid
gold; two
tone, rec-
tangular roll
end, raised
figure dial;
17 j. $220

A91 — 14k
yellow solid
gold; rec-
tangular
knife edge,
bar end,
raised figure
dial; 17 j.
$220

14K $1000-1100   14K $750-850   14K $450-500

A93 — 14k
yellow solid
gold; rec-
tangular
knife edge
bezel, fancy
end, pink
dial; 17 j.
$250

A95 — 14k
yellow two
tone solid
gold; rec-
tangular
curved,
R.F.D.; 17 j.
$260

A97 — 14k
yellow solid
gold; square
roll end, gold
figure dial;
17 j. $200

AGASSIZ

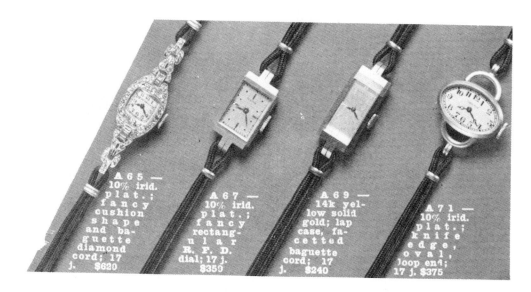

A 65 —
10% irid.
plat.;
fancy
cushion
shape
and ba-
guette
diamond
cord; 17
j. $620

A 67 —
10% irid.
plat.;
fancy
rectang-
ular
R. F. D.
dial; 17 j.
$350

A 69 —
14k yel-
low solid
gold; lap
case, fa-
cetted
baguette
cord; 17
j. $240

A 71 —
10% irid.
plat.;
knife
edge,
oval,
loop end;
17 j. $375

10-25% over gold
Not much market

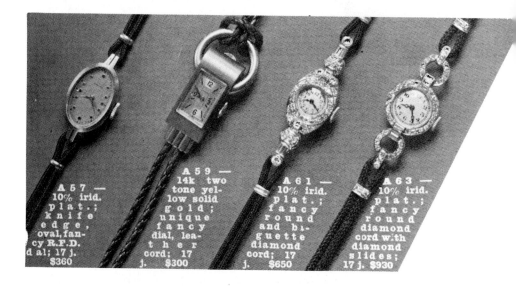

A 57 —
10% irid.
plat.;
knife
edge,
oval, fan-
cy R.F.D.
dial; 17 j.
$360

A 59 —
14k two
tone yel-
low solid
gold;
unique
fancy
dial, lea-
ther
cord; 17
j. $300

A 61 —
10% irid.
plat.;
fancy
round
and ba-
guette
diamond
cord; 17
j. $650

A 63 —
10% irid.
plat.;
fancy
round
diamond
cord with
diamond
slides;
17 j. $930

Astin Watch Co. S. A.

La Chaux-de-Fonds

Steel $10-15
18K $75-85

Steel $25-35
18K $125-150

5 1/4"

7 3/4-11"

8 3/4-12"

10 1/2"

56

57

Steel $25-35
18K $125-140

58

Steel $10-15
18K $90-100

59

Steel $125-150
18K $450-500

Steel $100-110
18K $175-200

Steel $125-150
18K $175-200

10 1/2"
53

13"
54

15 1/2"
55

18KYG $100–140
STEEL $20–30

18KYG $160–200
STEEL $20–30

18KYG $200–240
STEEL $90–120

18KYG $100–140
STEEL $10–20

18KYG $150–180
STEEL $70–100

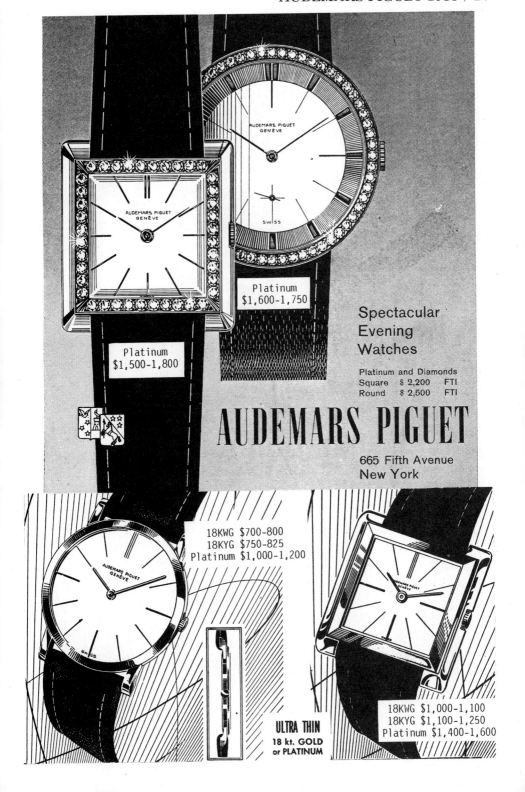

Platinum
$1,600-1,750

Platinum
$1,500-1,800

Spectacular
Evening
Watches

Platinum and Diamonds
Square $ 2,200   FTI
Round $ 2,500   FTI

AUDEMARS PIGUET

665 Fifth Avenue
New York

18KWG $700-800
18KYG $750-825
Platinum $1,000-1,200

18KWG $1,000-1,100
18KYG $1,100-1,250
Platinum $1,400-1,600

ULTRA THIN
18 kt. GOLD
or PLATINUM

Audemars Piguet Ltd.

Full Size Royal Oak
Steel $1,000-1,200
Steel & Gold $1,700-1,900
18K $5,000-5,500
Add for Diamond Bezel
$1,500-2,000

3/4 Size Royal Oak
Steel $1,200-1,500
Steel & Gold $2,000-2,200
18K $5,500-6,000

Diamond Bezel
18K $1,500-1,700

3/4 Size Royal Oak
Steel $800-1,000
Steel & Gold $1,300-1,450
18K $3,000-3,300

4153 477

7005

8638 424

18K $800-1,000

Diamond Bezel
Bracelet
18K $1,500-1,800

Skeleton
18K $4,500-5,000

4083

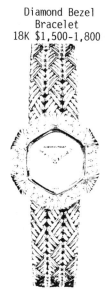

8746 485

4019

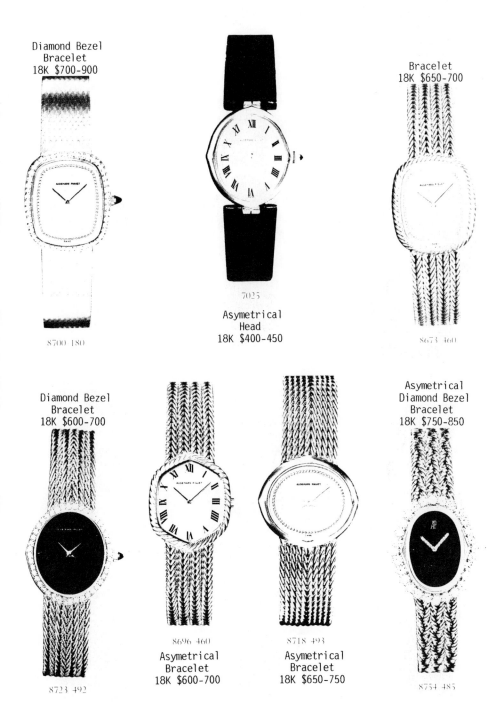

Diamond Bezel
Bracelet
18K $700-900

8700 180

7025

Asymetrical
Head
18K $400-450

Bracelet
18K $650-700

8673 460

Diamond Bezel
Bracelet
18K $600-700

8723 492

8696 460

Asymetrical
Bracelet
18K $600-700

8718 493

Asymetrical
Bracelet
18K $650-750

Asymetrical
Diamond Bezel
Bracelet
18K $750-850

8754 485

Bracelet
18K $1,100-1,250

4144 180

Strap
18K $1,150-1,275

4141

Bracelet-Quartz
Steel $700-800
Steel & Gold $1,200-1,350
18K $2,200-2,400

6005 477

Bracelet
18K $1,150-1,300

4032 470

Bracelet
18K $900-1,000

4079 469

Bracelet-Calendar
Automatic
18K $900-1,000

4137 469

Belforte "Voyager". Waterproof. Center seconds. 17J movement. Square, gold-filled case. ca 1962 . . . . $15—25

Benrus
21x33mm—CA 1940's
14K Yellow $175—250

Belforte "Nobility". Waterproof. Center seconds. Round chrome case. ca 1962 . . $7—18

Benrus "Dial-O-Rama". Waterproof. Hour & minute windows. 17J movement. Round chrome case. ca 1957. . . . . $100—125
Bracelet . . . . $2—4

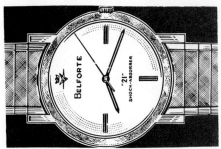

Belforte. Waterproof. Center seconds, 21J movement. Round, stainless steel case with florentine bezel. ca 1963. . . . . $10—15

Benrus "Golden Halo". Ladies, 17J movement. Rectangular gold-filled case and faceted single lugs. ca 1946. . . . .$5—10

Benrus
24x34mm—CA 1950's
3 Diamond dial—Step lugs
14K Yellow $200—250

BOREL
Ca 1954
14KYG Filled $40-60

Borei COCKTAIL watches are still being produced and can be bought wholesale from their office in Kansas City. After market value is from $35-100, depending on the head style & size in steel or plated.

U.S. DISTRIBUTION CENTER

ERNEST
BOREL / Mido

1008 Walnut Kansas City, MO 64106
816/421-2562

4330

4330B

4446

$50-75

4173

$125-175

4432

$75-100

Yellow cases. All available with choice of black or white dial, some with blue or brown dial.

NOUVEAU

1-Button Chronograph
Porcelain Dial
Steel $225-250
18K $550-625

Un seul poussoir
pour les 4 fonctions

Le chronographe
à 4 temps

avec remise en marche facultative

Porcelain Dial
Steel $150-175
18K $400-450

NOUVEAU

1-Button Chronograph
Porcelain Dial
Steel $200-250
18K $500-550

Simplicité
et précision

BOVET FRÈRES & C⁻ S. A.

FLEURIER (Suissse)

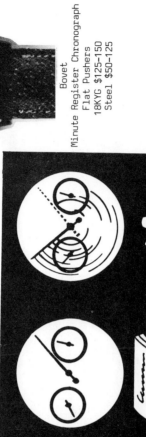

Breitling

Steel $400-440

Steel $500-550   Steel $600-675

Steel $200-250
18K $400-450

Steel $250-300
18K $450-500

Breitling

1939

10 1/2"   1941

Steel $400-450

Steel $350-400

Steel $275-325

Steel $175-200

Breitling
10 ¹/₂ ′′′′

757

Steel $1,300–1,400
18K $3,800–4,500

754

Steel $1,200–1,300
18K $3,500–4,000

756

Steel $1,000–1,150
18K $3,300–3,600

755

Steel $1,100–1,250
18K $3,700–4,100

753

Steel $300–400
18K $1,200–1,400

BROOKS

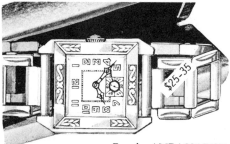

Brooks AMBASSADOR

No. 14020—10½ Ligne, 17 **Jewel** movement. Star 14 Karat gold filled two-tone case. Radium dial and hands. Two-tone link band to match. **$39.50**

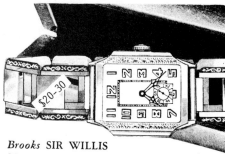

Brooks SIR WILLIS

No. 14021—10½ Ligne, 17 **Jewel** movement. White filled engraved case. Radium dial and hands. Latest flexible link band..... **$37.50**

No. 14022—*Brooks* **GOVERNOR**. Same as above, but in natural gold color filled case, with flexible link band to match. **$42.50**

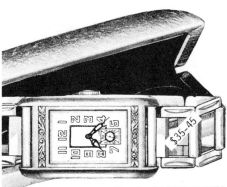

Brooks COMMANDER

No. 14023—9 Ligne, 17 **Jewel** movement. Star 14 Karat white gold filled case, curved to fit the wrist. Radium dial and hands. Link band. **$42.50**

Brooks LEXINGTON

No. 14024—9 Ligne, 17 **Jewel** movement. Star 14 Karat white gold filled case, curved to fit the wrist. Luminous dial and hands. Link band. **$49.50**

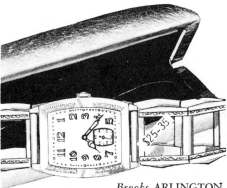

Brooks ARLINGTON

No. 14025—9 Ligne, 17 **Jewel** movement. Star 14 Karat solid gold white case, curved to fit the wrist. Luminous dial and hands. Link band. **$67.50**

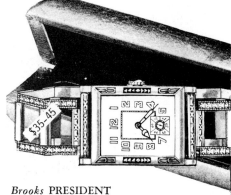

Brooks PRESIDENT

No. 14026—9 Ligne, 17 **Jewel** movement. Star 14 Karat white gold filled engraved case. Luminous dial and hands. Link band. **$49.50**

BROOKS

Brooks SCOUT
No. 14002—5/0 size, 6 Jewel movement. White permanent finish case. Radium dial and hands. Link band. **$13.50**

Brooks RANGER
No. 14001—5/0 size, 6 Jewel movement. White permanent finish engraved case. Radium dial and hands. Fine leather strap. **$11.50**

Brooks MARKS JR.
No. 14004—10½ Ligne, 6 Jewel movement. Permanent finish engraved two-tone case. Radium dial and hands. Link band..... **$16.50**

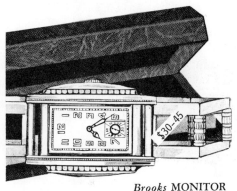

Brooks MONITOR
No. 14003—10½ Ligne, 6 Jewel movement. White permanent finish engraved case. Radium dial and hands. Link band. **$15.50**

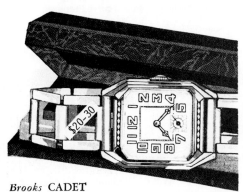

Brooks CADET
No. 14006—10½ Ligne, 7 Jewel movement. White permanent finish case of modernistic design. Radium dial and hands. Link band. **$18.50**

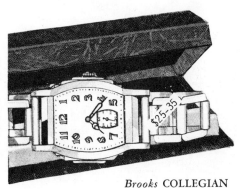

Brooks COLLEGIAN
No. 14005—5/0 size, 7 Jewel movement. White permanent finish case in modern step-design. Radium dial and hands. Link band... **$17.50**

Bristol "Ladies Octagon". Silvered dial. 7J or 15J, 9''' movement. Octagonal convertible, engraved case. ca 1918.
14K yellow gold. . . . .$40—60
25 Year yellow gold-filled . . . . 10—20

Bristol "Ladies Round". Silvered dial. 7J or 15J, 9''' movement. Round convertible, engraved case. ca 1918. 14K yellow gold . $40—60
25 Year yellow gold-filled . . . . 10—20

Bristol "Ladies Oval". Silvered dial, 7J or 15J, 9''' movement. Oval convertible, engraved case. ca 1918. 14K yellow gold . . . . . $60—80
25 Year yellow gold-filled . . . . 30—40

Brooks "Greenwich Jump Hour". Hour, minute & seconds windows. 9¾''', 17J movement. 14K white gold-filled, engraved rectangular case. ca 1933. . . . . $150—180

Brooks "Observer Jump Hour". Hour, minute & seconds windows. 10½''', 15J movement. Chrome tonneau case. ca 1933 . . . . $100—120

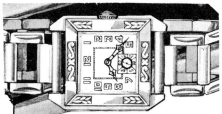

Brooks "Ambassador". Radium silvered dial & hands. 10½''', 17J movement. Tu-tone 14K gold-filled, engraved square case and molded lugs. ca 1933. . . . .' . . . .$45—65
Tu-tone bracelet. . . . . 7—18

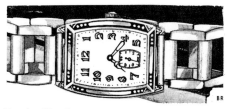

Brooks "Lexington". Luminous hands & dial, subsidiary seconds. 9''', 17J movement. 14K white gold-filled, engraved curved tonneau case. ca 1933. . . . .$20—30
Bracelet . . . . 4— 8

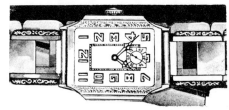

Brooks "Sir Willis". Radium silvered dial & hands, subsidiary seconds. 10½''', 17J movement. Yellow gold-filled, engraved rectangular case with carved-out corners. ca 1933 . $20—25
White gold-filled. . . . . 15—20
Bracelet . . . . 4— 8

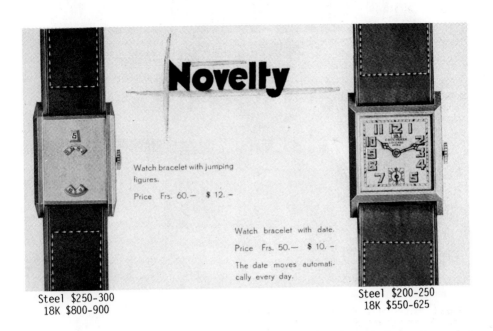

Novelty

Watch bracelet with jumping figures.

Price Frs. 60.— $ 12.—

Watch bracelet with date.

Price Frs. 50.— $ 10.—

The date moves automatically every day.

Steel $250-300
18K $800-900

Steel $200-250
18K $550-625

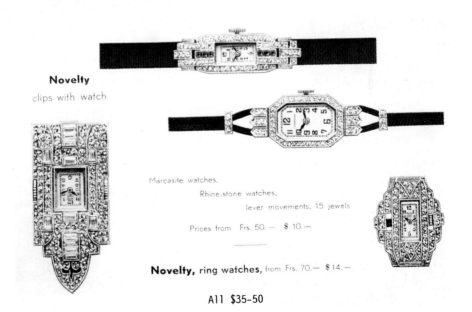

Novelty

clips with watch

Marcasite watches,

Rhine-stone watches,

lever movements, 15 jewels

Prices from Frs. 50.— $ 10.—

Novelty, ring watches, from Frs. 70.— $ 14.—

All $35-50

CHANCELLOR ✦ 14 kt. white gold case and 14 kt. woven gold mesh strap to match; 17 jewel movement; wafer thin case curved to fit the wrist . $150.00

14KWG Head $250
14KWG $150

14KWG $175

BANKER ✦ 15 jewel movement; radium dial . . . $24.75

14KWG $150

NORMAN ✦ 15 jewel radium dial; complete with bar link strap $37.50

14KWG $150

BREWSTER ✦ 15 jewel; radium dial; complete with woven mesh strap $37.50

14KWG $250

PRESIDENT ✦ 17 jewel movement; radium dial; curved to fit wrist; complete with woven mesh strap $50.00

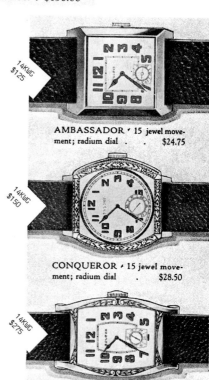

14KWG $125

AMBASSADOR ✦ 15 jewel movement; radium dial . . $24.75

14KWG $150

CONQUEROR ✦ 15 jewel movement; radium dial . $28.50

14KWG $275

TEMPLAR ✦ 15 jewel movement; radium dial . . . $37.50

14KWG $325

BUCKINGHAM ✦ 17 jewel; radium dial; curved to fit wrist $50.00

Bulova "Gold Curved Strap". Radium silvered dial. 17J movement. 14K green gold, engraved rectangular case. ca 1927. . . . . . . $250–300
14K white gold $250–300
14K white or green gold-filled. . . . $50–75

Bulova "Spartan". Round radium silvered dial, subsidiary seconds. 15J movement. Gold-filled tonneau case. ca 1928 . . . . $25–45

Bulova "Senator". Radium silvered dial. 15J movement. Engraved, gold-filled, rectangular case. ca 1928 . . . . $50–60

Bulova "Gold Strap". Radium silvered dial, subsidiary seconds. 15J movement. 14K white gold, engraved octagonal case. ca 1927 $175–210

Bulova "Banker". Radium silvered dial, subsidiary seconds. 15J movement. 10K yellow gold-filled tonneau case. ca 1927 . . . $50–60

Bulova "Treasurer". Radium silvered dial, subsidiary seconds. 15J movement. Engraved gold-filled tonneau case. ca 1928 . . . $60–80

Bulova "Gold Strap". Radium silvered dial, subsidiary seconds. 17J movement. 14K green gold case. ca 1927. . . . . $150–180

Bulova "Spencer". Radium silvered dial, subsidiary seconds. 17J movement. Engraved, white gold-filled, curved rectangular case. ca 1929 . . . . $75–85

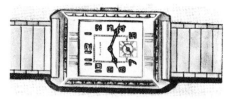

Bulova "Wellington". Radium silvered dial, subsidiary seconds. 17J movement. 14K gold engraved rectangular case. ca 1929 . . $175–210

Bulova "Watertite". Round dial, subsidiary seconds. 15J movement. Engraved, skeleton-type, gold-filled tonneau case. ca 1930. $85–105

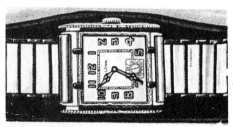

Bulova "Fleetwood". Radium silvered dial, subsidiary seconds. 17J movement. Tu-tone gold-filled, engraved rectangular case. ca 1929.
. . . . $75–95

Bulova "Commodore". Silvered dial, subsidiary seconds. 15J movement. Round chrome case. ca 1936 . . . . $10—20
Yellow plated top. . . . . 15—30
Bracelet . . . . 2— 3

Bulova "Argyle". Radium silvered dial, subsidiary seconds. 17J movement. 14K gold, engraved tonneau case. ca 1929 . . . $325–390

Bulova "Craftsman". Subsidiary seconds. 15J movement. Yellow gold plated, tonneau case. ca 1936. . . . . $65–80

Bulova "Sky King Tu-Tone". Subsidiary seconds. 17J movement. Tu-tone gold-filled, engraved tonneau case. ca 1932 . . . . $75–100

Bulova "Banker". Black dial, subsidiary seconds. 17J movement. Yellow gold plated, round case and large square lugs. ca 1936.
. . . . $50–70

Men's Bulova Watches

A VARIETY of handsome models. You can consult your Bulova with pride. Men who wear Bulova strap watches are proud of them, and they have a right to be, because Bulova watches are always true to their trust. They're accurate and dependable, and they're good looking as well. Each watch is sent in a beautiful presentation case.

$50-60 Good Looking
Surrey $37.50
$3.75 Down and $3.75 a Month
Engraved 14-K White Gold filled oxidized finish case with 15-Jewel Bulova movement; luminous dial and hands. Complete with bar link band.

You Pay No Interest or Carrying Charges When Buying from Loftis

We Prepay All Forwarding Charges and Guarantee Safe Delivery

$60-70 Remarkable Value
La Fayette $29.75
$2.97 Down and $2.97 a Month
Plain polish, 14-K White Rolled Gold plated, oval case, fitted with reliable 15-Jewel Bulova movement; luminous dial and hands. Complete with woven mesh band.

A Dependable Time-piece

Very Attractive

A Watch That Will Be Appreciated by the Man or Young Man
Envoy $24.75
$2.47 Down and $2.47 a Month
Now you can get a fine Bulova strap watch for as little as $24.75. There can be no reason now for anyone to be without a nationally famous Bulova watch. Patented methods of production have made it possible for Bulova Watch Co. to produce really fine timepieces of guaranteed quality and dependability. Plain polish, 14-K White Rolled Gold plated case. Curved back to fit the wrist. Fitted with 15-Jewel Bulova movement, radium dial and hands. Sent in a handsome presentation case.

We Are Authorized Distributors for Bulova Watches

$65-75
Very Attractive
Pres. Madison $60.00
$6.00 Down and $6.00 a Month
A real man's strap watch. Case is 14-K White Gold filled inlaid with black enamel. Has a 17-Jewel Bulova movement; radium dial and hands. Complete with woven mesh bracelet.

Our Immense Buying Power Is Your Gain

$75-85
Accurate Timekeeper
Cambridge $50.00
$5.00 Down and $5.00 a Month
Distinctive dust-proof case, 14-K White Gold filled, hand engraved. Has a 15-Jewel Bulova movement. Radium dial and hands. Complete with White Gold filled mesh band.

$60-70
Sturdily Built
Crusador $37.50
$3.75 Down and $3.75 a Month
Engraved 14-K White Gold filled, oval case with White Gold filled mesh band attached. Has a 15-Jewel Bulova movement. Radium dial and hands.

Satisfied Customers Everywhere Our Best Recommendation

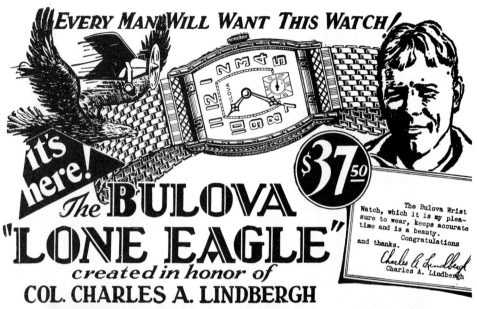

EVERY MAN WILL WANT THIS WATCH!

it's here!

The **BULOVA "LONE EAGLE"**

created in honor of
COL. CHARLES A. LINDBERGH

$37.50

The Bulova Wrist Watch, which it is my pleasure to wear, keeps accurate time and is a beauty. Congratulations and thanks.

Charles A. Lindbergh
Charles A. Lindbergh

$60-70

THE fact that Colonel Lindbergh has endorsed his Bulova Watch so enthusiastically will naturally add to your desire to possess this handsome "Lone Eagle" created expressly in his honor.

Then too, you'll like its good looking appearance, its handsomely engraved 14-K White Gold filled Case with non-breakable crystal in back to protect the movement from dust. Has 15-Jewel reliable Bulova movement. Latest style flexible link band—and as the years go by you'll like, above all, its accurate, dependable service. *Sent in a Beautiful Presentation Case.*

Lone Eagle, Man's Watch **$37.50**

Type 2 Spaceview
Steel $125-150
Gold Filled $150-175
14K $250-300
18K $300-350

What Apollo means

Apollo means the conquest of the moon. And soon man will be there. Bulova Accutron tuning-forks ordered for the Apollo project will help to guide him there, and back, by aiding in the navigation of the space-craft.

The tuning-fork systems use thin metal blades to produce the precise frequencies required by the electronic navigation instrumentation. Bulova electronic master timers aboard the five human orbiter satellites have already mapped out 10 potential landing sites for the Apollo astronauts. The timers synchronised the spacecraft's photographic sub-system.

And Bulova Accutron long-duration timers will be part of a sophisticated electronic package left on the surface of the moon.

The self-powered electronic instrument packages will send back to earth information on unsupervised, pre-programmed operations for periods up to 12 months.

In these, and many other ways, Bulova research and engineering are bringing the moon and stars a little closer to us all.

Today, as well as being involved in applications for timing devices in space, Bulova offers more than 60 different Bulova Accutron wristwatches.

Model of lunar landing vehicle in new Apollo display now available to all Bulova Accutron jewellers.

BULOVA ACCUTRON

Bulova UK Limited
3 Charles St., Berkeley Square, London W1

With Dial
$100–120
Spaceview
$200–250

ACCUTRON ASTRONAUT "A"
White, stainless steel case, waterproof*, shock-protected, sweep second hand, hack setting mechanism,
rotating 24 hour bezel, 24 hour indicator, black luminous dial and hands,
adjustable stainless steel band.
$175.00

With Dial
$50–60
Spaceview
$175–200

ACCUTRON "210"
Yellow and White combination, 14K
gold bezel ring, stainless steel case,
waterproof*, shock-protected, sweep
second hand, luminous dial and
hands, applied markers on dial, adjustable yellow and white combination band.   **$175.00**

18K $1,800–2,000

ACCUTRON ASTRONAUT "C"
Yellow, 18K gold case, waterproof*,
shock-protected, sweep second hand,
luminous dots and hands, hack setting mechanism, rotating 24 hour
bezel, 24 hour indicator, gold dial
with applied figures, 18K gold adjustable band.   **$1000.00**

With Dial
$40–50
Spaceview
$125–150

ACCUTRON "214"
White, stainless steel case, waterproof*, shock-protected, applied
markers, sweep second hand, alligator lizard strap.   **$125.00**

Type 2 Spaceview
10KYGF $150–175

ACCUTRON SPACEVIEW "H"
Yellow, 10K gold filled bezel, stainless steel back, transparent dial
lets you see spaceview movement,
waterproof*, shock-protected, luminous hands and dots, sweep second
hand, adjustable band.   **$150.00**

With Dial
Steel $120–140
10KGF $140–160
Spaceview
$125–150

ACCUTRON "202"
Yellow, 10K gold filled bezel, stainless steel back, waterproof*, shock-
protected, sweep second hand, calf
strap, RAILROAD APPROVED. Also in
all stainless steel case.   **$125.00**

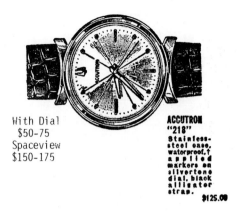

With Dial
$50-75
Spaceview
$150-175

ACCUTRON "218" Stainless-steel case, waterproof.† applied markers on silvertone dial, black alligator strap. **$125.00**

With Dial
$40-50
Spaceview
$125-150

ACCUTRON "411" Yellow, 10K gold filled case, stainless steel back, waterproof*, shock-protected, sweep second hand, applied figures on dial, alligator lizard strap. **$135.00**

With Dial
Steel $45-55
14K $250-300
Spaceview
$160-180
14K $300-350

ACCUTRON "223" Electronic timepiece. White, .Stainless steel case. Waterproof*. Luminous. **$125.00** In 14K yellow gold, **$200.00**

With Dial
$40-50
Spaceview
$125-150

ACCUTRON "412" Yellow, 10K gold filled bezel, stainless steel back, waterproof*, shock-protected, sweep second hand, luminous hands and dots, applied figures on dial, alligator strap. **$135.00**

NOTE: Original 214 metal bands marked Accutron are valued at $5-15.
Leather straps marked Accutron are $5-10.

NOTE: The model numbers do not appear on the watch. Case numbers are stamped with ink on the inside case back. The year made is on the outside case back (M=1960 N=1970) plus the year (M6=1966).

With Dial
$40-50
Spaceview
$125-150

ACCUTRON "400" Yellow, 10K gold filled case, waterproof*, shock-protected, applied figures on dial, sweep second hand, alligator strap. **$150.00**

With Dial
$40-50
Spaceview
$125-150

ACCUTRON "413" Yellow, 10K gold filled bezel, stainless steel back, waterproof*, shock-protected, sweep second hand, applied markers on dial, adjustable band. **$150.00**

With Dial
$40-50
Spaceview
$135-160

ACCUTRON "417"
10K gold-filled, stainless-steel
back, waterproof,† adjustable
mesh bracelet with fold-over
buckle. $150.00

With Dial
14K $250-300
Spaceview
14K $350-400

ACCUTRON "513"
Yellow, 14K gold case, waterproof*,
shock-protected, sweep second hand,
applied markers on dial, adjustable
band. $250.00

With Dial
$40-50
Spaceview
$125-150

ACCUTRON "420"
10K gold-filled, waterproof,†
luminous dots and hands, adjustable mesh bracelet with
fold-over buckle. $175

14K $200-250

ACCUTRON "514"
Yellow, 14K gold, sweep second
hand, shock-protected, applied markers on dial, Florentine engraved
bezel, alligator strap. Also in White.
          $200.00

ACCUTRON "505"
Yellow, 14K gold case, applied marker dial, waterproof*, shock-protected,
alligator strap. Also in 14K white
gold. $200.00

With Dial
14K $350-400
18K $400-450
Spaceview
14K $400-450
18K $450-500

With Dial
14K $200-250
Spaceview
14K $250-300

ACCUTRON "560"
Yellow, 14K gold case and matching
14K gold adjustable mesh band.
Waterproof*, shock-protected, applied dial markers. $395.00

NOTE: **Accutron "505"** appears on the cover
as an original **type one (1) Spaceview.**
All of the round 214 Accutrons could have
come from the factory as a Spaceview with
a **401 spacer ring** taking the place of a
dial with the chapter ring printed on the
crystal or with a standard dial. The
later **type two (2) Accutron Spaceview
Model "H"** came from the factory without a
dial and used a **524 reflector chapter
ring.** All **214 Accutrons** set from the
back.

With Dial
18K $300-350
Spaceview
18K $450-500

ACCUTRON "602"
Yellow, 18K gold case, waterproof*,
shock-protected, sweep second hand,
applied markers on dial, alligator
strap with 18K gold buckle. $300.00

Steel
$50

$750-900
18K
$1,600-1,920

Butex
37mm—CA 1950's
Split second—Chronograph—Square pushers
Gold filled $800-900

Steel
$20

Cartier

18K $4,000-4,500

> * All values are given for the head only
>   unless the band is included in the
>   description.
> * Read page 12 before using this book
>   to value your wrist watch.
> * Values are given for a mint watch
>   with original dial, movement and
>   case.

18K $4,500-5,000

18K $5,500-6,000

Cartier

INTERNATIONALLY RENOWNED
JEWELLERS SINCE 1847

Movements by
Jager Le Coultre

14K $250 - 350

Bracelet
14K $650 - 850

Bracelet
14K $500 - 600

Bracelet
Backwind
14K $650 - 750

Bracelet
Backwind
18K $650 - 750

Ladies' Magnificent Gold Watches — From an extensive collection in exclusive contemporary designs . . . all with the finest Swiss movements. Left to right in 14kt gold; $115; $210; $235; $330; in 18kt gold, $360.

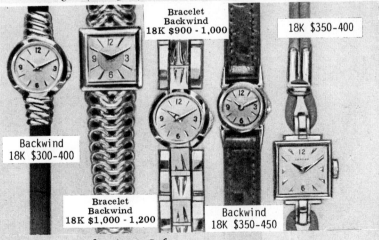

Bracelet
Backwind
18K $900 - 1,000

18K $350-400

Backwind
18K $300-400

Bracelet
Backwind
18K $1,000 - 1,200

Backwind
18K $350-450

The Time of Your Life — wrist watches of exceptional beauty and accuracy, all with finest Swiss movements. From our wide collection in 18kt gold. Left to right: $205; $450; $360; $215; $155 . . . Prices include Federal Tax. Illustrated actual size.

Cartier, synonymous with finest quality and value

FIFTH AVENUE AND 52 STREET, NEW YORK 22, N. Y.   PLaza 3-0111

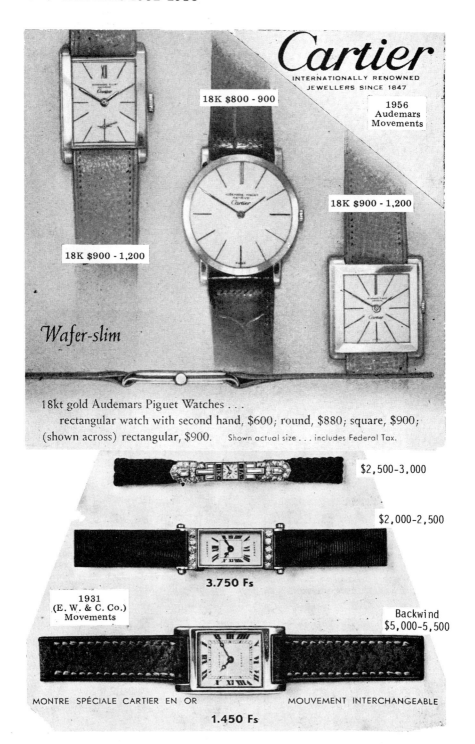

Cartier

INTERNATIONALLY RENOWNED
JEWELLERS SINCE 1847

1956
Audemars
Movements

18K $800 - 900

18K $900 - 1,200

18K $900 - 1,200

Wafer-slim

18kt gold Audemars Piguet Watches . . .
rectangular watch with second hand, $600; round, $880; square, $900;
(shown across) rectangular, $900.   Shown actual size . . . includes Federal Tax.

$2,500-3,000

$2,000-2,500

3.750 Fs

1931
(E. W. & C. Co.)
Movements

Backwind
$5,000-5,500

MONTRE SPÉCIALE CARTIER EN OR   MOUVEMENT INTERCHANGEABLE

1.450 Fs

Certina Watches

FOR THAT CERTAIN TIME

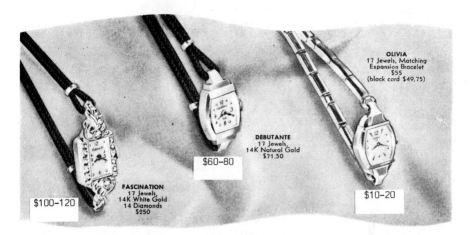

OLIVIA
17 Jewels, Matching
Expansion Bracelet
$55
(black cord $49.75)

DEBUTANTE
17 Jewels,
14K Natural Gold
$71.50

$60–80

FASCINATION
17 Jewels,
14K White Gold
14 Diamonds
$250

$100–120

$10–20

HONORED BY WATCH CONNOISSEURS OF SIXTY NATIONS

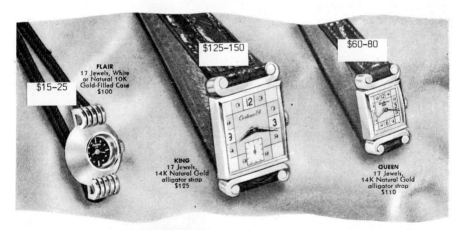

FLAIR
17 Jewels, White
or Natural 10K
Gold-Filled Case
$100

$15–25

$125–150

$60–80

KING
17 Jewels,
14K Natural Gold
alligator strap
$125

QUEEN
17 Jewels,
14K Natural Gold
alligator strap
$110

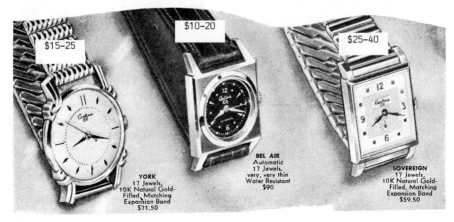

$15–25

$10–20

$25–40

YORK
17 Jewels,
10K Natural Gold-
Filled, Matching
Expansion Band
$71.50

BEL AIR
Automatic
17 Jewels,
very, very thin
Water Resistant
$90

SOVEREIGN
17 Jewels,
10K Natural Gold-
Filled, Matching
Expansion Band
$59.50

Certina "Gold Oval". Plain champagne dial. 14K gold oval case with engraved Roman numerals on bezel. ca 1969 . . . . . $75—100

Champ. Subsidiary seconds. 9¾''', 15J movement. 14K WGF, engraved tonneau case. ca 1928 . . . . $15—25

Certina. Round, gold-filled case with wide mesh bracelet. ca 1969 . . . . $35—50

Champ. Subsidiary seconds. 9¾''', 15J movement. 14K WGF tonneau case. ca 1928 $15—30

Certina "Gold Interchangeable". Ladies. 14K gold cushion case. Hinged lugs for interchangeable bands. ca 1969. . . . . $60—80

Champ. Ladies. 6½''', 15J movement. 14K gold engraved tonneau case. ca 1928 . . . . . $40—80
Gold-filled . . . . 10—20

CHAMP

Imported since 1898 by D. C. Percival & Co., Inc., 373 Washington Street, Boston, Mass. Offered a line to the wholesale trade from $15 to $250.

Champ. Ladies. 5¾''', 15J movement. 18K gold, engraved rectangular case. ca 1928. . . . . $45—85

Champ. Subsidiary seconds. 10½''', 15J movement. 14K WGF square case. ca 1928 . $15—25

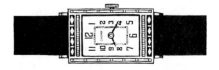

Champ. Ladies, 5¾''', 15J movement. 18K gold, engraved rectangular case. ca 1928. . . . . $40—80

David Mycko has been in close touch with the Character, Political and Advertising Wrist Watch Market for the past twelve years, and he has done the pricing of the character watches. He is a member of the NAWCC, Inc., attending most of the regional and national shows and many of the chapter meetings that have a trading session or mart. During the last three years he has attended all the major toy sales held in the United States as an active buyer, seller and observer of price trends.

The prices in this book are based on what a wrist watch will sell for to a collector. Recorded here are some actual recent sales of rare or expensive watches, and averaged top values for the more common types which never get much attention but which are usually bought and sold on a one-on-one basis.

No attempt has been made to predict the future prices but only to report the recent happenings in the market place among knowledgeable collectors and dealers.

This book does not indicate the high prices asked and many times received by Madison Ave., or Long Island, NY, or Melrose Ave., CA jewelry stores, auction houses, & antique dealers at the major shows, or, for that matter, any sale that would have to help support high overhead, travel and marketing expenses such as fancy showrooms, wages, and expensive advertising. Perhaps the values given in this book could be considered high whole-sale or low retail.

This book is not a price list but an indication of value. It does not tell the buyer what he should pay but what he might expect to buy or sell at the **top price** level. Values in this book are based on the following concepts of retail value: **The price a knowledgeable collector or investor who wants the wrist watch and has the money, will pay another collector or dealer who knows the value.** Consequently, no watch sales have been used that occur among individuals and dealers who have no market information or the perception of actual supply and demand.

Use the values given in this book as a guide, but, more importantly, use your own judgment based on your knowledge or desires of your particular collecting area and circumstances.

Remember, the price you pay must ultimately be your own, and is the value of the Character Wrist Watch to you at that particular moment.

Despite the fact that the values shown are based on sales between knowledgeable persons, there are still many wrist watches for sale at **bargain prices.** In other words, many wrist watches have not been **discovered** by collectors, and, consequently, are available at prices far below those they will warrant when their real importance becomes generally known. It is our hope that this book will be of real value to you by helping you build your collection for the least possible cost and with a good chance for future value appreciation.

An unusual market situation exists at this time. **BRADLEY TIME** closed it's doors for good in 1986 and residing in their warehouses were large numbers of some of the later issues. These Character Wrist Watches in New Old Stock **(NOS)** have found their way into the market place at what looks like bargain prices. A lot less of these watches exist than there are collectors and not everyone has access to them. Collectors tend to collect what is readily available and interest appears to be increasing for these attractive & well made pieces.

Pre-World War II pieces are very **hard to find,** along with **many recent contemporary pieces.** Prices have risen dramatically in the recent past.

Roy has collected or rather threw back and kept over 500 different **Character, Advertising or Political Watches** he has acquired over the years.

Recent events since the issue of Character Book 3: In a conversation by phone at press time, David indicated that there has been a surge upward in the **pre 1960's** copyrighted character watch asking prices. From the recent telephone calls received by Roy, Sherry and David, there is greater interest in **Bradley,** and the **W7** pieces also. 9/30/89

We know there are many more watches of which we have no illustrations. Send black & white or color 35mm photos of your watches "about 120% of actual size" and we will give you credit under acknowledgments for small help and "special thanks" for large help. **If your watch is not shown in Book 3 or this Book 4, it only means we don't have a picture of it.**

Send your pictures or old point-of-sale catalogs or sales literature illustrating character watches to Roy Ehrhardt 10101 Blue Ridge, Kansas City, Missouri 64134. Phone (816) 761-0080.

Abbott & Costello
Abbott & Costello Enterprises
The "Oldies" Series
Bradley-Quartz Analog-1986
HK Case-Japan Movement & Dial
White plastic case/strap
A&C 1 Head-34x39mm $35-40
A&C 2 Head-24x28mm $40-45

Black plastic case/strap
A&C 3 Head-34x39mm $35-40
A&C 4 Head-24x28mm $40-45
See-thru Layout Box $15-20

Abbott & Costello
Abbott & Costello Enterprises
The "Oldies" Series
Bradley-Quartz Analog-1986
HK Case-Japan Movement & Dial
Gold tone top-Stainless back
A&C 5 Head-32x38mm $50-60
A&C 6 Head-24x30mm $40-50
Layout Box $15-20

Alice in Wonderland
Walt Disney Productions
U.S. Time-Analog-1950
Chrome plated top-Stainless back
AIW 1 Head 25x37mm $50-60
Cup box $100-110

Alice in Wonderland
Walt Disney Productions
Timex-Analog-1958
Chrome plated top-Stainless back
AIW 4 Head 24x32mm $40-50
Box plastic statue $125-135
Box porcelain statue $125-135

Alice in Wonderland
Animated-Mad Hatter
Walt Disney Productions
New Haven-Analog-1953
Stainless steel case
AIW 2 Head $125-135
Box $100-110

Alice In Wonderland
Animated Hands
Walt Disney Productions
Bradley-Swiss Analog-1973
Gold Tone Base Metal Case
AIW 6 Head 25x32mm $40-50
Box $20-25

Walt Disney's
**ALICE IN
WONDERLAND**
Colorful Alice on dial. Pink case
and washable pink band.

Alice in Wonderland
Walt Disney Productions
U.S. Time-Analog-1955
AIW 3 Head $50-60
Box $100-110

*NOTE: All measurements are taken from
tip of lug to tip of lug and across the
smallest diameter.*

Alice In Wonderland
Moving Mad Hatter
Wotania-Swiss Analog-Ca 1972
Gold tone top-Base metal back
Embossed Lion Rampant case back
AIW 7 Head 25x32mm $50-70

Alice In Wonderland
Webster-Swiss Analog
Gold tone top-Base metal back
AIW 8 Head 29x35mm $20-30

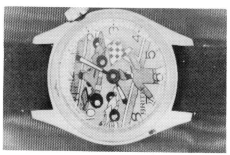

Automobile Racing
Moving Checker Flag
Britix-Corona-HK Analog-Swiss Parts
Gold tone top-Stainless back
AUR 2 Head 26x33mm $20-30

Apollo 15
Reflector-Dustproof
HK Dial-Swiss Analog
Chrome plated top-Stainless back
APO 1 Head 34x41mm $100-125

CHARACTER IDENTIFICATION CODES

The 3 letter identification code preceding the number is usually made up using the first two letters of the first name and the first letter of the last name. Exceptions occur because of the desire not to have duplicates which confuse the computer. These codes make possible more precise telephone and mail order descriptions.

Arthur Fiedler-"Mr. Pops"-Original
Stamped on case back
Constructa Watch Ltd.
Swiss Analog-On movement & case
Gold tone top-Stainless back
ARF 1 Head 34x42mm $60-75

Bambi
Animated Ears-WDP
Ingersoll (U.S. Time)-Analog-1949
White metal case
BAM 1 Head 29x40mm $200-250
Birthday Friends Box $200-250

Character Watches Listed Alphabetically
By First Names

Barbie
Mattel, Inc.–1973
Bradley-Swiss Analog
Clear base acryl case–Vinyl strap
BAR 5-Head 31x36mm $50-70

Magnifying Crystal
BAR 6-Head 34x34mm $50-70
Roll box $20-25

The values in the
Character section
were done by
David A. Mycko

Babe Ruth
Jura Watch Co-Swiss-Ca 1949
Florescent Dial-Steel color case
BAB 1 Head 32x41mm $300-400
Baseball Box $500-550

A SPECIAL THANKS TO:
Phil Summers
Kansas City, MO
*for the use of his character
watch research.*

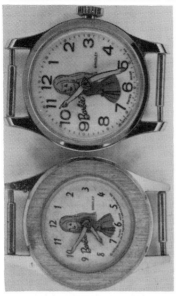

Barbie
Animated Hands-Mattel Inc.
Bradley-Swiss Analog-1978
Gold tone top-Base metal back
BAR 7 Head 26x33mm $50-60
BAR 8 Head 26x33mm $50-60
Pop up box $20-25

A SPECIAL THANKS TO:
Robert "Bob" Arnold,
Atlas, MI
for the use of his Character
Watch research.

Basketball Players
Swiss Unmarked
International Precision Time Ltd.
Remex-HK Analog-Sweep second
Gold tone top-Base metal back
BAP 1 Head 26x33mm $15-20

Batman
Gilbert-Swiss Analog-1966
Black plastic case
BAT 1 head 42x64mm Est. $400-450
Box $75-100

Batman
D.C. Comics Inc.
Swiss Analog-1977
Gold tone base metal top
Stainless steel back-Stick hands
Navy blue leather strap
Yellow stitching
BAT 2 Head Small $250-300
BAT 3 Head Large $350-400
Box $50-60
Ring $15-20

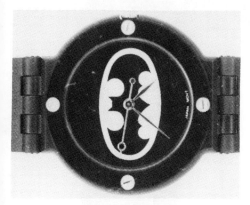

Batman
Embossed D.C. Comics Inc.-1989
Quintel-Japan Quartz Analog
HK Assembly
Ladies movement-Plastic insert
ABC Company-Miyota Co.-Sweep second
Consort Fashion Corps.
Clear plastic box-Stainless back
Black or white plastic top
PVC black or white plastic strap
Brass stud rivets
Watch & Box at retail 8/89 $30
BAT 4 Head 35mm
BAT 5 Head 27mm

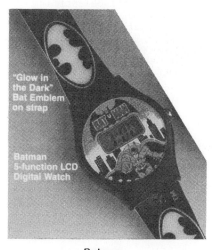

"Glow in the Dark" Bat Emblem on strap

Batman 5-function LCD Digital Watch

Batman
Embossed D.C. Comics Inc.-1989
5 function LCD-China Assem.
Ladies movement-Plastic insert
Consort Fashion Corps.
Clear plastic box
Black plastic top-Stainless back
Black "glow in the dark"
Bat Emblem strap
Watch & Box at retail 8/89 $12
Bat 7 Head 23x32mm

Batman
MY 9-12-86-Colored dial
Cosmo-HK Analog
Gold tone top-Stainless back
Sweep second-Yellow dial
Watch at wholesale 6/89 $20
BAT 6 Head 34x40mm

A SPECIAL THANKS TO:
William "Bill" Selover
St. Augustine, FL
for the use of his Character
Watch research.

Battlestar Galactica
Animated Seconds
Universal City Studios
Bradley-Swiss Analog-1979
Chrome top-Base metal back
BAG 1 Head 29x36mm $45-55
Pop up box $15-20

A SPECIAL THANKS TO:
Maggie Kenyon
New York, NY
for the use of her Character
Watch research.

NOTE: all values are given for a mint
original head & band

Bears Playing
Moving Bear
Wotania-Swiss Analog
Gold tone top-Base metal back
Embossed Lion Rampant case back
BEP 1 Head 25x32mm $25-35

Beatles
4 Beatles Faces on Seconds Disc
(Apple Corps Ltd.-HBL Ltd.-1989)
PG Time Ltd.-Swiss Analog
Hong Kong Assembly
Chrome plated case-Red & blue hands
Stainless expansion band
Watch, Box & Card retail 6/89 $30
Black trivia card
BEA 1 Head 32x38mm

Beethoven-Original
Animated Hands
Offbeat Time Co.
Windert-Swiss Analog-Sweep second
Gold tone top-Base metal back
BET 1 Head 32x40mm $40-50

Bert & Ernie
"Sesame Street Birthday"
Jim Henson Muppets
Bradley-Swiss Analog-1980
Chrome plated top-Base metal back
B&E 4 Head 26x32mm $35-45
B&E 5 Watch & Record $150-175

Beetle
Moving Eyes
Wotania-Swiss Analog
Gold tone top-Base metal back
Embossed Lion Rampant case back
BEL 1 Head 25x32mm $35-45

Betty Boop
Animated Mickey Hands
Bright Ideas S.F., Ca-K.F.S.-1989
Swiss Quartz Analog-HK Assembly
Gold tone top-Base metal back
Sweep Second
Ladies movement-Plastic insert
Watch at retail 6/89 $45
BEB 2 Head 32x38mm-No box

Big Bad Wolf
Moving Wolf
Lakeside Games
Division of Leisure Dynamics, Inc.
Red plastic strap with
Three Little Pigs
Plastic skeleton case
BBW 2 Head 37x46mm $35-45

Big Bird
Sesame Street-Jim Henson Muppets
Animated Hands
Bradley-Swiss Analog-1974
Chrome plated top-Base metal back
BIG 1 Head 29x36mm $35-45
BIG 2 Head 29x37mm $35-45
BIG 3 Head 30x37mm $35-45
Roll box $20-25
Pop up box $20-25

Big Bird
Sesame Street-Jim Henson Muppets
Animated Hands
Bradley-Swiss or HK Analog-1974
Chrome plated top-Stainless back
BIG 4 Head 26x33mm $35-45
BIG 5 Head 26x33mm $35-45
BIG 6 Head 26x33mm $35-45
Pop up Box $20-25

*NOTE: all values are given for a mint
original head & band*

Big Bird
Sesame Street-Jim Henson Muppets
Animated Hands
Bradley-Swiss or HK Analog-1978
Chrome plated top-Stainless back
BIG 7 Head   27x34mm $35-45
BIG 8 Moving 26x33mm $110-125
Roll box $20-25
Pop up Box $20-25

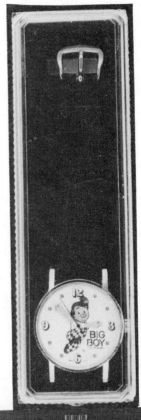

Big Boy-The Original
(Shoney's Restaurants)
Animated Hands-Sweep second
Evacosta-Swiss Analog-7J
Chrome plated top-Base metal back
BIB 3 Head 32x41mm $60-75
Flat layout box $2-7

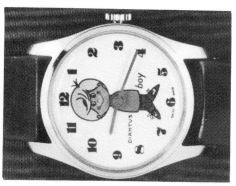

Black Hole
Walt Disney Productions
Bradley-Swiss-1979
Black cycolac case
Black plastic & metal strap
BLH 1 Head 35x40mm $35-45
Pop up box $20-25

Boy, Yellow Hair
Stick Hands
Diantus-Swiss Analog
Chrome plated top-Stainless back
Clear plastic straps
BOY 1 Head 30x36mm $15-25

Boy & Girl
Moving Eyes
Ruhla-Swiss Analog
Chrome plated top-Stainless back
BOG Head 27x35mm $30-40

Bobby
Swiss Unmarked-Prototype watch
Swiss Analog-Sweep second
Gold tone top-Stainless back
BOB 1 Head 31x36mm
For Information Only

Boy Scout
Animated Hands
Ingersoll-Analog-1934
Chrome plated case-Leather strap
BOY 2 Head $250-275
Box $100-125

New Haven Official
"Boy Scout" 7 Jewel.
Dependable Boy Scout
watch, streamlined Gold
Plated case; curved to fit
wrist. Radium dial with
Official Boy Scout Seal,
7 jewel movement. Un-
breakable crystal. De-
tachable leather strap.
Gift box.

Boy Scout
New Haven-Analog-1935
BOY 3 Head 28x38mm $125-150
Box $100-125

Bozo
Animated Hands
Capitol Records Inc.
Basic-Swiss Analog
Chrome plated-Base metal case
Red plastic/leather strap
BOZ 1 Head 31x36mm $50-60

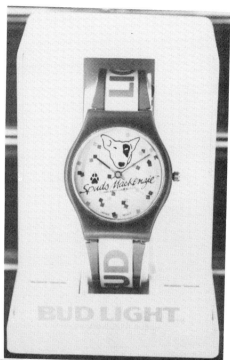

Buck Rogers-Imitation
"In the 25th Century"
No copyright-Colored dial
Westclox USA Analog Ca 1970s
Converted pocket watch
Chrome plated case
BUR 1 Head 50mm $30-40
Flat layout box & papers $5-10

Bud Light-"Spuds MacKenzie"-Face
Anheuser-Busch-1986
ABC Co-Japan Quartz Analog
HK Assembly
Blue plastic top-Stainless back
Ladies movement-Plastic insert
Blue plastic straps
marked "Bud Light"
BUL 2 Head 35x41mm $45-60
Box $10-20

> *Character Watches Listed Alphabetically*
> *By First Names*

Bud Light-"Spuds MacKenzie"-Party
Anheuser-Busch-1986
ABC Co-Japan Quartz Analog
HK Assembly
Blue plastic top-Stainless back
Ladies movement-Plastic insert
Yellow plastic straps
marked "Bud Light"
BUL 3 Head 35x41mm $45-60
Box $10-20

Bud Light-"Spuds MacKenzie"-Surfer
Anheuser-Busch-1986
ABC Co-Japan Quartz Analog
HK Assembly
Blue plastic top-Stainless back
Ladies movement-Plastic insert
White plastic straps marked
"Bud Light"
BUL 1 Head 35x41mm $45-60
Box $10-20

Note: BRADLEY TIME was a company organized about 1950 to market Character Advertising, Political & other Special Watches, and did so with hundreds of examples. They held the Disney Contract from 1972 to 1985. BRADLEY closed forever in 1986.

Butterfly-Eastman
Moving Eyes
Swiss Analog-Ca 1975
Gold tone top-Base metal back
BUT 1 Head 25x32mm $25-35

Bud Light-"Spuds MacKenzie"-Face
Anheuser-Busch-1986
ABC Co-Japan Quartz Analog
HK Assembly
Blue plastic top-Stainless back
Ladies movement-Plastic insert
White plastic straps marked "Bud Light" with colored confetti
BUL 1 Head 35x41mm $45-60
Box $10-20

PROTOTYPES

I have in my collection many one off crude prototypes prepared for competition by the designers to try for management acceptance. These were followed by more sophisticated examples without movements to show dealers & wholesalers to get their feeling of future market acceptance, and have either failed or made it into production. Many times the dials are printed on the reverse of other dials already in their product line. These are interesting in their somewhat crude state as an indication of creative thinking by the dial and/or watch designers. These make an interesting sideline for the advanced collector.

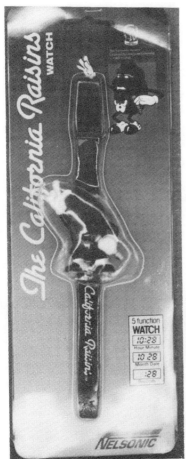

California Raisins-Sunglasses
Nelsonic-CalRab Inc.-1988
Japan 5 function LCD-HK Assem.
Purple plastic case
Black vinyl strap marked "The
California Raisins"
Watch & blister pak
retail 6/89 $20
CAR 1 Head 35x45mm

California Raisins-Singer
Nelsonic-CalRab Inc.-1988
Japan 5 function LCD-HK Assem.
Purple plastic case
Black vinyl strap
Watch & blister pak
retail 6/89 $20
CAR 2 Head 35x45mm

Captain Marvel
Fawcett Pub. Inc.
Marvel Import-Swiss Analog-1948
Aluminium Case
CAM 1 Head 33x41mm $125-145
Box $300-325

Care Bears
American Greetings Corp.
Bradley-Swiss Analog-1983
Gold tone top-Stainless back or
Chrome plated top-Stainless back
CAB 1 Head 24x31mm $15-20
CAB 2 Head 27x34mm $15-20
CAB 3 Head 27x34mm $15-20
Pop up box $5-10

Care Bears
American Greetings Corp.
Bradley-HK Analog-1983
Plastic top-Stainless back
Assorted colors
CAB 4 Head 30x33mm $15-20
Box $5-10

Care Bears
Bradley Time-Analog-Ca 1983
Chrome Case-Blue Strap
CAB 7 Head ??x??mm $15-20
Pop up box $5-10

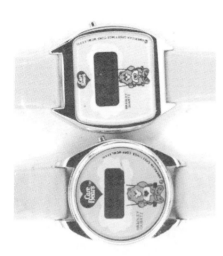

Care Bears
American Greetings Inc.
Bradley-Quartz-LCD-Ca 1984
Chrome Case-White Strap
Month-Date-Hour-Minute-Seconds
CAB 8 Head 26x31mm $10-20
Pop up box $5-10

Care Bears
American Greetings Corp.
Bradley-HK-Quartz LCD-1983
Chrome plated top-Stainless back
CAB 5 Head 26x33mm $15-20
CAB 6 Head 26x33mm $15-20
Pop up box $5-10

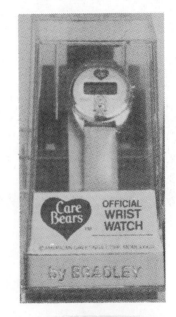

Care Bears
Pop up-"Closed"
Bradley Time-Quartz LCD-Ca 1984
Month-Date-Hour-Minute-Seconds
Blue Plastic Case & Band
CAB 9 Head-Closed 29x30mm $15-25
Pop up box $5-10

Care Bears
Those Characters from Cleveland
Bradley-HK Analog-1986
Plastic case/heart
CAB 10 Head 29x30mm $20-35
Box $5-10

Cat
Moving Eyes
Ruhla-Swiss Analog
Chrome plated top-Stainless back
CAA 2 Head 27x35mm $35-45

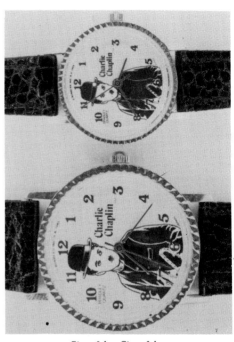

Charlie Chaplin
Bubbles, Inc. S.A.
The "Oldies" Series
Bradley-Quartz Analog-1985
HK Case-Japan Movement & Dial
Gold tone top-Stainless back
CHC 5 Head-32x38mm $50-60
CHC 6 Head-24x30mm $40-50
Layout Box $20-25

Cathy
Universal Press Syndicate
Bradley-Swiss Analog-1982
Chrome plated top-Base metal back
CAT 1 Head 27x32mm $35-40
CAT 2 Head 26x33mm $35-40
Box $10-15

NOTE: A 1987 book by
HOWARD BRENNER titled
COLLECTING COMIC CHARACTER
CLOCKS AND WATCHES
(ISBN 0-89689-062-7)
will be very useful in your collecting,
ESPECIALLY the INTRODUCTION.

Available from:
COLLECTOR BOOKS
P.O. Box 3009
Paducan, KY 42002-3009
1-800-626-5420

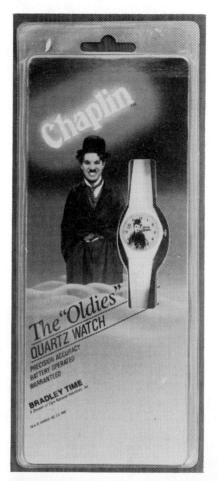

Charlie Chaplin
Bubbles, Inc. S.A.
The "Oldies" Series
Bradley-Quartz Analog-1985
HK Case-Japan Movement & Dial
White plastic case/strap
CHC 1 Head-34x39mm $50-60
CHC 2 Head-24x28mm $40-50

Black plastic case/strap
CHC 3 Head-34x39mm $50-60
CHC 4 Head-24x28mm $40-50
See-thru Layout Box $20-25

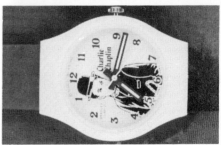

Charlie Chaplin
"Runs Backwards"
Bubbles, Inc. S.A.
The "Oldies" Series
Bradley-Analog-1977
Red buckle strap-Black hole strap
White plastic top-Stainless back
CHC 7 Head 33x40mm $125-140
See-thru layout box $25-30

Chipmunks
Bagdasarian Productions Inc.
Bradley Time-Analog-Ca 1984
Chrome Case-Red Strap
CHI 1 Head 28x34mm $35-45
CHI 2 Head 24x31mm $30-40
Pop up box $20-25

American and European
CHARACTER
Wrist Watch Price Guide Book 3
illustrates and values over 900
character wrist watches, ordering
information follows the text of this
book.

"CINDERELLA"......in the
"Slipper" Gift Box...$6.95

Cinderella
Ingersoll-U.S. Time-1950
Chrome top-Stainless back
CIN 1 Head 25x37mm $35-45
Plastic Slipper box $150-175

Cindy
Moving Shoe
Wotania-Swiss Analog
Gold tone top-Base metal back
Embossed Lion Rampant case back
CIY 1 Head 25x32mm $25-35

Chipmunks
Bradley Time-Quartz LCD-Ca 1984
Chrome Case-Red Strap
Month-Date-Hour-Minute-Seconds
CHI 3 Head 26x31mm $15-20
Pop up box $5-10

Cindy
Moving Shoe
Basis-Swiss Analog
Gold tone top-Base metal back
CIY 2 Head 26x32mm $20-25

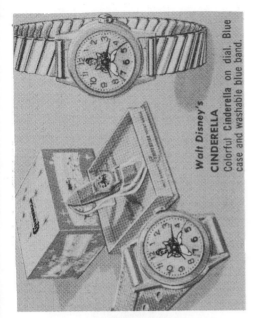

Cinderella
U.S. Time-Analog-1955
CIN 2 Head $35-40
Plastic Slipper Box $150-175

Cinderella
Walt Disney Productions
Bradley-Swiss Analog-1971
Gold tone top-Base metal back
CIN 4 Head 22x27mm $25-35
CIN 5 Head 26x32mm $25-35
CIN 6 Head 26x33mm $25-35
CIN 7 Head 29x35mm $25-35
Box $15-20

Cinderella
Walt Disney Productions
Timex Analog-1958
Chrome plated top-Stainless back
CIN 3 Head 24x32mm $50-60
Box plastic statue $150-170
Box porcelain statue $150-170

NOTE: all values are given for a mint
original head & band

Cinderella
Walt Disney Productions
Bradley-Swiss Analog-Ca 1971
Gold tone top-Base metal back or
Chrome plated top-Base metal back
CIN 8 Head 26x33mm $25-35
CIN 9 Head 26x30mm $25-35
CIN 10 Head 27x33mm $25-35
Roll Box $15-20

Cinderella
Walt Disney Productions
Animated Hands
Bradley-Swiss Analog-Ca 1972
Gold tone top-Base metal back or
Chrome plated top-Base metal back
CIN 12 Head 26x33mm $40-50
CIN 13 Head 26x32mm $40-50
CIN 14 Head 26x32mm $40-50
Roll Box $10-15

Cinderella
Webster Watch Co.
Swiss Analog-1972
Gold tone top-Base metal back
CIN 3a Head 26x32mm $20-25

Cinderella
Walt Disney Productions
Animated Hands
Bradley-Swiss Analog-1975
Gold tone top-Base metal back
CIN 15 Head 25x33mm $25-35
Box $10-15

*In an interview, Gable once said, "I've spent a lot of time learning to be an actor. I'm still learning. I don't know how you go about learning to be a personality, but I do know how you learn to go about being an actor, and I work at it. It's a profession I'm proud of." Gable was always known to study his lines and the characters he was portraying diligently. *

Clark Gable (Memories Collection)
Gable Estates & Company-1987
Product of Harilela Bob Ltd.-HBL
HK Quartz Analog-Sweep Second
Black plastic top-Base metal back
Black straps w/ paragraph on Gable
Black Trivia Card
CLG 1 Head 40x49mm
Head, Box & Card at retail 6/89 $40

INFORMATION WANTED by EDITOR ROY EHRHARDT

For the preparation of future issues of this book and other clock and watch books, we need additional new and different information. Here are some samples of what we need.

Wrist Watch Point of Sale Booklets and Factory Product Catalogs, and other advertising that illustrates and describes wrist watches. We especially need information on Patek Philippe, Rolex, Audemars Piguet, Vacheron & Constantin, Cartier, Tiffany, Universal Geneve, Concord, Corum, and other lesser known Foreign and American companies.

Clocks, Wrist or Pocket Watch Periodicals, both Horological and Jewelry Trades (all languages and dates, 1850 to 1980).

Clock and Watch Auction Catalogs. Any auction house, both old and new issues.

Let me know what you have. Roy Ehrhardt, 10101 Blue Ridge, P.O. Box 9808, Kansas City, MO 64134, or phone 816-761-0080.

Clash of the Titans
Metro Goldwyn-Mayer Film
Bradley-Swiss Analog-1981
Chrome plated top-Base metal back
COT 1 Head 30x36mm $35-40
Box $10-15

Colonial Gentlemen
Moving Arm
Wotania-Swiss Analog
Gold tone top-Base metal back
Embossed Lion Rampant case back
COG 1 Head 25x32mm $25-35

Clowns
Moving Arm
Wotania-Swiss Analog
Gold tone top-Base metal back
Embossed Lion Rampant case back
CLO 2 Head 25x32mm $45-60

Clowns
Moving Arm
Criterion-Swiss Analog-HK Dial
Chrome plated top-Stainless back
Winder at 2-Ca 1975
CLO 3 Head 30x35mm $25-30

Commemorative Eagle Dial
Commemorative Series
Engraved Liberty Bell on case back
Registered Edition 1776-1976
Bradley Time-Swiss Analog-1973
Gold tone top-Base metal back
COE 1 Head 34x42mm $60-75

Cowboy Bronco Buster
Moving Man
Economic-Swiss Analog
Gold tone top-Base metal back
COB 1 Head 25x32mm $45-60

Cookie Monster
Muppets Inc.-Animated Hands
Bradley-Swiss Analog-Ca 1971
Chrome top-Base metal back
COM 1 Moving Head-26x33mm $110-125
COM 2 Head-26x33mm $35-40
COM 3 Head-29x36mm $35-40
Pop up box $15-20

Cowboy Gunfighter
Moving Gun
Arios Ltd.-Swiss Analog
Gold tone top-Base metal back
COG 1 Head 25x32mm $45-60

Cool Cat-W7-Sheraton
(Dial Only)
Stamped on case back Cool Cat
Warner Bros. Seven Arts Inc.
Sheffield-Swiss Analog
Gold tone top-Base metal back
See Wile E. Coyote WEC 1 for Case
COC 1 Head 30x36mm $200-225

Cowboy Robber
Moving Gun
Wotania-Swiss Analog
Gold tone top-Base metal back
Embossed Lion Rampant case back
COR 2 Head 25x32mm $40-50

Cowboy, Space Gun
Remex-HK Analog
Gold tone top-Stainless back
Sweep second
COS 1 Head 26x34mm $20-30

Cub Scouts
"Cubs-Wolf's Head"-1950
Kelton-Ingersoll-Analog
Chrome plated top-Stainless back
CUS 1 Head 24x35mm $30-40

Cowgirl
Moving Gun
Wotania-Swiss Analog
Gold tone top-Base metal back
Embossed Lion Rampant case back
COG 2 Head 25x32mm $50-70

Cub Scouts
"Cubs-Wolf's Head"-1978
Timex-Analog Calendar
Chrome plated top-Stainless back
CUS 2 Head 30x37mm $50-60

Cowgirl (Annie Oakley)
Moving Gun
Case marked Muros Watch Factory
Swiss Analog-1951
Probably sold by New Haven
Chrome plated case
COG 1 Head 32x41mm $200-250

Daffy Duck
W7-Shearton
Swiss Analog-Ca 1972
Gold tone top-Base metal back
DAD 1 Head 30x37mm $200-225
Birthday Box $100-125

DALE EVANS
Official WATCH and JEWELRY SET

Features a slender chrome plated watch with stainless
steel back, expansion bracelet. Autographed picture of
Dale Evans and Buttermilk on dial. Lovely necklace
with official Dale Evans "Lucky Horseshoe" pendant
in rhodium finish. In clear-view 3-D gift box.
42W28- 560   Retail $8.50

Dale Evans
Bradley Time-Ingraham-1957
Made in Chrome, Blue, Pink & Gold
DAE 5 Head 25x37mm $75-85
Box $150-175

Dale Evans & Buttermilk-Reflector
No copywrite-Optical animation
Ingraham-Analog-Ca 1960
Chrome plated case
DAE 7 Head 25x37mm $185-215
Dial Illustrated Only
See ROY 16 For Case

Dale Evans Watch. Year after year, it's always a top favorite of girls! Has full color picture of Dale Evans and Buttermilk on dial. Large numerals are easy to read. Watch has precision Swiss movement: anti-magnetic, shockproof and electrically timed for accuracy. Chrome case, leather strap. Beautifully gift boxed.

**DALE
EVANS**

Dale Evans
Bradley Time-Swiss-Ca 1962
Chrome plated-Stick hands
DAE 6 Head $50-60
Box $100-120

Daisy Duck
Animated Hands
Ingersoll-U.S. Time-Ca 1948
Steel color case
DAS 1 head 29x40mm $200-250
Birthday Box $200-250

NOTE: All measurements are taken from tip of lug to tip of lug and across the smallest diameter.

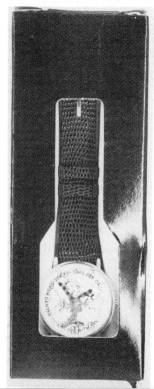

FRONTIER-SCOUT. Slim, oblong Chrome plated case. Stainless steel back. Genuine leather strap and western fittings. In captivating 3-dimensional, full color, Clear-Vue presentation gift package.
42W22-338   Retail **$4.95**

DELUXE FRONTIER-SCOUT. Same as above with matching Expansion Bracelet.
42W23-407   Retail **$5.95**

Davy Crockett
Ingraham-Analog-1951
Chrome plated top-Stainless back
DAC 2 Head 24x37mm $100-125
Box $200-225

Dan Quayle-Unmarked
Misplaced numbers on dial
Animated necktie/hands
Quartz Analog-Gold tone case
Stamped on case back China
on plastic sticker
Watch & Box at retail 6/89 $40
DAQ 1 Head Medium

Dem. Donkey-Original
Animated Hands
Dirty Time Company-1970
Windert-Swiss Analog
Chrome plated case
DED 1 Head 34x40mm $85-110

Dick Tracy
Moving Western Six Gun
"New Haven Clock & Watch Co"
marked on case & dial
Chic. Trib-USF 1951-on dial
Swiss Analog-Stainless steel case
DIT 8 Head 33x41mm $250-300

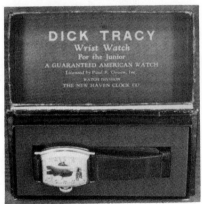

A SPECIAL THANKS TO:
William "Bill" Selover
St. Augustine, FL
for the use of his Character
Watch research.

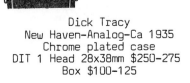

New Haven
"Dick Tracy"
A popular character
watch. Chromium finish
case, curved to fit wrist.
Neat silvered dial. Un-
breakable crystal; length
1⅞ inches. Detachable
leather strap. Gift box.

Dick Tracy
New Haven-Analog-Ca 1935
Chrome plated case
DIT 1 Head 28x38mm $250-275
Box $100-125

Dizzy Dean
Everbrite-U.S.A.-1935
Steel color case
DIZ 1 Head $450-500
Box $200-250

Donald Duck
WDP-Animated Hands
Ingersoll-U.S. Time-Ca 1948
Steel color case
DON 2 Head 29x40mm $250-300
Birthday Box $200-250

Dopey
Same as above-Not Illustrated
DOP 1 Head 29x40mm $250-300
Birthday Box $200-250

Donald Duck
Animated Hands
Walt Disney Productions
Bradley-Swiss Analog-1974
Chrome plated top-Base metal back or
Gold tone top-Base metal back
DON 7 Head 29x36mm $50-60
DON 8 Head 30x36mm $50-60

Small Not Illustrated
DON 9 Head 23x29mm $35-40

Donald Duck
Animated Hands
Walt Disney Productions
Bradley-Swiss Analog-1973
Chrome plated top-Stainless back
or Gold tone top-Base metal back
DON 5 Head 25x33mm $50-60
DON 6 Head 29x36mm $50-60
Box $20-25
Roll box $20-25

A SPECIAL THANKS TO:
Tom & Claire LaRose
Greensboro, NC
for the use of their character
watch research.

Donald Duck
Animated Hands
Walt Disney Productions
Bradley-HK Analog-1982
Chrome plated top-Stainless back
DON 10 Head 27x34mm $50-60
DON 11 Head 26x33mm $50-60
DON 12 Head 26x32mm $50-60
DON 13 Head 26x33mm $50-60
Pop up box $20-25
Roll box $20-25

Donald Duck-Birthday
Animated Hands-Registered
Walt Disney Productions-1984
Bradley-HK Analog-Quartz Analog
Gold tone top-Stainless back
DON 14 Head 27x32mm $75-90
DON 15 Head 28x34mm $75-90
DON 16 Large Head $175-200
Picture frame box $25-30
Flat layout box $45-50

Donald Duck-Birthday
Animated Hands-Registered
Walt Disney Productions
Bradley-HK Quartz LCD-1984
Gold tone top-Stainless back
DON 17 Head 25x31mm $70-80
DON 18 Head 30x34mm $70-80

Doves-Girl
Girl w/ Moving Dove
Britix-Corona-HK Made-Swiss Parts
Gold tone top-Base metal back
DOV 1 Head 26x33mm $25-35
DOV 2 Same-Not Animated $15-25

Duckling, Ugly
Moving Eyes
Wotania-Swiss Analog
Gold tone top-Base metal back
Embossed Lion Rampant case back
DUU 1 Head 25x32mm $25-35

Elvis Presley (Memories Collection)
Mirror dial
Stamped on case back
1987-Elvis Presley Enterprises Inc.
Product of Harilela Bob Ltd.-HBL
Japan Analog-HK Assem.
Chrome plated case
Black leather strap
Watch, Box & Card retail 6/89 $35
ELP 10 Head 30x35mm

Ernie Keebler Watch

Emmett Kelly, Jr.
Green Stuff Licensing Corp.
The "Oldies" Series
Bradley-Quartz Analog-1985
HK Case-Japan Movement & Dial
White plastic case/strap
EKJ 1 Head 34x39mm $35-45
EKJ 2 Head 24x28mm $25-35

Black plastic case/strap
EKJ 3 Head 34x39mm $35-45
EKJ 4 Head 24x28mm $25-35
Flat Layout Box $10-20

Not illustrated-See WCF 5 & 6
Gold tone top-Stainless back
EKJ 5 Head 32x38mm $45-55
EKJ 6 Head 24x30mm $35-45
Layout Box $10-20

Ernie Keebler
LeJour-W. German Quartz Analog
HK Assembly
Ladies movement-Plastic insert
Chrome plated top-Stainless back
Black leather strap
ERK 1 Head 33x38mm $20-25
Box $5-10

Epcot Center Dragon
Walt Disney Productions-1982
Bradley-HK Analog
Chrome plated top-Stainless back
EPC 1 Head 26x32mm $20-30
Pop up box $5-10

Ernie
Jim Henson-Muppets Inc.
Bradley-Swiss Analog-1976
Chrome plated top-Stainless back
ERN 1 Head 26x33mm $35-45
Roll box $10-20

Ernie
Animated Hands
Jim Henson-Muppets Inc.
Bradley-Swiss Analog-1976
Chrome plated top-Stainless back
ERN 2 Head 26x32mm $35-45
ERN 3 Head 29x36mm $40-50
Roll box $10-20

Ernie
Jim Henson-Muppets Inc.
Bradley-HK Quartz LCD-1982
Chrome plated top-Stainless back
ERN 4 Head 26x33mm $15-20
Pop up box $5-10

A SPECIAL THANKS TO:
Bernie & Sue Edwards
Chicago, IL
for the use of their character
watch research.

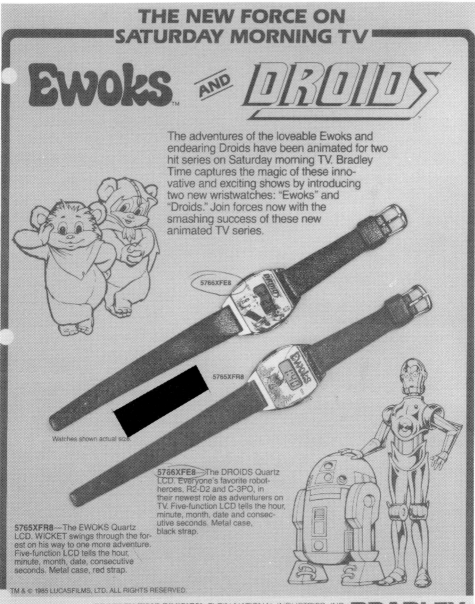

THE NEW FORCE ON SATURDAY MORNING TV

Ewoks™ AND DROIDS™

The adventures of the loveable Ewoks and endearing Droids have been animated for two hit series on Saturday morning TV. Bradley Time captures the magic of these innovative and exciting shows by introducing two new wristwatches: "Ewoks" and "Droids." Join forces now with the smashing success of these new animated TV series.

5766XFE8

5765XFR8

Watches shown actual size.

5766XFE8—The DROIDS Quartz LCD. Everyone's favorite robot-heroes, R2-D2 and C-3PO, in their newest role as adventurers on TV. Five-function LCD tells the hour, minute, month, date and consecutive seconds. Metal case, black strap.

5765XFR8—The EWOKS Quartz LCD. WICKET swings through the forest on his way to one more adventure. Five-function LCD tells the hour, minute, month, date, consecutive seconds. Metal case, red strap.

TM & © 1985 LUCASFILMS, LTD. ALL RIGHTS RESERVED.

BRADLEY TIME DIVISION, ELGIN NATIONAL INDUSTRIES, INC. 1115 BROADWAY, NEW YORK, NY 10010 • 212 243-0200 **BRADLEY**

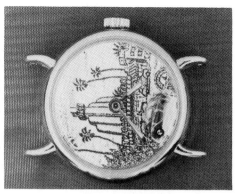

Fiat
Steering Wheel-17J
Rosco-Swiss Analog
Plastic & Chrome plated top
De Luxe Stainless back-Waterproof
FIA 1 Head 39x39mm $50-75

Fox Theater
Moving Car
Tali-1988-Hong Kong Analog
Craw lugs-Chrome plated case
FOT 1 Head 30x36mm $10-20

Flag of United States of America
Glory Time Co.-Swiss Analog-Ca 1970
Gold tone top-Stainless back
Red, white, blue strap
FLU 1 Large Head $30-40

Football Player
Moving Ball-Passing
Wotania-Swiss Analog
Gold tone top-Base metal back
Embossed Lion Rampant case back
FOP 2 Head 25x32mm $25-35

Frog-College
New Zoo Revue-1975
Criterion-HK Analog
Algor Watch Co.-Swiss Parts
Gold tone top-Stainless back
Sweep second
FRC 1 Head 31x39mm $20-30

Frog Prince/Princess
Diantus-Swiss Analog-Unmarked
Chrome plated top-Base metal back
FRP 5 Head 29x35mm $20-30

Frog Prince/Princess
Moving Frog
Wotania-Swiss Analog
Gold tone top-Base metal back
Embossed Lion Rampant case back
FRP 3 Head 25x32mm $25-35

Frog-Sperina
Moving Eyes
Swiss Analog-Ca 1975
Gold tone top-Base metal back
FRO 1 Head 25x32mm $25-35

Frog Prince/Princess
Moving Bird
Britix-Corona-Swiss Analog
Gold tone top-Base metal back
FRP 4 Head 25x32mm $25-35

G.O.P. Original
Animated Elephant Feet-Hands
"Dirty Time Co.-1970"
Windert-Swiss Analog-Sweep second
Chrome plated case
GOP 1 Head 33x39mm $85-110

A SPECIAL THANKS TO:
Steve & Marsha Berger
Algonquin, IL
for the use of their character
watch research.

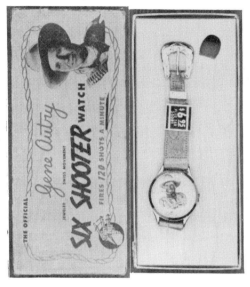

Gene Autry
Wilane-Swiss-1948
Steel color case
GEA 1 Head 33x33mm $150-175
Champion Box $150-175

Gene Autry
Animated moving gun
New Haven-1951
Steel color case
GEA 2 Head $250-275
Six Shooter Box $200-225

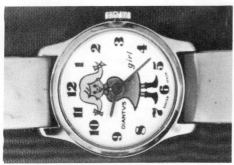

Girl, Pigtails
Stick Hands
Diantus-Swiss Analog
Chrome plated top-Stainless back
Plastic straps
GIR 1 Head 25x33mm $15-25

Gismo-Gremlins
Warner Bros. Inc.-1984
Nelsonic-HK Analog
Gold tone top-Stainless back
GIS 1 Head 27x34mm $30-40

A SPECIAL THANKS TO:
Howard Brenner
Rochester, NY
for the use of his character
watch research.

Goofy Backwards
Animated Hands Run Backwards
Walt Disney Prod.
Bradley-Helbros-17J-1972
Base metal bezel-Stainless back
GOO 1 Head 34x40mm $1,000-1,250
Box $100-125

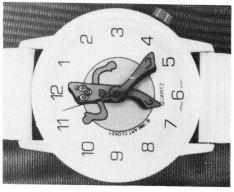

Gumby
Animated feet
Art Clokey-1986
Japan Quartz Analog-HK Assem.
White plastic top-Stainless back
Sweep second-White plastic straps
Watch & Box at retail 6/89 $30
GUM 2 Head 34x40mm

CHARACTER IDENTIFICATION CODES

The 3 letter identification code
preceding the number is usually made
up using the first two letters of
the first name and the first letter
of the last name. Exceptions occur
because of the desire not to have
duplicates which confuse the computer. These codes make possible more
precise telephone and mail order
descriptions.

Gumby-On Horse
Animated feet
Art Clokey-1986
Japan Quartz Analog-HK Assem.
White plastic top-Stainless back
Sweep second-White plastic straps
Watch & Box at retail 6/89 $30
GUM 3 Head 34x40mm

Groucho Marx
Not Illustrated
GRM 1 Same as Clark Gable CLG 1

Hansel & Gretel
Moving Witch
Wotania-Swiss Analog
Gold tone top-Base metal back
Embossed Lion Rampant case back
H&G 1 Head 25x32mm $25-35

Herself the Elf
American Greetings Corp.
Bradley-HK-Quartz LCD-1982
Gold tone top-Stainless back or
Chrome plated top-Stainless back
Her 2 Head 26x33mm $15-20
Her 3 Head 26x33mm $15-20
Pop up box $5-10

Heartbeat
Moving Beat
Nelson-Swiss Analog-Ca 1972-89
Gold tone top-Base metal back
Embossed Lion Rampant case back
Watch at retail 8/89 $10
HEA 1 Head 25x32mm

Herself the Elf
American Greetings Corp.
Bradley-HK Analog-1982
Gold tone top-Stainless back
HER 1 Head 27x32mm $15-20
Pop up box $5-10

Hockey Players
Moving Hockey Stick
Wotania-Swiss Analog
Gold tone top-Base metal back
HOP 1 Head 25x32mm $25-35

Holly Hobbie
Bradley-Swiss Analog-1978
Gold Color Base Metal Case
Stainless Steel Back
Spade hands-Yellow Vinyl Strap
HOL 1 Tank 24x31mm $20-25
HOL 2 Head 27x32mm $15-20
HOL 3 Head 30x35mm $15-20
Pop up box $5-10

Holly Hobbie
Bradley-HK Quartz LCD-1982
Gold Color Base Metal Case
Stainless Steel Back
HOL 5 Head 25x32mm $15-20
Pop up box $5-10

Holly Hobbie
Bradley Time-HK LCD-1982
Blue plastic-Stainless back
HOL 6 Head 26x32mm $10-15
Blister pak $5-10

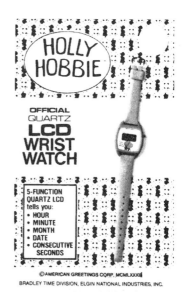

HOLLY HOBBIE

OFFICIAL
QUARTZ
LCD
WRIST
WATCH

5-FUNCTION
QUARTZ LCD
tells you:
• HOUR
• MINUTE
• MONTH
• DATE
• CONSECUTIVE
  SECONDS

©AMERICAN GREETINGS CORP. MCMLXXXI
BRADLEY TIME DIVISION, ELGIN NATIONAL INDUSTRIES, INC.

Holly Hobbie
American Greeting Card
Bradley-Swiss Analog-1980
Gold tone top-Stainless back
HOH 4 Head $15-20
Blister pak $5-10

"HOPALONG CASSIDY"... in
"Saddle Stand" Box . . $6.95

Hopalong Cassidy
Ingersoll-U.S. Time-1950
Chrome top-Stainless back
HOC 1 Small 25x37mm $50-60
Saddle Box $150-175

HOC 2 Regular 29x40mm $85-95
Brands Box $150-175

Howdy Doody
"It's Howdy Doody Time"
40th Anniversary Edition
Concepts Plus, Inc.-1987
N.B.C. Inc./K.F.S. Inc.
HK Analog-Sweep second
Chrome plated top-Stainless back
White plastic strap
Watch & Box at retail 6/89 $30
HOD 3 Head 30x35mm

Humphrey Bogart
Not Illustrated
HUB 1 Same as Clark Gable CLG 1

Hush Puppies
Moving Eyes-Registered
Rega-Israel-Swiss Analog
Stamped on case back
Rega Industries Ltd.
Chrome plated case
HUP 1 Head 29x35mm $100-125

James Dean (Memories Collection)
"Time Ran Out" on dial
Stamped on case back
James Dean Foundation 1987
Harilela Bob Ltd.-HBL
Japan Analog-HK Assem.
Chrome plated case
Steel expansion band
Watch, Box & Card retail 6/89 $35
JAD 1 Head 30x35mm

Irish Spring
"Ladies Like It Too"
Swiss Analog-Calendar
Gold tone top-Stainless back
IRS 1 Head 34x40mm $25-35

JEDI-Ewoks
Lucasfilm
Bradley Quartz-HK LCD-1983
Chrome top-Steel back
JEE 4 Head 27x35mm $15-20
Pop up box $5-10

JEDI-Ewoks-Wicket
Lucasfilms Ltd.
Bradley-HK Quartz LCD-1985
Chrome plated top-Stainless back
JEE 5 Head 26x31mm $15-20
Blister Pack $5-10

JEDI-Ewoks
Lucasfilm
Bradley-HK Analog-1983
Chrome top-Steel back
JEE 1 Head 27x35mm $35-45
JEE 2 Head 26x33mm $35-45
JEE 3 Head 27x34mm $35-45
Pop up box $10-15

JEDI-Ewoks-Wicket
TM & C-Lucasfilm Ltd.
Bradley-Swiss Analog-1981
Black plastic cycolac case
JEE 6 Head 35x41mm $35-45
Box $5-10

JEDI-Jabba the Hutt
Lucasfilms
Bradley-HK-Quartz LCD-1983
Chrome plated top-Stainless back
JEJ 2 Head 27x34mm $15-20
Box $5-10

Jenny Fair
Moving Eyes
Wotania-Swiss Analog
Gold tone top-Base metal back
Embossed Lion Rampant case back
JEF 1 Head 25x32mm $25-35

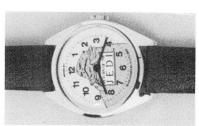

JEDI-Jabba the Hutt
Lucasfilm Inc.
Bradley-HK Analog-1983
Chrome plated top-Steel back
JEJ 3 Head 27x34mm $35-45
Pop up box $5-10

Jiminy Cricket
Animated Hands
Ingersoll-U.S. Time-Ca 1948
Steel color case
JIC 1 head 29x40mm $200-250
Birthday Box $200-250

JEDI-Jabba the Hutt
Lucasfilm
Bradley-HK Analog-1983
Chrome top-Steel back
JEJ 1 Head 27x35mm $35-45
Pop up box $10-15

Jimmy Carter
From Peanuts to President
Goober Time Co.-1976
Korean-Swiss-Hong Kong
Gold tone base metal bezel
Screw stainless steel back
JIM 1 Head 34x41mm $50-75
Box $10-15

Jimmy Carter President-Original
Timely Creations-1980
Swiss Analog-HK Assem.
Gold tone top-Stainless back
JIC 2 Head 33x40mm $50-75

Joker, The
Embossed D.C. Comics Inc.-1989
Quintel-Japan Quartz Analog
HK Assem.
Ladies movement-Plastic insert
ABC Company-Miyota Co.-Sweep second
Consort Fashion Corps.
Clear plastic box
Purple & green plastic top
Stainless back
PVC purple plastic strap
Brass stud rivets
Watch & Box at retail 8/89 $30
JOK 2 Head 35mm
JOK 3 Head 27mm

Joker, The
DABS & Co.-DC Comics Inc-1977
Swiss Analog-Stick hands
Gold tone base metal top
Stainless back-Navy blue leather
strap-Yellow stitching
JOK 1 Head $450-500
DABS Box see WON 1 $50-65

The Joker-"Comic Book DABS"
Illustrated above
Watch at wholesale 6/89 $45-65
JOK 5 Large Head
Various contemporary movements,
cases & straps
Superman, Wonder Woman,
Batman & Spiderman
(same as above)
See explanation on next page

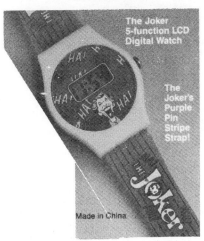

The Joker
5-function LCD
Digital Watch

The
Joker's
Purple
Pin
Stripe
Strap!

Made in China

Joker, The
Embossed D.C. Comics Inc.-1989
5 function LCD-China Assem.
Ladies movement-Plastic insert
Consort Fashion Corps.
Clear plastic box
Green plastic top-Stainless back
Purple "JOKER" pin stripe strap
Watch & Box at retail 8/89 $12
JOK 4 Head 23x32mm

DABS WRIST WATCHES

A note about **"Comic Book"** dial watches and other interesting ideas.

SUPERMAN, BATMAN, SPIDERMAN, WONDER WOMAN & The JOKER

On the original factory assembled DABS Watches, DABS & Co is printed on the dial, along with the 1977 DC Comic Inc., copyright. The 1977 DABS watches were sold to children by mail in limited quantities, and are moving out of reach of most collector's pocketbooks today. These are desirable as cartoon character watches not associated with comic art.

On the back of some DC Comics the five different 1977 DABS watches were illustrated by actual size facsimile prints of the dials. The 1977 **comic book** dials have the original advertising on the back identifying it as original artwork and not a copy machine or photographic reproduction. The after factory assembly using the original artwork from dials available on the **comic book's** back cover can be identified by the 1977 DC Comic Inc. copyright-trademark.

This assembly using the dials **comic book's** back cover is preserving original artwork which would otherwise be lost. **Comic book** dial watches are offered as examples of original period comic artwork to comic art collectors, in a new and constant visible form. They are beautifully printed in true comic colors, and are usually found glued over dials on new old stock Bradleys & other contemporary Swiss watches from the late 1970's, early 1980's.

As you can see from the **comic book's** back cover, illustrated on the page following Wonder Woman and at the end of the character section, anyone can preserve and create their own watch.

Original comic art is the reference point and power providing justification for future value appreciation for cartoon character watch collecting. Except for a few ahead of their time, cartoon and comic character watch collecting is the new kid on the block in the comic art field. The character watch has been a tag along for the children not noticed by the serious student until late years.

Character watch collectors and comic art collectors have interests in common, but not alike. The true comic art collectors desire is original artwork, which includes movie animation cells, story board drawings, Sunday newspaper strips and **comic books** by various artists and writers, and is a recognized commodity of value. Comic art collectors follow artists and writers with less emphasis on toys, premiums and novelties, such as watches.

Cartoon watch collectors are interested in characters and their personalities with identification through toys, premiums, and novelties, such as watches, with few knowing the artist, writer or even the publisher presenting the artist efforts.

American comic art, often called nostalgia, has been exhibited at such prestigious museums, as the Metropolitan Museum of Art in New York, since the 1930's. Critics have reviewed and recognized art in cartoons since the early political cartoons of the civil war.

An American phenomenon developed in the early part of this century called the Sunday funnies, typing Americans as a people who can "laugh at ourselves." We depicted our trials and woes of everyday life in Mutt & Jeff, Buster Brown, Bringing up Father, and the Katzenjammer Kids, among a few.

The 1930's being a depression era, premiums and give a ways were born to stimulate business and supply low cost gifts for children whose parents had little extra money. Also, during that time **comic books** came into existence and our characters now had lives and personalities beyond Sunday strips limited 1930's pace. The Golden Age of Comic Art is recognized as beginning in 1938 and lasting through 1955.

Since the 1950's new artists and writers during our post war economic boom created multitudes of toys, premiums and watches for newly affluent parents who wanted to give their children all they themselves wanted when they were young. Thus a separation occurred between comic art and comic toys, watches or premiums. The parents knew the background of the gift of the Mickey Mouse, Batman or Orphan Annie watch, the child just appreciated the cartoon face, later collecting examples of character watches. Now comic art, cartoon and character watch collectors are recognizing each other as related even though the watches, toys and premiums were not art but merchandise created in contemporary time. Many times the collector of comic art had just as soon have the box as the toy or watch.

Character watches are now big business many times being released simultaneously with a new characters movie debut or re-issue aimed specifically for the collectors market.

What the future holds for us in collecting is serious business as evidenced by prices commanded for early comic and cartoon character watches, and the fast rising prices caused by collector demand of contemporary pieces. Political, advertising & gimmick watches are gaining in popularity also. **If you have no DABS, this will have to do you.**

William "Bill" Selover

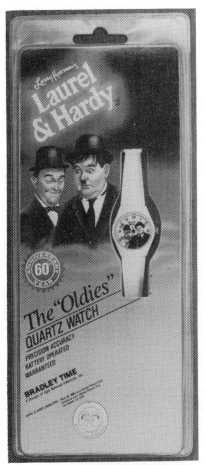

Laurel & Hardy
Larry Harmon Pictures Corp.
The "Oldies" Series
Bradley-Quartz Analog-1985
HK Case-Japan Movement & Dial
White plastic case/strap
L&H 1 Head-34x39mm $50-60
L&H 2 Head-24x28mm $40-50

Black plastic case/strap
L&H 3 Head 34x39mm $50-60
L&H 4 Head 24x28mm $40-50
See-thru layout box $10-20

Jumprope
Moving Girl
Economic-Swiss Analog
Gold tone top-Base metal back
JUM 1 Head 25x32mm $25-35

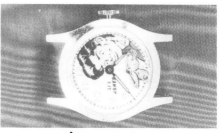

Li'l Abner-Donkey
Moving Donkey-USF 1951
Case marked Muros Watch Co.
Swiss Analog
Probably sold by New Haven
Chrome plated case
LIA 2 Head 32x41mm $275-325
Box $125-150

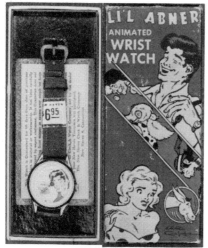

Li'l Abner-Flag
Moving Flag-USF 1951
Case & Movement marked
New Haven Clock & Watch Co
Swiss Analog-Chrome plated case
LIA 1 Head 32x41mm $225-250
Box $125-150

ANIMATED CHARACTER WATCHES for "LITTLE CHARACTERS"

Li'l Abner—The mule actually nods its head 120 times a minute! 6⁹⁵

Texas Ranger – His trusty gun 'shoots" – (moves back and forth!) 6⁹⁵

Cowgirl—For the girls who love adventure in true western style. 6⁹⁵

Dick Tracy—His automatic gun "shoots"120 times every minute! 6⁹⁵

Dec. 1951 - Saturday Evening Post

Lion
Moving Eyes
Ruhla-Swiss Analog
Chrome plated top-Stainless back
LIO 1 Head 26x35mm $30-40

NOTE: All measurements are taken from
tip of lug to tip of lug and across the
smallest diameter.

NOTE: all values are given for a mint
original head & band

Little Hans-Piet
Moving Eyes
Rega-Israel-Swiss Analog
Swiss Lutzker Corp.
Stamped on case back
VSA Pat. 2 988 870
Chrome plated top-Stainless back
LIH 1 Head 30x38mm $35-45

Little Red Riding Hood
Moving basket
Wotania-Swiss Analog
Gold tone top-Base metal back
Embossed Lion Rampant case back
LRR 3 Head 25x32mm $30-40

A SPECIAL THANKS TO:
Patrick Ryan
Rockport, MA
for the use of his character
watch research.

Lone Ranger
Ca 1951
LOR 2 Head $110-125
Western Box $150-175

Lone Ranger
New Haven-Ca 1939
Chrome top-Stainless back
LOR 1 Head 26x39mm $200-225
Box $150-175

Lone Ranger
Lone Ranger Television Inc.
Bradley-Swiss & Hong Kong-1980
Base metal top-Stainless back
LOR 3 Head 29x37mm $65-75
Pop up box $10-15

Lone Ranger
No copywrite-Colored dial
Q&Q-HK Analog-Ca 1976
Gold tone top-Stainless back
LOR 4 Head 32x38mm $40-60

LUV
(Came with Truck)-Chevrolet Time
Swiss Analog-Ca 1970s
Gold tone top-Base metal back
LUV 1 Large Head $100-125

Mad-30th Anniversary Edition
"What, Me Worry?"-Animated Hands
(Alfred E. Newman)
Embossed E.C. Publication Inc.-1987
Concepts Plus, Inc.
PG Time Ltd.-Swiss Analog-HK Assem.
Chrome plated top-Stainless back
Red pigskin leather strap
Watch & Box at retail 6/89 $25
MAD 1 Head 32x37mm

Mad-Collectible
"What, Me Worry?"-Animated Hands
(Alfred E. Newman)
Embossed E.C. Publication Inc.-1987
Concepts Plus, Inc.
PG Time Ltd.-Swiss Analog-HK Assem.
Chrome plated top-Stainless back
Red plastic strap
Watch & Box at retail 6/89 $25
MAD 2 Head 32x37mm

Mad-Limited Edition
"What, Me Worry?"-Animated Hands
(Alfred E. Newman)
Embossed E.C. Publication Inc.-1987
Concepts Plus, Inc.-HK Assembly
PG Time Ltd-Swiss Quartz Analog
Chrome plated top-Stainless back
Red pigskin leather strap
Watch & Box at retail 6/89 $25
MAD 4 Head 32x37mm

Majorette-Reflector
No copywrite-Optical animation
Ingraham-Analog-Ca 1960
Chrome plated case
MAJ 2 Head 25x37mm $75-100

Mad-Designer
"What, Me Worry?"-Animated Hands
(Alfred E. Newman)
Embossed E.C. Publication Inc.-1987
Concepts Plus, Inc.-HK Assembly
PG Time Ltd-Swiss Quartz Analog
White plastic top-Stainless back
White plastic strap
Watch & Box at retail 6/89 $25
MAD 3 Head 32x37mm

Marilyn Monroe
"Not Illustrated"
No copywrite-Colored dial
Q&Q or Quemex-HK Analog-Ca 1980's
Gold tone top-Stainless back
MAM 5 Head 33x38mm $40-60

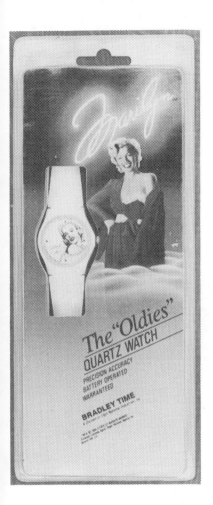

Marilyn Monroe
The "Oldies" Series
Estate of Marilyn Monroe
Bradley-Quartz Analog-1985
HK Case-Japan Movement & Dial
White plastic case/strap
MAM 1 Head-34x39mm $35-45
MAM 2 Head-24x28mm $35-45

Not illustrated-See WCF 5 & 6
Gold tone top-Stainless back
MAM 3 Head-32x38mm $35-45
MAM 4 Head-24x30mm $35-45
See-thru layout box $10-15

A SPECIAL THANKS TO:
Micheal Orloff
Valley Forge, PA
for the use of his character
watch research.

Masters "He-Man"
Mattel Inc.
Bradley-Quartz LCD-Ca 1983
Chrome Case-Black Strap
Month-Date-Hour-Minute-Seconds
MAH 2 Head 26x31mm $10-15
Blister pac $5-10

Masters "Skeletor"
Mattel Inc.
Bradley-Quartz LCD-Ca 1983
Chrome Case-Black Strap
Month-Date-Hour-Minute-Seconds
MAH 3 Head 26x31mm $10-15
Box $5-10

Marilyn Monroe
(Memories Collection)
1987-Estate of Marilyn Monroe
Japan Analog-HK Assem.
Chrome plated case
Steel expansion band
Watch, Box & Card retail 6/89 $35
MAM 6 Head 30x35mm

Masters "He-Man"
Mattel Inc.
Bradley-Flashing Quartz LCD
Month-Date-Hour-Minute-Seconds
Black Plastic Case/Strap-Ca 1984
MAH 5 Head 31x46mm $50-60
Pop up box $25-30

"I KEEP TIME FOR 1½ MILLION HAPPY CHILDREN"

MICKEY MOUSE WATCHES

BY Ingersoll

Already 1½ million children are learning punctuality with Mickey Mouse Watches — and parents are as happy about it as the children. The movements are standard Ingersoll make — dependable and sturdy. Pocket watch and fob, $1.50 in a gift box.

MICKEY MOUSE WRIST WATCH, complete with bracelet, now only $2.95. The demand is so heavy that there is often a scarcity. Buy for Christmas now.

MICKEY MOUSE ALARM CLOCK, $1.50. Teaches early rising to children. Standard Ingersoll clock and alarm mechanisms.

"THREE LITTLE PIGS". As delightful as Mickey. Pocket watch and fob, $1.50. Wrist watch, $2.95. Alarm clock, $1.50.

This Page is for Information Only.

"MICKEY MOUSE" . . . . in the
"Presentation" Gift Box . . **$6.95**

Mickey Mouse
Animated Hands
Walt Disney Productions
Timex-Analog-1958
Chrome plated top-Stainless back
MIC 10 Head 24x32mm $40-50
Box plastic statue $125-150
Box porcelain statue $125-150

Mickey Mouse
Ingersoll-U.S. Time-1950
Animated-Chrome case-Red strap
MIC 8 Head 25x37mm $45-55
Strap $10-15
Friends Box $125-140
Mickey Box 1958 $125-140

Walt Disney's
MICKEY MOUSE
Mickey tells time with his hands.
Red case and washable red vinylite
band.   Retail price $6.95

Mickey Mouse
U.S. Time-Analog-1955
MIC 9 Head $45-55
Box $125-140

Mickey Mouse
Animated Hands
Walt Disney Productions
Bradley-Swiss Analog-1972-76
Gold tone top-Base metal back or
Chrome plated top-Base metal back
MIC 14 Head 25x33mm $35-45
MIC 15 Head 26x33mm $35-45
MIC 16 Head 29x36mm $35-45

Mickey Mouse-Sportsman
Animated Hands
Bradley-Swiss Analog-Calendar
Screw back-Waterproof-1973
Silver Tone Base Metal Case
Stainless Back-Rotating Bezel
Cut Out Black Plastic Strap
Sweep Second
MIC 18 Head 32x38mm $55-70
Box $15-20

Mickey Mouse
Animated Hands
Walt Disney Productions
Bradley-Swiss Analog-Ca 1974
Base Acryl case/colors
MIC 24 Head 33x33mm $50-60

Magnifying Crystal
MIC 25 Head 34x43mm $75-95
Box $10-15

Mickey Mouse
Animated Hands
Walt Disney Productions
Bradley-Swiss Analog-1976
Base acryl plastic/colors
MIC 34 Head 35x44mm $50-60
MIC 35 Head 31x36mm $50-60
Box $10-20

Mickey Mouse-Time Teacher
Walt Disney Productions
One blue & one white hand
Bradley-Swiss Analog-Ca 1973
Chrome plated top-Base metal back
MIC 20 Head 29x36mm $25-35
Box $10-15

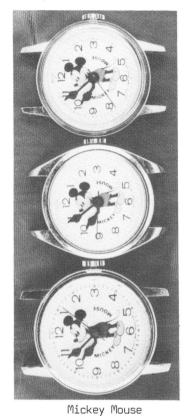

Mickey Mouse
Animated Hands-"Moving Head"
Walt Disney Productions
Bradley-Swiss Analog-1976-78
Chrome plated top-Stainless back
MIC 26 Head 26x33mm $110-125
MIC 27 Head 29x33mm $110-125
Layout box $10-20

Mickey Mouse
Animated Hands
Walt Disney Productions
Bradley-Swiss Analog-1976-78
Chrome plated top-Stainless back
or Gold tone top-Base metal back
MIC 38 Head 29x36mm $35-45
MIC 39 Head 27x35mm $35-45
MIC 40 Head 34x41mm $50-70
Layout box $20-25

Mickey Mouse
Magnifying Crystal
Animated Hands
Walt Disney Productions
Bradley-Swiss Analog-Ca 1976
Base acryl plastic/colors
MIC 33 Head 40x40mm $70-95
Box $10-20

Mickey Mouse
Bradley-Swiss-Digital-1976
Chrome plated top-Base metal back
MIC 36 Head $20-30
Box $5-10

Mickey Mouse-Digital
Walt Disney Productions
Bradley-Swiss-Digital-1976
Base metal back
Bushed chrome plated top
MIC 37 Head 32x37mm $25-35
MIC 37a Gold tone top $25-35
Box $5-10

Mickey Mouse-Auto Racer
Walt Disney Productions
Bradley-Swiss Analog-1978
Black base acryl case
Black vinyl & metal strap
MIC 59 Head 40x45mm $70-90
Box $10-15

*Walt Disney Productions licensed
Bradley Time Division of Elgin
National Watch Co. to produce &
market their Character Watches in
"1972 & Ended in 1985".*

Mickey Mouse
Animated Hands
Walt Disney Productions
Bradley-Swiss Analog-1978
Chrome plated top-Base metal back
MIC 55 Large $125-150
MIC 56 Medium $50-60
MIC 57 Medium $50-60
Box $10-20

Mickey Mouse-Auto Racer
Walt Disney Productions
Bradley-Swiss Analog-1978
Black base acryl case
Black vinyl & metal strap
MIC 60 Head 34x40mm $65-85
Box $10-20

Mickey Mouse-Accutron
Not Illustrated-WDP
Bulova-Tuning Fork-Day,Date-Ca 1977
Chrome plated waterproof case
MIC 210 Head Large $250-300

Mickey Mouse-Sportsman
Bradley-Swiss Analog Calendar-1978
Chrome Plated Base Metal Top
Steel Back-Rotating Bezel
Sweep seconds-Stick hands
Waterproof Snap Back
MIC 61 Head 31x38mm $85-100
MIC 62 Head 31x38mm $85-100
Box $10-20

Mickey Mouse
"Motorcycle Helmet"
Walt Disney Productions
Bradley-Swiss Analog-Ca 1979
Red plastic case/strap
MIC 102 Head 31x38mm $150-175
Box $20-25

Mickey Mouse
Animated Hands
Walt Disney Productions
Bradley-Swiss & HK Analog-1978-82
Chrome plated top-Stainless back
or Gold tone top-Base metal back
MIC 64 "Smallest Mickey" $25-35
MIC 65 Head 21x28mm $35-45
MIC 66 Head 27x32mm $35-45
MIC 67 Head 27x32mm $35-45
Box $10-20

Mickey Mouse
Walt Disney Productions-1969
Timex-Analog-Plastic insert
Chrome plated top-Stainless back
MIC 201 Head 31x38mm $75-100
Flat layout box $10-20

Mickey Mouse-Sport
Animated Seconds
Walt Disney Productions
Bradley-Swiss Analog-1978
Chrome plated top-Base metal back
Head 30x37mm
MIC 87 Basketball $45-60
MIC 88 Tennis $45-60
MIC 89 Football $45-60
MIC 90 Baseball $45-60
Roll box $10-20

Mickey Mouse-Disco
Animated Hands
Walt Disney Productions
Bradley-Swiss Analog-1980
Chrome plated top-Stainless back
MIC 102a Head 29x37mm $100-115
Record & Box $150-175

NOTE: all values are given for a mint
original head & band

Mickey Mouse
Animated Hands-Walking
Bradley Time-Swiss Quartz-Ca 1984
18K Solid Gold Coin Case
MIC 182 His 18K Est. $2000
MIC 183 Her 18K Est. $1850

Mickey Mouse
Flip Top 5 Function LCD
Bradley-Hong Kong Quartz LCD-1984
Plastic Top-Stainless Steel Back
Black Vinyl Strap
MIC 192 Head 41x42mm $40-50
Box $10-20

Mickey Mouse
74 Golf Classic
Walt Disney World
National Team Championship
Walt Disney Productions
Helbros Electric Calendar-1974
Gold tone top-Stainless back
MIC 200 Head 34x41mm $200-250

Mickey Mouse
WDP
Ingersoll-U.S. Time-1948
20th Birthday Series
MIC 6 Head 29x40mm $150-175
Birthday Box $200-250

Minnie Mouse
Animated Hands
Walt Disney Productions
Timex-Analog-1958
Chrome plated top-Stainless back
MIN 2 Head 24x32mm $45-55
Box plastic statue $125-150
Box porcelain statue $125-150

Minnie Mouse
Animated Hands
Walt Disney Productions
Bradley-Swiss Analog-1975
Chrome plated top-Base metal back
MIN 6 Head 34x40mm $55-65
MIN 7 Head 34x40mm $55-65
Box $15-25

Minnie Mouse
Animated Hands
Walt Disney Productions
Bradley-Swiss Analog-1975
Gold tone top-Stainless back
MIN 5 Head 26x33mm $30-40
Box $10-20

Minnie Mouse
Animated Hands-Magnifying Crystal
Walt Disney Production
Bradley-Swiss Analog-1978
Base acryl lucite/colors
MIN 11 Head 30x36mm $50-75
Box $10-15

Minnie Mouse
Bradley Time-Quartz LCD-Ca 1984
Chrome Case-Red Strap
Month-Date-Hour-Minute-Seconds
MIN 21 Head 25x31mm $15-20
Box $5-10

Minnie Mouse
"Moving Head"
Animated Hands
Walt Disney Production
Bradley-HK Analog-1980
MIN 12 Head 26x33mm $110-125
MIN 13 Head 26x33mm $110-125
Flat layout box $25-35

American and European
CHARACTER
Wrist Watch Price Guide Book 3
illustrates and values over 900
character wrist watches, ordering
information follows the text of this
book.

Miss Piggy
Picco-Hanson Associates Inc.-1980
17J-Japan Analog
Chrome plated case
MIP 2 Head 30x38mm $25-35
Round display box $10-20

Minnie Mouse
Walt Disney Productions
Bradley-HK-Quartz LCD 1984
Plastic case assorted colors
MIN 22 Head 26x31mm $15-20
Blister pack $5-10

NOTE: All measurements are taken from
tip of lug to tip of lug and across the
smallest diameter.

Mouse-Love
Adorable Sales-1970
Swiss Analog
Magnifying Crystal-Red plastic case
MOL 1 Head 25x42mm $100-125

Monopoly
Animated Hands
Parker Bros. 1935-1986
Armitron-Japan Quartz Analog
Black acrylic top-Stainless back
MON 1 Head 23x35mm $40-60

Mouse-Love
Pendant
Adorable Sales-1970
Webster-Swiss Analog
MOL 2 Head $75-100

Mouse-Marshall
Moving Dog
Unmarked-Swiss Analog
Gold tone top-Base metal back
MOM 1 Head 25x32mm $25-35

Mouse-Tongue Showing
Animated hands-Swiss Unmarked
Tinted dial-Blue, yellow, green
Tradear Limited-HK Analog-Ca 1970's
Chrome plated top-Stainless back
Screw back-Water tight
MOT 1 Head 28x35mm $30-40

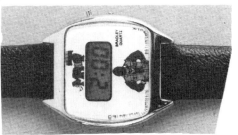

Mr. "T"
Bradley Time-Quartz LCD-Ca 1983
Chrome case-Black strap
One button five function LCD
MRT 1 Head 26x31mm $25-35
Box $5-10

Mouse, Yellow Ears
Animated Hands-Swiss Unmarked
International Precision Time Ltd.
HK Analog-Sweep Second
Chrome plated top-Base metal back
MOY 1 Head 26x33mm $20-25

Mr. "T"
And His Dog "Dozer"-Ca 1984
Bradley Time-Flashing Quartz LCD
Month-Date-Hour-Minute-Seconds
Black Plastic Case/Strap
MRT 3 Head 31x46mm $50-75
Box $25-35

Mr. "T"
And His Dog "Dozer"
Bradley Time-Analog-Ca 1980
Chrome or gold tone case-Black strap
MRT 1 Head 27x34mm $25-35
Box $5-10

Opel
Steering Wheel
Old England-Swiss Analog-Ca 1969
Base metal top-Stainless back
Sweep seconds-Pierced vinyl strap
OPE 1 Head 39x39mm $55-75

Orphan Annie
Harold Gray-New Haven-Analog
Chrome plated case-1936
ORA 2 head 26x39mm $160-175
Box $125-150

New Haven
"Orphan Annie"
A popular character watch. Chromium finish case, curved to fit wrist. Neat silvered dial. Unbreakable crystal; length 1 7/8 inches. Detachable leather strap. Gift box.

Orphan Annie
New Haven-Analog-1935
Chrome plated case
ORA 1 Head 28x38mm $250-275
Box $150-175

PAC-MAN
Bally Midway Mfg. Co.
Bradley-Swiss Analog-1980
Base metal top-Stainless back
PAC 1 Head 29x37mm $35-45
Pop up box $5-10

Oscar the Grouch
Muppets Inc.-Animated Hands
Bradley-Swiss Analog-Ca 1971
Chrome top-Base metal back
OTG 1 Head 25x33mm $35-45
OTG 2 Head 29x36mm $40-60
Pop up box $5-10

PAC-MAN, MS.
Bally Midway Mfg. Co.
Animated Seconds
Bradley-Swiss Analog-1980
Base metal top-Stainless back
PAC 2 Head 27x34mm $35-50
Pop up box $5-10

Owl-Graduate
New Zoo Revue-1975
Philmar Watch Co-Swiss Analog
Gold tone case
OWG 1 Head 22x41mm $20-30

Panda
Swiss Unmarked-Prototype watch
Swiss Analog-Sweep Second
Gold tone top-Stainless back
PAN 1 Head 29x35mm
For Information Only

Pepsi Cola
"You've Got a Lot to Live"-Ca 1965
Swiss Analog
Chrome plated top-Base metal back
PEC 1 Head Small $40-50

Pinocchio
Moving Jiminy Cricket
Wotania-Swiss Analog
Gold tone top-Base metal back
Embossed Lion Rampant case back
PIN 3 Head 25x32mm $25-35

Peter Pan
Moving Tinkerbell
Wotania-Swiss Analog
Gold tone top-Base metal back
Embossed lion rampant on case back
PEP 1 Head 25x32mm $25-35

Pinocchio
Moving Jiminy Cricket
Webster Watch Co.-1974
Gold tone top-Base metal back
PIN 4 Head 25x32mm $25-35

Pinocchio
Animated Hands-WDP
Ingersoll-U.S. Time-1948 back
Steel color case
PIN 1 Head 29x40mm $200-250
Birthday Box $200-250
Birthday cake box $300-325

Pinto
Moving Back Legs
Came with Pinto Car
Trice-Swiss Analog
Gold tone top-Base metal back
PIT 2 Head 36x41mm $65-85

Pluto
WDP
Ingersoll-U.S. Time-1948
Steel color case
PLU 1 Head 29x40mm $200-250
Birthday Box $200-250

Pro Celeb-Forest Hills
Bradley-Swiss Analog
Gold tone top-Base metal back
PRC 1 Head 33x40mm $15-25

Puppet-Girl
Moving Puppet
Wotania-Swiss Analog
Gold tone top-Base metal back
PUP 1 Head 28x32mm $25-35

Popeye
Animated Hands
King Features Syndicate Inc.
Bradley-Swiss Analog-Ca 1974
Chrome top-Base metal back
POP 2 Head 29x36mm $100-110
POP 3 Sweep 29x36mm $100-110
Pop up box $15-25
Flat layout box $25-40

Quick Draw McGraw
H-BP
Bradley Time-Swiss Analog
Gold tone top-Base metal back
QUD 1 Head 29x35mm $100-125

Raggedy Ann
Animated Hands
The Bobbs-Merrill Co. Inc.
Bradley Time-Swiss Analog-1971
Base acryl assorted color case
RAG 3 Head 31x36mm $20-30
RAG 4 Head 34x34mm $35-45
Box $10-15

Raggedy Ann & Andy
Animated-Seesaw Hearts
The Bobbs Merrill Co, Inc.-1975
Louis Marx & Co., Inc.
Japan-Analog-MARX buckle
Red plastic case-Yellow strap
RAG 5 Head 41x46mm $35-50

Character Watches Listed Alphabetically By First Names

Raggedy Ann
Animated Hands-Magnifying Crystal
The Bobbs-Merrill Co. Inc.
Bradley-Swiss Analog-1971
Chrome & gold tone top
Base metal back
RAG 1 Head 26x33mm $15-20
RAG 2 Head 26x33mm $15-20
Pop up box $5-10

Robin Hood
Swiss Analog-Ca 1958
Chrome plated case
ROH 4 Est. $150-175

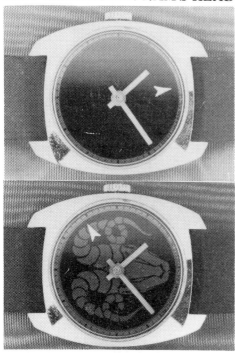

Ram's Head
Lucerne Enterprises Inc.-1977
Polarized plastic seconds disc
Bradley-Swiss Analog
Gold tone top-Base metal back
RAH 1 Head 29x35mm $30-45

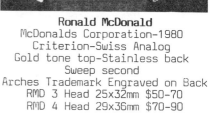

Robo Force
CBS Inc.
Robot Maxx Steele-Blue Dial
Bradley Time-Analog-Ca 1984
Chrome Case-Black strap
ROB 1 Head 27x34mm $15-20
Pop up box $5-10

Ronald McDonald
McDonalds Corporation-1980
Criterion-Swiss Analog
Gold tone top-Stainless back
Sweep second
Arches Trademark Engraved on Back
RMD 3 Head 25x32mm $50-70
RMD 4 Head 29x36mm $70-90

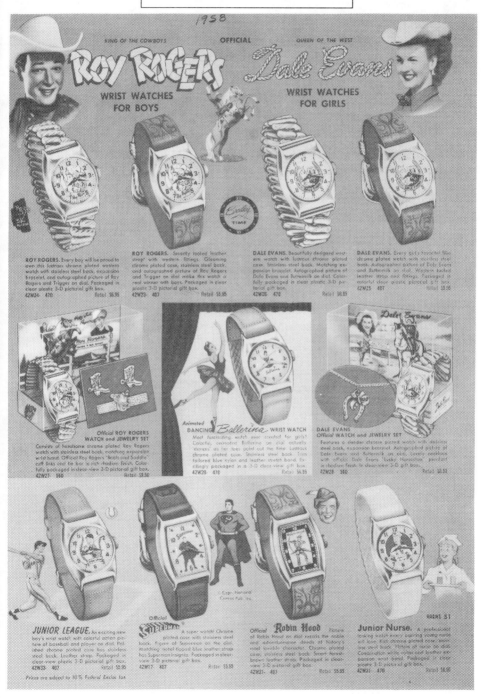

Skateboarder
Animation missing
Hafner-Swiss Analog
Gold tone top-Base metal back
SKA 1 Head 29x35mm $25-35

NOTE: all values are given for a mint
original head & band

Scales of Justice
Lucerne Enterprises Inc.-1977
Polarized plastic seconds disc
Bradley-Swiss Analog
Gold top-Base metal back
SOJ 1 Head 34x41mm $30-45

Smurf & Smurfette
Animated Hands
Wallace Berrie & Co-Peyo
Bradley Time-Analog-CA 1983
Chrome case-Blue strap
SMU 1 Smurf   27x31mm $20-25
SMU 2 Smurfette 27x31mm $20-25
Pop up box $5-10

Scooby Doo
Hanna Barbera Productions Inc-1978
Picco-Singapore-Swiss Analog-7J
Tan plastic case/strap-Sweep second
SCD 1 Head 31x32mm $50-75

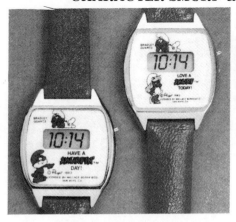

Smurf & Smurfette
Wallace Berrie & Co-Peyo
Bradley Time-Quartz LCD-Ca 1983
Chrome case-Blue strap
Month-Date-Hour-Minute-Seconds
SMU 3 Smurf   26x31mm $10-15
SMU 4 Smurfette 26x31mm $10-15
Pop up box $5-10
Blister pak $5-10

NOTE: *All measurements are taken from
tip of lug to tip of lug and across the
smallest diameter.*

Snoopy Tennis-Yellow Dial
Animated Hand/Tennis Racket-1976
Moving Ball on Rotating Disc
United Feature Syndicate, Inc.-1958
Chrome plated top-Stainless back
SNO 4 Head 32x37mm $50-60
Doghouse box $10-20

Snoopy
United Feature Syndicate, Inc.
Clouds on Rotating Polarized Disc
Swiss Analog-Ca 1970
Black plastic case and strap
SNO 6 Head Medium $40-50
Doghouse Box $10-20
Strap $10-20

Snoopy
Animated Hands-Black or red dial
United Feature Syndicate, Inc.
Timex-Swiss Analog-1971
Chrome plated top-Base metal back
SNO 5 Medium Head $100-150
Doghouse box $10-20

"SNOW WHITE" . . . . **in the**
"Magic Mirror" Box . . . **$6.95**

Snow White
Ingersoll-US Time-1950
Chrome Top-Stainless back
SNW 1 Head 25x37mm $30-40
Mirror Box $150-175

Snow White
Animated hands
Bradley Time-Swiss Analog-1973
Gold tone top-Base metal case
Leather strap
SNW 5 Head 25x32mm $35-45
Roll box $5-10

Soap Box Derby-1936
All American-Cheverolet
Waltham-6/0s-15J-Analog
SBD 1 Movement & Dial Only
For Information Only

Snow White-Seven Dwarfs
Moving Witch
(Only Dark Haired Fairy
Tale Princess)
Wotania-Swiss Analog
Gold tone top-Base metal back
Embossed Lion Rampant case back
SNW 6 Head 25x32mm $25-35

Soap Box Derby
Waltham Premier-870-9J-Analog
Keystone Victory 10KRGP Case
Engraved Chevrolet Motor Div.
Award All American-Soap Box Derby
City Champion 1940-Won by
Dan Linehan on case back
SBD 2 Head 27x37mm Est. $300-400

Snow White
WDP-(Walt Disney Prodctions)
Ingersoll-USA Analog-Ca 1947
Chrome plated top-Base metal back
SNW 7 Head 27x39mm $225-250
Box $150-175

Soccer
Moving Ball
Wotania-Swiss Analog
Gold tone top-Base metal back
Embossed Lion Rampant case back
SOC 2 Head 25x32mm $25-35

Space Man-Eastman
Moving Eyes-Israel
Chrome plated top-Stainless back
SPM 1 Head 26x33mm $35-45

CHARACTER RESEARCH

We are really just beginning to learn what is the correct case, movement, strap & hands to go with a given dial. It seems to us watches made to sell to the public were at first made in limited amounts because of the inability to predict the number of sales. It seems to us upon a close look at a watch like BAB 1 that after the first run it was sold out and by the time the merchandiser returned to the factory for additional orders either that particular case & style or movement was no longer in production. BAB 1 has been verified to be original in at least two unmarked cases, making the exacta case the most desirable. This practice is much more evident in Bradley, especially Mickey Mouse.

Soccer
Moving Leg & Ball
Economic-Swiss Analog
Gold tone top-Base metal back
SOC 3 Head 25x32mm $25-35

Soccer
Swiss Unmarked
Moving Leg & Ball
Chancellor-Swiss Analog
Gold tone top-Base metal back
SOC 4 Head 26x32mm $25-30

Space-Planet Surface
Erwin Triebold-Mumpf Swiss-No. 102
Swiss Analog-1969
Gold tone top-Base metal back
SPP 1 Head 26x32mm $30-40

Spiro Agnew-Original
Animated Hands
DTC-"Dirty Time Co."-Ca 1973
Swiss Analog
Gold tone top-Base metal back
SPA 7 Head Large $40-50

Spiro Agnew
"Original"-Ca 1973
Stick hands-Ribbed bezel
Webster-Swiss Analog
Chrome plated top-Base metal back
SPA 6 Head 35x42mm $40-50
Plastic Packaging $2-5

Spiro Agnew
Animated Hands
Swiss Unmarked-Ca 1973
Swiss Analog
Gold tone top-Base metal back
SPA 8 Head Large $40-50

Sport Billy-FIFA
Moving Soccer Foot
Sports Billy Productions-1979
Bradley-Swiss Analog
Chrome plated top-Stainless back
SPB 2 Head 30x36mm $50-65
Pop up box $5-10

Note: BRADLEY TIME was a company organized about 1950 to market Character Advertising, Political & other Special Watches, and did so with hundreds of examples. They held the Disney Contract from 1972 to 1985. BRADLEY closed forever in 1986.

Star Trek-Mr. Spock
Paramount Pictures Corp.
Bradley-Swiss Analog-1979
Chrome plated top-Base metal back
STM 1 Head 29x36mm $50-70
Box $5-10

Star Wars-Darth Vader
20th Century Fox Film Corp-1977
Bradley-Swiss Analog
Chrome Plated Top-Base Metal Back
Sweep second-Stick hands
Vinyl strap-Grey Dial
SWV Head 29x37mm $50-70
Pop up box $5-10

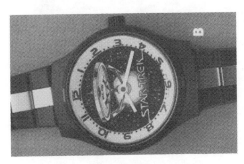

Star Trek
Spaceship U.S.S Enterprise
Paramount Pictures Corp.
Bradley-Swiss Analog-1980
Black cycolac plastic case
STS 1 Head 35x41mm $50-70
Box $5-10

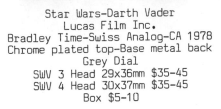

Star Trek-Kirk & Spock
Paramount Pictures Corp.
Bradley-Swiss Quartz-Analog-1980
Chrome plated top-Stainless back
STKS 1 Head $10-15
Box $5-10

Star Wars-Darth Vader
Lucas Film Inc.
Bradley Time-Swiss Analog-CA 1978
Chrome plated top-Base metal back
Grey Dial
SWV 3 Head 29x36mm $35-45
SWV 4 Head 30x37mm $35-45
Box $5-10

Star Wars-"R2 D2" & "3 CPO"
Bradley-Hong Kong Analog-CA 1982
Chrome plated top-Stainless back
Black star filled sky dial
SWR 9 Head 28x35mm $55-65
SWR 10 Head 30x36mm $55-65
Pop up box $5-10

Star Wars-"R2 D2" & "3 CPO"
Lucas Film Inc.
Bradley-Swiss Analog-Ca 1977
Chrome or gold top base metal case
Blue star filled sky dial
Stick hands-Black/blue vinyl strap
SWR 2 Head 34x41mm $60-70
SWR 3 Head 34x41mm $60-70
Pop up box $5-10

Star Wars-Darth Vader
Lucasfilm Inc.-1979
Bradley-Swiss Analog
Black cycolac plastic case
SWV 5 Head 35x40mm $35-45
Box $5-10

Star Wars-"R2 D2" & "3 CPO"
Lucas Film Inc.-1983
Bradley Time-Quartz Musical LCD
Plays Star Wars theme alarm
Programed Approaching Tie Fighter
Black plastic case/Pierced strap
SWR 11 Head 35x42mm $15-25
Box $10-15

American and European
CHARACTER
Wrist Watch Price Guide Book 3
illustrates and values over 900
character wrist watches, ordering
information follows the text of this
book.

Strawberry Shortcake
American Greetings Corp.
Bradley Time-Quartz LCD-Ca 1981-84
Chrome case-Red strap
Month-Date-Hour-Minute-Seconds
STS 10 26x32mm $5-10
STS 11 26x35mm $5-10
STS 12 20x27mm $5-10
Blister pak $5-10

Strawberry Shortcake
American Greetings Corp.
Bradley-Hong Kong Analog-Ca 1980
Chrome case-Red vinyl strap
STS 1 24x31mm $10-15
STS 2 27x33mm $10-15
STS 3 27x33mm $10-15
STS 4 27x34mm $10-15
STS 5 24x30mm $10-15
Box $5-10

*NOTE: All measurements are taken from
tip of lug to tip of lug and across the
smallest diameter.*

Superman
DC Comics Inc
Bradley-Swiss Analog-1962
Chrome plated top-Base metal back
SUP 12 Head 30x36mm $60-75

Superman-Leaping
Embossed DC Comics Inc.-1986
UD-Akita-Japan Quartz Analog
HK Assembly
Red plastic top-Stainless back
Ladies movment-Plastic insert
Black vinyl strap
Watch & Box at retail 6/89 $30
SUP 9 Head 34x40mm

Superman
No copyright-Colored dial-Ca 1980
Quemex-HK Analog-Swiss parts
Gold tone top-Stainless back
Sweep second hand
SUP 8 Head 33x38mm $40-60

Superman & Lois Lane
Embossed DC Comics Inc.-1986
UD-Akita-Japan Quartz Analog
HK Assembly
White plastic top-Stainless back
Ladies movement-Plastic insert
Blue vinyl strap
Watch & Box at retail 6/89 $30
Box same as SUP 9
SUP 10 Head 34x40mm

Superman—Flying
Embossed DC Comics Inc.-1986
UD-Akita-Japan Quartz Analog
HK Assembly
Black plastic top-Stainless back
Ladies movment-Plastic insert
Black vinyl strap
Watch & Box at retail 6/89 $30
SUP 13 Head 34x40mm

Superman—Lois Lane
Embossed DC Comics Inc.-1986
UD-Akita-Japan Quartz Analog
HK Assembly
White plastic top-Stainless back
Ladies movement-Plastic insert
White vinyl strap
Watch & Box at retail 6/89 $30
Box same as SUP 9
SUP 11 Head 34x40mm

Tarzan
Edgar Rice Burroughs Inc.
Bradley-Swiss Analog-1983
Gold tone top-Stainless back
TAR 4 Head 27x34mm $35-45
Pop up Box $5-10

Tennis Players
Moving Tennis Racket
Tennis ball on moving plastic disk
as second hand-Ca 1980's
Corona-HK-Swiss Analog
Chrome plated case
TEP 1 Head 33x38mm $20-30

Tarzan
No copyright-Colored dial
Q&Q-HK Analog-Ca 1976
Gold tone top-Stainless back
TAR 5 Head 32x38mm $40-60

Tennis Players
Moving Tennis Racket
Wotania-Swiss Analog
Gold tone top-Base metal back
Embossed Lion Rampant case back
TEP 2 Head 25x32mm $25-35

Teeter Totter
Moving Teeter
Wotania-Swiss Analog
Gold tone top-Base metal back
Embossed Lion Rampant case back
TET 1 Head 25x32mm $25-35

The Three Stooges
Animated Hands
Norman Maurer Productions Inc.-1985
The "Oldies" Series
Bradley-Quartz Analog-HK Case
Japan movement & dial
White plastic case & strap
TTS 7 Head 24x28mm $125-150
Pop up box $10-20

Tom Thumb
World Wide Watch Co Inc
Swiss Analog
Chrome plated top-Base metal back
TOT 1 Head 29x36mm $40-60

Tweety
Animated Hands-Hearts on Dial
Unmarked Swiss
HK-Swiss Analog-Sweep second
Chrome plated top-Stainless back
TWE 1 Head 35x42mm $75-100

Tom & Jerry
MGM/UA Entertainment Co.
The "Oldies" Series
Bradley-Quartz Analog-1985
HK Case-Japan Movement & Dial
White plastic case/strap
T&J 2 Head 34x39mm $35-45
T&J 3 Head 24x28mm $25-35

Black plastic case/strap
T&J 3 Head 34x39mm $35-45
T&J 4 Head 24x28mm $25-35
See-thru Layout Box $10-15

United States Army
Army Seal-"Glory Time Co"
Windert Watch SA-Swiss Analog
Dirty Time Co. Case
Gold tone top-Base metal back
Sweep second hand
USA 1 Head 35x40mm $20-30

United States Navy
Navy Seal-"Glory Time Co"
Windert Watch SA-Swiss Analog
Dirty Time Co. Case
Gold tone top-Base metal back
Sweep second hand
USN 1 Head 35x40mm $20-30

Volleyball Players
Moving Arm-Ca 1980's
Volleyball on moving plastic
disk as second hand
Corona-HK-Swiss Analog
Red top-Chrome plated back
VOP 1 Head 34x38mm $20-30

"Wile E. Coyote"
Warner Bros. Seven Arts-W7
Sheraton-Swiss Analog-Ca 1972
Gold tone top-Base metal back
WEC 1 Head 30x36mm $200-225

W.C. Fields
W.C. Fields Productions Inc.
The "Oldies" Series
Bradley-Quartz Analog-1985
HK Case-Japan Movement & Dial
Gold tone top-Stainless back
WCF 5 Head 32x38mm $55-70
WCF 6 Head 24x30mm $35-50
Layout Box $15-25

Winnie the Pooh
Animated Hands
Walt Disney Productions
Bradley-Swiss Analog-1977
Chrome plated top-Base metal back
or Gold tone top-Base metal back
WIP 3 Head 27x32mm $30-40
WIP 4 Head 26x33mm $20-30
Box $10-15

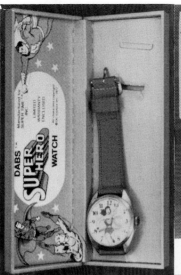

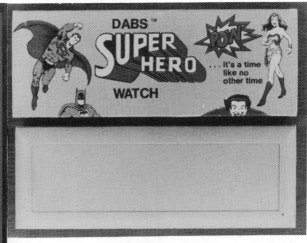

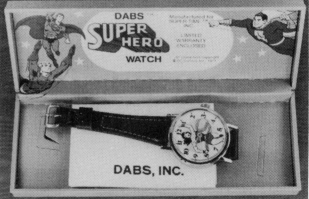

The following all used the same box: Batman, Superman, Spiderman, The Joker & Wonder Woman. These were issued in 1977 and were known as the DABS Watches.

Wonder Woman
DABS & Co.-D.C. Comics
Marvel Comics Group
Swiss Analog-1977
Gold tone base metal top
Stainless steel back
Blue leather strap-yellow stitching
WON 1 Head 34x40mm $85-100
WON 2 Head 26x32mm $75-90
Box $50-65

"DABS" Comic Book Back

Woody Woodpecker
Animated Hands
Walter Lantz Productions, Inc.
Endura-Swiss Analog-1972
White plastic case
Magnifying Crystal
WOW 4 Head 38x42mm $75-100

Woody Woodpecker & Friend
Moving Woodpecker
Basis-Swiss Analog-Unmarked
Gold tone top-Base metal back
WOW 5 Head 26x38mm $45-55

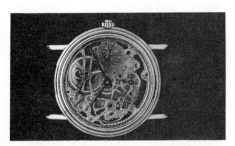

Chopard
29mm—CA 1980's—Skeletonized
Yellow Gold Decorated Bridges
Lady's 18k Polished Yellow Gold Case
$3,000-3,500

Chopard
Lady's—14x32mm—CA 1970's
Diamond and sapphire bezel
White gold $400-500

Chopard
Bracelet—14x34mm—CA 1970's
Lady's—Diamond and ruby bezel
White gold $600-700

Chopard
30mm—Modern—17 Jewels—Bracelet
Onyx—coral and diamond bezel
Lady's 18k Textured Yellow Gold
$800-1,000

Chopard
Lady's 32x14mm—CA 1980's
Hinged lug—Diamond and emerald
Yellow gold $400-500

Chopard
Lady's—15mm—CA 1960's
1.20 Carat—56 diamonds—Bracelet
18K White $400-500

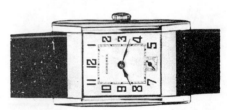

Chronex. Silvered dial, black enameled figures,
subsidiary seconds. 7J movement. Chrome
finished, curved, molded rectangular nickel
case. ca 1932 . . . .$20—35

Chopard
Lady's—14x32mm—CA 1970's
Diamond bezel and lugs
White gold $300-400

Chronex. Silvered dial, luminous hands and
numerals, subsidiary seconds. 15J movement.
14K white gold-filled, faceted rectangular
case. ca 1932 . . . .$25—45

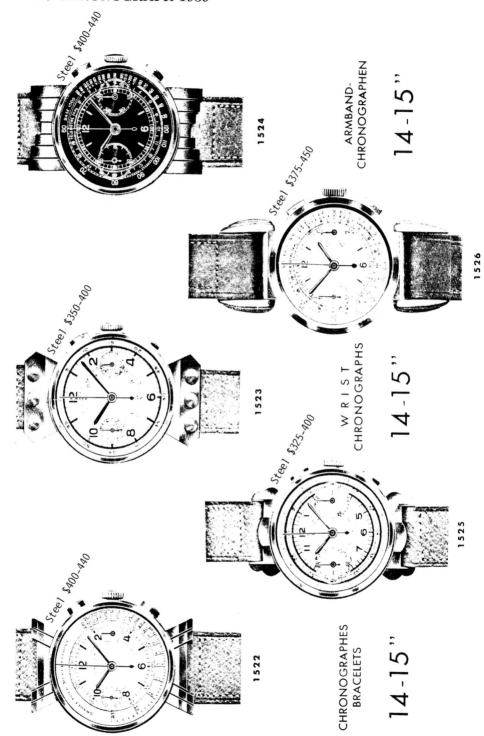

Steel $400-440

1524

ARMBAND-
CHRONOGRAPHEN

14-15"

Steel $375-450

1526

Steel $350-400

1523

W R I S T
CHRONOGRAPHS

14-15"

Steel $325-400

1525

Steel $400-440

1522

CHRONOGRAPHES
BRACELETS

14-15"

Steel $900-1,000
18K $2,000-2,200

427

Wrist Split second Timer.

Steel $75-100
18K $175-200

1527

14/15"

**Wrist - chronographs, with
12 hours register.**

Steel $60-75
18K $150-175

1528

Steel $60-75
18K $150-175

1529

WRIST - CHRONOGRAPHS

Steel $350-400

1516

Steel $425-475

1517

Steel $375-425

1518

Steel $325-375

1519

Steel $300-350

1520

Steel $350-400

1521

WRIST-CHRONOGRAPHS 13" WITH REGISTER

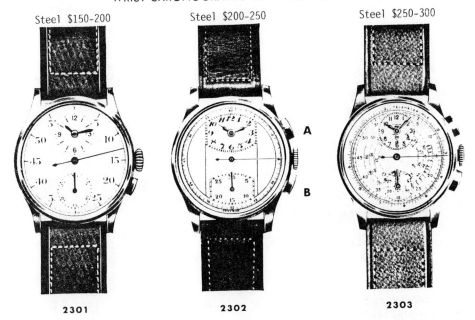

Steel $150-200 Steel $200-250 Steel $250-300

A

B

2301   **2302**   **2303**

CHRONOGRAPH 11¼" - 13"
WITH TURNING BEZEL
allowing to register up to 60 Minutes

* All values are given for the head only unless the band is included in the description.
* Read page 12 before using this book to value your wrist watch.
* Values are given for a mint watch with original dial, movement and case.

Steel $150-200

Steel $50-70

411

2003

13" 1/5 of second, start, stop and back action from the side pusher, also obtainable with Pulsometer dial and Yachting Timer 5 Minutes. (See Mod. 353, page 12.)

Steel $350-400

1502

Wrist-Chronograph for aviator
TURNING BEZEL WITH INDEX

CHRONOGRAPHE 15"

Steel $150-200

1505

With turning bezel

Recording up to 12 hours.

13"

Steel $150-175
18K $400-450

1162

14"

Steel $150-175
18K $400-450

1530

CHRONOGRAPHES-
WATERPROOF

Latest technical improvements. Non-magnetic. **Incabloc** Shock-absorber

WRIST-
CHRONOGRAPHS

14-15"

Steel $325-375

1509

Steel $300-350

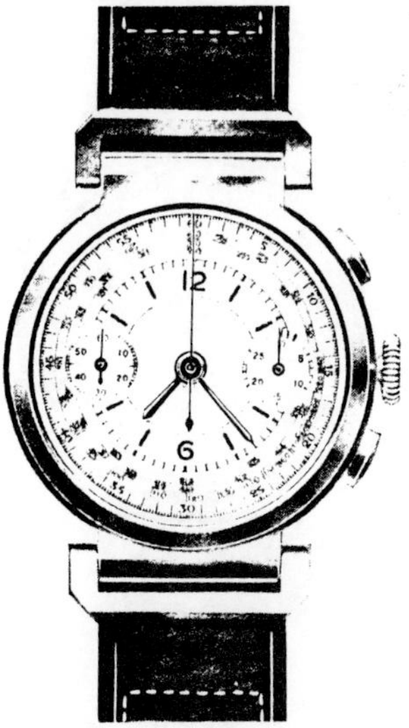

1510

Steel $250-300

1511

Steel $350-400

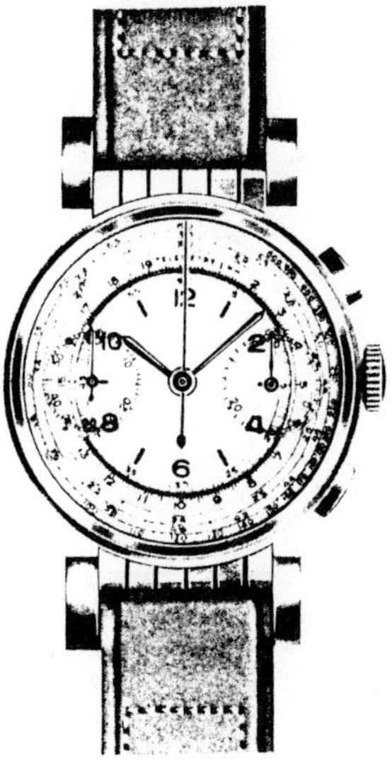

1512

Steel $325-375

1513

Steel $325-375

1515

WRIST
CHRONOGRAPHS

14-15"

Steel $200-250

Steel $100-125
18K $200-250

Steel $75-100
18K $200-225

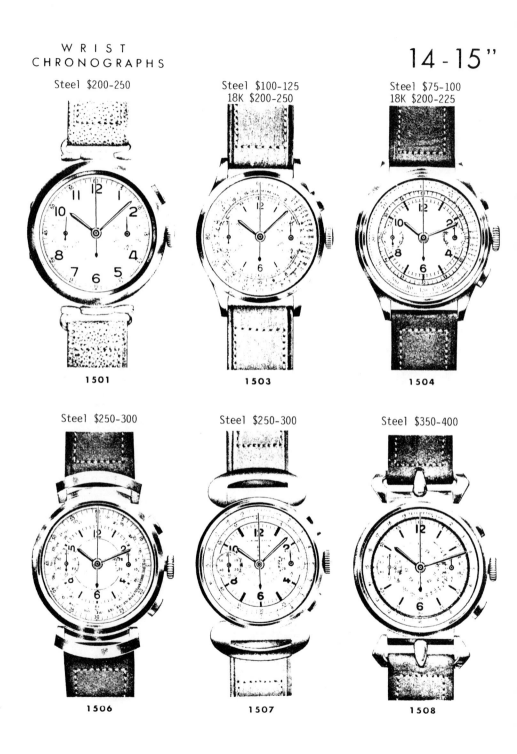

1501

1503

1504

Steel $250-300

Steel $250-300

Steel $350-400

1506

1507

1508

WRIST-
CHRONOGRAPHS

13"

Steel $350-400

1159

Steel $300-350

1161

Steel $300-350

1158

Steel $50-60

1163

CHRONOGRAPHES
BRACELETS

13"

Steel $275-300

1157

Steel $250-300

1160

WRIST - CHRONOGRAPHS

13"

Steel $50-60
18K $150-200

1151

Steel $75-100

1152

Steel $150-175
18K $300-350

1153

Steel $100-125
18K $200-250

1154

18K $225-250

1155

18K $275-300

1156

Steel $150-175
18K $300-350

Steel $125-150
18K $300-350

2001

2002

11 1/4"

11 1/4 - 13"

10 1/2"
Steel $150-175

1004

With **TURNING BEZEL, recording up to 12 hours.**

THE SMALLEST WRIST
CHRONOGRAPH WITH REGISTER

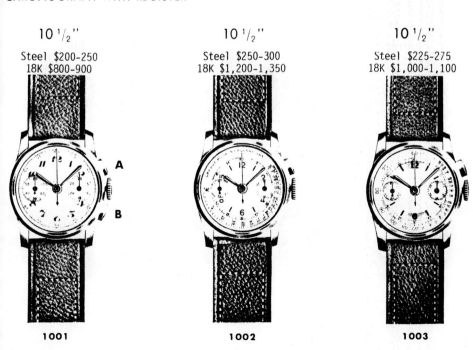

10 1/2"
Steel $200-250
18K $800-900

A

B

1001

10 1/2"
Steel $250-300
18K $1,200-1,350

1002

10 1/2"
Steel $225-275
18K $1,000-1,100

1003

1936

CORTÉBERT WATCH Co
LA CHAUX-DE-FONDS

Cortébert - Art - Technique
Maison Fondée en 1790 invite les
grossistes étrangers et les horlogers
suisses à visiter son stand à la Foire
de Bâle où les modèles les plus mo-
dernes seront exposés. Un choix de
classe, une qualité garantie et une ex-
périence de 150 ans engagent certainement à donner la préférence à la mar-
que Cortébert, de réputation mondiale.

1940

18KYG
$150-180

18KYG $50-70   18KYG $60-80

Cortebert
22x30mm—CA 1950's
Hidden lugs
18K Yellow $200—300

Cortebert
Digital—38mm—CA 1932
Glasgow hallmarks
18K Yellow $700-800

Croton "Aquamedio". Sweep second, radium dial, 9J or 17J, waterproof stainless steel case. ca 1941. $10-20

Croton "Sportsleader". Center seconds. 17J movement. Round, chrome plated top, stainless steel, waterproof case. ca 1962. . . . $5—10

Croton "Aquamatic". Waterproof, nonmagnetic radium dial, 17J, self-winding. Stainless steel. ca 1941 . . . . $5-10

Croton "Cruiser". Subsidiary seconds. 17J movement. Round, chrome plated top, stainless steel back. ca 1962. . . . .$6—12

Croton "President". 12-diamond silver dial. 17J, thin movement. 18K yellow gold, round thin case. ca 1961. . . . . $120-140
Without diamond dial $100-120

Croton "Buccaneer". Subsidiary seconds. 17J movement. Stainless steel, waterproof case. ca 1962. . . . .$5—10

Croton "Aquadatic". Center seconds, date window at 3. 17J, self-winding movement. Round stainless steel case. ca 1962 . . .$10—15

Croton "Sportsman". Center seconds. 17J movement. Round, chrome plated top, stainless steel back. ca 1962. . . . .$5—10

$20-35

$20-35

CY 971—CYMA, 6/0 size, 15 jewels, Star Stellar quality, white or green case, detachable lugs and buckle, radium numerals **$30.00**

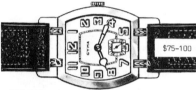

$75-100

CY 972—CYMA, 10½ ligne, 15 jewels, white R. P. chromium special link case, detachable lugs and buckle, radium numerals **$30.00**

$35-50

CY 973—CYMA, 10½ ligne, 15 jewels, Stellar quality, white or green case, detachable lugs and buckle, radium numerals **$32.00**

$20-35

CY 974—CYMA, 10½ ligne, 15 jewels, Stellar quality, white or green engraved case, detachable lugs and buckle, radium numerals. **$33.00**

$25-40

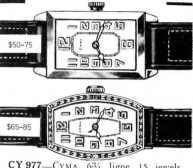

$50-75

$65-85

CY 977—CYMA, 6¾ ligne, 15 jewels, Stellar quality, white or green engraved case, detachable lugs and buckle, radium numerals......**$36.00**

$50-75

CY 978—CYMA, 10/0 size, 15 jewels, Stellar quality, white or green case, detachable lugs and buckle, radium numerals **$37.50**

$65-90

CY 979—CYMA, 10/0 size, 15 jewels, Stellar quality, white or green engraved case, detachable lugs and buckle, radium numerals....**$38.50**

$125-150

CY 980—CYMA, 10½ ligne, 15 jewels, white R. P. chromium finish, enamel bezel, special link case, detachable lugs and buckle **$40.00**

$20-35

No. D 942—11½ Ligne, *Doric* **AMBASSADOR** movement. Luminous dial and hands. 14 Karat White Rolled Gold Plate case. **Guaranteed 10 Years.** Gold filled bracelet to match. **$22.50**

No. D 943—11½ Ligne, *Doric* **AVIATOR** movement. Radium dial and hands. 14 Karat Natural Rolled Gold Plate case. **Guaranteed 10 Years.** Open link gold filled bracelet. **$24.50**

No. D 944—10½ Ligne, *Doric* **MINISTER** movement. Luminous dial and hands. Handsome white engraved case. Attractive link band to match. **$18.50**

No. D 945—10½ Ligne, *Doric* **ADMIRAL** movement. Radium dial and hands. Modernistic white case. Smart link band to match. **$20.50**

No. D 946—10½ Ligne, *Doric* **MONTICELLO** 17 Jewel movement. Luminous dial and hands. 14 Karat Natural Rolled Gold Plate case. **Guaranteed 10 Years.** Gold filled band to match. **$31.50**

No. D 947—10½ Ligne, *Doric* **GOVERNOR** 17 Jewel movement. Radium dial and hands. 14 Karat White Rolled Gold Plate case. **Guaranteed 10 Years.** Gold filled band to match. **$33.50**

No. D 948—10½ Ligne, *Doric* **VIRGINIAN** 17 Jewel movement. Luminous dial and hands. Attractive white case. New open link band. **$25.50**

No. D 949—10½ Ligne, *Doric* **STATESMAN** 17 Jewel movement. Radium dial and hands. Handsome white carved case. Open link band to match. **$27.50**

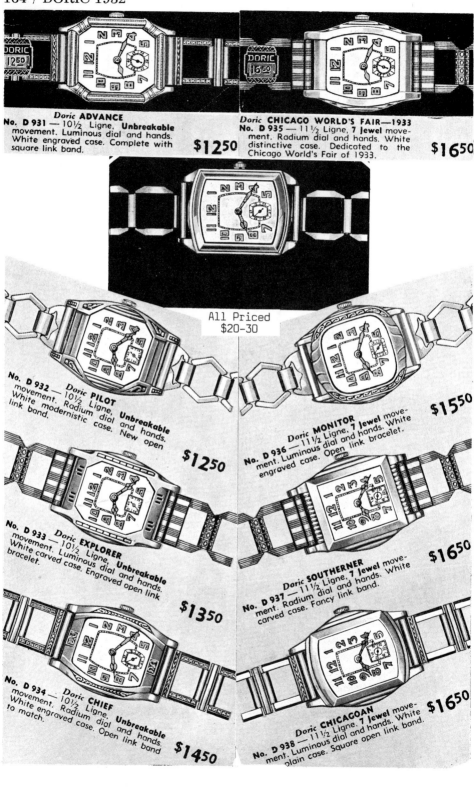

Doric ADVANCE
No. D 931 — 10½ Ligne, **Unbreakable** movement. Luminous dial and hands. White engraved case. Complete with square link band.

$12⁵⁰

Doric CHICAGO WORLD'S FAIR—1933
No. D 935 — 11½ Ligne, **7 Jewel** movement. Radium dial and hands. White distinctive case. Dedicated to the Chicago World's Fair of 1933.

$16⁵⁰

All Priced
$20-30

Doric PILOT
No. D 932 — 10½ Ligne, **Unbreakable** movement. Radium dial and hands. White modernistic case. New open link band.

$12⁵⁰

Doric MONITOR
No. D 936 — 11½ Ligne, **7 Jewel** movement. Luminous dial and hands. White engraved case. Open link bracelet.

$15⁵⁰

Doric EXPLORER
No. D 933 — 10½ Ligne, **Unbreakable** movement. Luminous dial and hands. White carved case. Engraved open link bracelet.

$13⁵⁰

Doric SOUTHERNER
No. D 937 — 11½ Ligne, **7 Jewel** movement. Radium dial and hands. White carved case. Fancy link band.

$16⁵⁰

Doric CHIEF
No. D 934 — 10½ Ligne, **Unbreakable** movement. Radium dial and hands. White engraved case. Open link band to match.

$14⁵⁰

Doric CHICAGOAN
No. D 938 — 11½ Ligne, **7 Jewel** movement. Luminous dial and hands. White plain case. Square open link band.

$16⁵⁰

DOXA 1936.

$20-25

$10-15

$75-100

$5-10

$5-10

$150-200

$10-15

$5-10

$75-100

$5-10

$125-150

$15-20

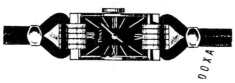

Doxa-Ladies-Cord
Ca 1939-13x30mm
Tutone-Yellow body
with white lugs
18KYG Head $100-125

Doxa-Asymetrical-Strap
Ca 1939-20x40mm
Tutone-Yellow back-Pink top
18KYG Head $800-900

18K $350-400

Doxa-Asymetrical-Ladies
Ca 1939-Bracelet
Diamonds
18KYG Head $400-450
Steel $25-35

18K $125-150

Doxa-Ladies-Cord
Ca 1939-17x30mm
Diamonds
18KYG Head $100-125

Steel $15-20

Steel $10-15

Doxa-Asymetrical-Strap
Ca 1939-19x42mm
Hidden lugs
18KYG $750-850

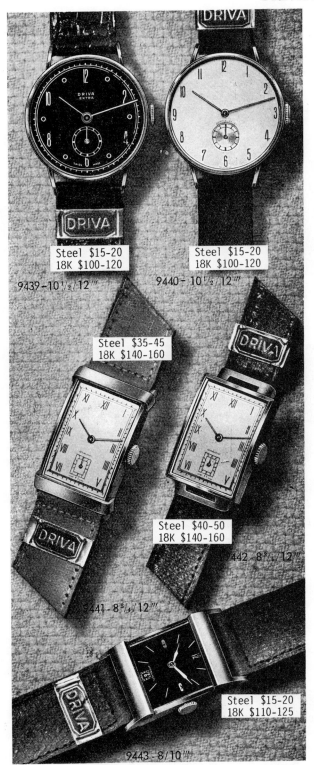

DRIVA WATCH Cᵒ·
3, RUE DU MONT-BLANC
GENÈVE

Steel $15-20
18K $100-120

9439 - 10½/12‴

Steel $15-20
18K $100-120

9440 - 10½/12‴

Steel $35-45
18K $140-160

Steel $40-50
18K $140-160

9442 - 8¾/12‴

9441 - 8¾/12‴

Steel $15-20
18K $110-125

9443 - 8/10‴

EBEL

LA CHAUX-DE-FONDS

Ref. 16003 — Ultra thin Staybrite Steel or Gold   Steel $100-120
18K $200-225

Ref. 16006 — Ultra thin Staybrite Steel or Gold   Steel $110-130
18K $225-240

Ref. 3060 — 18k red Gold
18K $90-100

Ref. 11565 — Staybrite Steel
Steel $50-60

Ref. 1431 — 18k red Gold, Rubis and Diamonds   18K $200-225

Ref. 9255 — 18k red Gold, Rubis and Diamonds   18K $100-125

Flat
$1,500-1,800

18KYG $200-240

18KYG $50-75

18KYG $70-110

18KYG $50-75

18KYG $60-85

18KYG $50-75

18KYG $50-75

18KYG $50-75

18KYG $40-60

18KWG & Diamonds
10/20% over salvage

18KYG $40-60

EBERHARD & CO

18KYG
$175-215

1278

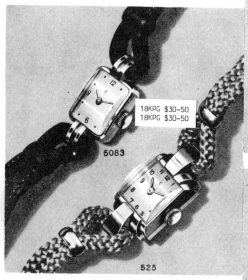

18KPG $30-50
18KPG $30-50

5083

525

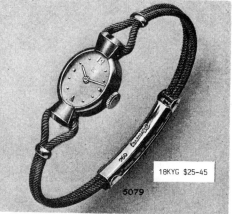

18KYG $25-45

5079

18KPG $30-50
18KYG $30-50

531

980

18KPG
$300-360

ELGIN NATIONAL WATCH CO.
Elgin, Illinois 1867-1953

Wrist watches are like women. Everyone's idea and ideal varies. Realizing this, the case makers tried to make a watch to please everyone by letting their designer's imagination run wild. Therefore, we have literally thousands of case styles, dial colors, case and dial metals, and combinations thereof. In 1931, Elgin offered over 300 different wrist watches and each year some would be dropped from the line and new ones were added in the hope of finding a winner. What we have selected for this book is just a sampling of their more interesting watches. The U.S. manufacture of Elgins stopped in the mid-fifties, and thereafter many watches were sold that were Swiss made but marked with the Elgin name.

ELGIN NATIONAL WATCH CO.
1874 – Mid 1900's

Serial No.	Date	Serial No.	Date	Serial No.	Date
101	1867	7,000,000	1897	21,000,000	1918
100,000	1870	8,000,000	1899	22,000,000	1919
200,000	1874	9,000,000	1900	23,000,000	1920
400,000	1875	10,000,000	1903	26,000,000	1923
500,000	1877	11,000,000	1904	29,000,000	1926
600,000	1879	13,000,000	1907	33,000,000	1929
700,000	1880	14,000,000	1909	34,000,000	1933
800,000	1881	15,000,000	1910	36,000,000	1936
1,000,000	1882	16,000,000	1911	38,000,000	1939
2,000,000	1886	17,000,000	1912	41,000,000	1942
3,000,000	1888	18,000,000	1914	43,000,000	1945
4,000,000	1890	19,000,000	1916	45,000,000	1948
5,000,000	1893	20,000,000	1917	50,000,000	1953
6,000,000	1895				

Note: EA Numbers were taken from American Pocket Watches Beginning to End, by Ehrhardt-Meggers 1987, Advertised on a page in the back of this book.

ELGIN NATIONAL WATCH CO.
Elgin, Ill. — 1874—Present

NAME CHANGES

National Watch Co.
Chicago, Ill.
1864–1874 Name Change
The Elgin National Watch Co.
Elgin, Ill.   1874—Present

NOTE: Name still used on imported Swiss wrist watches.

EA 258   Elgin National Watch Co.
5/0 Size—Hunting—Gilt or Nickel
Model 1—Pendant Set—¾ Plate

EA 255   Elgin National Watch Co.
0 Size—Open Face—Gilt or Nickel
Model 3—Pendant Set—¾ Plate

EA 259   Elgin National Watch Co.
5/0 Size—Open Face—Gilt or Nickel
Model 2—Pendant Set—¾ Plate

EA 256   Elgin National Watch Co.
3/0 Size—Hunting—Gilt or Nickel
Model 2—Pendant Set—¾ Plate

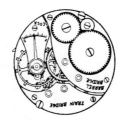

EA 257   Elgin National Watch Co.
3/0 Size—Open Face—Gilt or Nickel
Model 3—Pendant Set—¾ Plate

EA 260   Elgin National Watch Co.
10/0 Size—Open Face—Gilt or Nickel
Model 1—Pendant Set—¾ Plate

8/0 Size
Model 16 & 17
G 641-642

10/0 Size
G630

1st American
Automatic
G 607

15/0 Size
Model 3
G 557-558-559

8/0 Size
Model 16 & 17
Sweep Second G 467

Lip R 40 Cal
(Swiss) G 657

A Schild (Swiss)
1477-1563
G 634

15/0 Size
Model 4
G 670-671-672-673

8/0 Size
Model 20
G 680-681-682-683

8/0 Size
Model 7
G 554-555-556

6/0 Size
Self Wind
G 760-761

15/Size
Model 2
G 623-624-625-626

8/0 Size
Model 8 Sweep Second
G 532-533-534-535
G 536-537-538-539

A. Schild (Swiss)
1361, 1423, 1584
Sweep Second—Self Wind
G 654

A Schild (Swiss)
1320—1422—1607
Self Wind—Sweep Second
G 653

13/0 Size
G 716

EA 261   Elgin National Watch Co.

*Wrist watch movements smaller than 0 Size
are not collected unless they are in a nice
case. Some of the Elgin small size are illustrated on this page and have a value of
$1—20, depending on the buyer.*

G = Grade

13/0 Size
Some Digital G 718

21/0 Size
Model 3
Sweep Second G 547

21/0 Size
Model 4
G 617-618-619

Model 1
G 660-661-662

13/0 Size
Digital
G 717-719-721

21/0 Size
Model 2
G 533-535-541

G 803

20/0 Size
G 700-701-702
G 703-704-705

13/0 Size
Sweep Second G 724

21/0 Size
Model 9
G 655-656

Font 62
Sweep Second G 632

20/0 Size
G 740

13/0 Size
G 711-712-713-714-715

21/0 Size
Model 9
G 650-651

G 666 Sweep Second

20/0 Size
G 703

G = Grade

161
18/0S-15J-Embossed dial
Made 1929-Form fitting lugs
161 14KWGF Head $50-60

205
15J-Embossed dial-Luminous dot dial
White back & bezel
with green spur lugs
Made 1928
205 14KYGF Head $80-90

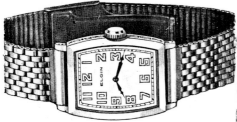

200-CLUBMAN
10/0S-17J or 15J
Made 1930-31
200 14KWGF Head $45-55

207-CLUBMAN
10/0S-15J-Luminous dot dial & hands
Made 1928-1930-Special curved head
207 14KWGF Head $55-65

201-TOUCHDOWN
10/0S-7J-Unusual dial
Made 1928-1931
201 14KWGF Head $45-55

208
10/0S-15J-Luminous dot dial & hands
Made 1928-1929
208 14KYGF White & black bezel
Head $75-85
216 14KGF White, Green Center
Head $85-100

203
10/0S-7J-Luminous dot embossed
dial & hands-Made 1928-1929
203 14KWGF Head $65-75
217 14KWGF with green center
Head $85-100

210
10/0S-15J-Luminous dot dial & hands
Made 1928-1929-Enameled Head
14K Solid Gold
210 Black & White Head $500-550
211 Green & White Head $500-550

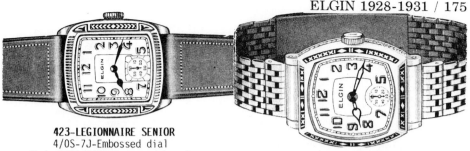

423-LEGIONNAIRE SENIOR
4/0S-7J-Embossed dial
Made 1928-1931-Engraved bezel
423 14KYGF Head $25-35

429-THRIFT
4/0S-7J-Luminous dot dial & hands
Made 1930-31-Engraved
429 Nickel Chromium plated
Head $30-40

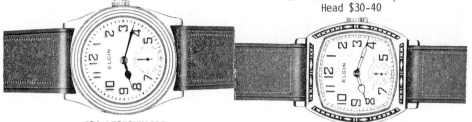

424-LEGIONNAIRE
4/0S-7J-Embossed dial
Made 1929
424 Nickel Chromium Plated
Head $25-35

430-LEGIONNAIRE-THRIFT
4/0S-7J-Luminous dot dial & hands
Made 1929-1931-Engraved & oxidized
430 Nickel Chromium plated
Head $30-40

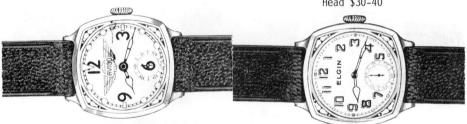

426-AVIGO-THRIFT
4/0S-7J-Air Corps specification dial
Luminous dot dial & hands
Made 1929-1931
426 Nickel Chromium Plated
Head $35-45

431-THRIFT
4/0S-7J-Luminous dot dial & hands
Made 1930-31
431 Nickel Chromium Plated
Head $35-45

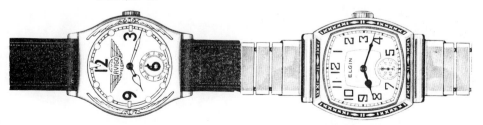

428-AVIGO
4/0S-7J-Air Corps specification dial
Made 1929-1931-Engraved & oxidized
428 Nickel Chromium Plated
Head $35-45

432-LEGIONNAIRE
4/0S-7J-Raised figure dial
Made 1929-Engraved & oxidized
432 Nickel Chromium Plated
Head $40-50

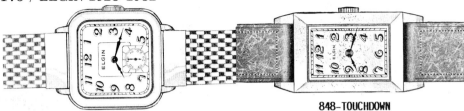

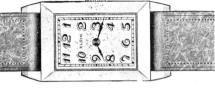

698
6/OS-17J-Embossed figure dial
Made 1928-1929-Extended center
698 14KWGF Head $45-55
WGF Mesh Band $5-7

848-TOUCHDOWN
18/OS-7J-Embossed dial
Made 1929-1931-Hinged lugs
848 14KWGF Head $85-100

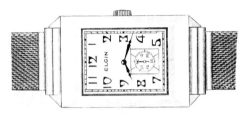

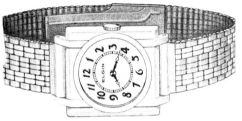

699
6/OS-15J-Embossed dial
Made 1929-Tu tone-Butler finished
699 14KGF White & Yellow Head $60-70
WGF Mesh Band $5-7

901-CLUBMAN
18/OS-17J-Raised yellow bars
Made 1930-31
901 14KWGF Heads $100-150

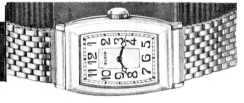

805-CLUBMAN
18/OS-17J-Luminous dial & hands
Made 1929-1931
805 14KGF White Head $70-80

906-CLUBMAN
18/OS-17J or 15J-Tonneau shape
Made 1930-31
906 14KWGF Head $60-70
1026 14KYGF Head $60-70

814-PRESENTATION
18/OS-17J-Made 1929-1932
814 14KYG Head $225-250
836 14KGG & 14KWG Head $450-500
837 14KWG Head $200-225
14KG Band $275-325

934-CAMPUS
18/OS-7J-Engraved
Made 1930-31-Tonneau
934 Nickel Chromium Plated
Head $40-50

467-CAMPUS
4/0S-7J-Full luminous dial & hands
Made 1930-31-White back & bezel
467 14KGGF Head $70-80

663
6/0S-Curved case-Luminous dial
Made 1928-Engraved
663 14KWGF Head $60-70
664 14KGGF Head $60-70

472-HOME RUN
4/0S-17J-Engraved
Made 1930-1932
472 14KWGF Head $45-55

665-CLUBMAN
6/0S-17J-Luminous dial & hands
Butler finish panel on dial
White back-Made 1928-1931
Engraved extended center
665 14KGGF Head $60-70

486
4/0S-7J-Embossed dial
Made 1932-1933-Engraved case
486 Nickel Chromium Plated
Head $40-50
Chronium plated band $3-5

667-HOME RUN
6/0S-15J-Special dial with plated
figures-Made 1928-1931
Engraved & oxidized
667 14KWGF Head $90-110

494
4/0S-17J-Enamel
Made 1932-1933
494 14KWGF Head $225-250
GF Flexible band $5-10

669-CAMPUS
6/0S-7J-Special dial with
plated figures
Made 1928-1931-Engraved & oxidized
669 14KWGF Head $65-75

433-THRIFT
4/0S-7J-Numerals set outside dial
in black enamel-Made 1930-31
433 Nickel Chromium Plated
Head $200-250

455-STATES
4/0S-17J-Luminous tutone dial
& hands-Green engraved-Extended
center-White back & bezel
Made 1929-1930-31
455 14KYGF Head $85-100
14KGF Kreisler Strap $5-10

436-LEGIONNAIRE SENIOR
S694-7J-Raised figure dial
Made 1928-1932
436 14KWGF Head $55-65

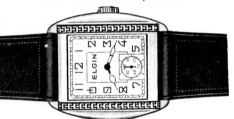

456-AMERICAN EFFICIENCY
4/0S-17J-Luminous dot dial & hands
Made 1928-1931
456 14KWGF Head $65-75

440-THRIFT
4/0S-7J-Numerals set in black
enamel bezel-Made 1930-31
440 Nickel Chromium Plated
Head $175-200

462-AMERICAN EFFICIENCY
4/0S-17J-First American Efficiency
dial-Made 1928-1932
462 14KWGF Head $60-70

442
4/0S-7J-Sweep second hand
Made 1932-1934-Early Doctor's
442 14KWGF Head $65-75

464-AMERICAN EFFICIENCY
4/0S-17J-Special dial
Made 1928-1932-Engraved
464 14KWGF Head $65-75

310-COMRADE
3/0S-7J-Raised figure dial
Made 1930-31-Engraved
310 Nickel Chromium Plated
Head $35-45

413-LEGIONNAIRE SENIOR
4/0S-7J-Full luminous dial & hands
Made 1928-1931-TuTone
413 14KWGF Head $45-55
416 14KGGF Head $45-55

317-BOY SCOUT
3/0S-7J-Aviation type luminous
dot dial-Made 1932-1937
317 Nickel Chromium Plated
Head $150-175

417-LEGIONNAIRE
4/0S-7J-Full luminous dial & hands
Made 1928-1929-Tutone with
green center-White Back & bezel
417 14KYGF Head $65-75

402-LEGIONNAIRE
4/0S-Embossed luminous dial
Made 1928
402 Nickel Chromium Plated
Head $40-50

418-SENIOR
4/0S-7J-Luminous dot embossed dial
& hands-Made 1928-1931
418 14KWGF Head $45-55
419 14KGGF Head $45-55

405
Embossed dial or
Luminous dot dial & hands-Made 1928
405 14KGF White or Green Head $55-65

422-LEGIONNAIRE-THRIFT
4/0S-7J-Luminous dial & hands
Made 1929-1931
422 Nickel Chromium Plated
Head $175-200

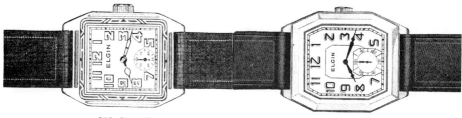

670-STATES
6/0S-15J-full luminous dial & hands
Made 1928-1931-Engraved & oxydized
670 14KWGF Head $60-70

677-HOME RUN
6/0S-15J-Raised figure dial
Made 1928-1931
677 14KWGF Head $50-60

671-STATES
6/0S-15J-Luminous dot dial & hands
Made 1929-1931-Hidden lugs
671 14KWGF Head $70-80

676-SENIOR
6/0S-7J-Full luminous dial & hands
Made 1928-1955-Engraved
676 Nickel Chromium Plated
Head $50-60
676 14KYGF Head $60-70

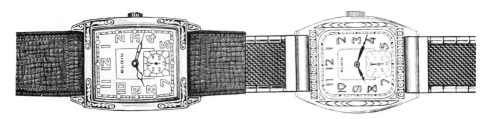

673-SENIOR
6/0S-7J-Embossed luminous dial
Made 1929-1931-Engraved
673 Nickel Chromium Plated
Head $60-70

687
6/0S-15J-Made 1928-1929-Engraved
687 Nickel Chromium Plated
Head $55-65
Nickel Chronium plated Band $3-5

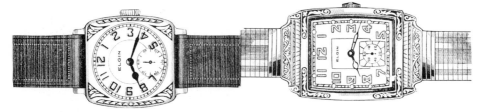

674-THRIFT
6/0S-7J-Embossed dial
Made 1929-1931
674 Nickel Chromium Plated
Head $55-65

693
6/0S-7J-Luminous dot dial & hands
Made 1928-1929-Engraved
693 Nickel Chromium Plated
Head $100-125
Nickel Chromium Band $3-5

219
10/0S-7J-Luminous dot dial & hands
Made 1929-TuTone
Green extended center
White back & bezel
219 14KGF White & Green Head $75-85

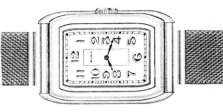

233
10/0S-7J-Raised figure dial
Made 1929
233 14KWGF Head $65-75

220-TOUCHDOWN
10/0S-7J-Raised figure dial
Made 1929-1931
220 14KWGF Head $60-70

241-TOUCHDOWN
10/0S-7J-Made 1930-31
241 14KWGF Head $55-65

229
10/0S-15J-Luminous dot dial & hands
Made 1929-Engraved
229 14KWG Head $225-250

242-PARISIAN
10/0S-15J-Flexible lugs
Made 1930-1932
242 14KWG Head $600-650
243 14KGG Head $650-700

231
10/0S-7J
Made 1932
231 14KWGF Head $55-65

311-COMRADE
3/0S-7J-Raised figure dial
Made 1930-1931-Engraved
311 Nickel Chromium Plated
Head $35-45

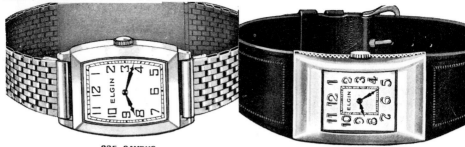

935-CAMPUS
18/0S-7J-Tonneau
Made 1930-31-Plain polished case
935 Nickel Chromium Plated
Head $35-45

942-CAMPUS
18/0S-7J-Curved case
Made 1930-31-Hidden lugs
942 Nickel Chromium Plated
Head $65-75

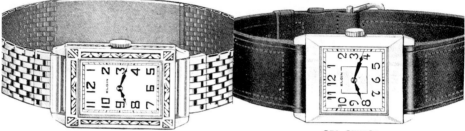

936-CAMPUS
18/0S-7J-Rectangular-Engraved
Made 1930-31
936 Nickel Chromium Plated
Head $60-70

951-SENIOR
18/0S-7J-Polished case
Made 1930-31
951 Nickel Chromium Plated
Head $40-50

940-CAMPUS
18/0S-7J-Curved engraved case
Made 1930-31
940 Nickel Chromium Plated
Head $65-75

952-SENIOR
18/0S-7J-Engraved case
Made 1930-31
952 Nickel Chromium Plated
Head $60-70

941-CAMPUS
18/0S-7J-Curved case
Made 1930-31-Engraved sides
941 Nickel Chromium Plated
Head $60-70

1013-CLUBMAN
18/0S-17J-White with Yellow Lugs
Made 1930-1932
1013 14KYGF Head $70-80

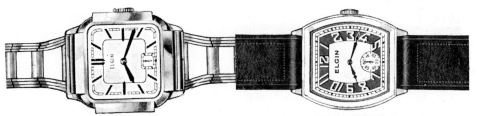

1483
4/0S-17J-Embossed dial
Made 1936
1483 10KYGF Head $55-65

1601-CLUBMAN
6/0S-15J-Full luminous dial & hands
Raised figure dial-Made 1930-31
1601 14KWG Head $200-225

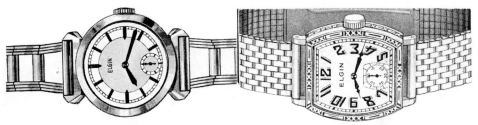

1485
4/0S-17J-Embossed dial
Made 1936
1485 10KYGF Head $35-45

1622-CLUBMAN
6/0S-17J or 15J
Made 1930-31
1622 14KWG Head $175-200

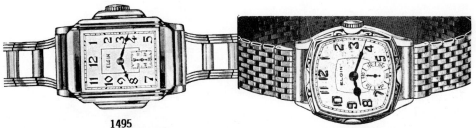

1495
4/0S-17J-Embossed dial
Made 1936
1495 10KYGF Head $60-70
1494 10KWGF Head $60-70

1631-HOME RUN
6/0S-15J
Made 1930-31-Engraved bezel
1631 Nickel Chromium Plated
Head $50-60

1600-HOME RUN
6/0S-15J
Made 1930-31
1600 14KWGF Head $65-75
1615 14KGGF Head $65-75
Same as 1615

1638
6/0S-17J-Full luminous dial
Made 1934-Engraved center
1638 14KGF White & Green
Head $45-55

1245
18/0S-17J-Raised figure dial
Made 1935-1937
1245 14KYG Head $150-175

1445
4/0S-7J-Raised figure dial
Made 1935-1936
1445 10KYGF Head $55-65

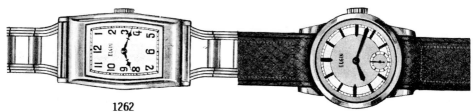

1262
18/0S-7J-Embossed dial
Made 1935-1938-SS back
1262 10KYGF Head $65-75
Same as 1260

1464
4/0S-7J-Embossed dial
Made 1936-1937
1464 10KYGF Head $25-35

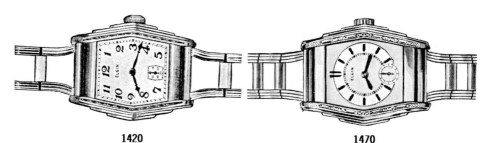

1420
4/0S-7J-Embossed dial
Made 1934-1936
1420 10KYGF Head $60-70

1470
4/0S-17J-Embossed dial
Made 1936-Engraved bars
Veritas metal
1470 10KYGF Head $65-75

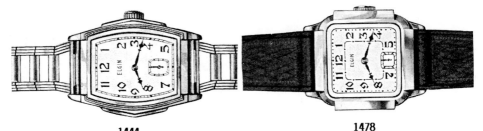

1444
4/0S-17J-Embossed dial
Made 1935-1936-SS back
1444 10KYRGP Head $50-60

1478
4/0S-7J-Embossed dial
Made 1936-1937
1478 Veritas Metal Head $55-65
1477 10KYGF Head $55-65

1063
18/0S-7J-Engraved bezel
Made 1932
1063 Nickel Chromium Plated
Head $55-65
Nickel Chromium plated Band $3-7

1136
18/0S-15J-Engraved bezel
Made 1933-1934-Recessed crown
1136 14KWGF Head $75-85
GF Link Band $5-7

1093
18/0S-17J-Recessed Crown
Made 1932-1934-Hidden lugs
1093 14KWGF Head $85-95
1094 14KYGF Head $85-95

1139
18/0S-15J-Polished bezel
Made 1934-1934
1139 14KWGF Head $55-65

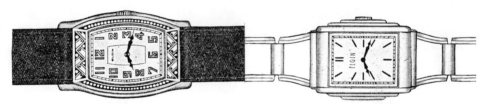

1068
18/0S-15J-Engraved bezel
Made 1932
1068 14KWGF Head $75-85

1212
18/0S-15J-Embossed or arabic dial
Made 1933
1212 10KWGF Head $60-70
1213 10KYGF Head $65-75

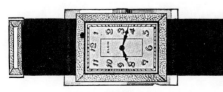

1095
18/0S-15J-Inlaid enamel dial
Made 1932-Recessed crown
1095 14KWG Head $140-160
1096 14KYG Head $160-180

1233-DOCTOR WILLIAM OSLER
18/0S-15J-Sweep second hand
Made 1935-1940
1233 14KGF Yellow Head $95-115

1812-LEGIONNAIRE
8/0S-15J-Reverse etched dial
Made 1937-Champfered bezel
1812 Veritas metal Head $45-55

1877-LEGIONNAIRE
8/0S-15J-Raised figure dial
Made 1937
1877 10KYGF Head $45-55

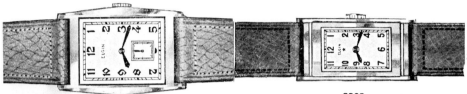

1867-CAVALIER
8/0S-7J-Embossed dial
Made 1937-1939
1867 10KYGF Head $55-65

2203
18/0S-17J-Curved dial raised figures
Made 1937-1939
2203 14YKG Head $150-175

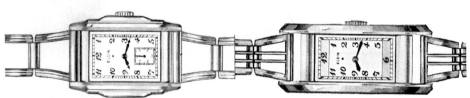

1871-LEGIANNAIRE
8/0S-15J-Raised figure dial
Made 1937-1938
1871 10KYGF Head $60-70

2237
18/0S-17J-Extremely curved
dial with raised figures
Made 1937-1939
2237 10KYGF Head $80-90
Same as 2241

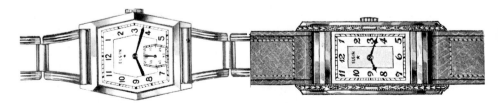

1873-LEGIONNAIRE
8/0S-15J-Raised figure dial
Made 1937-1938
1873 10KYGF Head $60-70

2243-STREAMLINE
18/0S-15J-Curved dial raised figures
Made 1938-1939
2243 10KYGF Head $85-100
Same as 2261

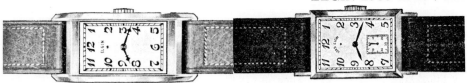

2247-STREAMLINE
18/0S17J-Curved dial raised figures
Made 1938-1939
2247 14KYG Head $75-85

3500-LORD ELGIN
15/0S-21J-Curved dial raised
blue figures
Made 1939-1940-Hand made case
3500 Platinum Head $700-800

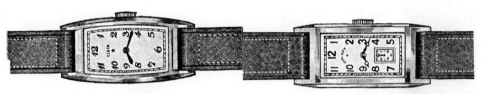

2271-STREAMLINE
18/0S-17J-Curved dial raised blue
figures-Made 1939
2271 10KYGF Head $65-75

3509-LORD ELGIN STREAMLINE
15/0S-21J-Curved dial raised figures
Made 1939-1940-Rectangle
3509 14KYGF Head $55-65

2839-LEGIONNAIRE STREAMLINE
8/0S-15J-Curved dial raised figures
Made 1938-Engraved bezel-Tonneau
2839 10KYGF Head $60-70

4501-LORD ELGIN
21J-Applied gold dot dial
Made 1941-1942
4501 Platinum Head $800-900

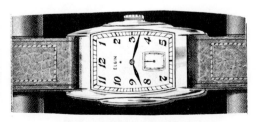

2847-CRUSADER STREAMLINE
8/0S-17J-Curved dial raised figures
Made 1938-1939-Tonneau
2847 14KYGF Head $60-70

4502-LORD ELGIN
21J-Applied gold dot dial
Made 1941-1942-Asymetrical case
4502 14KYG Head $300-350
4502 14KPG Head $350-400

4503-LORD ELGIN
21J-Curved dial raised figures
Made in 1941
4503 14KYG Head $175-200

4601-LORD ELGIN
21J-Flexible lugs-Drivers
Made 1941-1942
4601 14KYGF Head $75-85
4601 14KPGF Head $85-100

4504-LORD ELGIN
21J-Applied gold dot dial
Made 1941-1942
4504 14KYG Head $150-175

4602-LORD ELGIN
21J-High curved crystal
Flexible lugs-Drivers
Made 1941-1942
4602 14KPGF Head $85-100

4506-LORD ELGIN
21J-Extremely thin case
Made 1941-1942
4506 14KYG Head $120-140

4603-LORD ELGIN
21J-High curved crystal
Made 1941-1942-Tutone
4603 14KYGF & 14KPGF Head $85-100

4507-LORD ELGIN
21J-Curved dial
Made 1941
4507 14KYG Head $225-250

4604-LORD ELGIN
21-High curved crystal
Made 1941
4604 14KYGF Head $50-60

4605–LORD ELGIN
21J-Black dial
Made 1941
4605 14KYGF Head $65-75

4609–LORD ELGIN
21J-Pastel blue minute
track on silvered dial
4609 14KYGF Head $40-50
4609 14KWGF Head $40-50

4606–LORD ELGIN
21J-Made 1941-1942
4606 14KYGF Head $65-75
4606 14KPGF Head $75-85

4610–LORD ELGIN
21J-Applied gold dot dial
Made 1942
4610 14KYGF Head $60-70

4607–LORD ELGIN
21J-Spherical dial
Made 1941
4607 14KYGF Head $65-75

4608–LORD ELGIN
21J-Extremely thin
Made 1941
4608 14KYGF Head $40-50

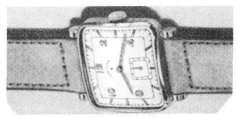

4802–LORD ELGIN
21J-Made 1941-42
4802 14KYGF Head $45-55

5505-DELUXE
15/0S-Spherical or silver
finish dial-Made 1941
5505 10KYGF Head $50-60
5505 10KPGF Head $55-65

5510-DELUXE
15/0S-17J-High curved crystal
Made 1941-42
5510 10KYGP Head $50-60
5510 10KPGP Head $55-65

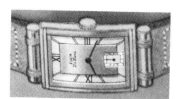

5506-DELUXE
15/0S-Arabic Silver finish dial
Made 1941-Covered lugs
5506 10KYGF Head $80-90

5511-DELUXE
15/0S-17J-Made 1941
5511 10KYGF Head $40-50

5507-DELUXE
15/0S-Made 1941
5507 10KYGF Head $70-80

5512-DELUXE
15/0S-17J-High curved crystal
Made 1942
5512 10KYGF Head $45-55
5512 10KPGF Head $50-60

5508-DELUXE
15/0S-Silver finish dial
Made 1941-Lobe lugs
5508 10KYGF Head $60-70
5508 10KPGF Head $65-75

5513-DELUXE
15/0S-17J-Made 1941-42
5513 10KYGF Head $30-40

5532-RIDGEWOOD
15/0S-Embossed gold figures
Made 1958-Black enamel lugs
5532 10KYGF Head $75-85

5702-DELUXE
8/0S-Spherical dial
Made 1941
5702 10KYGF Head $40-50

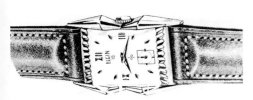

5539-SYCAMORE
15/0S-Embossed gold dial
3 Roman numerals-Hi curved crystal
Made Ca 1958-Extended lugs
5539 10KYGF Head $90-110

5703-DELUXE
8/0S-Made 1941
5703 10KYGF Head $65-75

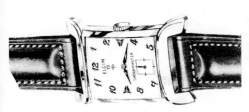

5575-GULFPORT
15/0S-Embossed gold figures
Hi curved crystal
Made Ca 1958-Shockmaster
5575 10KYGF Head $65-75

5706-DELUXE
8/0S-17J-Flexible lugs-Drivers
Made 1941-42
5706 10KYGF Head $75-85

5701-DELUXE
8/0S-Spherical dial
Made 1941-42-Covered lugs
5701 10KYGF Head $75-85
5701 10KPGF Head $85-100

5707-DELUXE
8/0S-17J-Made 1941
5707 10KYGF Head $40-50

5708-DELUXE
8/0S-17J-Drivers-Made 1941
5708 10KYGF Head $50-60
5708 10KPGF Head $55-65

6503
15/0S-Made 1941
6503 10KYGF Head $70-80

5805-PERSHING
13/0S-18K applied gold dots
Black dial-Made Ca 1958
Black depressed minute track
5805 10KYG Head $70-80

6554-OCEANSIDE
15/0S-Embossed gold figures
Made Ca 1958-Shockmaster
6554 10KYRGP Head $65-75

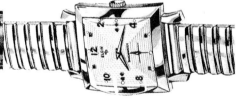

5917-SPINNER
10 1/2L-17J-Embossed semi blocked
full figure-Nite Glo-Sweep second
Made Ca 1958-Steel back
5917 10KYRGP Head $30-40

6761-PANAMA
8/0S-Embossed gold figures-Nite Glo
Made Ca 1955-58-Steel back
6761 10KYRGP Top Head $50-60

5918-DOLPHIN
10 1/2L-17J-Embossed figures
Made Ca 1958-Steel back
5918 Chrome Head $20-30

6805-NAUTILUS
11 1/2L-Luminous figures-Sweep
second-Unbreakable crystals
Made Ca 1958-Shockmaster
6805 Stainless Steel Head $30-40

4803-LORD ELGIN
Green hour field on silvered dial
21J-Made 1941
4803 14KYGF Head $45-55
4803 14KPGF Head $55-65

5501-DELUXE
15/0S-Curved dial
Made 1941-Curved Rectangle
5501 14KYG Head $200-250

4821-LORD ELGIN-Cranbrook
8/0S-Black enamel inlay bezel
applied figure dial-Made Ca 1958
4821 14KYGF Head $65-75

5502-DELUXE
15/0S-Roman index dial
Made 1941-T lugs
5502 10KYGF Head $75-85

4824-LORD ELGIN Rochester
8/0S-Applied figure dial
Made Ca 1958
4824 14KYGF Head $55-65

5503-DELUXE
15/0S-Flexible lugs
Made 1941-Drivers Watch
5503 10KYGF Head $85-100

4876-LORD ELGIN Brentwood
8/0S-21J-Embossed figures
Shock master-Nite glo dial Made
Ca 1956-58-Waterproof 4876
Stainless Steel Head $20-30

5504-DELUXE
15/0S-Spherical dial
Made 1941
5504 10KYGF Head $65-75

Elgin Produces First
U. S. Automatic Watch

Production of the first automatic, self-winding watch movement ever made in the United States has been announced by the Elgin National Watch Company, produced after ten years of intensive research work interrupted by the company's conversion to military production during World War II.

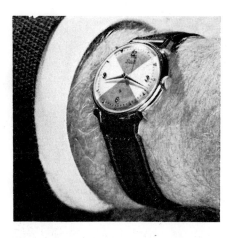

First American-made automatic, self-winding watch, introduced by Elgin National Watch Company after 10 years' research and development work, and which is said to eliminate most common weaknesses of previous self-winding watches. The timepiece will not be generally available until early next year.

According to J. G. Shennan, president, automatic timepieces similar to foreign makes have been produced here experimentally for several years, but large scale production had been delayed until Elgin could design a movement eliminating most common weaknesses. The new automatic model will not be generally available until early next year, he said.

Features of the new watch will be simplicity of construction, sturdiness and ease of servicing. Three sweep-second-hand models are included. All have unbreakable crystals, and are equipped with Elgin's exclusive Dura-Power mainsprings.

The winding movement is readily removable, and consists of one winding rachet wheel and pawl, eliminating intermediate wheels and pinions, which are delicate and difficult to service.

The rotor has sturdy pivot function in heavy jewels, eliminating excessive side shake and much damage from rough usage.

6811-DANTE
17J 9 1/4L-Embossed white figures
Black dial-Sweep second
Made Ca 1958-Shockmaster
6811 Stainless Steel Head $20-30

6823-CAVALIER
11 1/2L-Embossed gold figures
Sweep second-Self winding
Made Ca 1955-58-Shockmaster
6823 10KYGF Head $25-30

6818-SURF
9 1/4L-Embossed gold figures
Sweep second-Self winding
Made Ca 1958
6818 10KYGF Head $15-20

6824-PENSACOLA
11 1/2L-Embossed gold figures
Sweep second-Self winding
Made Ca 1958-Shockmaster
6824 10KYRGP Head $25-30

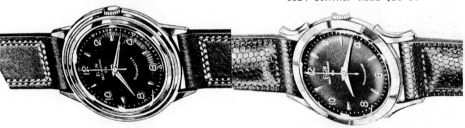

6821-NIAGARA
17J 11 1/2L-Embossed white figures
6811black sweep second-Self winding
Made Ca 1958-Shockmaster
6821 Stainless Steel Head $10-15

6825-LAKESHORE
17J 11 1/2L-Embossed gold figures
Black dial-Sweep second-Self winding
Made Ca 1958-Shockmaster
6825 10KYRGP Yellow Head $20-30

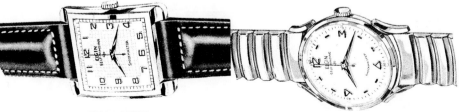

6822-LANCER
9 1/4L-Embossed gold figures
Black dial-Sweep second-Self winding
Made Ca 1955-58-Shockmaster
6822 10KYGF Head $30-40

6834-KENTWOOD
17J 11 1/2L-Raised figures
Sweep second-Black or Nite Glo dial
Made Ca 1958-Shockmaster
6834 Chrome Head $10-15
6834 14KYG Head $100-150

6905-CARRIBEAN
9 1/4L-Applied studs-Waterproof
Made Ca 1958-Shockmaster
6905 14KYG Head $115-130

7502-LORD ELGIN-Crestwood
21J 13/0S-21J-Applied figures
6 diamond dial-Made Ca 1956-58
Shockmaster
7502 14KYRGP Head $15-20
7502 14KYG Head $100-125
7502 14KWG Head $100-125

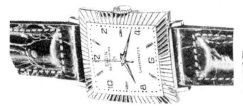

6908-SEABROOK
11 1/2L-Embossed figures
Sweep second-Self winding
Shock & waterproof
Made Ca 1958-Shockmaster
6908 14KYG Head $110-125

7503-LORD ELGIN-Henslee
13/0S-21J-Applied figures-Nite Glo
Made Ca 1956-58-Shockmaster
7503 14KYG Head $100-125

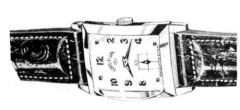

7500-LORD ELGIN-Scarsdale
13/0S-21J-Applied figures dial
High curved crystal
Made Ca 1956-58-Shockmaster
7500 14KWG Head $125-150
7500 14KYG Head $150-175

7512-LORD ELGIN-Vista
13/0S-Sweep second-Silver dial
Wrap around crystal-Applied figures
Made Ca 1957-Shockmaster
7512 14KYG Head $110-125

7501-LORD ELGIN-Aberdeen
21J 13/0S-21J-Applied figures
High curved crystal
Made Ca 1956-58-Shockmaster
7501 14KYG Head $150-175

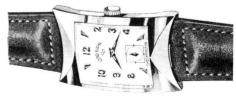

7575-LORD ELGIN IVANHOE
23J 13/0S-Applied figures
Made Ca 1958-Shockmaster
7575 14KYG Head $175-200

7579-LORD ELGIN SARASOTA
21J 13/0S-Applied figure-Nite Glo
Made Ca 1958-Shockmaster
7579 14KYG Head $140-155

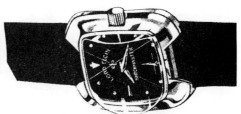

7603-LORD ELGIN TOWNSMAN
13/0S-21J-Applied gold studs
Black dial-Made Ca 1956-58
7603 14KYGF Head $90-110

7600-LORD ELGIN RANDALL
21J 13/0S-21J
Raised seven gold figures
Four faceted trylons dial
High curved crystal
Made Ca 1956-58-Shockmaster
7600 14KWGF Head $55-65

7606-LORD ELGIN BLACK KNIGHT
21J-Black textured dial
Made Ca 1956-Shockmaster
7606 Stainless Steel Head $60-70
7606 14KYRGP Head $70-80
7606 14KYG Head $170-200

7601-LORD ELGIN OXFORD
13/0S-21J-18K applied gold figure
Black or white dial
Made Ca 1956-58-Shockmaster
7601 14KYGF Head $75-85

7607-LORD ELGIN WESTWOOD
13/0S-Embossed indexes
Made Ca 1958
7607 14KYGF Head $40-50

7602-LORD ELGIN MILLBROOK
13/0S-21J-Embossed gold figures
Hi curved crystal
Made Ca 1956-Shockmaster
7602 14KYGF Head $60-70

7609-LORD ELGIN CHESWICH
13/0S-21J-Embossed figures
Made Ca 1956-58-Shockmaster
7609 14KYGF Head $60-70

7610-LORD ELGIN SPARTAN
21J 13/0S-Raised gold figures
Made Ca 1958-Shockmaster-Nite Glo
7610 14KYGF Head $60-70

7614-LORD ELGIN DUNBAR
13/0S-Applied diamond kites
Made Ca 1958-Asymetrical
7614 14KYGF Head $70-80

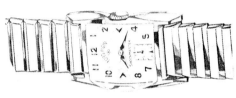

7611-LORD ELGIN PORTLAND
13/0S-21J-Embossed gold figures
Made Ca 1956-58-Shockmaster
7611 14KYGF Head $70-80

7615-LORD ELGIN BARRISTER
13/0S-Shock resistant
Applied figures
Made Ca 1958-Shockmaster
7615 10KYGF Head $40-50
7615 10KYG Head $110-125

7612-LORD ELGIN ASHFORD
21J 13/0S-Hi raised gold figures
Made Ca 1958-Shockmaster
7612 14KYGF Head $55-65

7617-LORD ELGIN SABRE
13/0S-Reverse etch
Diamond shaped markers
Made Ca 1958
7617 14KYGF Head $30-40

7613-LORD ELGIN CAMELOT
21J 13/0S-Hi raised gold figures
High flat crystal
Made Ca 1958-Shockmaster
7613 14KYGF Head $45-55

7618-LORD ELGIN Gaylord
13/0S-Wrap around
Crystal-Silver dial
Made Ca 1957-Shockmaster
7618 14KYGF Head $20-30

7619-LORD ELGIN Celestial
23J 13/0S-Shock resistant
Wrap around crystal
White on dark dial-Nite Glo
Made Ca 1957-Shockmaster
7619 14KWGF Head $20-30

7680-LORD ELGIN WAKEFIELD
13/0S-21J-18K Applied gold figures
Made Ca 1956-58
7680 14KYGF Head $20-30

7675-LORD ELGIN FAIRWAY
21J 13/0S-21J-Raised eight gold
figures-Four markers on dial
High curved crystal
Made Ca 1956-58-Shockmaster
7675 14KYGF Head $65-75

7681-LORD ELGIN TARPON
21J 13/0S-Applied gold figures
Nite Glo Dial-High curved crystal
Made Ca 1958
7681 14KYGF Head $45-55

7678-LORD ELGIN CLUBMAN
13/0S-21J-Black enamel bezel
Made Ca 1956-58-No figures dial
7678 14KYGF Head $40-50

7684-LORD ELGINS Meridian
13/0-Gilt dial-Sweep second
Waterproof snapback case-Shockmaster
Wrap around crystal-Made Ca 1957
7684 14KYRGP Head $15-20

7679-LORD ELGIN GARRISON
13/0S-18K applied gold figures
Nite Glo Dial
Made Ca 1958-Shockmaster
7679 14KYGF Head $55-65

7685-LORD ELGIN Panorama
23J 13/0-Silver dial-Shock resistant
Sweep second-Waterproof snapback
case-Wrap around crystal
Made Ca 1957-Shockmaster
7685 14KYGF Head $15-20

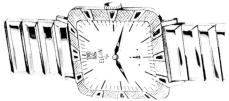

9501-HURON
13/0S-Embossed gold figure
Black dial-Enamel bezel
Made Ca 1958-Steel back
9501 10KYRGP Top Head $55-65

9510-DARWIN
13/0S-Hi raised gold figures
Made CA 1958-Steel back
9510 10KYRGP Top Head $55-65

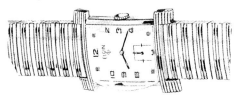

9504-ARDMORE
13/0S-Embossed gold figures
Made Ca 1958-Steel back
9504 10KYRGP Top Head $70-80

9511-CALDWELL
13/0S-Embossed gold figures
Made Ca 1958-Steel back
9511 10KYRGP Top Head $60-70

9507-LAWSON
19J 13/0S-Embossed gold figures
Made Ca 1958-Steel back
9507 10KYRGP Top Head $60-70

9512-ALL AMERICAN
13/0S-Fancy dial-No figures
Markers on dial-Enamel bezel
Made Ca 1958-Steel back
9512 10KYRGP Top Head $55-65

9509-STANWOOD
19J 13/0S-Embossed gold figures
Made Ca 1958-Steel back
9509 10KYRGP Top Head $20-30

9519-SPORTSMAN
13/0S-17J-Gold enamel indexes
on bezel
Made Ca 1957-Steel back
9519 10KYRGP Top Head $55-65

9583-TRINIDAD
13/0S-Embossed 4 white figures
Made Ca 1958-Shockmaster
9583 Stainless Steel Head $20-25

9587-DIRECT READING
13/0S-17J-Hour & minute discs
Snapback waterproof-Shock resistant
Made Ca 1957-Digital
9687 10KWRGP Top Head $200-225
9687 10KYRGP Top Head $200-225

9584-MIDSHIPMAN
13/0S-Raised 6 semi block gold
figures & 6 teardrops-Steel back
Made Ca 1958-Shockmaster
9584 10KYRGP Top Head $15-20

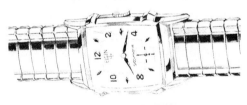

9585-NORTHBROOK
13/0S-Raised 5 gold figures
& 6 markers-Nite Glo-Steel back
Made Ca 1958
9585 10KYRGP Top Head $45-55

ABBREVIATIONS
18K = Solid Gold
14K = Solid Gold
G = Green
GF = Gold Filled
GP = Gold Plated
N = Nickel
PG = Pink Gold
R = Rolled
RGP = Rolled Gold Plate
S = Silver
Steel = Stainles Steel
WG = White Gold
YG = Yellow Gold

NOTE: This Elgin section has a large number of case styles. These case styles and prices would be about the same for a similar watch made by Bulova, Gruen, Waltham, Illinois and Hamilton, and could be effective for a time span of 1925 - 1960.

9586-AQUATIC
13/0S-17J-Waterproof
Raised figures-Nite Glo
Made Ca 1958-Shockmaster
9586 Chrome Head $15-20

* *All values are given for the head only unless the band is included in the description.*
* *Read page 12 before using this book to value your wrist watch.*
* *Values are given for a mint watch with original dial, movement and case.*

This is the Ford award watch. The Ford 23-jewel
Elgins are beautifully engraved with employee's name.
Some companies further personalize their Elgins with
their company emblem on the dial.

ELGIN *National Watch Company*

14KYG $150-180
14KGF $50-60

**IF HE'S THE
CAPABLE TYPE:**

He can build a boat or
a business with equal
ease. He'll like the
Matterhorn

Self-winding. Water-
proof* Shockmaster.
14K natural gold case.
Nite-Glo dial, dress
watch by day, lumi-
nous by night.

14KYG $100-120

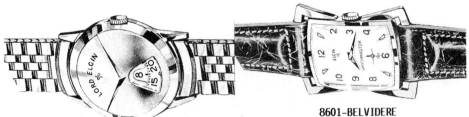

7775-LORD ELGIN DIRECT READING
21J 13/0S-Shockproof-Waterproof
Twelve block figures-Direct reading
Made Ca 1958-Digital
7775 14KYGF Head $175-200

8601-BELVIDERE
19J 13/0S-Raised eight gold figures
Four gold trylons dial
High dome crystal
Made Ca 1958-Unusual lugs
8601 10KYGF Head $75-85

7776-LORD ELGIN DIRECT READING
13/0S-Full figured disk
Made Ca 1958-Digital
7776 10KGF Yellow Head $250-300

8602-COLUMBUS
13/0S-Embossed square simi blocked
Made Ca 1958-Shockmaster
8602 10KYGF Head $35-45
8602 10KPRGF Head $40-50

8500-HAMMOND
13/0S-Embossed gold figures
Hi curved crystal
Made Ca 1958-Shockmaster
8500 10KYG Head $115-130

8603-HOLCOMB
13/0S-No figures-Simulated textured
design Hi curved dial
Made Ca 1958-Shockmaster
Enamel bezel
8603 10KYGF Head $55-65

8600-DANBURY
19J 13/0S-Embossed gold figures
Made Ca 1958-Shockmaster
8600 10KYGF Head $55-65

8604-GARFIELD
13/0S-Embossed figures-Textured dial
Made Ca 1958-Shockmaster
8604 10KYGF Head $35-45

8605-GARDNER
13/0S-Embossed gold figures
High curved crystal-Covered lugs
Made Ca 1958-Shockmaster
8605 10KYGF Head $60-70

8677-ALASKAN
19J 13/0S-Raised three gold figures
eight tryonds Nite glo dial
Curved crystal
Made Ca 1958-Shockmaster
8677 10KYGF Head $55-65

8606-EVEREST
13/0S-Embossed gold figures
Diamond markers-Hi curved crystal
Made Ca 1958-Shockmaster
8606 10KYGF Head $50-60

8678-PALM SPRINGS
13/0S-19J-Waterproof
Raised 8 gold indexes, 4 keystones
Made Ca 1958-Shockmaster
8678 10KYGF Head $40-50

8607-PARKTON
13/0S-Hi raised figures-Nite Glo
Made Ca 1958-Shockmaster
8607 10KYGF Head $70-80

8700-PERSHING
13/0S-Appliedr gold studs-Black dial
Made Ca 1958-Shockmaster
8700 10KPG Head $100-125

8609-CAMPAIGNER
13/0S-19J-Shock resistant
Full figure
Made Ca 1958
8609 10KYGF Head $85-95

9500-AVERY
13/0S-Embossed gold figures
Made Ca 1958-Steel back
9500 10KYRGP Top Head $60-70

9520-SABRE
13/0S-Reverse etch-Printed numerals
Made Ca 1958-Steel back
9520 10KWRGP Top Head $15-20

9577-STARBOARD
13/0S-Embossed gold figures
Made Ca 1958-Steel back
9577 10KYRGP Top Head $70-80

9521-SABRE
13/0S-Reverse etch-Diamond
shaped markers-Made Ca 1958
Shockmaster
9521 Stainless Steel Head $20-25

9579-ONTARIO
13/0S-Embossed white figures
Nite Glo-Made Ca 1958
9579 Steel back-Chrome head $45-55

9575-LAKEVIEW
13/0S-Embossed gold figures
Made Ca 1958-Shockmaster
9575 10KYGP Head $35-45

9580-EVERGLADE
13/0S-Embossed figures-Rose dial
Nite Glo-Made Ca 1958
9580 Stainless Steel Head $20-25
9580 Chrome Head $15-20

9576-NASSAU
13/0S-Raised figures-Nite Glo
Made Ca 1958-Shockmaster
9576 10KYRGP Head $15-20

9582-NORFOLK
13/0S-Embossed white figures
Made Ca 1958-Shockmaster
9582 Chrome Head $55-65

1940

Steel $75-85
18K $225-250

Steel $15-20
18K $95-110

Steel $1,000-1,200
18K $2,500-2,750

14KYGF $375-450
14KWGF $325-400

ERNEST BOREL & C°S.A.
Neuchatel

HERMES
ERBO

18K $150-175

1956

*One of the world's
finest self-winding
watches.
Complete calendar
(date, day of the
week, month, and
moon phases).*

1940

18K $100-120

346	GF	$50-60
4107	GF	$50-60
3170	GF	$20-25
1582	GF	$25-30
1426	GF	$30-35
1427	GF	$30-35
1429	GF	$45-55
3180	GF	$30-35

3170

1582

1426

1427

346

4107

1429

3180

Eska

14KYG
$60–75

14KYG
$90–110

14KYGT
$60–75

14KYG
$90–110

14KYG
$60–75

14KYG
$90–110

14KYG
$90–110

14KYG
$60–75

14KYG
$145–175

14KYG
$60–75

14KYG
$150–180

14KYG
$60–75

333
Pink or yellow solid
gold or 14 K gold
filled

14KYGF $35-45
14KYG $110-125
14KPG $120-135

440
Classic square,
heavy domed
crystal, yellow or
pink solid gold or
14 K gold filled

14KYGF $25-35
14KYG $100-115
14KPG $110-125

410
Short rectangular
curved solid yellow
or pink gold or 14 K
gold filled

14KYGF $40-50
14KYG $125-140
14KPG $135-150

394
Square pink or
yellow solid gold or
14 K gold filled also
available without
sweep second
hand)

14KYGF $25-35
14KYG $100-115
14KPG $110-125

327
Curved to fit the
wrist solid yel-
low or 14 K gold
filled

14KYGF $60-70
14KYG $150-175

332
Solid yellow
gold or gold
filled (also avail-
able with sweep
second hand)

14KYGF $15-20
14KYG $100-115

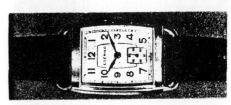

415
Yellow gold
filled

14KYGF $45-55

350
Solid yellow
gold or 14 K
gold filled (also
available with-
out sweep
second hand)

14KYGF $60-70
14KYG $150-175

A SPECIAL THANKS TO:
*William "Bill" Meggers, Jr.
Ridgecrest, CA
for the use of his wrist
watch research.*

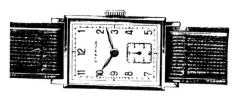

388
Narrow bezel, rectangular in solid yellow gold or stainless steel

Steel $25-35
14KYG $110-120

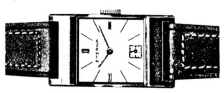

395
Streamlined with heavy domed crystal (Synthetic Sapphire) in solid yellow gold or stainless steel

Steel $30-40
14KYG $110-120

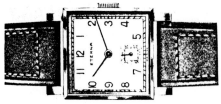

345
A *he-man's* watch in a very substantial case, yellow or pink solid gold or stainless steel

Steel $30-40
14KYG $125-140
14KPG $125-140

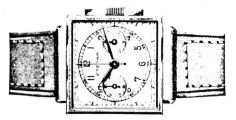

436
Square Chronograph, the perfect time-piece for sportsmen and scientists stainless steel

Steel $1,000-1,200

414
Short rectangular in solid yellow gold, gold filled or stainless steel

Steel $25-35
14KYGF $35-45
14KYG $110-120

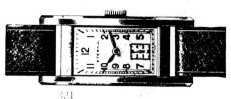

321
Curved to fit the wrist in solid gold or stainless steel

Steel $40-50
14KYG $150-175

397
Narrow bezel with sweep second hand (Doctor's watch) in stainless steel

Steel $35-45

347
A watch of perfect distinction, solid yellow gold or stainless steel

Steel $45-55
14KYG $125-140

ETERNA

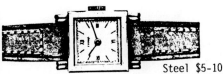

Steel $5-10
14KYG $50-60

291
For sportswear, yellow
solid gold or stainless
steel

Steel $10-15
14KYG $60-70

142
Yellow or pink heavy
solid gold case or
stainless steel

149
Conservative style in
solid yellow or pink
gold, 14 K gold filled or
stainless steel

Steel $15-20
14KYG $65-75

296
Unusual style in pink
solid gold or stainless
steel

14KYG $60-70

294
A compromise between
formal and sportswear
in yellow solid gold or
stainless steel

Steel $20-25
14KYG $75-85

290
A combination of
square and circle in
solid yellow gold or
stainless steel

14
Unusual pattern in solid
gold or stainless steel

Steel $5-10
14KYG $50-60

120
A tiny affair in pink
solid gold

Steel $10-15
14KYG $55-65

152
Barrel shaped, yellow
solid gold or stainless
steel

Steel $10-15
14KYG $55-65

151
Dressy model with flexi-
ble ends in yellow solid
gold or stainless steel

Eterna "Gold Strap". Black dial, subsidiary seconds. 17J movement. Rectangular, 14K gold case. ca 1946. . . . . $225–270

Eterna "Automatic". Waterproof, center seconds. Round case. ca 1948. 14K GF $10–20 Stainless Steel 7–14

Eterna "Gold Strap". Silver, black or rose, tu-tone dial, subsidiary seconds. 17J movement. Square case. ca 1942. 14K gold . . . $125–150 Stainless steel 10– 20

Eterna-Matic Centenaire. Matte dial, 33mm. slim 18K gold round case. ca 1960 . $100–120

Eterna "Thin Waterproof Gold". Subsidiary seconds. 14K gold, round case. ca 1940. . . . . $100–120

Evkob "Tu-tone Plated Strap". Radium numerals, subsidiary seconds. 10''', 15J movement. White & green rolled gold plate, chromium finish, three piece tonneau case. ca 1928. . . . . $75–90

Eterna "Gold Strap". Subsidiary seconds. 14K gold, round case. ca 1940 . . . . . . $100–125

Evkob "Tu-tone Plated Strap". Radium numerals, subsidiary seconds. 10''', 15J movement. Green & white rolled gold plate, chromium finish, three piece tonneau case. ca 1928. . . . . $30–45

TACHOMETER

To measure speed over a fixed course: Start the chronograph when crossing the starting line and stop it when the finish line is crossed. The sweep second hand will show the exact speed in miles per hour on the Tachometer scale, which is based on a measured mile.

TELEMETER

To measure the distance of an incident by sound: Start the chronograph when the flash of a barrage or lightning is seen; stop it when the noise is heard. The sweep hand will show the distance of the incident in miles on the Telemeter dial.

Steel $300-350

Steel $400-450

8061W6025—Gallet Double Button Chronograph. 17J movement with unbreakable mainspring. Features dial with black background. Radium hands and numbers. Telemeter and Tachometer tracks on dial. Stainless steel case guaranteed water resistant. **Sugg. Retail $124.20**

8056W9165—Gallet Calendar Chronograph. Latest type Calendar watch shows day, date and month. 30-minute register, 17J movement, time-out feature. 12-hour totalizer. Water and shock resistant stainless steel case.
Suggested Retail $189.00

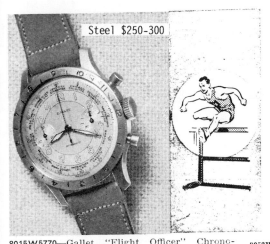

Steel $250-300

Steel $100-125

8015W5770—Gallet "Flight Officer" Chronograph. Hour control and world time in this well-known 17J double button model. Stainless steel water resistant case, 30-minute register, luminous dial, leather strap.

Suggested Retail $119.00

8052W5075—Double-Button Gallet Chronograph. Plain dial, 30-minute register, 17 jeweled high quality movement, steel case, time-out feature, 12 hour totalizer. For aviators, automobile and motor boat racing. Shock resistant. **Suggested Retail $104.70**
8053W5075—Radium, Telemeter and Tachometer Dial. After timing a measured mile, the sweep-second hand will show the miles per hour on the Tachometer scale. **Suggested Retail $104.70**

Steel $100-120
YRGP Top-Steel Back
$110-125

Steel $175-200

8040W3600—Gallet Wrist Alarm. 17J shock resistant movement. Sweep-second. Radium dial, raised figures, water resistant case. Top crown controls alarm. Lower crown for regular winding and setting. Stainless Steel case. **Suggested Retail $74.20**

8041W3800—In Yellow Rolled Gold Plated top. Steel back. **Suggested Retail $78.65**

8050W5075—Stainless Steel Gallet Chronograph. Radium, Telemeter and Tachometer dial. Fine quality 17J movement, shock and water resistant, 45-minute register. **Suggested Retail $104.70**

8051W5075—Radium dial only. **Suggested Retail $104.70**

Steel $175-200

Steel $200-225
14KYG $1,200-1,350

8048W3120—Telemeter and Tachometer Dial—Double Button Gallet Chronograph. 30-minute register. 17J movement. Steel back case with time-out feature. Excellent for speed recording. On the 8048W3120 after timing the measured mile, sweep-second hand will show the miles per hour. **Sugg. Retail $64.35**

8049W3120—Same as above with Plain Dial. **Suggested Retail $64.35**

8054W5770—Double-Button Gallet Chronograph. Radium, Telemeter and Tachometer Dial. Stainless Steel case, water and shock resistant. 17-jewel Gallet movement. 12-hour totalizer makes watch invaluable for timing gas consumption for aviators and other uses where long period timing is necessary. **Suggested Retail $119.00**

8055W13250—Same in 14K Yellow Gold case. **Suggested Retail $273.00**

Note: All chronographs have incabloc and unbreakable mainsprings
All watches shown are 66% of actual size.

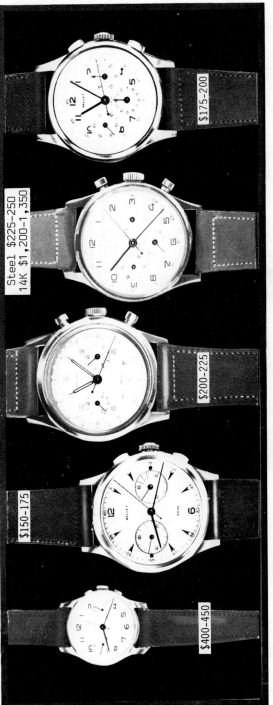

Steel $225-250
14K $1,200-1,350

$175-200

$200-225

$150-175

$400-450

GALLET WORLD'S SMALLEST CHRONOGRAPH

Smallest chronograph ever made. Features; double button 30 minute register, 17 jewels, 10½ ligne movement, unbreakable mainspring. Incabloc shock resistance, anti-magnetic and stainless steel case. Ideal for sports and general timing.

#932—17J GALLET
. . . $134.00

GALLET CHRONOGRAPH

No. 1293—17-jewel, 14 ligne, stainless steel chronograph. Raised modern stick dial. Unbreakable type mainspring, Incabloc. Anti-magnetic. No. 1293/7R—Same with telemeter, tachometer.
No. 1294—Same as above except yellow gold filled top and raised gilt dial.

#1293—17J, 14L GALLET—
Stainless steel $105.60

#1293/7R—17J, 14L GALLET;
Luminous dial $105.60

#1294—17J, 14L GALLET;
Yellow gold plated top $112.80

FINE QUALITY STAINLESS STEEL GALLET CHRONOGRAPH

Incabloc feature, 14 ligne, 17-jewels, 45-minute register, water-resistant.
Unbreakable mainspring.

#1034—GALLET; Plain dial
$112.30

#1034R—GALLET; Rad.
dial $112.30

#1034/7—GALLET; Tel. &
tach. dial... $112.30

#1034/7R—GALLET; Rad.
Tel. & tach. Dial... $112.30

DOUBLE-BUTTON GALLET CHRONOGRAPH

Stainless-steel case. Water-resistant.* 14 ligne; 17-jewel Gallet movement. 12-hour totalizer makes watch invaluable for timing gas consumption, for aviators, and where long period timing is necessary.
Unbreakable mainspring.

#1033—GALLET; Plain dial
$127.20

#1033/7—GALLET; Tel. &
tach. dial... $127.20

#1033/7R—GALLET; Rad. tel.
& tach. dial ... $127.20

#1033/7RB—GALLET; Same
with black dial ... $131.00
(on cover)

#1133/7R—14K GALLET; Tel.
& tach. dial $297.60

NEW DOUBLE-BUTTON GALLET CHRONOGRAPH

30-minute register; 14 ligne; 17-jeweled high quality movement; steel case; time-out feature; 12-hour totalizer for aviators, automobile and motor boat racing. After timing a measured mile the sweep-second hand will show the miles per hour on the Tachometer scale.
Unbreakable mainspring.

#1030—GALLET; Plain dial
$113.50

#1030/7—GALLET; Tel. &
tach. dial.... $113.50

#1030/7R—GALLET; tel. &
Tach. Rad. dial $113.50

Steel $200-225
14K $600-800

$200-225

$275-300

Steel $300-330
18K $1,200-1,350

$150-175

DRESS CHRONOGRAPH

Fashionable stick figure dial with telemeter and tachometer. Gold plated top. 17-jewel precision movement. 30-minute register. Incabloc shock resistance. Anti-magnetic. Glacidur balance. Steel back case.

#1022 — 17J GALLET $75.60
#1923 — 14K GALLET $239.30

GALLET DECIMAL CHRONOGRAPH WITH TIME-OUT FEATURE MINUTE DIVIDED INTO HUNDREDTHS

Fine 14 ligne, 17-jewel movement. 45 minute register. Easy to read decimal dial divides minute into hundredths. Stainless steel case. Unbreakable mainspring.

#1034/10 — 17J GALLET water resistant $112.30
#993/10 — 17J GALLET $103.20

GALLET "FLIGHT OFFICER" CHRONOGRAPH

Precision, 13-ligne, 17-jewel movement with double push action. Black radium dial. Rotating bezel featuring hour control and world time. Unbreakable mainspring. Glacidur balance, water-resistant stainless steel case.

#953B — As shown $134.00
#953 — WH Rad Dial $127.20
#1027 * 17J GALLET,
Stick Fig. dial $127.20
#1027B * — 17J GALLET,
Stick Fig. Black dial $127.20

*Tel. & Tac. dials; no world time.

GALLET CALENDAR CHRONOGRAPH

No. 998—Shown above. Latest Calendar Watch shows day, date, and month. 30-minute register; 17-jeweled excellent quality movement; 14 ligne; water-resistant steel case; time-out feature. 12-hour totalizer. No. 1998—14 Kt. Same movement. Water-resistant.

#998—17J GALLET $232.00
#1998—14K, GALLET... $429.00
#999—17 jewel Gallet. Same as above but with phases of the moon.
$242.40

DOUBLE-BUTTON GALLET CHRONOGRAPH 45-MINUTE REGISTER

13¾ ligne; 17-jeweled dependable movement. Steel case with time-out feature. For aviators, automobile and other speed recording. Dust proof buttons Unbreakable mainspring

#1023/7 —GALLET—Tel. & Tach. dial $66.00
#1023—GALLET—Plain dial $66.00
#1023/7R—GALLET— Tel. & rach. Rad. dial $66.00

GRANA

Made by Kurth Freres, Grenchen, Switzerland. Retail price range from $45 to $500, in gold, gold-filled and stainless steel cases, for all ages—men, women, boys & girls. ca 1946

Goering, Elaine. 6½''', 15J movement. 14K, 10 year, rolled gold plate, molded rectangular case. ca 1933 . . . . $10—20
12K gold-filled bracelet . . . . 5—10

Grana
24x34mm—CA 1930's
Curvex—Hunter
Polished enamel on cover
18K Yellow $1,400—1,600

Grana "Gold Strap". Luminous numerals & hands, subsidiary seconds. 14K gold rectangular case. ca 1946 . . . . $100—125

Grana. Center seconds. Round, 14K gold case. ca 1946. . . . . $100—125

Grandjean, Henry—Repeater
36mm—CA 1920's—2 Gongs
Slide activated—Minute repeater
Converted Pocket Watch E$6,000—7,200

Grana "Ladies Gold Cord". 14K gold, molded square case. ca 1946 . . . . $60—80

HOW TO DATE YOUR GRUEN WATCH

My list of watch calibers and their dates of manufacturing was compiled from several letters I received from Henry Doepke, who was the head of the service department when the company was moved out of Cincinnati in the late 1950's. This type of list doesn't take into account that the watch may have been stored at the factory or cased at the factory years after the movement was made. I have no idea how their case factory operated in regard to cases.

This list of dates is more accurate for the older less popular movements because usually they only made one run of movements. The more popular models, like the lady's 275 model, probably had several runs of movements. This list contains the first year of manufacture of the first run. I hope this list will be as useful to you as it has been to me.

MOVEMENT #	1st YEAR	MOVEMENT #	1st YEAR	MOVEMENT #	1st YEAR
LVI	PRE 1910	90	1910	181-183	1932
LVII	PRE 1910	91	1910	200-201	1919
LDG	PRE 1910	92-93	1917	202-203	1919
UUT	1916	94-95	1914	210-211	1939
UT	1912	96-97	1917	240-241	1919
UV	1923	98-99	1915	250	1920
VE	1910	100-101	1915	252-253	1920
V1	1910	103	1917	260-261	1920
V11/2	1910	105	1925	266	1920
V2	1910	106-1067	1928	267	1920
V21/2	1915	107-1077	1927	270-271	1936
V3	1910	109	1928	270SS-271SS	1937
V4	1910	115-116	1925	272	1938
V5	1913	1157-1158	1926	275	1947
V6	1910	1159	1926	280	1936
V7	1921	117	1925	285	1948
1-2	PRE 1910	119	1928	290	1940
3-4	PRE 1910	120-121	1916	291	1941
5-6	PRE 1910	123	1930	295	1946
7-8	PRE 1910	124-125	1915	300-301	1920
9-10	PRE 1910	126-127	1916	305	1927
20-21	1914	128-129	1919	306	1934
24-25	1910	130-131	1919	307	1932
30-31	1910	132-133	1919	311	1935
34-35	1910	135	1935	313	1928
45	1911	137-138-139	1919	3137	1930
47	1915	1397	1919	315	1929
50-51	1911	140-141	1919	3157	1930
52-53	1910	142-143	1919	325	1930
54-55	1910-11	145-146-147	1920	3251	1931
56	1910	148-149	1920	327	1932
57-58	1911	151	1921	328	1934
60-61	1911	153	1924	329	1933
62-63	1911	155	1924	330	1937
64-65	1911	157	1925	331	1928
75	1910	159-1597	1931	333	1928
80-81	1910	161-1617	1930	335	1948
80B	1910	163-165	1929	337-338	1928
82-83	1910	167-168	1936	341-342-343	1932
84-85	1914	169	1932	334	1934
86-87	1914-15	176-177	1920	344	1934
88-89	1915	179	1925	345-347	1935

MOVEMENT #	1st YEAR	MOVEMENT #	1st YEAR	MOVEMENT #	1st YEAR
350	1938	715	1930	873	1925
355	1935	716	1924	877	1928
360	1952	717	1926	877JH	1931
370	1948	719-723	1931	881	1933
380-381	1939	720-721	PRE 1910	881SS	1934
385	1946	724-725	1914	885	1935
390	1934	730-732	1914	900-901	PRE 1920
401	1917	740	PRE 1910	903	PRE 1920
402-403	1919	746	PRE 1910	910SS ALARM	1954
405-406	1938	750-752	1914	920SS ALARM	1955
405SS-406SS	1939	754	1921	975-976	1936
410-411	1939	756	1920	997	1917
410SS-411SS	1941	758	1923	ANNIVERSARY	1924
415-416	?	760-761	1914		
415CA	1953	764	1914		
420-421	1942	765-766	PRE 1910		
420SS-421SS	1942	771	PRE 1910	Prepared By:	
422-423	?	773	PRE 1910	Charles Cleves	
425-426	1945	775	PRE 1910	Bellevue, Kentucky	
425SS	1946	785	1924	(606) 491-0354	
430-431	1940	794-795	1918		
435	1940	796-797	1918		
440	1946	800-801	1914		
450	1946	802-803	1915		
460	1947	804-805	1914		
465-467-469	1935	806-807	1915		
470	1948	808-809	1915		
480	1951	811-812-813	1915		
485-487	1935	816-817	1920		
500-501	1936	818-819	1921		
500DD-501DD	1936	820-821	PRE 1920		
502	1936	822-823	1922		
520	1936	824-825	1922		
530-531	1936	826	PRE 1920		
540-541	1936	827	1922		
550 RES IND	1956	830-831	PRE 1920		
580-581-582	1936	833	1922		
610-611	1916	835	1924		
621-613	1916	835SS	1925		
615	PRE 1910	8357	1930		
616-617	PRE 1910	8357SS	1931		
620-621	1917	837	1920		
622-623	PRE 1910	838-839	1921		
626-627-629	1918-20	840-841	1918		
630-631	PRE 1910	843	1919		
633	1918	845	1919		
640-641	1920	847	PRE 1920		
643	PRE 1910	849	1919		
647	PRE 1910	850	1920		
650	1918	852	1920		
660-662	PRE 1910	854	1920		
675-677DD	1934	857	PRE 1920		
676-678	1934	859	PRE 1920		
680DD	1934	861	1921		
681	1934	862-863	PRE 1920		
707	1925	864-865	PRE 1920		
712	1924	866-867	PRE 1920		
713	1924	870-871	PRE 1920		

Gruen Attachments for Women's Wrist Watches

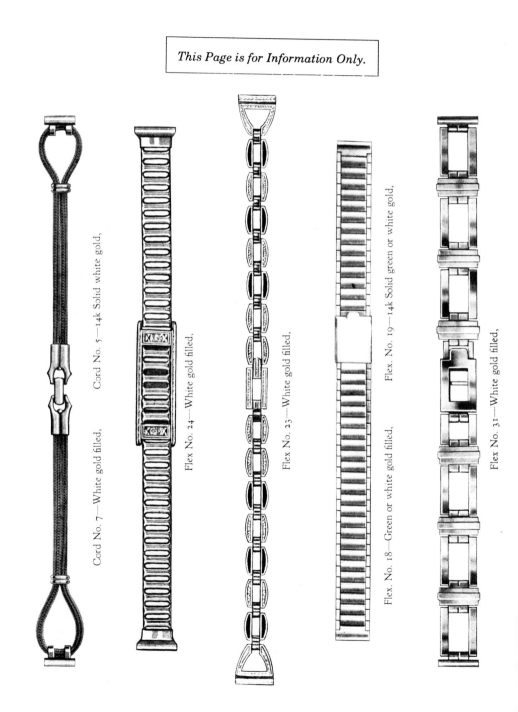

Cord No. 7—White gold filled,

Cord No. 5—14k Solid white gold,

Flex. No. 24—White gold filled,

Flex. No. 23—White gold filled,

Flex. No. 18—Green or white gold filled,

Flex. No. 19—14k Solid green or white gold,

Flex. No. 31—White gold filled,

Attachments for Women's Gruen Wrist Watches

This Page is for Information Only.

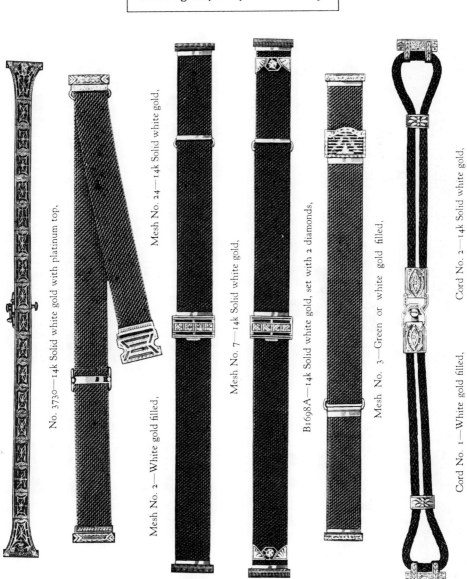

No. 3730—14k Solid white gold with platinum top,

Mesh No. 24—14k Solid white gold,

Mesh No. 2—White gold filled,

Mesh No. 7—14k Solid white gold,

B1698A—14k Solid white gold, set with 2 diamonds,

Mesh No. 3—Green or white gold filled,

Cord No. 2—14k Solid white gold,

Cord No. 1—White gold filled,

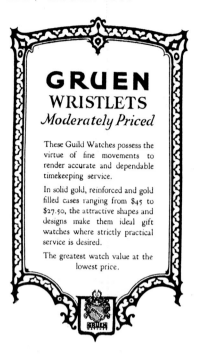

GRUEN
WRISTLETS
Moderately Priced

These Guild Watches possess the virtue of fine movements to render accurate and dependable timekeeping service.

In solid gold, reinforced and gold filled cases ranging from $45 to $27.50, the attractive shapes and designs make them ideal gift watches where strictly practical service is desired.

The greatest watch value at the lowest price.

☆WR82—14k White gold filled case, reinforced with extra gold. 15 jewel movement,

☆WR99—14k White gold filled case, reinforced with extra gold. 15 jewel movement,

WR83—14k White gold filled case, reinforced with extra gold. 15 jewel movement,

NOTE: *This Gruen catalog was prepared for a German Exhibition in 1930, and has a large number of case styles.*
These case styles and prices would be about the same for a similar watch made by Bulova, Elgin, Waltham, Illinois and Hamilton, and could be effective for a time span of 1925 - 1935.

☆☆WR100—14k White gold filled case, reinforced with extra gold. 15 jewel movement,

☆WR6—14k White gold filled case, reinforced with extra gold. 15 jewel movement,

GRUEN
WRISTLETS
Moderately Priced

> ✳ *All values are given for the head only*
> *unless the band is included in the*
> *description.*
> ✳ *Read page 12 before using this book*
> *to value your wrist watch.*
> ✳ *Values are given for a mint watch*
> *with original dial, movement and*
> *case.*

$15-20

☆WR75—14k White gold filled case,
reinforced with extra gold. 15 jewel
PRECISION movement,

$65-75

WG3—14k Solid white gold case,
15 jewel movement,

With second hand WG4

$15-20

☆☆WR4—14k White gold filled case,
reinforced with extra gold, fancy dial,
15 jewel movement,

$15-20

WR81—14k White gold filled case,
reinforced with extra gold. Engraved
and inlaid with black enamel. 15 jewel
movement,

$15-20

WR89—14k White gold filled case,
reinforced with extra gold. Engraved
and inlaid with black enamel. 15 jewel
movement,

The Gruen Cartouche Orné

Car. 367 — 14k White gold filled case
reinforced with extra gold, inlaid with
green and black cloisonne enamel.
15 jewel movement,

Orné 63

14k Solid white gold Crown-Guard case
Inlaid with blue and black enamel
17 jewel PRECISION movement,

Orné 54

14k Solid white gold case inlaid with
green cloisonne enamel
15 jewel movement,

Car. 372 — 14k White gold filled case,
reinforced with extra gold, inlaid with
green and black cloisonne enamel
15 jewel movement,

Orné 59

14k Solid white gold case inlaid with
red and black cloisonne enamel
15 jewel movement,

☆Car. 371—14k White gold filled case,
reinforced with extra gold, inlaid with
2 tone blue cloisonne enamel
15 jewel movement,

Orné 12

14k Solid white gold case inlaid in a
contrast of light and medium blue
cloisonne enamels
15 jewel movement,

Orné 57

14k Solid white gold case inlaid with
blue and black cloisonne enamel
15 jewel movement,

The Gruen Cartouche Orné

From Paris

Solid white and filled reinforced gold, exquisitely inlaid in cloisonne enamel-bright. colors and motifs highly modern.

An ideal wristlet for sports wear or whenever an effect of ultra smartness is desired.

A gift dainty and chic.

Orné 54 Cord
14k Solid white gold case inlaid with green cloisonne enamel
15 jewel movement,
$80-90

$90-105
Orné 53
14k Solid white gold case inlaid with red and black cloisonne enamel
15 jewel movement,

$90-105
☆Car. 369 — 14k White gold filled case, reinforced with extra gold, inlaid with dark blue cloisonne enamel
15 jewel movement,

$110-125

1

Orné 5

1 14k Solid white gold case, cloisonne enamel inlaid, in a dashing black and yellow Czecho design. Fitted with fancy brown sport leather strap and buckle
15 jewel movement,

$140-160

2

Orné 14

2 18k Solid white gold case inlaid with cobalt blue, dark cadmium, emerald green and black cloisonne enamel
17 jewel PRECISION movement,

$85-100

3

Orné 4
☆

3 14k Solid white gold case inlaid in a delightful Forget-me-not flower cloisonne design, in dark blues and yellow. Fitted with fancy blue leather sport strap and buckle
15 jewel movement,

$75-85

4

Orné 11

4 14k Solid white gold case inlaid in cloisonne enamel in powder blue and ultramarine
15 jewel movement,

Other Nurses' Watches with Sweep Second Hands

☆WR48—14k White gold filled case,
reinforced with extra gold. 15 jewel
movement,

$15-20

14KWGF
$15-20

14KGG
$75-85

14k White gold filled case, reinforced
with extra gold, with leather strap.
15 jewel movement,
☆☆(*Strap 16*)

14k Solid green gold case,
(*Strap 17*)

Small **GRUEN** WRIST WATCHES *in solid gold*

$85-100

☆WG17 — 18k Solid white gold case
15 jewel PRECISION movement,

$85-100

WG18L—18k Solid white gold case
Engraved and inlaid with black enamel
15 jewel PRECISION movement, with
applied solid gold numeral dial,

$90-115

WG9 — 18k Solid white gold case
15 jewel movement,

$55-65

☆WG12—18k Solid
white gold case
15 jewel movement,

$65-75

WG14 — 18k Solid
white gold case
15 jewel movement,

$60-70

WG19 — 18k Solid
white gold case
15 jewel movement,

$60-70

WG15 — 18k Solid
white gold case
15 jewel movement,

GRUEN

☆Car. 365—14k White gold filled case, reinforced with extra gold. Bright and antique finished engraving. 15 jewel movement,

14k Gold filled case, reinforced with extra gold. Antique finished engraving, 15 jewel movement,
☆☆(Car. 388, White)   (Car. 402, Coin)

☆Car. 421—14k White gold filled case, reinforced with extra gold. 15 jewel movement,

☆Car. 413—14k White gold filled case, reinforced with extra gold. 15 jewel movement,

Car. 412—14k White gold filled case, reinforced with extra gold. 15 jewel movement,

Car. 385—14k White gold filled case, reinforced with extra gold. 15 jewel movement,

Car. 423—14k White gold filled case. 15 jewel movement,

Car. 414—14k White gold filled case, reinforced with extra gold. Antique finished engraving. 15 jewel movement,

☆☆Car. 383—14k White gold filled case. 15 jewel movement,

Car. 410—14k White gold filled case. 15 jewel movement,

$20-25

☆☆Car. 222—14k White gold filled
case, reinforced with extra gold.
15 jewel movement,

14k Solid white gold case,
Car. 398,

$20-25

Car. 224—14k White gold filled case,
reinforced with extra gold, with decorated expanding bracelet. 15 jewel
movement,

$15-20

☆Car. 221—14k White gold filled case,
reinforced with extra gold. 15 jewel
movement,

14k Solid white gold case,
Car. 397,

The
GRUEN
NURSE'S
Cartouche

Right in clinic and hospital, with
the help of the medical profession
who asked for it, the new Nurses'
Cartouche (*patent applied for*)
was perfected.

In solid and reinforced white
gold, in the popular rectangular
shape and fitted with the rugged
Cartouche movement, this watch
has a second hand for pulse
reading and, if desired, a special
expanding band for slipping the
watch to the upper arm when
duty requires the hands to be free.

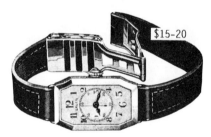

$15-20

☆☆Car. 223—14k White gold filled
case, reinforced with extra gold, leather
strap with Gruen Expanding Buckle
15 jewel movement,

$20-25

☆Car. 224—14k White gold filled case,
reinforced with extra gold, leather strap
with Gruen Expanding Buckle. 15 jewel
movement,

The GRUEN CARTOUCHE
in special designs

The 14k gold filled reinforced case is an improved construction found only in Gruen Guild Watches. A center lamination of strong base metal is surfaced on both sides by sheets of solid gold several times the weight and thickness required by the Federal Gold Filled Standard.

This method yields a watch case containing as much gold as many thin solid gold cases, yet sufficiently strong for adequate protection.

Ladies' sport wristlet with leather strap.

☆Car. 341 — 14k White gold filled Crown-Guard case, reinforced with extra gold. 15 jewel movement,

Ladies' sport wristlet with leather strap.

☆☆Car. 338 — 14k White gold filled Crown-Guard case, reinforced with extra gold. 15 jewel movement,

Ladies' sport wristlet with leather strap.
Car. 242—Semi-Cartouche, 14k White gold filled case, reinforced with extra gold, bright and antique finished engraving, 15 jewel movement,
With silk ribbon
Car. 192,

Sport wristlet with leather strap for the active lady who prefers the simplicity of tailored things

14k White gold filled case reinforced with extra gold. 15 jewel PRECISION movement,
Strap 19, White
Regular adjusted movement,
☆Strap 113, White

☆☆Car. 295—14k White gold filled case, reinforced with extra gold. Antique finished engraving, 15 jewel movement,
With gold-filled bracelet, as illustrated,

☆Car. 399 — 14k White gold filled case, reinforced with extra gold. 15 jewel movement,

☆☆Car. 400 — 14k White gold filled case, reinforced with extra gold. 15 jewel movement,

The GRUEN CARTOUCHE *in special designs*

Car. 368—14k White gold filled case, reinforced with extra gold. Inlaid with black and white enamel. 15 jewel movement,

☆Car. 366—14k White gold filled case, reinforced with extra gold. Inlaid with black and white enamel. 15 jewel movement,

☆Car. 404—14k White gold filled case, reinforced with extra gold. Inlaid with black enamel. 15 jewel movement,

Car. 370—14k White gold filled case, reinforced with extra gold. Inlaid with black and white enamel. 15 jewel movement,

14k Gold filled case, reinforced with extra gold. 15 jewel movement, with silk ribbon,
(Car. 403, White) (Car. 436, Coin)
With gold filled Guild bracelet, as illustrated,

☆Car. 294—14k White gold filled case, reinforced with extra gold. 15 jewel movement, $

Car. 434—14k White gold filled case, reinforced with extra gold. Inlaid with black enamel. 15 jewel movement,

GRUEN
CARTOUCHES
in
Reinforced and Gold Filled Designs

A Gruen Cartouche in the popular rectangular shape at this low cost of $37.50 and $35 is a real achievement.

Here are illustrated timepieces which will deliver a dependable and trouble-free service equal to the beauty of their case designs— in every sense watches worthy of the recognized prestige carried by the Gruen name on the dials.

15-jewel Cartouche movements in reinforced and gold filled cases.

☆☆Car. 107 — 14k White gold filled case. 15 jewel movement,

$15-20

$15-20

14k Gold filled case, reinforced with extra gold. 15 jewel movement,

☆
Car. 408, White, Antique finished engraving

Car. 384, White, Engraved

Car. 418, Green, Engraved

$10-15

☆☆Car. 173—14k White gold filled case. 15 jewel movement, With gold filled mesh bracelet, as illustrated,

$10-15

☆Car. 401—14k White gold filled case, reinforced with extra gold, with silk ribbon. 15 jewel movement,

With gold filled Guild bracelet, as illustrated,

$10-15

☆Car. 172—14k White gold filled case. 15 jewel movement, With gold filled Guild bracelet, as illustrated,

$10-15

☆Car. 106 — 14k White gold filled case. 15 jewel movement,

$10-15

☆☆Car. 389 — 14k White gold filled case, reinforced with extra gold. 15 jewel movement, $2

$95-110

WG21 — 18k Solid
white gold case
Engraved and inlaid
with black enamel
15 jewel movement,

Small GRUEN WRIST WATCHES in solid gold

Plain, easily read dials are but one
feature of these extraordinarily
dainty watches.

Employing a round movement —
some in the Gruen PRECISION
grade insuring highest accuracy
— the cases are symmetrical and
unusually handsome in design.

For the woman who wants a
really fine timepiece; character-
istically different and conservative in appearance, these wrist
watches should appeal.

$110-125

WG16 — 18k Solid
white gold case
Engraved and inlaid
with black enamel
15 jewel movement,

$75-85

WG10 — 18k Solid white gold case
15 jewel movement,

$60-70

WG13 — 18k Solid white gold case
15 jewel movement,

$70-80

WG29 — 14k Solid white gold case.
15 jewel movement,

$65-75

WG8 — 18k Solid white gold case
15 jewel movement,

$70-80

WG20 — 18k Solid white gold case,
engraved and inlaid with black enamel
15 jewel movement,

Moderately priced Gruens
Cased in Solid Gold

$65-75

☆Car. 181—14k Solid white gold case.
Engraved and inlaid with black enamel.
15 jewel movement,
With 17 jewel PRECISION movement,
Car. 204,

$55-65

☆Car. 405—14k Solid white gold case.
15 jewel movement,
With 17 jewel movement,
Car. 451

$65-75

Car. 140—14k Solid white gold case.
Inlaid with black enamel. 15 jewel
movement,

$65-75

Car. 406—14k Solid white gold case.
15 jewel movement,
With 17 jewel movement,
Car. 452

$70-80

Car. 91—18k Solid white gold case.
Inlaid with black enamel. 15 jewel
movement, 6

$55-65

☆Car. 314—14k Solid white gold case.
15 jewel movement,

$50-60

☆☆Car. 12 — 14k
Solid white gold case.
15 jewel movement,

$55-65

☆☆Car. 409 — 14k
Solid white gold case.
Antique finished en-
graving. 15 jewel
movement, $

$45-55

☆Car. 10—14k Solid
white gold case. 15
jewel movement,

Moderately priced Gruens
Cased in Solid Gold

☆Car. 435—14k Solid white gold case.
15 jewel movement,

Car. 437—14k Solid white gold case.
15 jewel movement,

☆Car. 373—14k Solid white gold case.
15 jewel movement,

Car. 314 Cord—14k Solid white gold
case. 15 jewel movement,

☆Car. 313—14k Solid white gold case.
15 jewel movement,

☆Car. 409 Flex. 23—14k Solid gold case, with gold-filled bracelet, 15 jewel
movement, $60

Car. 438—14k Solid white gold Crown-Guard case. 15 jewel movement,

With 15 jewel PRECISION movement Car. 443,

$50-60

$55-65

14k Solid white gold case with gold filled mesh bracelet. 15 jewel movement,

(Car. 288—Antique finish)
(Car. 425—Bright engraved)
With silk ribbon,

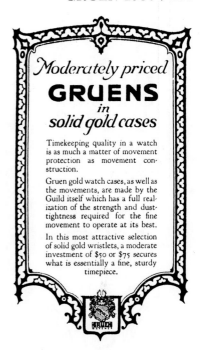

Moderately priced
GRUENS
in
solid gold cases

Timekeeping quality in a watch is as much a matter of movement protection as movement construction.

Gruen gold watch cases, as well as the movements, are made by the Guild itself which has a full realization of the strength and dusttightness required for the fine movement to operate at its best.

In this most attractive selection of solid gold wristlets, a moderate investment of $50 or $75 secures what is essentially a fine, sturdy timepiece.

$60-70

14k Solid gold case, with gold-filled bracelet, 15 jewel movement,
(Car. 416—Flex. 31, White) ☆☆ (Car. 417—Flex. 31, Coin)
Introducing the newest development in watch design—the bracelet shown above is part of the watch. The watch itself fits naturally into a design whose motif is carried out all the way around the wrist, making a single harmonious unit. Logical, new, a marked advance over the usual attached bracelet or ribbon—an original Gruen Guild creation.

$50-60

Car. 424—14k Solid white gold case.
15 jewel movement,

$60-70

14k Solid gold case. 15 jewel movement,

(Car. 416, White)   (Car. 417, Coin)

$55-65

☆☆Car. 387 — 14k Solid white gold Crown-Guard case. 15 jewel movement,

With solid gold mesh bracelet, as illustrated,

15 jewel PRECISION movement (Car. 442)
With silk ribbon,
With mesh bracelet,

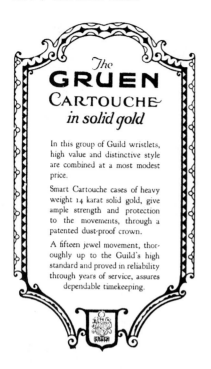

The GRUEN CARTOUCHE *in solid gold*

In this group of Guild wristlets, high value and distinctive style are combined at a most modest price.

Smart Cartouche cases of heavy weight 14 karat solid gold, give ample strength and protection to the movements, through a patented dust-proof crown.

A fifteen jewel movement, thoroughly up to the Guild's high standard and proved in reliability through years of service, assures dependable timekeeping.

$50-60

Car. 376—14k Solid white gold case
15 jewel movement,

With 17 jewel movement,
Car. 447

$55-65

Car. 375—14k Solid white gold case
15 jewel movement,

With 17 jewel movement,
Car. 446

$55-65

☆Car. 381—14k Solid white gold case.
15 jewel movement,
With 17 jewel movement,
Car. 450

$65-75

☆Car. 374—14k Solid white gold case,
with Crown-Guard and sport strap.
15 jewel movement,

$55-65

☆☆Car. 377—14k Solid white gold
case. 15 jewel movement,
With 17 jewel movement,
Car. 448

$55-65

☆☆Car. 348—14k Solid white gold
case. 15 jewel movement,
With 17 jewel movement,
Car. 445

The GRUEN CARTOUCHE

Daintiness with durability is achieved in these small rectangular wristlets by a movement which utilizes the entire case space for larger and stronger parts.

In plain, hand-chased and enamel-inlaid solid white gold cases, any one of this charming array will grace the wrist of a woman and assure her a regular and dependable timekeeping service.

$75-85

Car. 93 — 18k Solid white gold case. Inlaid with black enamel. 17 jewel PRECISION movement,

$70-80

Car. 96 — 18k Solid white gold case, with antique finished engraving 17 jewel PRECISION movement,

$60-70

Car. 26—18k Solid white gold case. 17 jewel PRECISION movement,

$60-70

Car. 210—18k Solid white gold case. 17 jewel PRECISION movement,

$50-60

☆Car. 205—14k Solid white gold case with silk ribbon. 17 jewel PRECISION movement,
With gold filled Guild bracelet, as illustrated,

$60-70

☆Car. 380—18k Solid White gold Crown-Guard case. 17 jewel PRECISION movement,

$60-70

Car. 379—14k Solid white gold Crown-Guard case. 17 jewel PRECISION movement,

$55-65

14k Solid gold Crown-Guard case. 17 jewel PRECISION movement
(Car. 419, Coin) ☆ (Car. 433, White)

Fine gold designs in the **GRUEN** CARTOUCHE

A watch, to be fully enjoyed, must have a reputation or social standing in the eyes of one's friends, in addition to being useful and beautiful.

In selecting a Gruen wristlet such as those exquisitely small models pictured here, you enjoy the certainty that you have presented a watch of genuine worth and a countrywide prestige.

$70-80

$50-60

☆☆Car. 103 — 14k Solid white gold case. 15 jewel movement,

15 jewel PRECISION movement, Car. 285,

With Solid gold mesh bracelet, as illustrated,

Car. 227—14k Solid white gold case, 15 jewel movement,

With 15 jewel PRECISION movement Car. 284,

$55-65

Car. 30—18k Solid white gold case. 18 jewel Extra PRECISION movement,

$50-60

☆☆Car. 206—14k Solid white gold case. 17 jewel PRECISION movement,

$55-65

Car. 279 Mesh—14k Solid white gold case and mesh bracelet. 15 jewel PRECISION movement,

$60-70

Car. 293—14k Solid white gold case. Engraved and inlaid with black enamel. 15 jewel PRECISION movement, With 17 jewel PRECISION movement, Car. 392, $85

$60-70

Car. 207—14k Solid white gold case, inlaid with black enamel, 17 jewel PRECISION movement,

$55-65

14k Solid gold Crown-Guard case. 15 jewel PRECISION movement, (Car. 307 White) ☆ (Car. 420 Coin)

GRUEN
Cartouche

$55-65

☆Car. 439—14k Solid white gold case.
with silk ribbon. 15 jewel
movement,
With gold-filled Guild bracelet,
as illustrated,
With 17 jewel PRECISION movement,
as illustrated
Car. 390,

$60-70

Car. 440—14k Solid white gold case.
15 jewel movement,
With 17 jewel PRECISION movement,
Car. 391,

$60-70

☆☆Car. 309—14k Solid white gold
Crown-Guard case. 15 jewel PRECISION
movement,

$60-70

☆Car. 178—14k Solid white gold case.
15 jewel movement, 16
With 17 jewel PRECISION movement,
Car. 202,

$65-75

Car. 290 Cord—14k Solid white gold
case. 15 jewel PRECISION movement, 70

$70-80

Car. 90—14k Solid white gold case.
15 jewel movement, 5'

$50-60

Car. 278 Cord—14k Solid white gold
case. 15 jewel PRECISION movement, "

The Gruen Cartouche

Cases of Solid Gold

$60-70

Car. 375 Mesh Cord—14k Solid gold case, with gold filled mesh cord. 15 jewel movement,
With 17 jewel movement,
Car. 446 Mesh Cord

$55-65

Car. 265—14k Solid white gold case. 15 jewel movement,

$65-75

Car. 337 Flex 23—14k Solid white gold case, with gold filled bracelet. 15 jewel movement,

$50-60

Car. 234 Cord—14k Solid white gold case with silk cord attachment, 15 jewel movement,

$50-60

☆☆Car. 378 Cord—14k Solid white and coin gold case, with silk cord attachment, 15 jewel movement,
With 17 jewel movement,
Car. 449 Cord

$65-75

Car. 348 Flex—14k Solid white gold case, with gold filled bracelet. 15 jewel movement,
With 17 jewel movement,
Car. 445 Flex

The Gruen Cartouche
Cases of Solid Gold

$65-75

☆☆Car. 234 — 14k
Solid white gold case.
15 jewel movement,

$65-75

Car. 233—14k Solid
white gold case
15 jewel movement,
,40

$70-80

☆Car. 337—14k Solid white gold case.
Antique finished engraving, 15 jewel
movement,

$50-60

☆Car. 347—14k Solid white gold case.
15 jewel movement, ⟩
With 17 jewel movement,
Car. 444

$70-80

☆Car. 230—14k Solid white gold case.
15 jewel movement,

$55-65

☆Car. 269 Mesh—14k Solid white gold
case. 15 jewel movement,
With mesh bracelet, as illustrated,

$75-85

Car. 377 Mesh—14k Solid white gold
case with gold filled mesh bracelet,
15 jewel movement, $
With 17 jewel movement,
Car. 448 Mesh

$65-75

Car. 231—14k Solid white gold case.
With antique finished engraving. 15 jewel
movement,

Moderately Priced
GRUEN
DIAMOND
WATCHES

A wrist watch bearing the name "Gruen" is a possession in itself of which any woman may well be proud.

But when, at these most modest prices, such a famed watch may be obtained with its case set in diamonds, the joy of ownership is doubled.

For then, to the daily usefulness of such a watch, is added the desirability of a fine piece of jewelry.

Car. 778—14k Solid white gold case set with 2 diamonds. 15 jewel movement,

☆☆Car.153—14k Solid white gold case set with 2 diamonds, 15 jewel movement

☆☆Car. 350—14k Solid white gold case set with 2 diamonds. 15 jewel movement

☆☆Car. 349—14k Solid white gold case set with 2 diamonds, 15 jewel movement

Car. 780—14k Solid white gold case set with 2 diamonds. 15 jewel movement,

Car. 774—14k Solid white gold case set with 2 diamonds and inlaid with black enamel, 15 jewel movement,

Car. 773—14k Solid white gold case, set with 2 diamonds, 15 jewel movement,

Car. 772—14k Solid white gold case, set with 2 diamonds, 15 jewel movement,

Car. 775—14k Solid white gold case set with 4 diamonds and inlaid with black enamel, 15 jewel movement,

☆Car. 782—14k Solid white gold case set with 2 diamonds. 15 jewel movement,

☆Car. 781—14k Solid white gold case set with 2 diamonds. 15 jewel movement,

Gruen Diamond
Cartouche Watches
Cased in Solid Gold

☆Car. 250—14k Solid white gold case set with 4 diamonds and inlaid with black enamel, 15 jewel movement,

$80-95

☆☆Car. 220—14k Solid white gold case set with 2 diamonds and 4 synthetic sapphires, 15 jewel movement,

$65-75

☆Car. 351—14k Solid white gold case set with 4 diamonds, 15 jewel movement

$70-80

☆☆Car. 23—14k Solid white gold case set with 4 diamonds, 15 jewel movement

$85-100

Car. 785 Mesh—14k Solid white gold case, filled mesh bracelet, set with 4 diamonds, 15 jewel movement,

$75-85

Car. 244—14k Solid white gold case set with 2 diamonds and inlaid with black enamel, 15 jewel movement,

$95-110

Car. 784—14k Solid white gold case set with 2 diamonds and 4 sapphires, 15 jewel movement,

$75-85

☆Car. 184—14k Solid white gold case set with 2 diamonds and inlaid with black enamel, 15 jewel movement,

Gruen Diamond
Cartouche Watches
Cased in Solid Gold

☆☆Car. 121 — 14k Solid white gold case set with 4 diamonds and 2 synthetic sapphires; 15 jewel movement,

$65-75

Car. 352—14k Solid white gold case set with 4 diamonds, 15 jewel movement,

$65-75

$70-80

Car. 787—14k Solid white gold case, set with 4 diamonds and 2 sapphires, 15 jewel movement,

$75-85

Car. 750—14k Solid white gold case set with 2 diamonds and inlaid with black enamel, 15 jewel movement,

$65-75

☆☆Car. 765 — 14k Solid white gold case set with 4 diamonds. 15 jewel movement

$80-95

☆Car. 786—14k Solid white gold case, set with 4 diamonds. 15 jewel movement,

$95-110

☆Car. 255 Mesh Cord—14k Solid white gold case and mesh cord set with 6 diamonds. 15 jewel movement,

$65-75

Car. 245—14k Solid white gold case set with 2 diamonds and inlaid with black enamel, 15 jewel movement,

$70-80

☆☆Car. 783 — 14k Solid white gold case, set with 2 diamonds. 15 jewel movement,

Gruen Diamond Cartouche Watches
Cased in Solid Gold

☆☆Car. 771—14k Solid white gold case set with 8 large diamonds, 15 jewel movement,

Car. 760—14k Solid white gold case and set with 6 diamonds; inlaid with black enamel; 15 jewel movement,

Car. 753—14k Solid white gold case set with 4 diamonds and inlaid with black enamel. 15 jewel movement,

Car. 751—14k Solid white gold case set with 2 diamonds and inlaid with black enamel. 15 jewel movement,

Car. 155—14k Solid white gold case set with 4 diamonds. 15 jewel movement,

Car. 757—14k Solid white gold case set with 4 diamonds and inlaid with black enamel, 15 jewel movement,

Car. 788—14k Solid white gold case, set with 4 diamonds. 15 jewel movement, $110

Car. 759—14k Solid white gold case and set with 6 diamonds; inlaid with black enamel. 15 jewel PRECISION movement,

Car. 761—14k Solid white gold case engraved and set with 8 diamonds, 17 jewel PRECISION movement,

Car. 756—14k Solid white gold case and set with 4 diamonds. inlaid with black enamel. 15 jewel movement,

Gruen Diamond Cartouche Watches
Cased in Solid Gold

☆Car. 353—14k Solid white gold case set with 6 diamonds. 15 jewel PRECISION movement

$150-175

Car. 305—18k Solid white gold case with platinum top set with 22 diamonds. 17 jewel PRECISION movement

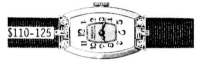

Car. 331—14k Solid white gold case, with 8 diamonds, including 4 baguettes, set in platinum. 17 jewel PRECISION movement

☆Car. 160—14k Solid white gold case set with 10 diamonds, 17 jewel PRECISION movement

$100-120

☆Car. 189—14k Solid white gold case set with 12 diamonds and 8 reconstructed sapphires, 17 jewel PRECISION movement

☆Car. 256 Mesh Cord—14k Solid white gold case and mesh cord, set with 6 diamonds, 17 jewel PRECISION movement

$175-200

Car. 303—18k Solid white gold case with platinum top set with 18 diamonds, 17 jewel PRECISION movement

$80-90

Car. 795—14k Solid white gold case set with 8 diamonds. 15 jewel movement

$75-85

Car. 257—14k Solid white gold case set with 6 diamonds, 17 jewel PRECISION movement

Gruen Diamond
Cartouche Watches
Cased in Solid Gold

$110-125

☆Car. 356—18k Solid white gold case
with 8 diamonds, including 2 baguettes,
set in platinum. 17 jewel PRECISION
movement

$100-120

Car. 317—14k Solid white gold case,
with 8 diamonds, including 2 baguettes,
set in platinum. 17 jewel PRECISION
movement

$80-90

Car. 252—14k Solid white gold case set
with 6 diamonds. 15 jewel PRECISION
movement

$75-85

Car. 259—14k Solid white gold case
set with 6 diamonds. 17 jewel PRECISION
movement

$75-85

☆Car. 766—14k Solid white gold case
set with 8 diamonds, 15 jewel movement

$70-80

Car. 793—14k Solid white gold case,
set with 6 diamonds. 15 jewel movement

$65-75

☆☆Car. 770—14k Solid White gold case set with 6 diamonds
and inlaid with hard black enamel, smart black silk adjustable cord
with gold loops and clasp, 15 jewel movement

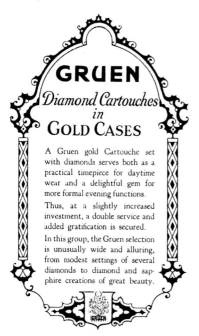

GRUEN
Diamond Cartouches
in
GOLD CASES

A Gruen gold Cartouche set with diamonds serves both as a practical timepiece for daytime wear and a delightful gem for more formal evening functions.

Thus, at a slightly increased investment, a double service and added gratification is secured.

In this group, the Gruen selection is unusually wide and alluring, from modest settings of several diamonds to diamond and sapphire creations of great beauty.

$90-110

Car. 319 Mesh Cord—14k Solid white gold case and mesh cord, 12 round and 2 baguette shaped diamonds set in platinum. 17 jewel PRECISION movement

$110-125

Car. 306 Mesh Cord—18k Solid white gold case with platinum top set with 18 diamonds, with 14k solid mesh cord, 17 jewel PRECISION movement

$275-325

☆Car. 329 Mesh—14k Solid white gold case and mesh bracelet with 32 diamonds set in solid platinum, 17 jewel PRECISION movement

$125-140

☆☆Car. 768—14k Solid white gold case and mesh bracelet set with 18 diamonds, 17 jewel PRECISION movement

$150-175

☆Car. 330—18k Solid white gold case with platinum top set with 30 round and 2 baguette shaped diamonds. 17 jewel PRECISION movement

$150-175

Car. 301—18k Solid white gold case with platinum top, set with 20 diamonds, 17 jewel PRECISION movement

$200-230

☆Car. 304—18k Solid white gold case with 4 large specially cut, cabochon green onyx. 14 diamonds set in platinum 17 jewel PRECISION movement

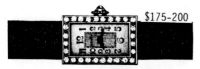

$175-200

Car. 194—18k Solid white gold case with platinum top, set with 28 diamonds. 17 jewel PRECISION movement

$175-200

Car. 324—18k Solid white gold case with platinum top, set with 22 diamonds. 17 jewel PRECISION movement

Exquisite Gruen Cartouche Watches

Platinum, Paved with Diamonds

$225-260

Solid iridium platinum
case set with 36 dia-
monds and 4 recon-
structed sapphires; 17
jewel PRECISION move-
ment
(Design C1077)

$200-230

Solid iridium platinum
case set with 34 dia-
monds and 4 recon-
structed sapphires; 17
jewel PRECISION move-
ment
(Design 3G1077)

$300-350

Solid iridium platinum
case set with 48
diamonds and 14 fine
reconstructed sap-
phires. 17 jewel
PRECISION movement
(Design J1077)

$150-175

$150-175

Solid iridium platinum
case set with 8 dia-
monds and 4 recon-
structed sapphires; 17
jewel PRECISION move-
ment
(Design A1077)

Solid iridium platinum
case set with 36 dia-
monds. 17 jewel
PRECISION movement
(Design M1077)

$165-185

Solid iridium platinum
case set with 10 dia-
monds. 17 jewel
PRECISION movement
(Design B1077)

Gruen Cartouche Watches

Platinum, Paved
with Diamonds

$275-315

Solid iridium platinum case paved with
44 diamonds and 12 fine reconstructed
sapphires; 17 jewel PRECISION movement
(Design H1077)

$150-175

Solid iridium platinum case paved with
32 full cut diamonds. 17 jewel PRECISION
movement
(Design 1W105)

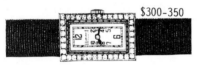

$300-350

Solid iridium platinum case paved with
40 diamonds and 30 fine reconstructed
sapphires; 17 jewel PRECISION movement
(Design 3M105)

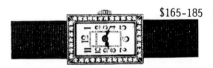

$165-185

Solid iridium platinum case paved with
38 diamonds. 17 jewel PRECISION
movement
(Design F1077)

$135-155

Solid iridium platinum case set with
28 diamonds. 17 jewel PRECISION
movement
☆(Design E1077)

$85-100

Solid iridium platinum case. Hand engraved. 17 jewel PRECISION movement
(Design I1077)

$175-200

Solid iridium platinum case paved with
46 diamonds. 17 jewel PRECISION
movement
(Design G1077)

$275-315

Solid iridium platinum case set with
40 diamonds. 17 jewel PRECISION
movement
(Design D1077)

Gruen Cartouche Watches

Platinum, Paved with Diamonds

$350-400

Solid iridium platinum case set with
52 diamonds and 8 black onyx. 17 jewel
PRECISION movement
(Design 4D105)

$400-450

Solid iridium platinum case set with
78 diamonds, the center diamonds of the
end pieces being rather large. 17 jewel
PRECISION movement
(Design 3S105)

$300-350

Solid iridium platinum case set with 44
diamonds and 4 black onyx. 17 jewel
PRECISION movement
(Design 4C105)

$425-475

Solid iridium platinum case set with 56
diamonds, including 2 of pentagon shape
and 16 genuine emeralds; 17 jewel
PRECISION movement
(Design 3Z105)

$375-425

Solid iridium platinum case set with
48 diamonds and 16 fine reconstructed
sapphires; 17 jewel PRECISION movement
(Design 3T105)

$325-365

Solid iridium platinum case set with
66 diamonds. The square cut diamonds
in end pieces are quite large. 18 jewel
Dietrich Gruen EXTRA PRECISION
movement
(Design A847-3797)

$300-350

Solid iridium platinum case set with 52
diamonds. 17 jewel PRECISION movement
☆(Design Z1077)

$375-425

Solid iridium platinum case set with
50 diamonds and 30 fine reconstructed
sapphires; 17 jewel PRECISION movement
(Design 3U105)

$250-300

Solid iridium platinum case set with
12 fine reconstructed sapphires and 48
diamonds, including 2 baguettes; 17 jewel
PRECISION movement
(Design N1077)

Exquisite Gruen Cartouche Watches

Platinum, Paved with Diamonds

$200–225

Solid iridium platinum case set with 44 diamonds. 17 jewel PRECISION movement
(*Design Y1077*)

$225–250

Solid iridium platinum case set with 52 diamonds. 17 jewel PRECISION movement
(*Design W1077*)

$225–250

Solid iridium platinum case set with 42 diamonds. 17 jewel PRECISION movement
(*Design 3P105*)

$235–255

Solid iridium platinum case set with 50 diamonds and 30 fine reconstructed sapphires 17 jewel PRECISION movement
(*Design 3L105*)

$200–225

Solid iridium platinum case set with 36 diamonds. 17 jewel PRECISION movement
(*Design X1077*)

$275–315

Solid iridium platinum case set with 48 diamonds including 2 baguettes. 17 jewel PRECISION movement
☆ (*Design 1B1077*)

$250–280

Solid iridium platinum case set with 46 diamonds and 18 fine reconstructed sapphires. 17 jewel PRECISION movement
(*Design S1077*)

$375–425

Solid iridium platinum case set with 30 fine reconstructed sapphires and 44 diamonds including 2 baguettes. 17 jewel PRECISION movement
(*Design O1077*)

GRUEN
Diamond Cartouches
in
PLATINUM

For those who feel a sentiment for the very best, these magnificent Gruen Watches will awaken an immediate appeal.

Cases of finest iridium platinum, fully paved with precious stones, serve as a proper setting for the remarkable Gruen *Precision* movements which make each one a timepiece of rare beauty and dependability.

If you have hoped to some day honor a dear friend with a perfect gift, nothing finer could be chosen to delight the most fastidious woman.

$325-375

Solid iridium platinum case set with 52 diamonds and 8 synthetic emeralds
17 jewel
PRECISION movement
Design 3O105)

$375-425

Solid iridium platinum case paved with 78 diamonds. 17 jewel
PRECISION movement
(Design 3Y105)

$225-250

Solid iridium platinum case set with 48 calibre sapphires and 52 diamonds, including 4 baguettes; 17 jewel
PRECISION movement
(Design L1077)

$325-375

Solid iridium platinum case set with 70 diamonds and 2 genuine oriental, square cut sapphires; 17 jewel
PRECISION movement
(Design 1W105-3780)

$300-350

Solid iridium platinum case set with 60 diamonds, 17 jewel PRECISION movement
(Design A626)

$350-400

Solid iridium platinum case set with 72 diamonds and 10 green onyx. 17 jewel
PRECISION movement
(Design 4E105)

$325-375

Solid iridium platinum case paved with 44 diamonds. Those in the end pieces are square cut. 17 jewel PRECISION movement
(Design 3Q105)

$375-425

Solid iridium platinum case set with 58 diamonds. The center diamonds of the end pieces being blue white and extra large. 17 jewel PRECISION movement
(Design 3W105)

Gruen Diamond-Set Baguette Watches
With silk cord attachments

$175-200

The simple effectiveness of this design is attained through the setting of 16 baguette-shape diamonds in the solid iridium platinum case. The black silk cord attachment is fitted with two platinum loops and clasp set with 14 small round diamonds; 17 jewel PRECISION movement
(Baguette 8)

$175-200

Solid iridium platinum case and silk cord attachment set with 48 diamonds, including 20 baguette and 2 hexagon-shape stones which cleverly conceal the cord fastenings 17 jewel PRECISION movement
(Baguette 9)

$150-175

A distinctly smart design is achieved through the small dial completely surrounded with 20 square-cut, 6 baguette-shape and 24 round diamonds set in a solid iridium platinum case with silk cord attachment and safety clasp with platinum loops set with 10 round diamonds, 17 jewel PRECISION movement
(Baguette 10)

$200-225

Solid iridium platinum case and cord bracelet attachments set with 42 diamonds including 10 baguette-shaped stones; 17 jewel PRECISION movement
(Baguette 11)

$200-225

Solid iridium platinum case and cord bracelet attachments set with 38 diamonds
(Baguette 12)

Gruen Bracelet Watches
Solid gold and gold filled designs

$150-175

14k Solid white gold case and bracelet
17 jewel PRECISION movement
(Car. 206 flex,

$200-230

14k Solid white gold case and bracelet
15 jewel movement
(Car. 103 flex.

$175-200

14k Solid white gold case and bracelet
15 jewel movement
(Car. 145 flex.

$50-60

14k White gold filled case and bracelet
15 jewel movement
(Car. 213 flex.

$45-55

14k White gold filled case and bracelet
15 jewel movement
(Car. 174 flex

$55-65

14k White gold filled case and bracelet
15 jewel movement
(Car. 107 flex.

$100-120

18k Solid white gold case, set with 10 diamonds, with
adjustable solid gold mesh cord and safety catch
17 jewel PRECISION movement—☆☆(Car. 769)

$150-175

18k Solid white gold case, platinum faced gold bracelet
set with 18 diamonds and 10 reconstructed sapphires
17 jewel PRECISION movement (Car. 189 flex)

$125-145

14k Solid white gold case and platinum faced gold bracelet,
set with 16 diamonds
17 jewel PRECISION movement—(Car. 160 flex)

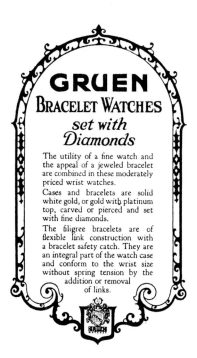

GRUEN
BRACELET WATCHES
set with
Diamonds

The utility of a fine watch and
the appeal of a jeweled bracelet
are combined in these moderately
priced wrist watches.

Cases and bracelets are solid
white gold, or gold with platinum
top, carved or pierced and set
with fine diamonds.

The filigree bracelets are of
flexible link construction with
a bracelet safety catch. They are
an integral part of the watch case
and conform to the wrist size
without spring tension by the
addition or removal
of links.

$175-200

18k Solid white gold case and platinum overlay bracelet with
20 diamonds set in platinum
17 jewel PRECISION movement—(Car. 362 flex)

$175-200

18k Solid white gold case with platinum top, platinum faced
gold bracelet, set with 18 diamonds and 4 reconstructed sapphires
17 jewel PRECISION movement—(Car. 215 flex)

$150-175

14k Solid white gold case and flexible platinum overlay bracelet with
18 diamonds set in platinum
17 jewel PRECISION movement—☆(Car. 328 flex)

$150-175

14k with gold case and platinum overlay bracelet with 12 diamonds
set in platinum
17 jewel PRECISION movement—(Car. 361 flex)

Gruen Bracelet Watches
Set with Diamonds

$150-175

14k Solid white gold case and platinum overlay bracelet,
set with 10 diamonds
17 jewel PRECISION movement—(Car. 360 flex)

$150-175

14k Solid white gold case and platinum overlay bracelet
set with 10 diamonds
17 jewel PRECISION movement—(Car. 359 flex)

$150-175

14k Solid white gold case and bracelet set with
6 diamonds
15 jewel PRECISION movement—(Car. 357 flex)

$175-200

14k Solid white gold case and bracelet, set with
6 diamonds
15 jewel PRECISION movement—(Car. 358 flex)

$200-230

14k Solid white gold case and bracelet, set with
6 diamonds and 4 synthetic sapphires
15 jewel movement—(Car. 121 flex)

$175-200

14k Solid white gold case and bracelet, set with 6 diamonds
15 jewel movement
☆(Car. 155 flex)

Crowning the many noteworthy achievements of the Gruen Guild are these gorgeous creations in platinum and precious stones.

Only a passion for beauty and a devotion to the highest principles of workmanship could produce such triumphs of the watchmaker's art.

Under the spell of the fine old traditions of medieval masters, craftsmen of the modern Gruen Guild have been inspired, in these rare watches, to do their very best.

GRUEN
Jeweled Bracelet
WATCHES

$375-425

Solid iridium platinum case and bracelet fully paved with 78 diamonds; 18 jewel Dietrich Gruen Extra Precision movement

(Design A847 flex)

$475-525

Solid iridium platinum case and mesh bracelet set with 180 diamonds, of which those in the watch case are full-cut stones; 17 jewel Precision movement

(Design 1W105 Diamond Mesh)

$625-685

Solid iridium platinum case and bracelet paved with 202 round and square-cut diamonds and 32 large, genuine Oriental sapphires which illuminate the entire setting; 18 jewel Dietrich Gruen Extra Precision movement.

(Design A Flex)

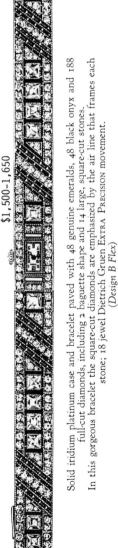

$1,500-1,650

Solid iridium platinum case and bracelet paved with 48 genuine emeralds, 48 black onyx and 188 full-cut diamonds, including 2 baguette shape and 14 large, square-cut stones.
In this gorgeous bracelet the square-cut diamonds are emphasized by the air line that frames each stone; 18 jewel Dietrich Gruen Extra Precision movement.

(Design B Flex)

GRUEN
Diamond-Set
BAGUETTE
WATCHES

Employing the remarkably small Gruen baguette movement, watches of the dainty gracefulness of these, have established a new vogue for distinctive wristlets.

Hand-wrought in platinum and set with first choice diamonds, originality of design is combined with the timekeeping reliability of fine, Gruen Guild movements.

Jewelers who search European markets for rare creations to please their most exacting customers, have found nothing which more adroitly proclaims the unusual in artistic watch craftsmanship.

$150-175

Solid iridium platinum case set with 62 diamonds, including 2 baguette shaped stones; 17 jewel PRECISION movement
(Baguette 5)

$275-300

Solid iridium platinum case set with 50 diamonds, including 2 triangular and 6 baguette shaped stones; 17 jewel PRECISION movement
(Baguette 1)

$375-425

Solid iridium platinum case and mesh bracelet, set with 57 diamonds, including 8 square cut, 6 baguette shaped and 6 pentagon shaped stones; 17 jewel PRECISION movement
(Baguette 3)

$250-300

Solid iridium platinum case with silk cord attachment, set with 64 diamonds including 20 baguette-cut stones, 17 jewel PRECISION movement
(Baguette 4)

$400-450

A bracelet watch of marvelous richness is this solid iridium platinum case and flexible bracelet set with 129 diamonds, including 10 baguette-shape stones. The round diamonds are full-cut and because of their large size contribute to the most striking effect of this bracelet; 17 jewel PRECISION movement
(Baguette 6)

$375-425

A regal simplicity recommends this solid iridium platinum case paved with 18 baguette-shape diamonds and the iridium platinum bracelet paved with 38 large, emerald-cut diamonds in matched, graduated pairs; 17 jewel PRECISION movement
(Baguette 7)

Gruen *Attachments*

$10-15

Mesh No. 20—Green or white gold filled with sliding buckle, adjustable to any size,

Mesh No. 21—14k, solid gold,

$200-225

Mesh No. 18—14k solid white gold,

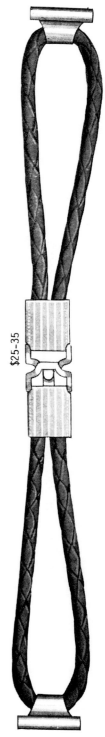

$25-35

Cord No. 3 (Braided leather)—Green or white gold filled,

Gruen Attachments for Men's Wrist Watches

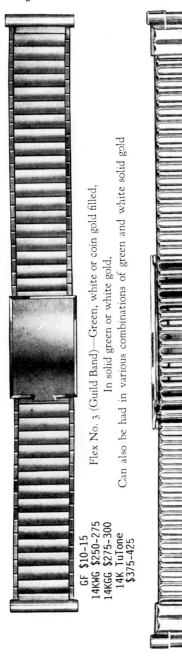

Flex No. 3 (Guild Band)—Green, white or coin gold filled,

In solid green or white gold,

Can also be had in various combinations of green and white solid gold

GF $10-15
14KWG $250-275
14KGG $275-300
14K TuTone
$375-425

Flex No. 11—Lord Wadsworth band, green or white gold filled,

$15-20

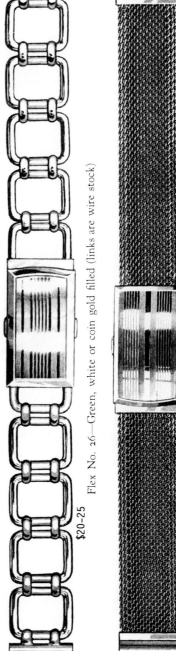

Flex No. 26—Green, white or coin gold filled (links are wire stock)

$20-25

Mesh No. 23—Green or white gold filled (single mesh).

$10-15

Gruen Wrist Watches for Men

$55-65

15 jewel movement
Nickel Tarnish Proof case
☆
(Strap 109,

$65-75

15 jewel movement
14k Gold filled case,
(Strap 134 Green)   (Strap 135 White)
With gold filled link band,
as illustrated,

$75-85

15 jewel movement
14k Gold filled case,
(Strap 143 Green) ☆ (Strap 144 White)

$65-75

15 jewel movement
14k Gold filled case,
(Strap 13, Green)   ☆   (Strap 14, White)

$65-75

15 jewel movement
14k Gold filled case,
(Strap 112 White)   (Strap 146 Coin)

Gruen Wrist Watches for Men

$60-70

15 jewel movement
Nickel Tarnish Proof case
☆
(Strap 130,

$50-60

15 jewel movement
Nickel Tarnish Proof case
☆
(Strap 128,

$45-55

15 jewel movement
Nickel Tarnish Proof case
☆☆
(Strap 111,

$70-80

15 jewel movement
Nickel Tarnish Proof case
☆☆
(Strap 129,

$75-85
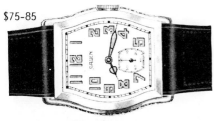

15 jewel movement
14k White gold filled Crown-Guard case
reinforced with extra gold
(Strap 115,

$5-10

15 jewel movement
Nickel Tarnish Proof case
☆☆
(Strap 110,

Wrist Watches for Men

Gruen

GF $70-80
14K $225-250

$60-70

15 jewel movement
14k Gold filled case
reinforced with extra gold
With curved crystal, center and back
of case,
(Strap 136, Green) ☆ (Strap 137, White)
With 17 jewel movement,
(Strap 156, Green)   (Strap 157, White)
With 17 jewel PRECISION movement
14k Solid gold case,
(Strap 172, White)   (Strap 173, Coin)

15 jewel movement
14k Gold filled case,
With curved crystal, center and back
of case
(Strap 140, White)   (Strap 141, Coin)
With 17 jewel PRECISION movement,
(Strap 159, White)   (Strap 160, Coin)

$65-75

$80-90

15 jewel movement
14k Gold filled Crown-Guard case
reinforced with extra gold
with leather strap,
(Strap 114, White) ☆ (Strap 145, Coin)
With 17 jewel movement,
(Strap 163, White)   (Strap 164, Coin)
With gold filled Guild band
as ilustrated,

15 jewel movement
14k Gold filled case,
(Strap 126 Green)   (Strap 127 White)

Gruen Wrist Watches for Men

$60-70

15 jewel movement
Nickel Tarnish Proof case
☆☆
(Strap 99,

$80-90

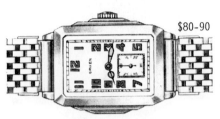

The Varsity
15 jewel movement
14k Gold filled case reinforced with extra
gold, filled link band,
(Strap 147, White)☆☆(Strap 148, Coin)
With 17 jewel movement,
(Strap 168, White)   (Strap 169, Coin)

$55-65

15 jewel movement
14k White gold filled case
With leather strap
☆☆(Strap 87,
With gold filled Armored edge mesh band
as illustrated, $42.50

$75-85

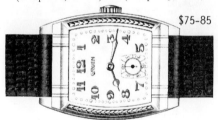

15 jewel movement
14k Gold filled case,
(Strap 133, White)   (Strap 142, Green)
With 17 jewel movement,
(Strap 161, White)   (Strap 162, Green)

$45-55

15 jewel movement
Nickel Tarnish Proof case
☆
(Strap 100,

$70-80

15 jewel movement
14k White gold filled case
Antique finished engraving
☆
(Strap 88,

GRUEN
WRIST WATCHES
for men

$325-365

17 jewel PRECISION movement
18k Solid white gold case
with curved back
(*Strap* 74,

$175-200

17 jewel PRECISION movement
14k Solid white gold case
(*Strap* 65,

$85-100

15 jewel movement
14k Gold filled Crown-Guard case,
reinforced with extra gold
Antique finished engraving,
(*Strap* 57 Green)   (*Strap* 58 White)

$85-100

15 jewel movement
14k White gold filled case, reinforced
with extra gold
Antique finished engraving
☆
(*Strap* 122,

$70-80

15 jewel movement
14k Gold filled case, reinforced with
extra gold.
☆☆
(*Strap* 121, White)   (*Strap* 125, Green)

$75-85

15 jewel movement
14k Gold filled Crown-Guard case,
reinforced with extra gold
with leather strap,
(*Strap* 27, Green) ☆☆ (*Strap* 28, White)
With gold filled mesh band
as illustrated,

$75-85

15 jewel movement
14k Gold filled case
Antique finished engraving,
(*Strap* 90, White) ☆☆ (*Strap* 124, Coin)

$175-200

17 jewel PRECISION movement
14k Solid green gold case
(*Strap* 10,

Smart
GRUEN
WRIST WATCHES
for men

Every man needs *two good watches*
—a pocket and wrist watch.
The pocket watch, of course, will
always hold its place as the more
dignified timepiece. The pocket
watch and chain are correct for all
evening wear—and such informal
affairs as the theatre or church.
The wrist watch is the timepiece
of convenience. For busy men
during busy hours at the office;
for summer comfort when no
vest is worn; for sports wear or
in winter when the time is
quickly at hand without opening
the overcoat or removing
the gloves.

$65-75

15 jewel PRECISION movement
14k White gold filled case
reinforced with extra gold
Antique finished engraving
(*Strap* 84,

$65-75

15 jewel PRECISION movement
14k White Gold filled case
reinforced with extra gold
with leather strap
☆
(*Strap* 72,
with gold filled mesh band
as illustrated,

$70-80

15 jewel PRECISION movement
14k White gold filled case
reinforced with extra gold
Antique finished engraving
with leather strap
(*Strap* 64,
With gold filled Guild band, as illustrated,

$225-250

17 jewel PRECISION movement
14k Solid green gold case
(*Strap* 12,

$75-85

15 jewel PRECISION movement
14k White gold filled case
reinforced with extra gold
Antique finished engraving
☆
(*Strap* 97,

7 Features — —

distinguish the new Gruen Quadron —
No other man's wrist watch has them all

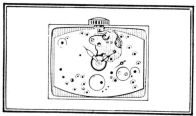

1 *New Rectangular Movement*

Instead of the usual round construction, this new rectangular movement fills out the entire case space, allowing larger and stronger parts.

2 *Curved to Fit the Wrist*

Although carrying a straight glass, the case and strap hugs the arm.

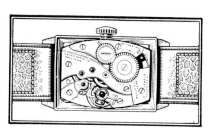

Dustproof Case Construction **4**

A collar on the winding stem employs the side of the case to give added strength and dust-tightness.

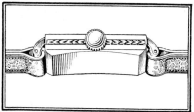

3 *Spring-locking Strap Pins*

No sewing required for the quick replacement of straps. Spring lock prevents accidental detachment.

The Gruen Precision Movement **6**

One of the world's finest watch movements and a feature of most of the new Quadrons. This *Precision* mark is the Guild's pledge of higher accuracy, finer quality and finish.

The Second-Hand **5**

A full length rectangular movement permits the second-hand at the proper position on the movement and dial, without extra parts.

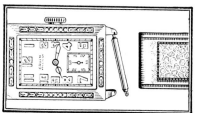

7 *Sweatproof Leather Strap*

Repels moisture, keeping strap neat.

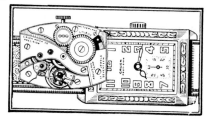

The New
GRUEN
QUADRON

The patented Gruen Quadron, with its *rugged rectangular movement which fills out the entire space within the case*, comes nearest to approaching pocket-watch time requirements in a timepiece for a man's wrist.

The *patented* Gruen Quadron possesses, in addition, *many distinguishing features not to be found in any other watch*. Every possible advantage has been incorporated to give the Quadron the ultimate in comfort, security and utility to please those men who admire fine things.

$250-275

Pat'd

17 jewel PRECISION movement
14k Solid white gold Crown-Guard case
(*Quad 58,*

$175-200

17 jewel PRECISION movement
14k Solid white gold Crown-Guard case
(*Quad 59,*

Sweatproof (Pat'd.)—Leather straps are used exclusively on all Gruen men's wrist watches.

GRUEN 1930 / 269

$275-315

17 jewel PRECISION movement
18k Solid white gold case
with radium or applied solid gold numeral
dial only
(*Quad 8,*

$275-315

17 jewel PRECISION movement
18k Solid white gold case
with radium or applied solid gold
numeral dial only
☆
(*Quad 11,*

$2,500-2,750

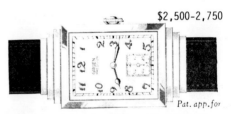

Pat. app. for

17 jewel PRECISION movement, gold finished and hand engraved in the old Guild manner
18k Solid white and green gold case with radium or applied solid gold numeral dial only
(*Quad 61,*

$325-365

Pat'd

15 jewel movement
14k Solid gold case,
(*Quad 16 Green*) ☆☆ (*Quad 17 White*)

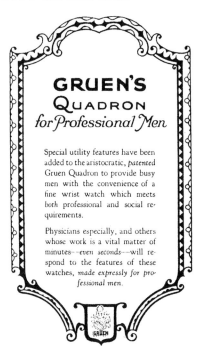

GRUEN'S
QUADRON
for Professional Men

Special utility features have been
added to the aristocratic, *patented*
Gruen Quadron to provide busy
men with the convenience of a
fine wrist watch which meets
both professional and social requirements.

Physicians especially, and others
whose work is a vital matter of
minutes--*even seconds*--will re-
spond to the features of these
watches, *made expressly for professional men.*

$300-340

17 jewel PRECISION movement
with extra large second-hand.
14k Solid white or green gold
case with strap and Gruen
Expanding Buckle,
(*Quad E39 Green*)
(*Quad E40 White*)

$500-550

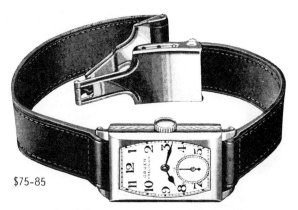

$75-85

17 jewel PRECISION movement with extra large
second-hand. 14k White gold filled case,
reinforced with extra gold, fitted with a strap
and Gruen Expanding Buckle for slipping the
watch to the upper arm when hands must be
free
☆
(*Quad E6,*

17 jewel PRECISION movement
with extra large second-hand.
18k Solid white gold case engraved and enameled, fitted
with strap and Gruen Ex-
panding Buckle
(*Quad E52,*

Gruen Quadrons

$300-355

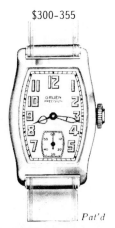

Pat'd

17 jewel PRECISION movement
14k Solid gold case
with leather strap,
(Quad 39, Green)   (Quad 40, White)
With gold filled Ben-Hur band, as
illustrated,

$95-110

15 jewel movement
14k Gold filled Crown-Guard case
reinforced with extra gold,
(Quad 64, White) ☆ (Quad 70, Green)
With gold filled link band,
as illustrated,

$275-300

17 jewel PRECISION movement
14k Solid green gold case
(Quad 77

$75-85

15 jewel movement
14k Gold filled case
reinforced with extra gold,
(Quad 68, Green) ☆☆ (Quad 69, White)
With gold filled woven band,
as illustrated,

Gruen Quadrons

$225-250

Pat'd

17 jewel PRECISION movement
14k Solid gold Crown-Guard case,
☆☆
(Quad 35, White)   (Quad 41, Green)

$125-140

17 jewel PRECISION movement
14k Gold filled case
reinforced with extra gold
Antique finished engraving,
☆☆
(Quad 21, White)   (Quad 65, Coin)

$70-80

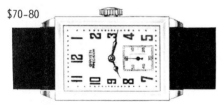

17 jewel PRECISION movement
14k Gold filled case
reinforced with extra gold
☆(Quad 15,

$95-110

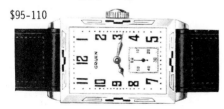

15 jewel movement
14k Gold filled case
reinforced with extra gold
Antique finished engraving,
☆
(Quad 79, Green)   (Quad 80, White)

$275-310

Pat'd

14k Solid white gold engraved and
antique finished Crown-Guard case
with gold filled mesh bracelet
(Quad 36 Mesh,

$75-85

15 jewel movement
14k Gold filled Crown-Guard case
reinforced with extra gold,
(Quad 63, White) ☆☆ (Quad 81, Coin)

$85-100

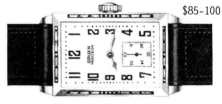

17 jewel PRECISION movement
14k Gold filled case
reinforced with extra gold
Antique finished engraving,
(Quad 47, Green)   (Quad 48, White)

$70-80

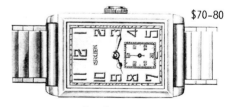

15 jewel movement
14k Gold filled case
reinforced with extra gold
with leather strap,
(Quad 37, Green) ☆☆ (Quad 38, White)
With gold filled Guild band, as
illustrated,

$450-500

17 jewel PRECISION movement
14k Solid white gold case
with leather strap

(Quad 67 White)
(Quad 76 Green)
With gold filled mesh band, as illustrated,

Pat. app. for

14KYG $500-550
With 14KP Band
⊥ $550-610 ⊥

17 jewel PRECISION movement
14k Solid gold case, with leather strap,
☆
(Quad 60, White)
(Quad 66, Coin)
With gold filled Guild band, as illustrated,

Pat. app. for

GRUEN
QUADRON

$375-425

17 jewel PRECISION movement
14k Solid gold case,

Engraved in antique finish
(Quad 50 Green)
(Quad 28 White)

Pat'd

$650-725

17 jewel PRECISION movement
18k Solid white gold case
Engraved in antique finish and inlaid in black enamel
(Quad 52, $125)

Pat'd

$325-365

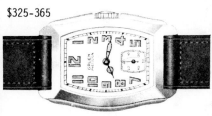

17 jewel PRECISION movement
18k Solid white gold Crown-Guard case
(Quad 51,

$350-380

15 jewel movement
14k Solid white gold case
☆
(Quad 23,

Pat'd

The
GRUEN
TECHNI-QUADRON

Ever striving for improvement and perfection, the Guild has produced a new type of wrist watch designed to serve the professional needs of technicians, doctors and other men who require exact time in seconds.

In this new Techni-Quadron the convenience and style of a smart wrist watch are combined with quick, accurate time reading features which assures a welcome for this watch from any man whose daily work demands constant, precise time.

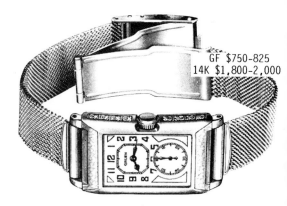

GF $750-825
14K $1,800-2,000

15 jewel movement
14k Gold filled Crown-Guard case,
reinforced with extra gold
Gold filled mesh band
(Quad 74 Mesh,

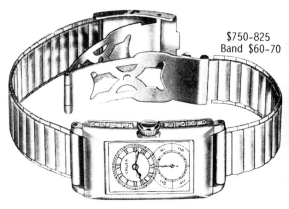

$750-825
Band $60-70

15 jewel movement
14k Gold filled Crown-Guard case,
reinforced with extra gold
Gold filled Guild band
(Quad 73 Guild,

$750-825
Band $45-55

15 jewel movement
14k Gold filled Crown-Guard case,
reinforced with extra gold,
☆☆
(Quad 72 Green)
(Quad 73 White)
14k Solid gold case
(Quad 75

$750-825

15 jewel movement
14k Gold filled Crown-Guard case,
reinforced with extra gold
(Quad 74,

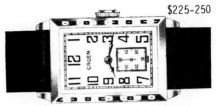

$225-250

15 jewel Quadron movement
14k White gold filled case
reinforced with extra gold
Inlaid with white and black enamel
(Quad 55,

$175-200

15 jewel movement
14k White gold filled case
reinforced with extra gold
Inlaid with white and black enamel
(Strap 102,

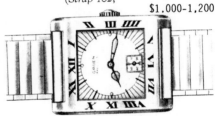

$1,000-1,200

The Centurion

17 jewel PRECISION movement
14k Solid gold case with numerals on
bezel and inlaid with hard black enamel
with leather strap,
(Strap 131, White)   (Strap 132, Coin)
With gold filled Guild band
as illustrated,

Gay
GRUEN
SPORT WATCHES
for men

The newest thing in men's
wrist watches — serious time-
keepers—brightened with the
smile of modern color-enamel
inlays.

Especially suitable for vacation
wear or travel, but quite as
desirable for every-day use by
the man who finds time for
cheerfulness in his day's work.

$175-200

15 jewel movement
14k White gold filled case
reinforced with extra gold
Inlaid with red and black enamel

(Strap 101,

$200-225

15 jewel movement
14k White gold filled case
reinforced with extra gold
Inlaid with green enamel

(Strap 103,

NOTE: *This Gruen catalog was
prepared for a German Exhibition in
1930, and has a large number of case
styles.*
*These case styles and prices would be
about the same for a similar watch
made by Bulova, Elgin, Waltham,
Illinois and Hamilton, and could be
effective for a time span of 1925 - 1935.*

GRUEN
SPORT WATCHES
for men

$225-250

A SPECIAL THANKS TO:
Joseph Conway
Newton, MA
for the use of his Gruen
wrist watch library.

$250-285

15 jewel Quadron movement
14k White gold filled case
reinforced with extra gold
Inlaid with red and black enamel
(*Quad* 56,

15 jewel Quadron movement
14k White gold filled case
reinforced with extra gold
Inlaid with black and green enamel
(*Quad* 54,

$300-350

$350-375

15 jewel PRECISION movement
14k Gold filled case
with numerals on bezel,
(*Strap* 138 White)   (*Strap* 139 Coin)

15 jewel movement
Nickel Tarnish Proof case
with numerals on bezel
☆(*Strap* 158,

$475-525

17 jewel PRECISION movement
14k Solid, combination white and green
gold Crown-Guard case
(Tank 18,

The famous
GRUEN
TANK

This good looking man's wrist watch has earned well merited distinction. It combines practical features with an attractive appearance.

In addition to its 17 jewel Precision movement, which assures greater accuracy and longer life, the patented case construction provides for the strap connections as part of the case itself.

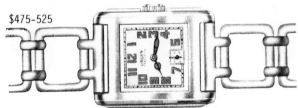

$475-525

17 jewel PRECISION movement
14k Solid, combination white and green
gold Crown-Guard case, with gold filled
link band
(Tank 18 Flex 26,

$225-250

17 jewel PRECISION movement
14k Solid gold case,
with leather strap,

☆
(Tank 4 Green)   (Tank 6 White)
With gold filled Guild band
as illustrated,

$225-250
Band $25-35

17 jewel PRECISION movement
14k Solid white gold case, with gold filled
Ben-Hur band,
(Tank 4 Ben-Hur Green)
(Tank 6 Ben-Hur White)

GRUEN'S
Sweep Second-Hand Strap Watches

$45-55

15 jewel movement with sweep second-
hand. 14k gold filled case, reinforced
with extra gold,
Black figure or radium dial

$150-175

15 jewel movement with sweep second-
hand. 14k Solid green gold case
Radium dial only
(*Strap 17,*

TANK

$75-85

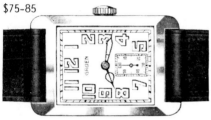

The Imperial Tank
15 jewel movement
14k Gold filled case
reinforced with extra gold,
(*Tank 19 White*)   (*Tank 21 Green*)
With 17 jewel movement

(*Tank 24 White*) ☆ (*Tank 25 Green*)

$325-375

The Imperial Tank
15 jewel movement
14k Solid gold case
Antique finished engraving,
(*Tank 23 White*)
17 jewel movement,
(*Tank 27 White*)

$375-435

17 jewel PRECISION movement
18k Solid gold case
Antique finished engraving
(*Tank 13 White,*

$250-300

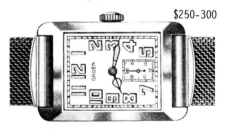

The Imperial Tank
15 jewel movement
14k solid gold case
with leather strap,
☆ (*Tank 22 White*)
With gold filled mesh band
as illustrated,
17 jewel movement
with leather strap,
(*Tank 26 White*)
With gold filled mesh band
as illustrated,

GRUEN

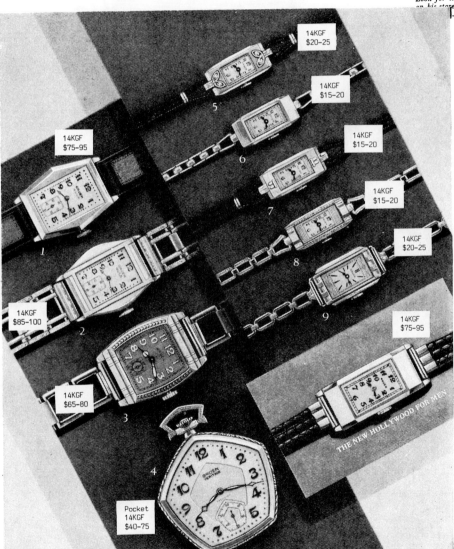

14KGF $20–25

14KGF $15–20

14KGF $15–20

14KGF $15–20

14KGF $75–95

14KGF $20–25

14KGF $85–100

14KGF $75–95

14KGF $65–80

Pocket 14KGF $40–75

THE NEW HOLLYWOOD FOR MEN

1. **Croydon,** a very modern watch that will give years of faithful Gruen service at the low cost of **$25.**

2. **Savoy,** a sturdy model any man will be proud to wear—**$18.75.**

3. **Brewster,** unusual value in a fine 15-jewel Gruen—**$29.75.**

4. **Pentagon VeriThin,** "America's Preferred Presentation Watch," 17-jewel *Precision* movement—**$75.**

5. **Tuxedo,** one of Gruen's timekeeping baguettes, set with four fine diamonds —**$49.75.**

6. **Vernon,** one of the most attractively designed Gruen baguettes at the moderate price of **$37.50.**

7. **Stoneleigh,** a slender baguette (no wider than a cigarette) most modestly priced at **$32.50.**

8. **Smithfield,** an outstanding example of the fine line of baguettes crafted by Gruen—**$42.50.**

9. **Beverly,** remarkable value in a Gruen, promising enduring style and timekeeping excellence—**$23.85.**

Hollywood, a new streamline model curved to the wrist, for the modern young man. Braided leather band— **$39.75.**

14KGF
$20-30

11

14KGF
$20-30

10

14KGF
$30-40

9

THE WATCH THAT TELLS SO

GIVE

THE PRECISION® WATC

8

14KYG $100-125
14KWG $90-110

7

14KGF
$20-30

6

14KGF
$30-40

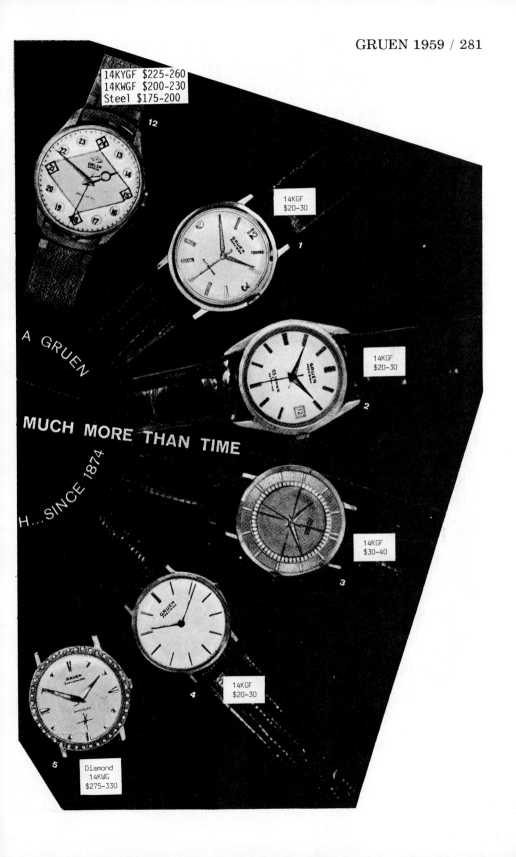

14KYGF $225-260
14KWGF $200-230
Steel $175-200

14KGF
$20-30

14KGF
$20-30

14KGF
$30-40

14KGF
$20-30

Diamond
14KWG
$275-330

A GRUEN

MUCH MORE THAN TIME

H...SINCE 1874

THE NEW GRUEN VERI-THIN
At Gruen Jewelers Only..$29⁷⁵ up

IT IS EASY to see that the new Gruen Veri-Thin, with its amazing streamline thinness, is a radically new *idea* in wristwatch design.

The radical new Gruen Veri-Thin movement is 50% thinner at sides and ends to fit the spherical arc of the case—yet working parts are *full-sized* for pocket-watch accuracy! Heretofore called "impossible," this new Gruen Veri-Thin movement is, we believe, the greatest advance in three hundred years of watch-making!

And Gruen has done this, not in a luxury watch, but in a wristwatch priced where every man can own one. See it today—at Gruen Jewelers only—from $29.75 up. Other Gruen watches from $24.75 to $250; with precious stones, up to $2500. Write for folder.

THE GRUEN WATCH COMPANY, TIME HILL, CINCINNATI, O., U. S. A. IN CANADA: TORONTO, ONTARIO

VERI-THIN PHANTOM, 15 jewels, yellow gold-filled case, Guildite back, with either black or silver dial $29.75

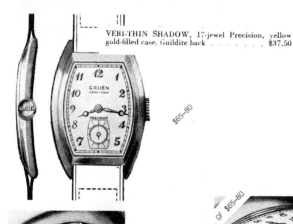

VERI-THIN SHADOW, 17-jewel Precision, yellow gold-filled case, Guildite back $37.50

HERE'S HOW IT'S MADE

This life-size diagram shows how the full-size, rugged working parts of the Veri-Thin movements are brilliantly arranged to fit completely within the thin, curved case without sacrificing accuracy or dependability. By this ingenious arrangement of the wheel-train, it is possible to slope the case downward on both ends and sides for extreme thinness and streamlined styling.

*REG. U. S. PATENT OFFICE
PATENTS PENDING

Copyright 1939, The Gruen Watch Company

VERI-THIN MERCURY, 17-jewel Precision, yellow gold-filled case $37.50

VERI-THIN BLADE, 15 jewels, yellow gold-filled case, Guildite back, matching flex band . $39.75

VERI-THIN TAPERFLOW, 17-JEWEL PRECISION, YELLOW GOLD-FILLED CASE, GUILDITE BACK . . . $33.75

Gubelin
25J-Ipsomatic-Swiss-1954
Moonphase triple calendar
Watertite-Self-winding
Stainless Steel Head $1,500-1,700
14KYG Top $1,700-1,900
18KYG Head $3,000-3,500

Gubelin
25J-Ipsomatic-Swiss-1954
Moonphase triple calendar
Self-winding
Stainless Steel Head $900-1,000
14KYG Head $1,250-1,500
18KYG Head $2,000-2,200

Gubelin
15J-Swiss-1954
14KYG Head $1,200-1,350
18KYG Head $1,500-1,650

Gubelin
25J-Ispomatic-Swiss-1954
Moonphase triple calendar
Self-winding
80 Micron Gold Plate $1,500-1,700
14KYG Top $2,200-2,500
14KYG Head $4,500-5,000
18KYG Head $5,000-5,500

Gubelin
15J-Swiss-1954
18KYG Head $2,000-2,200

Gubelin
17J-Swiss-1954
Stainless Steel $125-150
18KYG Head $250-300

A SPECIAL THANKS TO:
Ronald "Ron" & Pat Starnes
Tulsa, OK
for the use of his Wrist
Watch research.

Gubelin
Triple Chronograph-1954
17J-Swiss-Non-Magnetic-Waterlite
(Not waterlite head) $600-675
Stainless Steel $1,000-1,200
18KYG Head $3,500-4,000

Gubelin
17J-Swiss-1954
18KYG Head $375-425

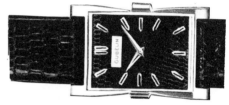

Gubelin
15J-Swiss-1954
18KYG Head $1,750-1,950

Gubelin
17J-Alarm-Swiss-1954
Waterlite
Stainless Steel Head $200-225
14KYG Top $250-300
18KYG Head $950-1,150

Gubelin
17J-Swiss-1954
Stainless Steel Head $110-125
18KYG Head $325-375

Gubelin
15J-Swiss-1954
14KYG Head $400-450
18KYG Head $450-500

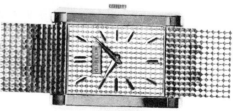

Gubelin
15J-Swiss-1954
18KG Bracelet Only $300-350
18KYG Head $450-500

Gubelin
21J-Swiss-1954
Self-winding
18KYG Head $375-425

Gubelin
25J-Ipsomatic-Swiss-1954
Self-winding-Waterlite
18KYG $700-775

Gubelin
18J-Swiss-1954
Very flat
Stainless steel head $75-85
18KYG Head $150-175

Gubelin
25J-Ipsomatic-1954
Self-winding-Waterlite
Stainless steel head $125-150
14KYG Top $150-175
18KYG Head $250-275

Gubelin
15J-Swiss-1954
Very flat-Waterlite
Stainless steel head $100-120
18KYG Head $225-250

Gubelin
17J-Swiss-1954
Waterlite
14KYG Head $200-225
18KYG Head $225-250

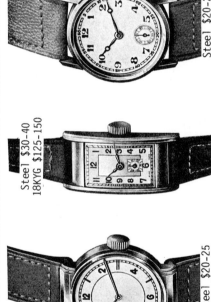

14KGF $40-50
Steel $25-35

14KGF $30-40
Steel $15-25

14KGF $55-75
Steel $40-50

14KGF $50-70
Steel $35-45

14KGF $40-50
Steel $25-35

STAND Parterre

14KGF $65-85
Steel $40-50

Hafis Jarproof Watches open up a **new Sales opportunity**, as the watch built to stand rough usage, with a style of its own, and a reputation for reliability and close timing. Our new calipers are masters of modern watchmaking. Sole selling rights for various markets available. Write for particulars to the manufacturers,

F. SUTER & Co,
HAFIS WATCH Co
BIENNE (SWITZERLAND)

HAMILTON WATCH COMPANY
Lancaster, Pa. U.S.A.
1893 to 1983

The Hamilton product catalog of 1911 does not show any wrist watches available at that time. The smallest pocket watch movement offered was 0 size, 17 jewel, and we have seen wrist watches made with round, converted pocket watch-style cases, with convertible or detachable bands. At this time, Hamilton was selling uncased 0 size movements, and in 1913, 6/0 size movements to the trade. The first Hamilton wrist watch to appear in their product catalog was a 6/0 size, 17 jewel, Grade 986, shown in the first illustration below. Hamilton went on to produce a long and varied line of case styles until they ceased U.S.A. production (in the 1960's) then used the Hamilton name on Swiss-made movements. Hamilton was a company of many firsts, including electric watches and the Computer Pulsar. They made fine watch movements and are considered by collectors to be the "Patek Philippe" of American wrist watch makers.

EA 325　　　　　　　Hamilton Watch Co.
0 Size—Hunting—Nickel
Model 1—Pendant Set—Bridge

Note: EA Numbers were taken from American Pocket Watches Identification and Price Guide Begining to End, by Ehrhardt-Meggers 1987, Advertised on a page in the back of this book.

EA 326　　　　　　　Hamilton Watch Co.
0 Size—Hunting—Nickel
Model 2—Pendant Set—Winding Wheels

HAMILTON WATCH COMPANY
1893 — 1948

Serial No.	Grade	Date	Serial No.	Grade	Date
1	936	1893	3,056,001	902	1926-28
2,000	7J	1894	3,100,001	916	1923-28
6,801	932	1894	3,135,001	918	1928-36
14,001	999	1895	3,200,001	912	1924-36
15,701	939	1900	4,025,301	987E	1928-37
20,501	999E	1896	A001	980B	1937-46
23,301	11J	1903	1B-001	999	1943-54
25,001	11J	1896-99	2B-001	999B	1943
30,001	11J	1896	2B-701	950B	1943
50,001	962	1896	C001	992B	1940-54
55,601	969	1898	E001	989	1928-36
70,001	976	1901	F101	995	1931-39
80,001	972	1902	G101	980	1934-51
104,001	940	1899	H1001	400	1929-32
150,001	924	1901	H50001	401	1930-33
200,001	926	1902	J1001	982	1935-51
400,001	924	1904	L101	997	1936-41
501,001	926	1906	M001	982M	1941-51
601,001	926	1908	N001	721	1939-49
710,001	993	1908	001	987	1937-48
900,001	940	1911	R001	923	1937-49
1,000,001	972	1913	S001	950B	1941-53
1,079,001	992L	1914	SS001	987S	1940-48
1,156,001	996L	1915	T001	911	1938-50
1,305,001	956P	1918	V001	911M	1941-50
1,648,001	992L	1924	X001	917	1936-54
1,831,001	920	1918	HWR001	H917	1938
1,882,901	900	1921-22	Y001	747	1947-54
2,000,001	988	1913-17	CY001	748	1948-54
1,989,001	194	1923	001A	750	1949-54
2,035,001	981	1919-23	001C	751	1950-54
2,327,001	992L	1925	001E	752	1951-54
2,538,001	974L	1929	001F	753	1951-54
2,567,001	992L	1930	001H	754	1952-54
2,611,001	950	1936	001K	756	1954
2,581,001	992E	1930-40	HW001	H980	1942-49
2,611,401	950E	1937	W001	980I	1942-48
3,000,001	922	1924-36			

EA 326A　　　　　　　Hamilton Watch Co.
0 Size—Hunting—Nickel
Model 3*—Pendant Set—¾ Plate

6/0 SIZE

GRADE 986

Open face, ¾ plate movt.
17 jewels, double roller

GRADE 986A

Open face, ¾ plate movt.,
17 jewels, double roller

GRADE 987

Hunting, ¾ plate movt.,
17 jewels, double roller

GRADE 987A

Hunting, ¾ plate movt.,
17 jewels, double roller

GRADE 987S

Hunting, ¾ plate movt.,
17 jewels, double roller

GRADE 979

Hunting, ¾ plate movt.,
19 jewels, double roller

8/0 SIZE

GRADE 747

Hunting, ¾ plate movt.,
17 jewels, double roller

GRADE 748
(one piece barrel bridge)

Hunting, ¾ plate movt.,
18 jewels, double roller,
direct drive center
seconds

GRADE 748
(two piece barrel bridge)

Hunting, ¾ plate movt.,
18 jewels, double roller.
direct drive center
seconds

12/0 SIZE

GRADE 752

Hunting, ¾ plate movt.
17 jewels, double roller

GRADE 753

Hunting, ¾ plate movt..
19 jewels, double roller

GRADE 754

Hunting, ¾ plate movt..
19 jewels, double roller

14/0 SIZE

GRADE 980
Open face, ¾ plate movt.,
17 jewels, double roller

GRADE 982
Open face, ¾ plate movt.,
19 jewels, double roller

GRADE 982M
Open face, ¾ plate movt.,
19 jewels, double roller

18/0 SIZE

GRADE 989
Open face, ¾ plate movt.,
17 jewels, double roller

21/0 SIZE

GRADE 995
Open face, ¾ plate movt.,
17 jewels, double roller

GRADE 721
Open face, ¾ plate movt.,
17 jewels, double roller

GRADE 750
Open face, ¾ plate movt.,
17 jewels, double roller

GRADE 751
Open face, ¾ plate movt.,
17 jewels, double roller

*Wrist watch movements smaller than 0 size
are not collected unless they are in a nice
case. Some of the Hamilton small size are
illustrated on this page and have a value of
$1—25, depending on the buyer.*

20/0 SIZE

GRADE 997
Open face, ¾ plate movt.,
17 jewels, double roller

*NOTE: There are many Swiss Contract
movements made for Hamilton that
are not shown in this book.*

22/0 SIZE

GRADE 911
Open face, ¾ plate movt.,
17 jewels, double roller

GRADE 911M
Open face, ¾ plate movt.,
17 jewels, double roller

BLADE
10K w/y GF.
$89.50

$75-95

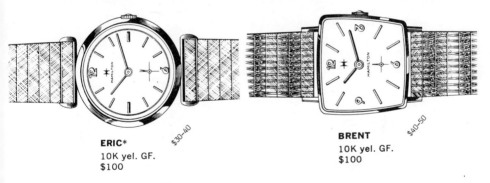

MEN'S MEDALLION WATCHES

- **22 JEWELS** - **HAND-APPLIED 14K GOLD NUMERALS AND MARKERS**
- **SHOCK-RESISTANT** - **ANTI-MAGNETIC**
- **UNBREAKABLE DYNAVAR MAINSPRING** - **FULLY ADJUSTED**

ERIC*
10K yel. GF.
$100

$30-40

BRENT
10K yel. GF.
$100

$40-50

* *Weatherproof (Waterproof-Dustproof with seals intact.)*

TRENT
10K w/y GF/ ssb,
alt. black dial.
Bracelet, $89.50
Strap, $79.50

$60-80

SEATON*
10K yél. GF, grey dial
rim, grey suede strap.
$89.50

$25-35

HAMILTON

MEN'S MEDALLION WATCHES

- 22 JEWELS • HAND-APPLIED 14K GOLD NUMERALS AND MARKERS
- FULLY ADJUSTED • SHOCK-RESISTANT • ANTI-MAGNETIC
- LIFETIME UNBREAKABLE DYNAVAR MAINSPRING • WEATHERPROOF MODELS

(Waterproof-dustproof with seals int

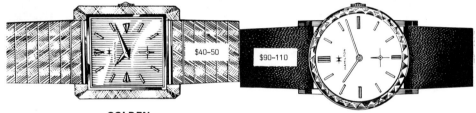

GOLDEN TEMPO "N"

10K yellow multi-color gold-filled case and bracelet.
Bracelet . $100.00

$40–50

ELLIOTT

14K yellow gold case, faceted crystal.
Strap . . . $125.00

$90–110

$125.00 to $85.00

$35–45

LINDSAY

10K yellow gold-filled case.
Bracelet . . $95.00

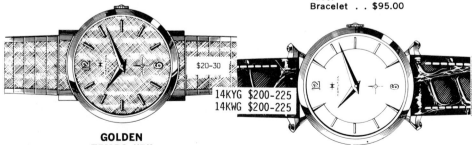

$20–30

14KYG $200–225
14KWG $200–225

GOLDEN TEMPO "R"

10K yellow gold-filled case with multi-color dial and bracelet.
Bracelet . $100.00

SIR ECHO

14K yellow or white gold case.
Strap . . . $125.00

FINE WATCHES

□ 17 JEWELS □ SHOCK-RESISTANT
□ ANTI-MAGNETIC □ UNBREAKABLE MAINSPRING

Waterproof (Waterproof-Dustproof with seals intact.)

$30-40

$30-40

$20-30

BOATSWAIN III*
10k yel. RGP/ssb.
$69.50

GALEN
10k yel. RGP/ssb.
$59.95

DATELINE S-575*
Calendar
SS case.
Bracelet, $59.95
Strap, $55

$25-35

SEA RANGER II*
10k yel. RGP/ssb.
Bracelet, $59.95
Strap, $49.95

FIRST MATE*
10k yel. RGP/ssb.
White or gold dial
Bracelet, $65
Strap, $55

$20-30

$30-40

VINCENT
10k yel. RGP/ssb.
$65

SEA BREEZE II*
10k yel. RGP/ssb.
$65

$20-30

SEA MATE II*
10k yel. RGP/ssb.
alt. black dial.
Bracelet, $59.95
Strap, $49.95

$20-30

THINLINE WATCHES

☐ ULTRA-THIN CASE DESIGNS ☐ 17 JEWELS
☐ SHOCK-RESISTANT ☐ ANTI-MAGNETIC
☐ UNBREAKABLE MAINSPRING

Weatherproof

$90-110

THINLINE 2024
14k yel. gold.
$150

$100-125

THINLINE 2019
14k w/y gold.
$175

$90-110

THINLINE 2017
14k w/y gold.
$150

$100-125

THINLINE 2021
14k yel. gold.
$175

$90-110

$100-125

THINLINE 2023
14k yel. gold.
$175

THINLINE 2022*
14k yel. gold.
$120

$90-110

$100-125

THINLINE 2025
14k yel. gold.
$160

THINLINE 2016*
14k yel. gold.
$120

$100-125

$90-110

THINLINE 2020
14k yel. gold.
$160

THINLINE 4007*
10k yel. GF.
$69.50

MEN'S SELF-WINDING WATCHES

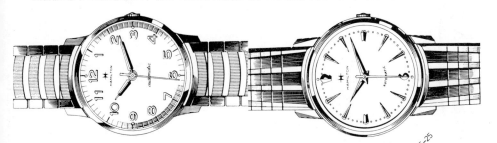

**ACCUMATIC
A-502**

Stainless steel case.
Bracelet . . $59.95
Strap $55.00

**ACCUMATIC
A-500**

Stainless steel case.
Bracelet . . $65.00
Strap $59.95

$15-25

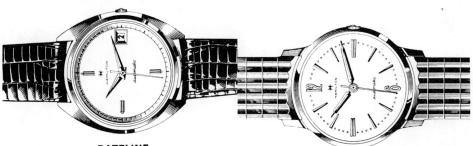

**DATELINE
A-576**
Calendar

Stainless steel case
and bracelet.
Bracelet . . $75.00
Strap $69.50

$15-25

**ACCUMATIC
A-503**

Stainless steel case.
Bracelet . . $59.95
Strap $55.00

$15-25

**ACCUMATIC
A-652**

10K yellow rolled
gold plate case,
stainless steel back,
alternate full nu-
meral dial.
Bracelet . . $75.00
Strap $65.00

$20-30

**THIN-O-MATIC
T-452**

10K yellow gold-filled
case, stainless steel
back.
Bracelet . . $89.50
Strap $79.50

$15-25

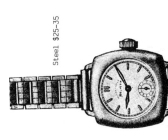

Forme A   Forme B   Forme C

The 13 lig. Wrist chronograph

lever movement, 17 jewels. 1st quality, Breguet hairspring, cut balance.
1/5 of seconds, recording 0—30 minutes.

The 16 lig. Wrist-Chronograph "B" quality

lever movement, 15 jewels, Breguet hairspring.

Ref. 420

13 lig. Wrist Timer

Ref. 351—354

lever movement, 7 jewels, stop on the balance system.
1/5th of seconds, recording 0—30 minutes.

permettent à la fabrique de chronographes et compteurs de sport

Ed. Heuer & Co., à Bienne

de vous livrer ses spécialités de haute précision aux prix du jour.

Réf. 351 C/N.

\$150-175

Réf. 358.

\$175-200

Réf. 2403/2/J.✕F.

\$400-450

Réf. 2403/2/H✕E.

\$375-425

For pilots, drivers, and divers.

Ideal for the man on the go. Superpressurized to work 50,000 feet in the air or 330 feet under the water. With silver or black dial, tachymeter outer rim or rotating minute/hour bezel for calculating time zone changes, remaining oxygen time, and so on. The luminous dial is exceptionally bright, for night flying and underwater use.

AUTAVIA TACHY
Model 1163 T
$ 215 (Corfam strap)
$ 230 (Steel bracelet)

AUTAVIA MH
Model 1163 MH
$ 215 (Corfam strap)
$ 230 (Steel bracelet)

Rotating bezel

The rotating outer bezel of the Autavia MH allows instant comparisons between time zones, elapsed and remaining oxygen time, or transit and departure times. A click-stop safety device prevents settings from being accidentally changed.

1. Time study

How efficient are your workers – and their machines? For that matter, are you operating at peak efficiency?

2. Racing

Check lap times, pit stops, elapsed time, or the lead one driver has over another. Keep track of time between check points in auto rallies.

3. Coaching

The coach can never leave his stop-watch home – it stays right on his wrist. (And the swimming coach can even wear his HEUER Automatic in the pool).

4. Ice Hockey

Keep track of penalty times – how much longer will your favorite player have to warm the penalty bench?

The Heuer Automatic Chronograph: a totally new type of watch!

Self-winding, with automatic 31-day calendar and 12-hour stop watch. A revolutionary development of Swiss watchmaking science. Elegance. Ruggedness. Precision.

Solid 18-carat gold case. Gold hour bars and luminous points, against silver-plated or champagne dial. Tachymeter graduations around outer edge. Water-resistant.

A sporting watch in formal dress.

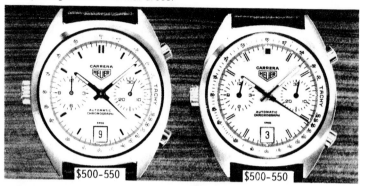

CARRERA Gold 18 ct.
Model 1158 S
$ 550 (Corfam strap)

CARRERA Gold 18 ct.
Model 1158 CH
$ 550 (Corfam strap)

Two "Carrera" models with stainless cases. Silver-plated or charcoal dial, with hour bars and luminous points. Tachymeter graduation for measuring average speeds. Semi-recessed press buttons. Water-resistant.

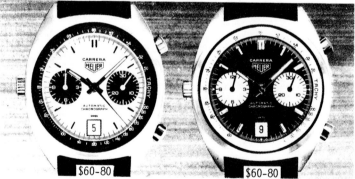

CARRERA Stainless Steel
Model 1153 S
$ 195 (Corfam strap)
$ 210 (Steel bracelet)

CARRERA Stainless Steel
Model 1153 N
$ 195 (Corfam strap)
$ 210 (Steel bracelet)

Tachymeter scale

The tachymeter scale on the Carrera and Autavia T automatically calculates miles per hour over a measured mile, kilometers per hour over a measured kilometer, or even units-per-hour of production capacity.

The scale can be read directly when one mile, kilometer or other unit is timed; for shorter distances, the dial indication must be multiplied by the fraction involved (e.g., for half a measured mile, read one-half the scale value), and for multiple units, the indication must be multiplied by the number of units measured.

How to use your Heuer Automatic Chronograph

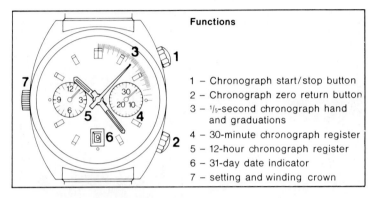

Functions

1 – Chronograph start/stop button
2 – Chronograph zero return button
3 – 1/5-second chronograph hand and graduations
4 – 30-minute chronograph register
5 – 12-hour chronograph register
6 – 31-day date indicator
7 – setting and winding crown

To time a continuous process:

● When whatever you're timing – say, an auto trip begins – press button 1. The large second hand (3) starts advancing 1/5 second at a time (3).

As it completes each full revolution, the hand on the small minute register dial (4) springs forward one minute. After 30 minutes, the hand on the 12-hour register (5) springs forward to register the first half hour.

At your destination, stop the chronograph by pressing button 1 again. Now you can read off your total time: 3 hours (dial 5), 22 minutes (dial 4), 35-2/5 seconds (dial 3).

To return the chronograph dials to zero again, just press button 2.

To time an intermittent process.

● If you want to know how much time during your auto trip you actually spend on the road, the process is only a little different.

Start timing as before with button 1. But press button 1 again at your first rest stop, to interrupt the timing. When you start off again, press button 1 once more, and timing will begin again from where it stopped.

Repeat this at every stop until you reach your destination. Since the timer was only operating this time while you actually drove, the total time will be somewhat shorter – perhaps only 2 hours, 18 minutes and 39-2/5 seconds. Divide your total mileage by this figure, and you'll know your average rate of speed.

Once you've read your total timing from the registers, you can return them once again to zero by pressing button 2.

Timing and time-keeping are independent.

The regular hour and minute hands run independently of the chronograph timer mechanism. You can time as many events as you like without affecting the accuracy of watch's normal time-keeping functions.

And, of course, you never have to wind your watch as long as you are wearing it – your normal wrist and arm movements will wind it for you. (That's why we put the winding crown on the left; it's practically superfluous).

Technical information

"Sunken rotor" automatic winding

The self-winding rotor of the HEUER automatic chronograph is a proven and patented design that allows the case to be conveniently and elegantly slim without cramping the watch and timing movements.

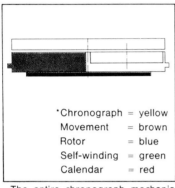

*Chronograph = yellow
Movement   = brown
Rotor   = blue
Self-winding = green
Calendar   = red

The entire chronograph mechanism is only 3 mm high, and is fastened to the time-keeping movement by only 3 screws.

Revolutionary new mechanism

The counter mechanisms form a separate unit, mounted and tested independently of the watch movement. This simplifies both production and maintenance, helping to assure years of reliability.

The watch movement itself

Precision movement with jeweled lever escapement, 17 jewels, "Incabloc" shock protection, unbreakable mainspring. Power reserve at least 40 hours.

Case and dial

All HEUER chronographs have water-resistant and dust-proof cases to meet US Government Test for Water Resistance. Modern luminous dials with $1/5$-second graduations and sculptured hour bars. Corfam or steel watch bands.

Initial winding

If the watch is not worn for more than 40 hours, it must be wound, like any other watch. Unless you are left-handed, this is most convenient when the watch is turned so that its winding crown is at the right. Turn it 4 or 5 turns in the direction of the date window to start it. Then put it on – your normal arm and wrist movements will keep it wound thereafter.

Setting the date

To change or set the date, pull out the crown and turn the hour hand back from 12 to 11 o'clock, then turn it forward again to 12:00 repeating until the correct date is set. The date will automatically jump forward one day every other time the hand passes 12.

34W24. 7 Jewels. **$17.00**
Leather Strap
Yellow rolled gold plate, stainless steel back case, raised numeral dial. Heavy flat crystal.

34W22. 17 Jewels. **$22.00**
Leather Strap.
34W23. 7 Jewels. **$16.50**
Leather Strap.
Yellow rolled gold plate, stainless steel back case, raised numeral dial.

34W1. 17 Jewels. **$39.50**
G.F. Expansion Bracelet.
34W2. 17 Jewels. **$29.50**
Leather Strap.
Yellow gold filled case, Incabloc movement, high flat crystal, raised numeral dial.

34W3. 17 Jewels. **$31.50**
G.F. Expansion Bracelet.
34W4. 17 Jewels. **$27.00**
Leather Strap.
Yellow rolled gold plate, stainless steel back case, Incabloc movement, high curved crystal, raised numeral dial.

34W26. 7 Jewels. **$19.00**
Yellow rolled gold plate, stainless steel back case, high crystal, raised figure dial, quality leather strap.

34W27. 7 Jewels. **$19.00**
Yellow rolled gold plate, stainless steel back case, high crystal, raised figure dial, quality leather strap.

34W11. 17 Jewels. **$26.00**
Leather Strap.
Yellow rolled gold plate, stainless steel back case, raised numeral dial, 4 facet crystal.

34W12. 17 Jewels. **$26.00**
G.F. Expansion Bracelet.
34W13. 17 Jewels. **$22.00**
Leather Strap
Yellow rolled gold plate, stainless steel back case, raised numeral dial.

Heyworth

34W5. 17 Jewels. **$31.50**
G.F. Expansion Bracelet.
34W6. 17 Jewels. **$27.00**
Leather Strap.
Yellow rolled gold
plate, stainless steel
back case, Incabloc
movement, high
curved crystal, raised
numeral dial.

34W7. 17 Jewels. **$26.00**
G.F. Expansion Bracelet.
34W8. 17 Jewels. **$22.00**
Leather Strap.
Yellow rolled gold
plate, stainless steel
back case, high curved
crystal, raised numer-
al dial.

34W9. 17 Jewels. **$26.00**
G.F. Expansion Bracelet.
34W10. 17 Jewels. **$22.00**
Leather Strap.
Yellow rolled gold
plate, stainless steel
back case, raised nu-
meral dial.

34W14. 17 Jewels. G.F. Expansion Bracelet **$26.00**
34W15. 17 Jewels. Leather Strap $22.00
34W16. 7 Jewels. Leather Strap $16.50
Yellow rolled gold plate, stainless steel
back case, raised numeral dial.

34W17. 17 Jewels. **$26.00**
G.F. Expansion Bracelet.
34W18. 17 Jewels. **$22.00**
Leather Strap.
Yellow rolled gold
plate, stainless steel
back case, high curved
crystal, raised numer-
al dial.

34W21. 17 Jewels $29.75
Yellow rolled gold plate, stainless steel
back case, fancy raised numeral and stick
dial, quality leather strap.

34W19. 17 Jewels. **$22.00**
Leather Strap
34W20. 7 Jewels. **$17.00**
Leather Strap
Yellow rolled gold
plate, stainless steel
back case, raised nu-
meral dial, high
curved crystal.

HEYWORTH

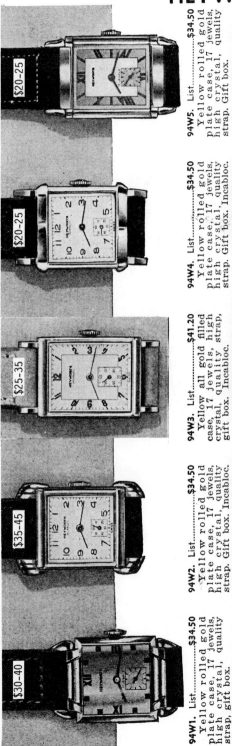

94W5. List..........**$34.50**
Yellow rolled gold plate case, 17 jewels, high crystal, quality strap. Gift box.

94W4. List..........**$34.50**
Yellow rolled gold plate case, 17 jewels, high crystal, quality strap. Gift box. Incabloc.

94W3. List..........**$41.20**
Yellow all gold filled case, 17 jewels, high crystal, quality strap, gift box. Incabloc.

94W2. List..........**$34.50**
Yellow rolled gold plate case, 17 jewels, high crystal, quality strap. Gift box. Incabloc.

94W1. List..........**$34.50**
Yellow rolled gold plate case, 17 jewels, high crystal, quality strap, gift box.

94W12. 17 jewels. List **$28.00**
94W13. 7 jewels. List **20.50**
Yellow rolled gold plate case, quality strap, gift box.

94W11. 17 jewels. List **$29.00**
Yellow rolled gold plate case, quality strap, gift box.

94W9. 17 jewels. List **$28.00**
94W10. 7 jewels. List **20.50**
Yellow rolled gold plate case, quality strap, gift box.

94W8. 17 jewels. List **$29.00**
Yellow rolled gold plate case, quality strap, gift box.

94W6. 17 jewels. List **$28.00**
94W7. 7 jewels. List **20.50**
Yellow rolled gold plate case, quality strap, gift box.

Watches shown ⅞ actual size.

$40-50

3003BR — (9¼″), 17 Jewel DRESS AUTOMATIC (360°), 10K Natural Goldfilled Case, Sweepsecond, Incabloc, with matching Goldfilled Expansion Bracelet $62.00

3006 — (9¼″), 17 Jewel DRESS AUTOMATIC (360°), 10K Natural Rolled Gold Plate Top, Steel Back, Sweepsecond, Incabloc $53.20

$20-25

$50-60

2099FH — 17 Jewel CHRONOGRAPH Service Watch, Chrome Top, Steel Back Swiss Case, Radium Dial. $52.60
2090FH — Same as the above but with regular Chrome Top, Steel Back Case. $46.00
2090FHST — Same as the above but with regular All Steel Swiss Case. $48.60

2053DRH — (8¾″), 17 Jewel, Rectangular SERVICE WATCH, 10K Natural Rolled Gold Plate Top, Steel Back Case, Sweepsecond, Incabloc, Water Repellent $43.90
2053DH — Same as the above but with Chrome Top, Steel Back Case $41.20

$20-25

$35-45

844 — (8¾″), 17 Jewel, 10K Natural Rolled Gold Plate Top, Steel Back Case, Dome Crystal $30.50
844/7 — Same as the above in 7 Jewel $25.20

$150-175
$150-175
$150-175
$175-200

2053RS — Same as the above but with Yellow Goldfilled Top, Steel Back Swiss Case $43.90

Cal. #11 — 17 Jewel, CALENDAR with Moon Phase, All Steel Swiss Case $66.50
Cal. #9 — Same as the above with Yellow Goldfilled Top, Steel Back Swiss Case. $79.80
Cal. #12 — Same as the above but with (360°) AUTOMATIC Movement, All Steel Case. $93.30

ALL PRICES KEYSTONE

Prices subject to change without notice.

HYDE PARK

Supplied to the trade by Emil Leichter Watch Co., New York, NY. a full line of designs and case metals for both men and women.

Hyde Park "Man's Gold". Subsidiary seconds. 17J movement. Square, 14K yellow gold case. ca 1946. . . . . $110–135

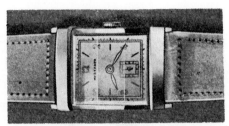

Hyde Park "Trifacet". Subsidiary seconds. 17J movement. 14K yellow gold rectangular, tri-facet case. ca 1947 . . . . $100–125

Hyde Park "Rhinestone Dial". Subsidiary seconds. 8¾''', 7J or 17J movement. Rectangular, yellow rolled gold plate case with scalloped edges. ca 1950. . . . . $60–80

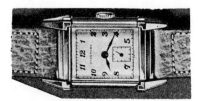

Hyde Park "Man's Plated Strap". Subsidiary seconds. 8¾''', 17J movement. Rectangular case, rolled gold plate top, stainless steel back. ca 1950. . . . . $35–45

Hyde Park "Rhinestone Dial". Subsidiary seconds. 8¾''', 7J or 17J movement. Yellow rolled gold plate rectangular case with scroll crystal. ca 1950 . . . . $40–50

Hyde Park "Automatic". Radium silvered dial, luminous hands & numerals, center seconds. 11¾''', 17J movement. Round chrome top case with steel back. ca 1950 . . . . $20–30

Hyde Park "Ladies Diamond & Gold". 17J movement. 14K white gold square case & diamond-set lugs. ca 1946 . . . . . . $75–95

* All values are given for the head only unless the band is included in the description.
* Read page 12 before using this book to value your wrist watch.
* Values are given for a mint watch with original dial, movement and case.

ILLINOIS

NOTE: Key model identifiers are underlined.

The EA Numbered Identification drawings and pictures have been perfected by William "Bill" Meggers for Illinois. All EA Drawings will eventually be brought up to these standards when enough time & researchers can be found to do the work. If you are interested in helping with this let me know. Roy.

ILLINOIS WATCH CO.
SPRINGFIELD WATCH CO.
Springfield, Ill. 1870-1928

NAME CHANGES

Organized as
SPRINGFIELD WATCH CO.
Springfield, Ill. 1870-1877

July 1877 Reorganized as
THE ILLINOIS SPRINGFIELD WATCH CO.
Springfield, Ill.

December 1878 Name change to
ILLINOIS WATCH CO., Springfield, Ill.

January 1928 Sold to
HAMILTON WATCH CO., Lancaster, Pa.

NOTE: Hamilton continued production in the factory at Springfield until 1933, then removed the remaining inventory to Lancaster, Pa. where it continued to assemble and sell Illinois watches until about 1948.

Serial No.		Date
1-	2,000	1872
2,411-	2,550	
3,001-	3,700	
4,001-	4,360	
4,401-	4,470	
5,001-	5,500	
2,301-	2,410	1873
2,551-	2,720	
3,701-	4,000	
4,361-	4,400	
4,471-	5,000	
5,501-	6,840	
7,001-	10,000	
2,001-	2,100	1874
2,721-	2,830	
6,841-	7,000	
2,101-	2,160	1875
2,831-	2,880	
2,211-	2,230	1876
2,881-	2,900	
2,201-	2,210	1877
2,231-	2,250	
2,261-	2,270	
2,901-	3,000	
51,401-	51,650	1878
58,001-	59,000	
96,401-	102,400	
112,101-	118,600	
50,601-	50,700	1879
51,651-	51,700	
54,901-	55,200	
57,001-	57,800	
118,601-	133,900	
150,301-	154,900	
46,001-	48,000	1880
50,701-	51,000	
55,201-	57,000	
57,801-	58,000	
61,001-	61,300	1880
65,001-	66,000	
69,401-	88,100	
102,801-	102,900	
133,901-	150,000	
154,901-	162,000	

Serial No.	Date
162,001	1881
235,000	1882
310,000	1883
390,000	1884
470,000	1885
552,001	1886
672,000	1887
792,000	1888
912,000	1889
1,030,001	1890
1,300,001	1896
1,400,000	1898

Note: EA Numbers were taken from American Pocket Watches Beginning to End, by Ehrhardt-Meggers 1987, Advertised on a page in the back of this book.

EA 500   Illinois Watch Co.
0 Size—Open Face—Nickel
Model 1—Pendant Set—¾ Plate

EA 500A   Illinois Watch Co.
0 Size—Hunting—Nickel
Model 2—Pendant Set—¾ Plate

EA 500B   Illinois Watch Co.
0 Size—Open Face—Nickel
Model 3—Pendant Set—True Bridge

EA 500C   Illinois Watch Co.
0 Size—Hunting—Nickel
Model 4—Pendant Set—True Bridge

EA 500D Same Specifications as EA 500
Price Range: $100—175
(Mostly InterState Chronometer)

EA 500E Same Specifications as EA 500A
Price Range: $100—175
(Mostly InterState Chronometer)

EA 503   Illinois Watch Co.
3/0 Size—<u>Open Face</u>—Nickel
Model 3—Pendant Set—Bridge
Movement, Dial & Hands weigh:
12 Dwt./18 Gr./0.6 Oz.
Dial Feet: 19.0, 38.5, 57.5 minutes
Case Screws: 4.0, 34.0 minutes

EA 503A   Illinois Watch Co.
3/0 Size—<u>Hunting</u>—Nickel
Model 4—Pendant Set—Bridge
Movement, Dial & Hands weigh;
12 Dwt./18 Gr./0.6 Oz.
Dial Feet: 19.0, 38.5, 57.5 minutes
Case Screws: 19.0, 49.0 minutes

EA 504   Illinois Watch Co.
6/0 Size—Open Face—Nickel
Model 1—Pendant Set—¾ Plate
<u>Regluar Barrel & Click</u>
Movement, Dial & Hands weigh:
6 Dwt./9 Gr./.3 Oz.
Dial Feet: 2.5, 21.0, 43.5 minutes
Case Screws: 4.0, 35.0 minutes

(Also made with bridges like 504A but
with above winding wheels & click)

Decision Diagram
EA 504C Same as 504A
But winding wheels are reversed
(I. E. Hunting)

EA 504C   Illinois Watch Co.
6/0 Size—Hunting—Nickel
Model 4—Pendant Set—Bridge
Regular Barrel—<u>Marked "607"</u>
Movement, Dial & Hands weigh:
6 Dwt./9 Gr.0.3 Oz.
Dial Feet: 12.5, 43.5 minutes
Case Screws: 19.0, 51.0 minutes

EA 504A   Illinois Watch Co.
6/0 Size—Open Face—Nickel
Model 2—Pendant Set—Bridge
Regular Barrel—<u>Round Click</u>
Movement, Dial & Hands weigh:
6 Dwt./9 Gr./0.3 Oz.
Dial Feet: 2.5, 21.0, 43.5 minutes
Case Screws: 4.0, 35.0 minutes

EA 504B   Illinois Watch Co.
6/0 Size—Open Face—Nickel
Model 3—Pendant Set—Bridge
<u>21 Jewel, Motor Barrel</u>
Movement, Dial & Hands weigh:
6 Dwt./9 Gr./0.3 Oz.
Dial Feet: 2.5, 21.0, 43.5 minutes
Case Screws: 4.0, 35.0 minutes

Decision Diagram
EA 504E Same as 504A
But winding wheels are reversed;

EA 504E   Illinois Watch Co.
6/0 Size—Hunting—Nickel
Model 6—Pendant Set—Bridge
Friction Jewels—<u>Marked "605 or 607A"</u>
Other Specifications same as EA 504C
Price Range: $5—20

EA 505   Illinois Watch Co.
12/0 Size—Hunting—Nickel
Model 1—Pendant Set—¾ Plate
Movement, <u>marked "207"</u>
Fifth Pinion for Second Hand
Movement, Dial & Hands weigh:
8 Dwt./13 Gr./0.5 Oz.
Dial Feet: 6.0, 35.0 minutes
Case Screws: 4.0, 23.0 minutes

EA 504D   Illinois Watch Co.
6/0 Size—Hunting—Nickel
Model 5—Pendant Set—Bridge
Motor Barrel—<u>Marked "601"</u>
Other Specifications same as EA 504C

EA 504F   Illinois Watch Co.
6/0 Size—Hunting—Nickel
Model 7—Pendant Set—Bridge
Friction Jewels—<u>Marked "605A"</u>
Other Specifications same as EA 504C

EA 506   Illinois Watch Co.
18/0 Size—Hunting—Nickel
Model 1—Pendant Set—¾ Plate
Movement <u>unmarked</u>
Movement, Dial & Hands weigh:
5 Dwt./8 Gr./0.3 Oz.
Dial Feet: 19.0, 46.0 minutes
Case Screws: 45.0 minutes

EA 506A   Illinois Watch Co.
18/0 Size—Hunting—Nickel
Model 2—Pendant Set—¾ Plate
Movement <u>Marked "807"</u>
Other Specifiactions same as EA 506

EA 506B   Illinois Watch Co.
18/0 Size—Hunting—Nickel
Model 3—Pendant Set—¾ Plate
Movement <u>marked "805" or "807A"</u>
Other Specifications same as EA 506

EA 506C   Illinios Watch Co.
18/0 Size—Hunting—Nickel
Model 4—Pendant Set—¾ Plate
Movement <u>marked "807B"</u>
Other Specifications same as EA 506

EA 506D   Illinois Watch Co.
18/0 Size—Hunting—Nickel
Model 5—Pendant Set—¾ Plate
Movement <u>marked "805A"</u>
Other Specifications same as EA 506

The two movements below are
ES 507 a sample of imported
Swiss movements marked "Illionis
Watch Co." with "Hamilton-Illinois"
on the dial. These, however, have
no Grade or Serial Number to
identify them.

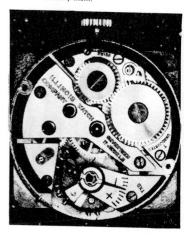

ES 507A   Illinois Watch Co.
XX Ligne—Hunting—Nickel
Pendant Set—¾ Plate
Movement marked "TXD Swiss"

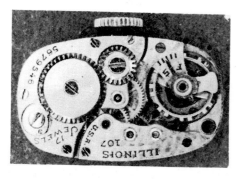

EA 507   Illinois Watch Co.
21/0 Size—Hunting—Nickel
Model 1—Pendant Set—¾ Plate
Movement <u>marked "105" or "107"</u>
Movement, Dial & Hands weigh:
2.6 Dwt./4 Gr./0.1 Oz.
Dial Feet: 6.0, 36.0 minutes
Case Screws: None

ES 507B   Illinois Watch Co.
XX Lignes—Hunting—Nickel
Pendant Set—¾ Plate
Movement marked "TXD Swiss"

ILLINOIS WATCH COMPANY
Springfield, Illinois
1869 to 1927

Hamilton bought the Illinois Company in 1927 and continued to operate in Springfield until 1933, and was then moved to Hamilton's main plant at Lancaster, Pa.

Illinois entered the wrist watch market about 1914 with ladies watches converted from their line of pocket watches. The first two illustrations are two styles of many offered during this period (1914–1925), which consisted of square, round, cushion, decagon, hexagon, cut-corner, etc., in solid gold and gold-filled, silver and base metal. Illinois (like most all other watch companies in the U.S.A.) offered to the trade uncased movements. Slowly at first, Illinois cased, timed and boxed wrist watches at the factory. Later, as rectangle and baguette movements were developed, case styles changed.

After about 1934, Illinois wrist watch advertisements disappeared and did not reappear until the mid-1950's when Hamilton offered wrist watches with the Illinois name on them. Many Hamilton wrist watches in the 400 Grade Series were made with Illinois movements with Hamilton markings that were either made from unfinished stock or of new manufacture.

As far as we can tell, there has not been any organized collecting of Illinois wrist watches at this time, and, as with all other companies, many Illinois wrist watches can be bought for less than the values shown here. There are some very high quality and beautiful Illinois movements.

Ron Starnes of Tulsa, Oklahoma gave us a lot of help with the Illinois section.

NOTE: The watches that were cased and timed at the factory were supplied with matching convertible bracelets and boxes but are not included in the values above. Illinois also sold movements only for custom cased watches.

Illinois "Ladies Ribbon". Dials various colors and finishes. Made in both 15J 6/0 size Grade 903, and 19J 6/0 size Grade 907, round movements. Open face with subsidiary seconds, hunting without. Case shapes include round, tonneau, cushion, decagon, hexagon and square, in various metals with matching ribbons and factory boxes. Ribbon & box not included in values. ca 1914 to 1925.

14K green gold	$60–80
14K yellow gold	60–80
14K yellow gold-filled	20–40
Silver	20–40

Illinois "Ladies Convertible". Dials various colors and finishes. Made in both 15J 6/0 size Grade 903, and 19J 6/0 size Grade 907. Round movements. Open face with subsidiary seconds, Hunting without. Case shapes are round, cushion, hexagon and decagon, in various metals. ca 1914 to 1925.

14K green gold	$60–80
14K yellow gold	60–80
14K green gold-filled	20–40
14K yellow gold-filled	20–40
Silver	20–40

The BILOXI
14K Gold Filled Case
Consumer price, $50.00

The BEVERLY
14K Solid Gold Case
Consumer price, $65.00

For conservative adornment the rich simplicity of the Biloxi and Beverly plain cases is unexcelled. The 17 jeweled movement is unparalled for accuracy

The LONG BEACH

The unusual engraved bezel of the Long Beach gives a slender effect very desirable for those of small wrists while its 14K gold filled case and 17 jeweled movement make it notable for beauty and accuracy alike.

Consumer price, $50.00

The ILLINOIS WATCH

HIGH GRADE
RIBBON WATCHES

18/0 Size   17 Jewels
Plain, Engraved and Inlaid Enamel Cases

All Cases Furnished in White Gold

18K SOLID GOLD ENGRAVED
18K SOLID GOLD ENAMELED
14K SOLID GOLD ENAMELED
14K SOLID GOLD ENGRAVED
14K GOLD FILLED ENGRAVED
14K GOLD FILLED ENAMELED
14K SOLID GOLD PLAIN
14K GOLD FILLED PLAIN

SPECIFICATIONS—18 0 MOVEMENT

Size Eighteen-0 or six and three-fourths ligne, 17 ruby and sapphire jewels, safety recoiling click, double roller escapement, tempered and hardened compensating balance, steel escape wheel, concaved and polished winding wheels.

SINCE 1870 AT
SPRINGFIELD, ILLINOIS

$60–80

The MARY TODD

The contrasting of jet black polished enamel, in a conventional design, in the 18K solid white gold case together with the 17 jewel movement makes the model one of rare beauty. Also supplied with full engraved bezel, 18K gold case.

Consumer price, $75.00
List - - - $86.00

$50–70

The BAR HARBOR

A richly engraved model notable for the good taste of its design and the high standard of its accuracy. Cased and fitted with 17 jewel movement 14K white solid gold.

Consumer price, $65.00
List - - - $74.00

$50–70

The DAYTONA

A charming model harmoniously decorated with polished surfaces and engraving. The case is 14K solid gold, the movement Illinois 17 jewels.

Consumer price, $65.00
List - - - $74.00

$20–30

The NEWPORT

A delicately engraved 14K white gold filled case with octagonal opening for its beautiful silvered dial and the accurate 17 jeweled movement are features of this very attractive model.

Consumer price, $50.00
List - - - $56.00

ILLINOIS

Sturdy 3-0 Size,
17 Jewel Strap Watches

These Illinois watches have proven their worth through many years of service. Thousands of these exceptional watches have checked the hours for men in all walks of life—in all parts of the United States and on the battlefields of France. The 3/0 size movement was used extensively by the United States Government during the late war. Each Illinois 3/0 is thoroughly dependable, and has masculine appeal.

◆ ◆ ◆

$125-150

The SKYWAY

For Air-Minded America. Designed to meet the particular requirements of aviation, this strapwatch is proving popular throughout the nation. In its makeup you will find no compromise with ordinary watch construction. Equipped with standard aeronautical dial, dust-proof case with screw back and bezel, 14K white gold filled case; extra strength crystal.

Suggested consumer price, $45.

$175-200

The GUARDSMAN

The Guardsman rotor-dial strapwatch is an unusual idea in men's wrist watches. The rotor-dial provides accurate timing of seconds—and has many advantages. In 14K white and green filled gold, plain or oxidized cases.

Suggested consumer price, $45.

A GREAT AMERICAN
WATCH SINCE 1870

ILLINOIS WRIST WATCHES

By L. Michael Fultz

"Whoever it was that supervised the design and marketing of the Illinois wristwatch during the 15 (at most) years of its indisputable greatness (1917-1932), clearly understood that the modern wristwatch should not only be designed to tell time, but to focus and further the wearer's notion of himself or herself as a player in that time. If Elgin was the Ford of its day, utility and little else, Illinois was the Supercharged Cord." (Quoted from Harry Bouras, Romantic Little Pieces of Time, published in Pen World Magazine.)

Illinois is emerging as the leader among U.S. made collectible wrist watches precisely because of the strength & style of its design. Illinois' stylistic trade-marks like the 9 o'clock seconds, the art deco style of the '20's cases, and geometric style of the early cases that make them a favorite with collectors for wear as well as acquisition. Unlike Elgin and Waltham, Illinois did not abandon the open face movement, rather, they adapted it into one of their trademarks.

Among the models most avidly sought by collectors are the 6/0 size gold-filled Picadilly (made in both white and green) and Ritz and Valedictorian (tu-tone, white bezel and back, yellow center). In the larger 3/0 size the Jolly Roger, Speedway and the early sterling cased watches are the most avidly sought. Among the solid gold models the Consul seems to be the most popular. Even ladies Illinois have become popular, the 18K Mary Todd Lincoln and the colorful enameled bezel Redonda are highly collectible.

The scarcity of many Illinois models offers an opportunity for appreciation in value. While other American manufacturers like Elgin and Waltham made tens of millions of wrist watch sized movements, Illinois' total production was a little over 800,000 movements in all wrist watch sizes (3/0, 6/0, 12/0, 18/0 and 21/0). The small number of O size movements cased as wrist watches is more than offset by the other sizes cased as pocket watches. Particularly scarce are the 12/0 size rectangular movements used in the Futura, Kenilworth, Rockliffe and similar models. Only about 40,000 of these movements were made in total which suggests some models may have had production totals of less than 5,000. Values for some stylish models like the Picadilly are now bid over $1,000. However, some much scarcer models are still selling for $100-300 when available.

Even the lowest grade Illinois movements are of better quality than its competitors. Others sold 7 jewel movements standard, Illinois cheapest was a 11 jewel, and the standard in most sizes was 17 jewels. Illinois top of the line 6/0 size 21 jewel movement is a beauty, with extra fancy damaskeening and matched all white sapphire jewels in gold settings & has a solid gold train wheels.

Many Illinois models have names; for a relatively comprehensive listing, see Vintage American & European Wrist Watch Price Guide, Book 1. Good advice (for value appreciation) is to buy only watches with Illinois marked cases, but case makers and case markings vary. Some models have numbers, some names, some both & some neither. Some model numbers cover more than one case style (and model name). Even Illinois advertising shows different cases with the same name. Some watches had different names depending on whether they were sold with a leather strap or a metal bracelet. For example, the Ritz has a strap, the Valedictorian has a bracelet, but the head on both is identical. Illinois made several models with solid gold cases, and some custom cased Illinois with solid gold cases are also known. Ladies models are somewhat harder to find than men's (though cheaper when found). However, they should be more plentiful (perhaps more ladies watches had solid gold cases and were scrapped).

Unlike most other makers, Illinois sold movements to Private Label sellers throughout the wrist watch era until its demise. For a collector, these private label watches increase the variety. Some are marked Illinois only on the movement and have private label dials (Spaulding & Co., etc.); some read both Illinois and the seller's name on both movement and dial (such as Santa Fe and Time King) and some are marked only with the seller's name on both movement and dial (Washington Watch Co., Burlington Watch Co., and certain department store brands like Marshall Field & Co.'s Ariston and Ultimus).

Much more study and research needs to be done on Illinois wrist watches. For example, although rumored to exist, there is as yet no documentation of Illinois double dial doctor's watches, or calendar watches or chronograph watches. Since no illustrations or advertising showing the complete watch have been found, the Southampton and the Enamel Bezel are known only from their names in an Illinois dial catalog (see Illinois Springfield Watches Identification and Price Guide, 1976 by Roy Ehrhardt). Much confusion surrounds Illinois' direct or rotor seconds 3/0 model; like the Southampton, no illustration of the complete watch has been found. However, these watches are occasionally found but serious questions remain about the correct case. Some are found in Major cases, some seem to be in inexpensive Star or Illinois Watch Case Co. Tivoli cases.

A group of collectors have formed the Illinois Wrist Watch Collectors, which publishes a newsletter devoted exclusively to Illinois wrists. For more information, contact L. Michael Fultz, 1535 West Adams Street, Chicago, Illinois 60607.

Illinois
Eagle* (top view)
Custom 15K solid green gold case
No casemaker's name
Note stars on bezel
Eagle's head/beaks are lugs
Star on crown
Probably custom made
15KG Head Est. $350-400

Eagle* (side view)
Note eagle head lugs holding
spring bars and that the end
of the steel spring bar forms
the eagle's eye

Admiral Evans
3/0S-Octogon shaped
Sterling case by
Illinois Watch Co of Elgin, IL
Sterling Silver $250-300

Illinois
3/0S-Cushion wire lug
Sterling silver case by Fahys
Metal dial, with integral
crystal protector
Sterling Head $450-500

Illinois
3/0S-Round wire lug
Sterling silver case by Fahys
Enamel dial marked with
Illinois Central railroad name
Sterling Head $250-300

Illinois
3/0S-Cushion sterling case
with hinged back by
Star Watch Case Co.-metal dial
Sterling Head $250-300

Skyway
3/0S-White G.F. case, screw back
and bezel, both with stars
By Wadsworth-Case marked
"211, Illinois Watch Springfield"
WGF Head $125-150

Speedway
3/0S-White G.F. case with engraved
bezel and lugs by Keystone
Case marked "Model #178"
WGF Head $125-150

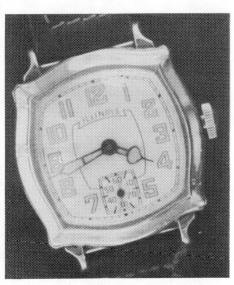

Jolly Roger
3/0S-Green G.F. case with plain
engraved bezel by Keystone
Case marked "Model #176"
GGF Head $250-300

Illinois
3/0S-White G.F. case with engraved
bezel and lugs by Keystone
Case marked "Model #178" and
identical, except for the bezel
to the Major and Speedway
WGF Head $125-150

Enamel Bezel
3/0S-White base metal case
by Keystone-Enamel dial
Metal Head $250-300

Marquis
6/0S-White G.F. plain bezel case
by Fahys-Case marked
"Illinois Watch Co. Special Model"
WGF Head $125-150

Picadilly
6/0S-Green G.F. case by Keystone
Case marked "Model #164"
GGF Head $650-700

Ritz
6/0S-White G.F. bezel and back
Yellow G.F. center case
by Wadsworth Case marked
"210 Illinois Watch Springfield"
Unusual black dial
Apparently from the factory
WGF Head $550-600

Southampton
6/0S–White G.F. case–Made by Fahy's
Marked "E/I" (probably for
Elgin/Illinois)–and "Shape Patented"
This is a plain bezel, I have
also seen an engraved bezel version
WGF Head $150–175

Tuxedo
18/0S–14K white gold case by Solidarity
Case marked "Illinois Watch
Special Model No. 151"
14KW Head $450–500

Canby
6/0S–14K yellow gold double hinged
case by Star
14KY Head $225–275

Consul
6/0S–14K white gold case by Solidarity
Case marked "Illinois Watch
Special Model No. 152"
14KW Head $450–500

INTERNATIONAL
WATCH CO.

18KYG $175-210

18KYG $150-180

18KYG $200-240

18KYG $150-180

18KYG $150-180

18KYG $150-180

18KYG $125-150

18KYG $150-180

18KYG $200-240

18KYG $150-180

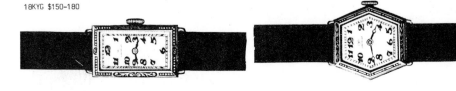

LA BELLE HORLOGERIE

DE HAUTE PRÉCISION

18KYG $550-650

18KYG $400-500

18KYG $450-550

MODÈLES I.W.C. „HERMET"
POUR LE SPORT

UHRENFABRIK
FABRIQUE D'HORLOGERIE
E. HOMBERGER-RAUSCHENBACH

Fabrique Juvénia, La Chaux-de-Fonds.

BRACELETS HOMMES JUVÉNIA

Réf. 3637

18K TuTone $1,250–1,400

Or rose et platine, glace cristal, cadran relief or.

Réf. 3641

18KYG $225–250

Or vert, glace cristal, cadran relief or.

Réf. 3642

18KYG $275–325

Or jaune, glace cristal, cadran relief or.

Réf. 3643

18KYG $250–275

Or vert, glace cristal, cadran relief or.

JUVENIA

DE TOUT TEMPS
À L'AVANT

6261

6909

6910

14KYG
$125-150

Steel
$15-25

Steel
$15-25

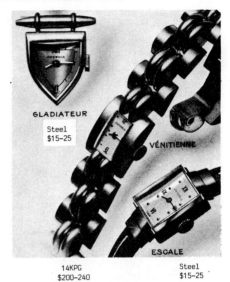

GLADIATEUR

Steel
$15-25

VÉNITIENNE

ESCALE

14KPG
$200-240

Steel
$15-25

6908

6907

6260

14KYG
$60-80

Steel
$15-25

Steel
$20-30

6912

6911

Steel
$15-25

14KYG
$50-70

6262

Steel
$35-45

AUTOMATIQUE, IMPERMÉABLE, PROTÉGÉE CONTRE LES CHOCS ET L'AIMANTATION

Gold bands on this page
10% over salvage

ISABEAU   14KYG
$60-80

14KYG
$225-270
PROMENADE

14KYG
$400-500
ALCANTARA

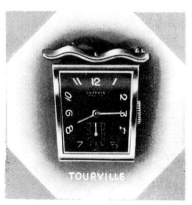

TOURVILLE

14KYGF
$20-30

14KYG
$140-170
MANHATTAN

JUVENIA
DE TOUT
TEMPS A
L'AVANT

AMIRAL

14KYG
$150-175

JUVENIA

Steel $15-25
Steel & Gold $35-45
18KYG $90-110
18KWG $80-100

$300-360

6882 SLIM, ⌀ 30 mm. stainless steel
7059 Stainless steel with gold bezel
6883 18 kt. yellow gold
7487 18 kt. white gold

$140-170

6747 SLIM, 18 kt. white gold, bezel with 45 diamonds

6747 SLIM, 18 kt. white gold, dial with diamonds

JUVENIA

Extra-thin

Steel $20-30
14KYGF $25-35

Steel $20-30
18KYG $90-110

7527 SLIMATIC ⌀ 30 mm. self-winding, stainless steel
7528 Same model 18 kt. yellow gold

7495A Stainless steel, satin finish bezel
7500 Gold plated

$20-30

7495B Stainless steel, bezel differently decorated

JUVENIA

7524 Ladies' style, stainless steel
7492 18 kt. yellow gold
7493 18 kt. white gold

Steel $10-20
18KYG $90-110
18KWG $90-110

Steel $20-30
18KYG $95-115

7556 Self-winding calendar, stainless steel
7558 18 kt. yellow gold

7554 Self-winding, Calendar, waterproof, stainless steel
7555 Same model gold plated

Steel $20-30
14KYGP $20-30

Steel $20-30
18KYG $90-110

7525 Stainless steel
7526 18 kt. yellow gold
7557 Same model self-winding, stainless steel

7582 Self-winding, waterproof, stainless steel
Same model with calendar

Steel $20-30

7181 Self-winding, Calendar, waterproof, stainless steel
7205 Same model gold plated with stainless steel back
7182 18 kt. yellow gold

Steel $20-30
14KYGP $25-35
18KYG $90-110

JUVENIA

18KYG $140-170
18KWG $130-160

$100-120

$100-120

$100-120

$100-120

7425 Rectangular shape, stainless steel

7272 Same model 18 kt. yellow gold (Polished or brushed bezel)

7473 Rectangular shape, oval opening, in 18 kt. yellow gold

7537 Rectangular shape 18 kt. yellow gold, crystal rim set with diamonds

7552 Same model 18 kt. white gold

7474 Rectangular shape, 18 kt. yellow gold

$100-120

7475 Rectangular across, oval opening 18 kt. yellow gold

Steel $30-40
RGP $35-45
18KYG $110-135
18KWG $105-130

Steel $30-40
RGP $35-45
18KWG $120-140
18KWG $110-130

6768 SLIM SQUARE, stainless steel

6979 gold plated

6769 18 kt. yellow gold

6894 18 kt. white gold

7433 Rectangular shape, stainless steel, curved bezel

7466 gold plated

7320 18 kt. yellow gold

7343 18 kt. withe gold

18×60

Steel $30-40
RGP $35-45
18KYG $110-130
18KWG $105-135

$120-140

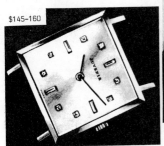

7434 Square shape, stainless steel, curved bezel

7471 gold plated

7275 18 kt. yellow gold

7342 18 kt. white gold

Steel $30-40
RGP $35-45
18KYG $120-180
18KWG $110-130

7476 Rectangular across 18 kt. yellow gold

Steel $30-40
RGP $35-45
18KYG $120-140

$145-160

6770 SLIM RECTANGULAR, stainless steel

6978 Same model gold plated

6771 Same model 18 kt. yellow gold

6895 Same model 18 kt. white gold

6894 SLIM SQUARE, 18 kt. white gold, dial with diamonds

7191 Square shape, stainless steel brushed bezel

7506 gold plated

7029 18 kt. yellow gold

JUVENIA

6650 SLIM, 18 kt. yellow gold

$325–390

7519 18 kt. yellow gold
7520 Same model 18 kt. white gold

$100–120

6952 SLIMATIC CALENDAR, self-winding, 18 kt. yellow gold
6725 Same model, but non-calendar

$350–420

JUVENIA Mystere

5733
MYSTERE PETITE
gold plated

$90–110

6147
MYSTERE LILLIPUT
gold plated

$50–70

6304
MYSTERE SQUARE LILLIPUT
gold plated

$50–70

6325
MYSTERE ELEGANCE LILLIPUT
gold plated

$65–85

A Practical, Serviceable Fountain Pen

Every child will be delighted to own one of these new Mickey Mouse Fountain Pens . . It is made with the same precision and care accorded only to highest priced pens . . It is not a toy—but a sturdily built pen that will give lasting service and satisfaction to child or adult . . Each pen is packed in an attractive Mickey Mouse Gift Box.

KINGSTON WATCHES

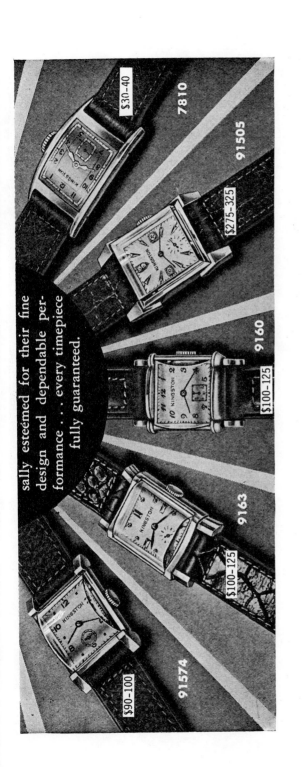

sally esteemed for their fine design and dependable performance . . . every timepiece fully guaranteed.

F7807. Natural 10k gold filled. Gold filled expansion bracelet. 17 jewels. **$47.50**

7810. Natural 10k rolled gold plate. Leather strap. 17 jewels. **$39.75**

7817. Natural 10k r.g.p. Steel back. Domed cyrstal. Leather strap. 17 jewels. **$34.75**

7817A. Natural 10k r.g.p. Steel back. Rock crystal. Leather strap. 17 jewels. **$34.75**

7817B. Natural 10k r.g.p. Steel back. Rock crystal. Leather strap. 17 jewels. **$34.75**

F7823. Natural 10k r.g.p. Steel Rhinestone dial. Gold filled expansion bracelet. Leather strap. 17 jewels. **$34.75**

7911. Natural 10k r.g.p. Steel back. Leather strap. 7 jewels. **$24.75**

7914. Natural 10k r.g.p. Steel back. Leather strap. 17 jewels. **$29.75**

9160. Natural 14k gold. Domed crystal. Leather strap. 17 jewels. **$65.00**

9163. Natural 14k gold. 18k gold markers on dial. Domed crystal. Alligator strap. 17 jewels. **$100.00**

91505. Natural 14k gold. 4 diamond and 8 18k gold markers on dial. Alligator strap. 17 jewels. **$210.00**

91574. Natural 14k gold. Domed crystal. Tufted leather strap. 17 jewels. **$65.00**

MONTRES LAVINA S. A.
VILLERET (SUISSE)

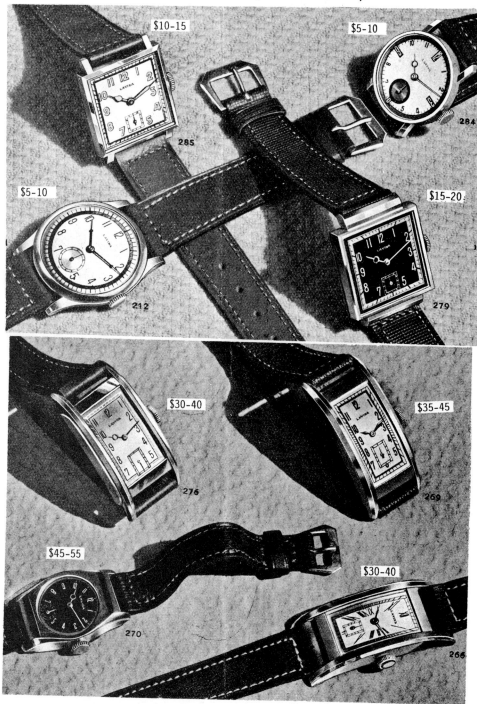

$10-15 285

$5-10 284

$5-10 212

$15-20 279

$30-40 276

$35-45 269

$45-55 270

$30-40 266

JAEGER-LeCOULTRE

HORLOGERIE DE LUXE

LAUSANNE [Suisse]

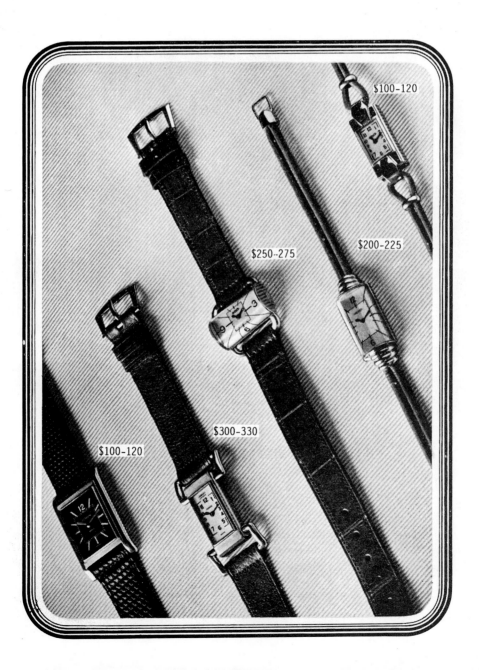

$100-120

$250-275

$200-225

$300-330

$100-120

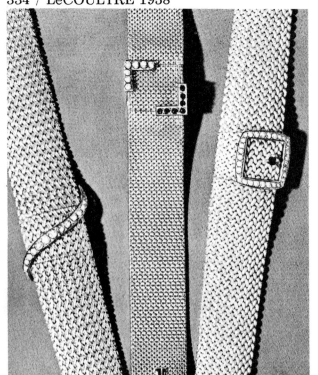

All Watches on
This page
10% to 20% over
Gold & Diamond Value

14KYG
$125-150

14KYG
$125-150

14KYG
$140-170

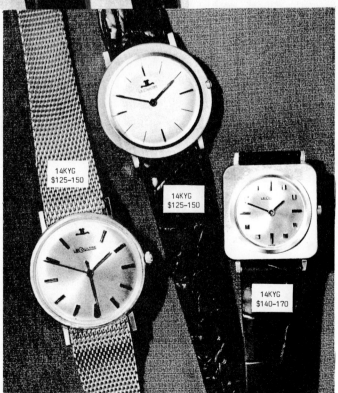

14KYG
$125-150

14KYG
$125-150

14KYG
$140-170

LE COULTRE

All 3 Heads
14KYG $90-110
14KWG $90-110
14KYGF $30-50

All 3 Heads
14KYG $130-150
14KWG $130-150
14KYGF $60-80

Steel
$100–120

Steel
$25–35

152
étanche

191

18KYG
$250–300

175
or

ÉLÉGANCE

LEMANIA

LUGRIN S.A. ORIENT (VALLÉE DE JOUX)

LÉONIDAS

Steel
$250-275

Réf. 717.
14 1/2 ''' chronographe-compteur
tachymètre 2 poussoirs.

Steel
$75-85

Réf. 465.
13'' chronographe-compteur
1/5 seconde.

Steel
$275-300

Réf. 716.
14 1/2 ''' chronographe-compteur
tachytélémètre 2 poussoirs.

Steel
$35-45

Réf. 441.
13''' compteur 1/5 sec.

Steel
$125-140

Réf. 461. 13'''
chron.-compt. 1/5 sec.

Léonidas Watch Factory Ltd.

Quelques types de sa production
du centenaire (1941)

Steel
$5-10

Steel
$150-175

14K
$300-335

Steel
$100-120

14K
$75-85

Steel
$150-175

Steel
$100-120

Steel
$175-200

GF $30-40

LOCUST

$30-40

L5048—10½ Ligne, Six Jewel Locust Movement, Cut Balance. White Rolled Plate Case. Woven Adjustable Mesh Band.......................... **$26.00**

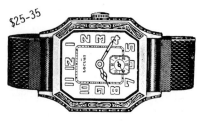

$25-35

L5046—10½ Ligne, Six Jewel Locust Movement, Cut Balance. White Rolled Plate Case, Adjustable Mesh Band.. **$25.00**

$25-35

L5047—10½ Ligne, 15 Jewel Locust Movement, Cut Balance. 14 Kt. White Gold Filled Case. White Link Band Adjustable Bracelet.......................... **$50.00**

$15-20

L5040—10½ Ligne, Six Jewel Locust Movement, Cut Balance. White Rolled Plate Case, with White Woven Adjustable Mesh Band...................... **$25.00**

Locust Wrist Watches for Men

When men first wore wrist watches it was considered good style to use a leather strap. Today fashion decrees a metal band—cleaner—more lasting—and more distinctive. The models shown have all the good qualities characteristic of Locust Watches—with the style feature added.

Every watch packed in a presentation box suitable for a gift.

Illustrations are ⅞ actual size.

LOCUST

$15-20

L5049—10½ Ligne, 15 Jewel Locust Movement, Cut Balance. White Rolled Plate Case, Flexible Weave Metal Band.......................... **$36.00**

$30-40

L5041—10½ Ligne, 15 Jewel Locust Movement, Cut Balance. White Rolled Plate Case. White Woven Adjustable Mesh Band....................... **$35.00**

$35-45

L5050—10½ Ligne, 15 Jewel Locust Movement, Cut Balance. White Rolled Plate Case. White Woven Adjustable Mesh Band....................... **$33.00**

$35-45

L5042—10½ Ligne, 15 Jewel Locust Movement, Cut Balance. White Rolled Plate Case, with White Woven Adjustable Mesh Band....................... **$38.00**

$30-40

L5051—8½x13 Ligne, 15 Jewel Locust Movement, Cut Balance. White Rolled Plate Case. Flexible Weave Metal Band.. **$43.00**

$30-40

L5043—8½x13 Ligne, 15 Jewel Locust Movement, Cut Balance. White Rolled Plate Case, with White Woven Adjustable Mesh Band.......................... **$40.00**

$10-15

L5052—9¾ Ligne, 15 Jewel Locust Movement. Cut Balance. White Rolled Plate Case. Curved to Fit the Wrist, with White Link Band Bracelet................ **$49.00**

$20-25

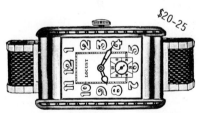

L5044—9¾ Ligne, 15 Jewel Locust Movement. Cut Balance. White Rolled Plate Case, Armored Mesh Adjustable Band **$45.00**

$60-70

L5053—9¾ Ligne, 15 Jewel Locust Movement. Cut Balance. White Rolled Plate Case. Armored Mesh Band........ **$50.00**

$25-35

L5045—9¾ Ligne, 15 Jewel Locust Movement. Cut Balance. White Rolled Plate Case. Flexible Weave Metal Band.. **$46.00**

No. 115-17J
14KYG $250-300

140T Longines Stopsecond Flyback
Second-setting Watch-17J
Natural Gold Filled $300-350

No. 117-17J
14KYG $300-350

143T Longines Nautical Watch
Stopsecond Telemeter-17J
Nautical Mile Reading
Stainless Steel $350-400

133F Longines-Weems
Second-setting Watch-15J
Natural Gold Filled Case
Steel $275-300
GF $300-325
14K $800-1,000

146T Longines Strap Chronograph
1/5 Second Telemeter-17J
Tachometer dial-Timeout Feature
Stainless Steel $450-500

13F Longines-Lindbergh
Small Size Lindbergh-15J
Hour-Angle watch
Gold Filled $1,800-2,000
Steel $2,000-2,200
Steel/Silver $2,200-2,400
14K $10,000-12,000

149T Longines Official LF
Nurses' or Ladies' Pilot Watch-17J
Sweepsecond Hand
Natural Gold Filled $50-60

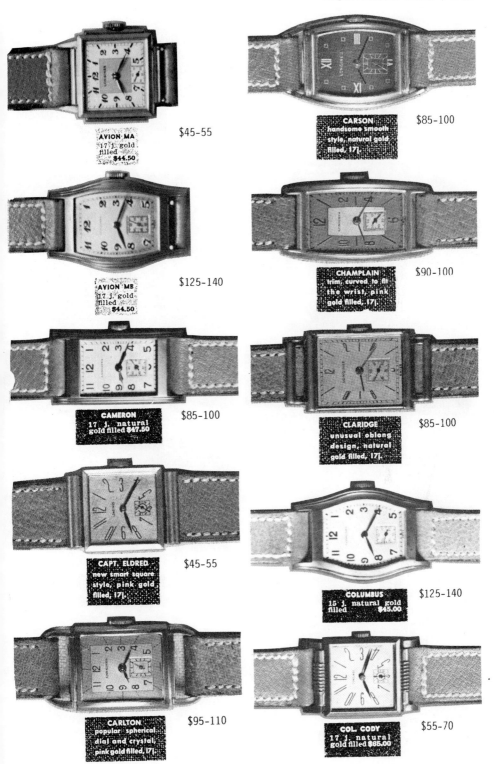

$45-55

AVION MA
17 j. gold.
filled
$44.50

CARSON
handsome smooth
style, natural gold
filled, 17j.
$85-100

$125-140

AVION MB
17 j. gold
filled
$44.50

CHAMPLAIN
trim, curved, to fit
the wrist, pink
gold filled, 17j.
$90-100

CAMERON
17 j. natural
gold filled $47.50
$85-100

CLARIDGE
unusual oblong
design, natural
gold filled, 17j.
$85-100

CAPT. ELDRED
new smart square
style, pink gold,
filled, 17j.
$45-55

COLUMBUS
15 j. natural gold
filled $45.00
$125-140

CARLTON
popular spherical
dial and crystal,
pink gold filled, 17j.
$95-110

COL. CODY
17 j. natural
gold filled $65.00
$55-70

$80-100

DIAMOND DIAL
WATCH
10% irid. platinum
17 j. $260.00

$450-500

CORONATION
PLATINUM
10% irid. platinum
17 j. $350.00

$1,150-1,250

DRAKE
simple, rectangu-
lar style, pink gold
filled, 17j.

$150-175

CORONATION STRAP

$200-240

Esquire — Yellow
gold filled; 17 j.
          $65

$35-50

David Belasco
Yellow gold filled;
17 j. $65

$85-100

ETHAN ALLEN
17 j. 14K pink gold
filled $60.00

$95-115

DAVID GARRICK
17 j. 14K yellow
gold filled $60.00

$175-200

FIFTH AVENUE B
14K yellow gold
17 j. $135.00

$325-350

GEORGE READE
17 j. natural gold
filled   **$55.00**

$115-140

FIFTH AVENUE H
14K yellow gold
17 j.   **$110.00**

$125-140

FIFTH AVENUE L
14K yellow gold
17 j.   **$110.00**

$65-80

153T LONGINES PROFESSIONAL
Sportsmen's or doctors' watch.
Sweepsecond hand. Stainless
steel, moisture-proof, 17J.

$45-55

FIFTH AVENUE R
14K yellow gold
17 j.   **$125.00**

$150-175

152T
LONGINES MOISTURE-PROOF
Sportsmen's watch. Stainless steel,
moisture-proof, 17J.

$40-50

FRANCIS KEY
sleek, wrist fitting
style, natural gold
filled, 17J.

$135-150

FRANK BACON
15 j. natural gold
filled   **$37.50**

$55-70

ALEXANDER BELL
sturdy, depend-
able, natural gold
filled, 15j.

$80-100

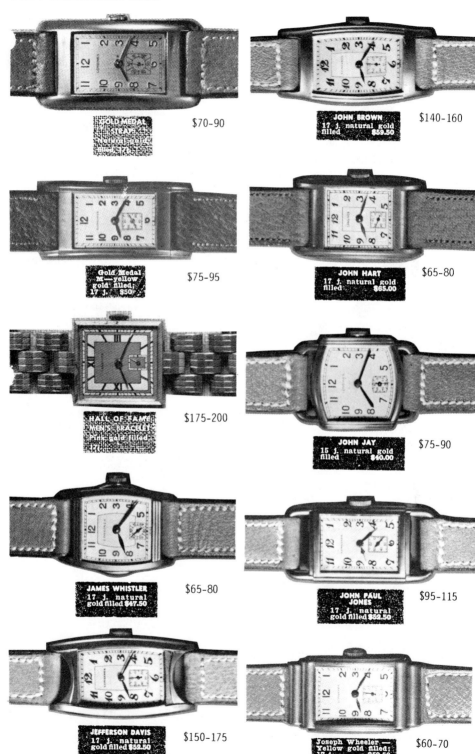

GOLD MEDAL STRAP — Natural gold filled $47.50 $70-90

JOHN BROWN 17 j. natural gold filled $59.50 $140-160

Gold Medal M — yellow gold filled; 17 j. $50 $75-95

JOHN HART 17 j. natural gold filled $65.00 $65-80

HALL OF FAME MEN'S BRACELET $175-200

JOHN JAY 15 j. natural gold filled $40.00 $75-90

JAMES WHISTLER 17 j. natural gold filled $47.50 $65-80

JOHN PAUL JONES 17 j. natural gold filled $52.50 $95-115

JEFFERSON DAVIS 17 j. natural gold filled $52.50 $150-175

Joseph Wheeler — Yellow gold filled; 17 j. $59.50 $60-70

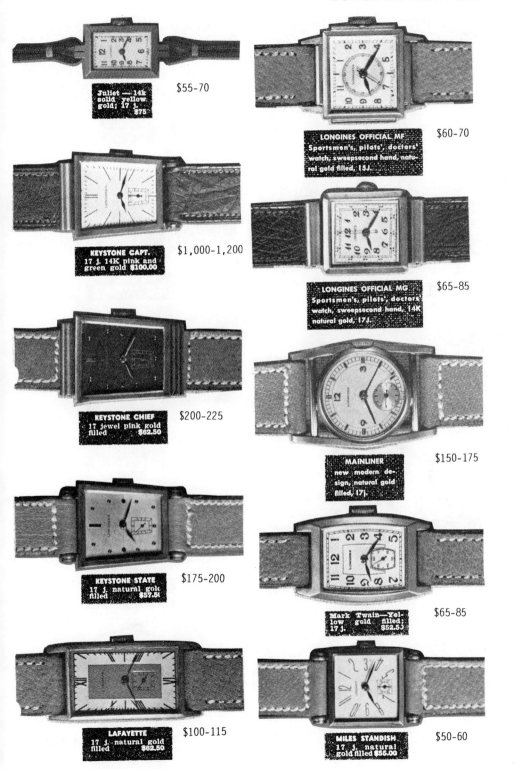

Juliet — 14k solid yellow gold; 17 j. $75 $55-70

LONGINES OFFICIAL MF Sportsmen's, pilots', doctors' watch, sweepsecond hand, natural gold filled, 15J. $60-70

KEYSTONE CAPT. 17 j. 14K pink and green gold $100.00 $1,000-1,200

LONGINES OFFICIAL MG Sportsmen's, pilots', doctors' watch, sweepsecond hand, 14K natural gold, 17J. $65-85

KEYSTONE CHIEF 17 jewel pink gold filled $62.50 $200-225

MAINLINER new modern design, natural gold filled, 17j. $150-175

KEYSTONE STATE 17 j. natural gold filled $57.50 $175-200

Mark Twain—Yellow gold filled; 17 j. $52.50 $65-85

LAFAYETTE 17 j. natural gold filled $62.50 $100-115

MILES STANDISH 17 j. natural gold filled $55.00 $50-60

MONTEREY smartly styled, stirrup ends, natural gold filled, 17 j.

$110-125

Official M — yellow gold filled; 17 j. $65

$150-175

Nathan Hale—Yellow gold filled; 17 j. $65

$115-130

PAR AVION MA 17 j. natural gold filled $44.50

$45-60

NATHANIEL HAWTHORNE 17 j. natural gold filled $50.00

$100-120

PAR AVION

$60-75

Official L— yellow gold filled; 17 j. $55

$15-25

PATRICK HENRY 17 j. natural gold filled $55.00

$70-85

Official L— solid yellow gold; 17 j. $65

$15-25

PETER COOPER 17 j. natural gold filled $42.50

$40-50

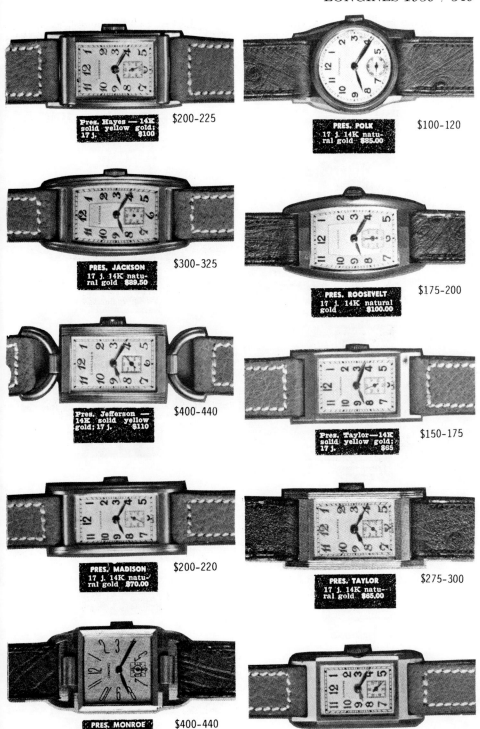

Pres. Hayes — 14K
solid yellow gold;
17 J. $100 $200-225

PRES. POLK
17 J. 14K natu-
ral gold $85.00 $100-120

PRES. JACKSON
17 J. 14K natu-
ral gold $89.50 $300-325

PRES. ROOSEVELT
17 J. 14K natural
gold $100.00 $175-200

Pres. Jefferson —
14K solid yellow
gold; 17 J. $110 $400-440

Pres. Taylor—14K
solid yellow gold;
17 J. $65 $150-175

PRES. MADISON
17 J. 14K natu-
ral gold $70.00 $200-220

PRES. TAYLOR
17 J. 14K natu-
ral gold $65.00 $275-300

PRES. MONROE
unusual style, 14K,
pink and green
gold, 17J. $400-440

Pres. Taft — 14K
solid yellow gold;
17 J. $75 $200-225

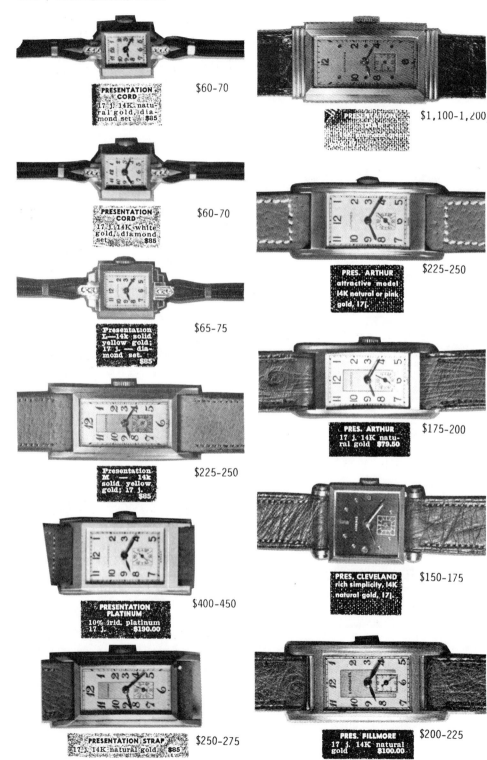

PRESENTATION CORD
17 J. 14K natural gold, diamond set $85

$60-70

PRESENTATION CORD
17 J. 14K white gold, diamond set $85

$60-70

Presentation L—14k solid yellow gold; 17 j. — diamond set $85

$65-75

Presentation M — 14k solid yellow gold; 17 j. $85

$225-250

PRESENTATION PLATINUM
10% irid. platinum 17 j. $190.00

$400-450

PRESENTATION STRAP
17 J. 14K natural gold $85

$250-275

PRESENTATION

$1,100-1,200

PRES. ARTHUR
attractive model 14K natural or pink gold, 17j.

$225-250

PRES. ARTHUR
17 j. 14K natural gold $79.50

$175-200

PRES. CLEVELAND
rich simplicity, 14K natural gold, 17j.

$150-175

PRES. FILLMORE
17 j. 14K natural gold $100.00

$200-225

FRES. VAN BUREN
modern style, 14K
pink and green
gold, 17j. — $400-425

SAMUEL CHASE
17 j. natural gold
filled $57.50 — $100-120

RALEIGH
ultra modern
style, natural and
pink gold filled, 17j. — $115-130

Stephen Douglas—
Yellow gold filled;
17 j. $67.50 — $90-110

ROBERT E. LEE
square with
stepped ends, pink
gold filled, 17j. — $65-80

STRATTON
modern stream-
lined style, pink
gold filled, 17j. — $80-100

ROBERT MORRIS
17 j. natural gold
filled $55.00 — $85-100

THOMAS EDISON
17 jewel pink gold
filled $60.00 — $110-130

ROMEO
17 j. 14K natu-
ral gold $75.00 — $175-200

THOMAS EDISON
popular square,
hinged ends, pink
gold filled, 17j. — $115-135

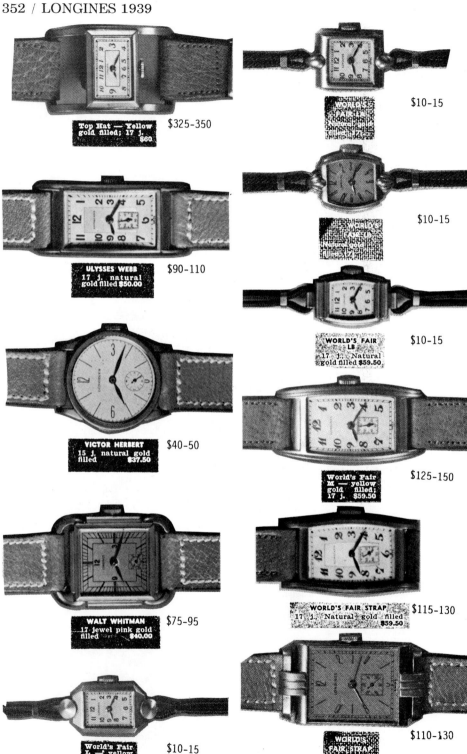

Top Hat — Yellow
gold filled; 17 j.
$60
$325-350

$10-15

ULYSSES WEBB
17 j. natural
gold filled $50.00
$90-110

$10-15

WORLD'S FAIR
L8
17 j. Natural
gold filled $59.50
$10-15

VICTOR HERBERT
15 j. natural gold
filled $37.50
$40-50

World's Fair
M — yellow
gold filled;
17 j. $59.50
$125-150

WALT WHITMAN
17 jewel pink gold
filled $40.00
$75-95

WORLD'S FAIR STRAP
17 j. Natural gold filled
$59.50
$115-130

World's Fair
L — yellow
gold filled;
17 j. $59.50
$10-15

$110-130

14K $100-120

150T LONGINES OFFICIAL LG Nurses' or ladies' pilot watch, sweepsecond hand, 14K natural gold, 17J.

YGF $10-15

AVION LA gold filled $44.50

YGF $10-15

GOLD MEDAL LB 17 j. natural gold filled $50

YGF $10-15

GOLD MEDAL LB 17 j. natural gold filled $50

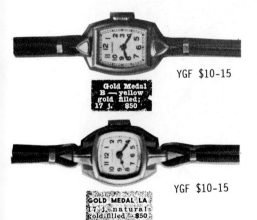

YGF $10-15

Gold Medal B — yellow gold filled; 17 j. $50

YGF $10-15

GOLD MEDAL LA 17 j. natural gold filled $50

YGF $10-15

YGF $10-15

AVION LB 17 j. gold filled $44.50

* All values are given for the head only unless the band is included in the description.
* Read page 12 before using this book to value your wrist watch.
* Values are given for a mint watch with original dial, movement and case.

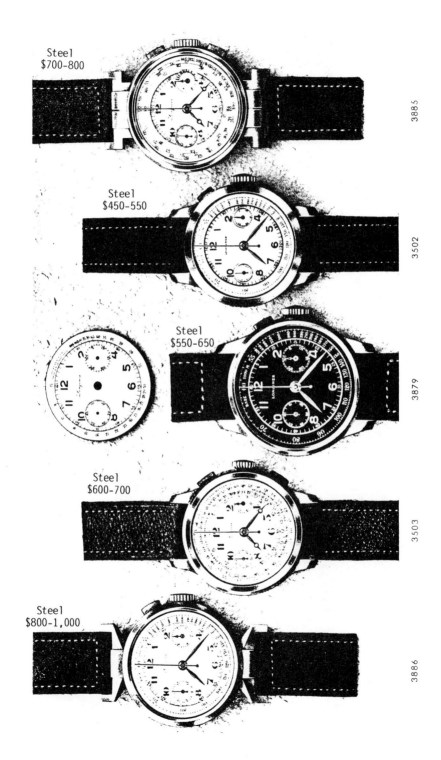

Steel
$700-800

3885

Steel
$450-550

3502

Steel
$550-650

3879

Steel
$600-700

3503

Steel
$800-1,000

3886

3901

3872

3871

3474

Steel $900-1,000

Steel $850-950
18K $2,000-2,200

Steel $750-850
18K $1,800-2,000

Steel $750-850
18K $1,500-1,700

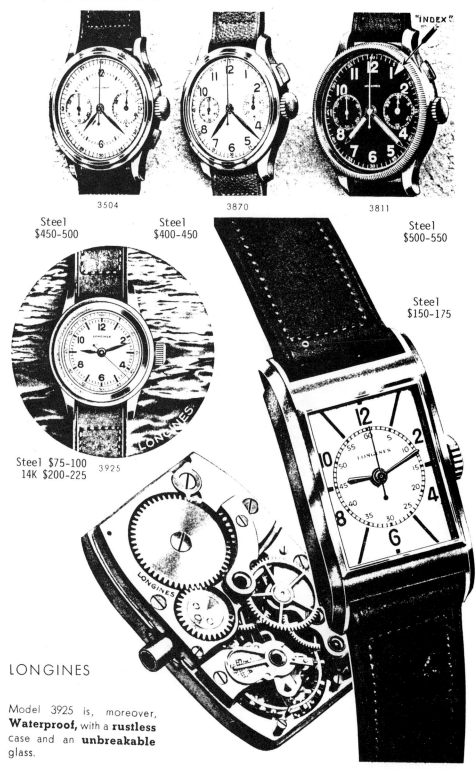

"INDEX"

3504
Steel
$450-500

3870
Steel
$400-450

3811
Steel
$500-550

Steel
$150-175

Steel $75-100
14K $200-225

3925

LONGINES

Model 3925 is, moreover,
Waterproof, with a **rustless**
case and an **unbreakable**
glass.

3906
Steel $50-60
14K $125-145

3718
Steel $175-200

3607
Steel $75-100
14K $150-175

3573
Steel $50-60
14K $110-130

3861
Steel $45-60
14K $110-130

3640
Steel $135-150
14K $250-275

3501
Steel $55-70
14K $155-175

All 14K
Solid Gold

$90-110

$150-175

$95-115

$200-225

$150-175

LONGINES 10 GRANDS PRIX

$30-45

$30-45

$35-50

$35-50

Longines Grand Prize

MEN'S AUTOMATIC ALL-PROOF® WATCHES

Left:
1006
Self-winding, All-Proof®,
stainless steel,
alligator strap

Center left:
1016*
Self-winding, All-Proof®,
stainless steel,
alligator strap

Center right:
1031
Self-winding, All-Proof®,
gold-filled top
with steel back,
alligator strap

Right:
1030
Self-winding, All-Proof®,
gold-filled top
with steel back,
alligator strap

NOTE: These watches are very hard to
sell because no one wants to wear them.
Pawn shops sell one ocassiionally to someone who wants a watch just to keep time.

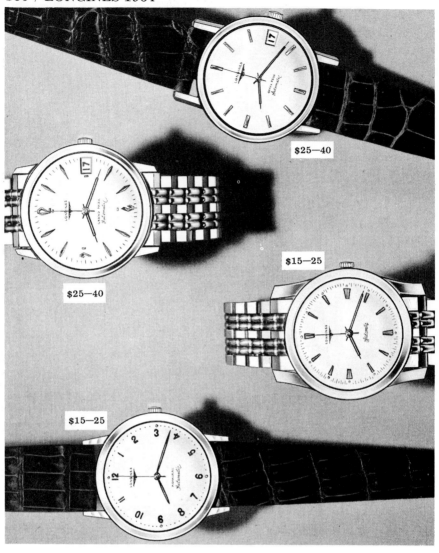

$25—40

$25—40

$15—25

$15—25

Longines Grand Prize Admiral

MEN'S STAINLESS STEEL AUTOMATIC ALL-PROOF® WATCHES

Left:
1350
Self-winding, All-Proof®,
sweep-second,
stainless steel,
alligator strap

Center left:
1300*
Self-winding, All-Proof®,
sweep-second,
stainless steel, with
matching link bracelet

Center right:
1372
Self-winding, All-Proof®,
sweep-second, calendar,
stainless steel, with
matching link bracelet

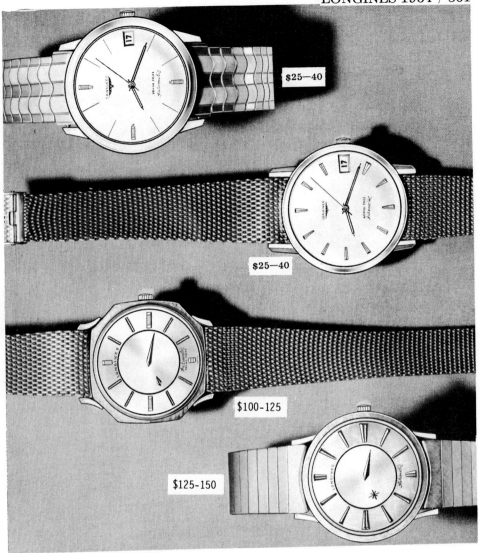

$25—40

$25—40

$100-125

$125-150

Longines Grand Prize

MEN'S GOLD-FILLED AUTOMATIC ALL-PROOF® WATCHES

Left:
1151
Self winding,
All-Proof®,
floating hour marker,
gold-filled, with
matching bracelet

Center left:
1153
Self-winding, All-Proof®,
floating hour marker,
gold-filled, with
deluxe mesh bracelet

Center right:
1491
Self-winding,
calendar, All-Proof®,
sweep-second,
gold-filled, with
deluxe mesh bracelet

Right:
1492

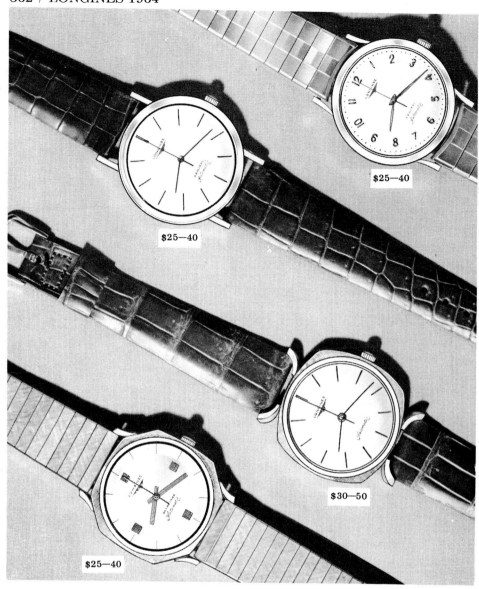

Longines Grand Prize

MEN'S GOLD-FILLED AUTOMATIC ALL-PROOF® WATCHES

Left:	*Center left:*	*Center right:*	*Right:*
1457	1458	1450	1451
Self-winding,	Self-winding,	Self-winding,	Self-winding,
All-Proof®,	All-Proof®,	All-Proof®,	All-Proof®,
sweep-second,	sweep-second,	sweep-second,	sweep-second,
gold-filled, with	gold-filled,	gold-filled,	gold-filled, with
matching bracelet	alligator strap	alligator strap	matching bracelet

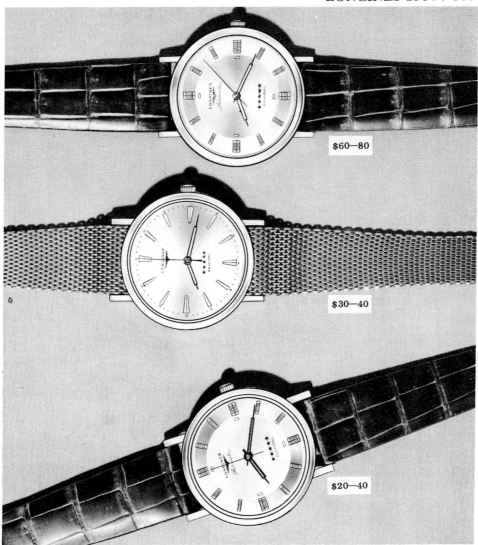

$60—80

$30—40

$20—40

Longines 5 Star Admiral

MEN'S AUTOMATIC ALL-PROOF® WATCHES

Left:
1380
Self-winding, All-Proof®,
sweep-second, stainless steel case,
alligator strap
$100.
_____
with matching bracelet
$110.

Center:
5013
Self-winding, All-Proof®,
sweep-second,
gold-filled case, with
deluxe mesh bracelet
$125.

Right:
1475
Self-winding, All-Proof®,
sweep-second,
14K gold top with steel back,
alligator strap
$125.
_____
with deluxe mesh bracelet
$140.

THE WORLD'S MOST HONORED WATCH
Official Watch of Leading Sports and Contest Associations Throughout the World.

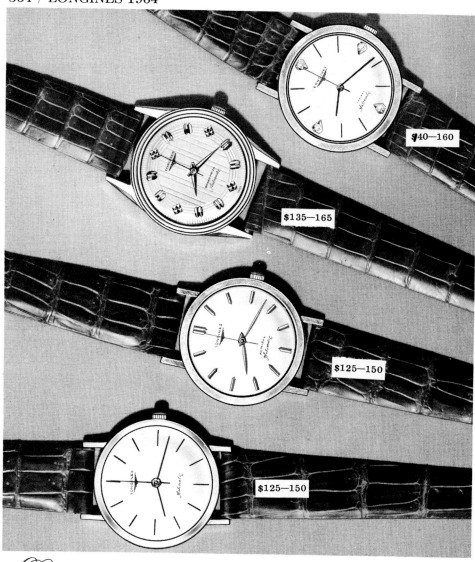

$140—160

$135—165

$125—150

$125—150

Longines
Grand Prize Admiral

MEN'S SOLID 14K GOLD AUTOMATIC ALL-PROOF® WATCHES

Left:
1516
Solid 14K yellow or white gold, self-winding, All-Proof®, sweep-second, alligator strap
$165.

Center Left:
1520
Solid 14K yellow gold, self-winding, All-Proof®, sweep-second, alligator strap
$175.

Center right:
1553*
Solid 14K yellow gold, self-winding, All-Proof®, sweep-second, alligator strap with 14K gold buckle
$185.
*Grand Prize

Right
1525
Solid 14K yellow or white gold, self-winding, dial set with 4 diamonds, All-Proof®, sweep-second, alligator strap with 14K gold buckle
$195.

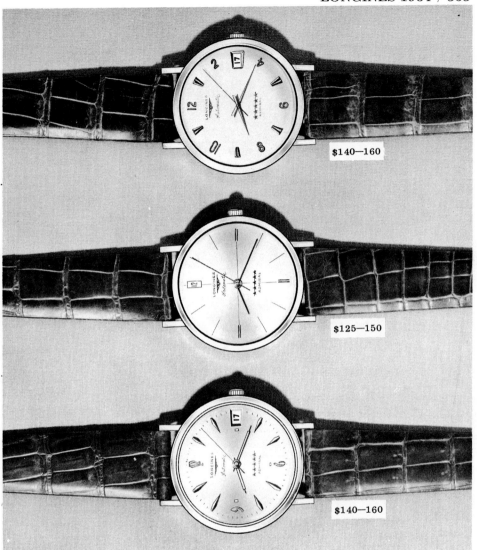

$140—160

$125—150

$140—160

Longines 5 Star Admiral

MEN'S AUTOMATIC AND CALENDAR ALL-PROOF® WATCHES

Left:
1485
Solid 14K yellow gold top, with stainless steel back, self-winding, calendar, All-Proof®, sweep-second, alligator strap
$135.

with matching deluxe mesh bracelet
$150.

Center:
1530
Solid 14K yellow gold, self-winding, All-Proof®, sweep-second alligator strap
$175.

Right:
1535
Solid 14K yellow gold, self-winding, calendar, All-Proof®, sweep-second, alligator strap with 14K gold buckle
$185.

THE WORLD'S MOST HONORED WATCH
Winner of Innumerable Prizes in Government Observatory Accuracy Contests

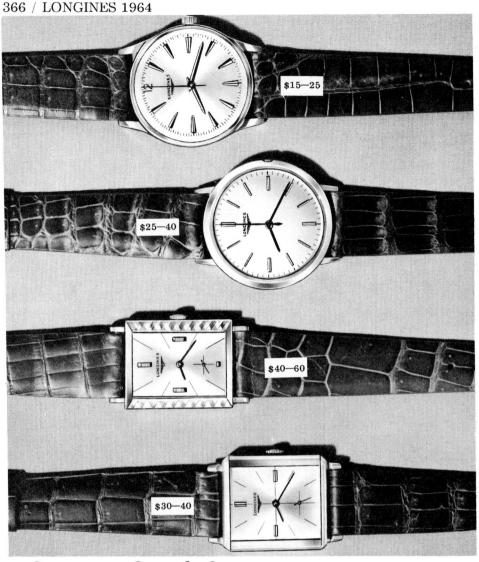

$15—25

$25—40

$40—60

$30—40

Longines Gold Medal and Olympian

MEN'S GOLD-FILLED AND STAINLESS STEEL WATCHES

Left:
2042
Men's Gold Medal, yellow
gold-filled, alligator strap
$71.50
___
with matching bracelet
$79.50

Center left:
2094
Men's Gold Medal, yellow
gold-filled, alligator strap
$79.50
___
with matching bracelet
$89.50

Center right
2090
Men's Gold Medal, yellow
gold-filled, sweep-second,
alligator strap
$79.50
___
with matching bracelet
$89.50

Right:
2016
Men's Olympian Stainless
Steel All-Proof®, sweep-
second, alligator strap
$71.50
___
with matching bracelet
$79.50

Longines Gold Medal

MEN'S GOLD-FILLED WATCHES

Left:	*Center left:*	*Center right:*	*Right:*
2206 Yellow or white gold-filled, alligator strap $90.	2205 Yellow or white gold-filled, alligator strap $90.	2215 Yellow gold-filled, alligator strap $95.	2210 Yellow or white gold-filled, dial with floating hour marker, with deluxe mesh bracelet $110.
with matching bracelet $100.	with matching bracelet $100.	with matching bracelet $105.	with matching bracelet $105.
with deluxe mesh bracelet $105.	with deluxe mesh bracelet $105.	with deluxe mesh bracelet $110.	with alligator strap $95.

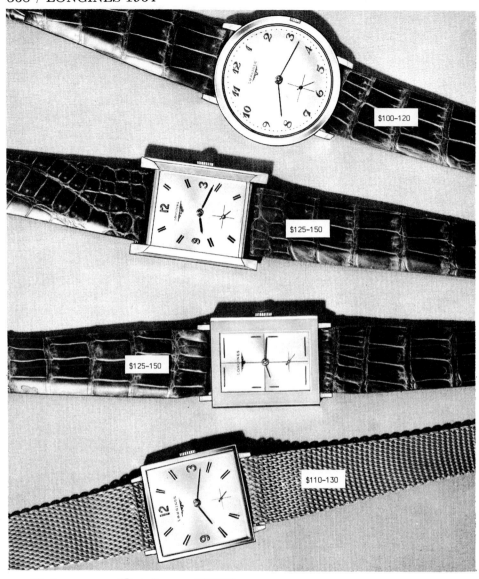

$100-120

$125-150

$125-150

$110-130

Longines World's Fair

MEN'S SOLID 14K GOLD DRESS WATCHES

Left:
2400
Solid 14K yellow gold
watch, with gold-filled
deluxe mesh bracelet
$115.
———
with alligator strap
$100.

Center Left:
2416
Solid 14K yellow gold,
alligator strap
$110.
———
with gold-filled deluxe
mesh bracelet
$125.

Center right:
2420
Solid 14K
yellow or white
gold, alligator strap
$110.

Right:
2405
Solid 14K yellow gold,
full numeral dial,
alligator strap
$110.
———
with gold-filled deluxe
mesh bracelet
$125.

THE WORLD'S MOST HONORED WATCH

$110–130

$110–130

$100–120

$150—200

Longines World's Fair

MEN'S SOLID 14K GOLD DRESS WATCHES

Left:	*Center left:*	*Center right:*	*Right:*
2507	2419	2508	2418
Solid 14K	Solid 14K yellow or	Solid 14K yellow gold	Solid 14K
yellow gold	white gold, with gold-filled	watch with gold-filled	yellow gold,
pocket watch	deluxe mesh bracelet	deluxe mesh bracelet	alligator strap
$125.	$125.	$140.	$110..
	with alligator strap	with alligator strap	with gold-filled
	$110.	$125.	deluxe mesh bracelet
			$125.

THE WORLD'S MOST HONORED WATCH
Winner of Innumerable Prizes in Government Observatory Accuracy Contests.

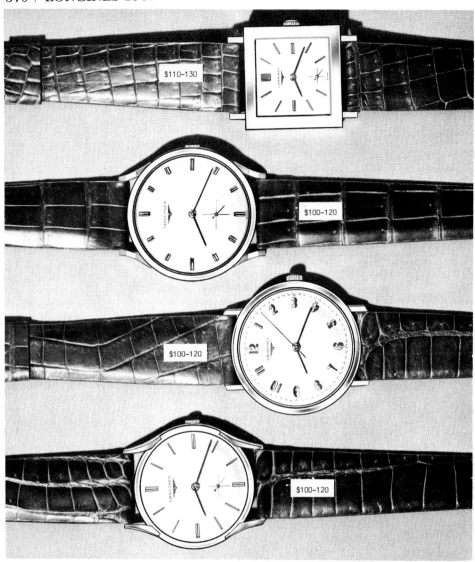

Longines World's Fair

MEN'S SOLID 14K GOLD DRESS WATCHES

Left:
2504
Solid 14K yellow
or white gold,
alligator strap
$125.

with gold-filled deluxe
mesh bracelet
$140.

Center left:
2509
Solid 14K yellow gold,
All-Proof®, sweep-second
alligator strap
$125.

with gold-filled deluxe
mesh bracelet
$140.

Center right:
2603
Solid 14K
yellow gold,
alligator strap
$135.

Right:
2500
Solid 14K yellow
or white gold,
alligator strap
$125.

with gold-filled deluxe
mesh bracelet
$140.

THE WORLD'S MOST HONORED WATCH

$110–130

$100–120

$100—125

$100—150

Longines World's Fair

MEN'S SOLID 14K GOLD ULTRA-THIN DRESS WATCHES

Left:
2611
Solid 14K yellow or
white gold,
alligator strap
$150.

Center left:
2612
Solid 14K
yellow gold,
alligator strap
$150.

Center right:
2617
Solid 14K yellow gold, alligator strap
$150.

with gold-filled deluxe mesh bracelet
$165.

Right:
2614
Solid yellow or
white gold,
alligator strap
$150.

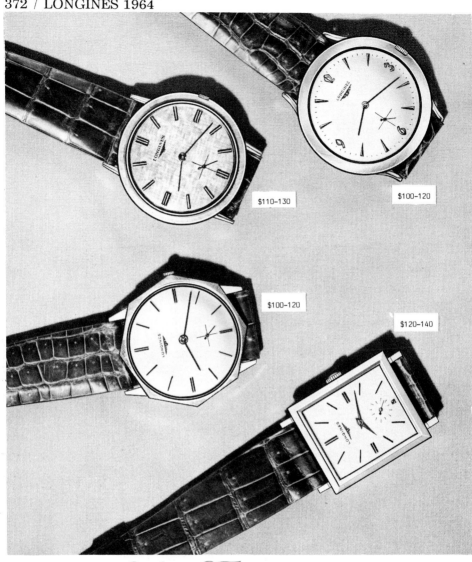

$110-130

$100-120

$100-120

$120-140

Longines World's Fair

MEN'S SOLID 14K GOLD DRESS WATCHES

Left:	Center left:	Center right:	Right:
2552 Solid 14K yellow gold, alligator strap $135.	2600 Solid 14K yellow gold, alligator strap $135.	2671 Solid 14K yellow or white gold, florentine finished gilt dial, alligator strap $150.	2607 Solid 14K yellow or white gold, alligator strap $150.
with gold-filled deluxe mesh bracelet $150.	with gold-filled deluxe mesh bracelet $150.		

THE WORLD'S MOST HONORED WATCH

The Watch of Great Pioneer Explorers and Aviators of our Times.

$100—125

$125—150

$120—140

$100—125

Longines World's Fair

MEN'S SOLID 14K GOLD DRESS WATCHES

Left:	*Center left:*	*Center right:*	*Right:*
2618 Solid 14K yellow or white gold, alligator strap. $150.	2690 Solid 14K yellow gold, alligator strap. $165.	2619 Solid 14K yellow gold, alligator strap. $150.	2695 Solid 14K yellow or white gold, with faceted synthetic sapphire crystal, alligator strap. $175.

THE WORLD'S MOST HONORED WATCH

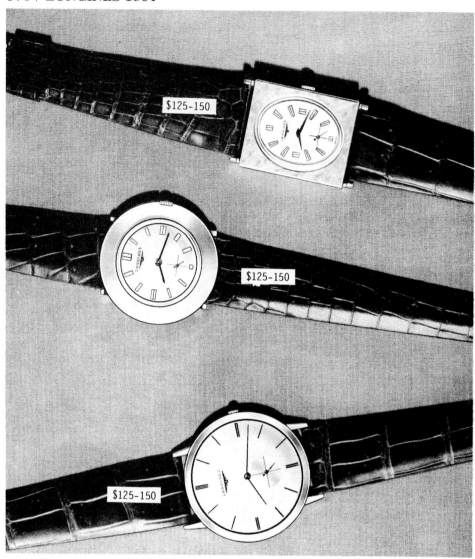

Longines World's Fair Deluxe

MEN'S SOLID 18K GOLD ULTRA-THIN DRESS WATCHES

Left:	*Center:*	*Right:*
2850	2854	2852
Solid 18K yellow gold, wafer-thin, alligator strap with 18K gold buckle.	Solid 18K yellow gold, wafer-thin, alligator strap with 18K gold buckle.	Solid 18K yellow gold, wafer-thin, alligator strap with 18K gold buckle.
$185.	$195.	$195.

THE WORLD'S MOST HONORED WATCH

Winner of Innumerable Prizes in Government Observatory Accuracy Contests.

Longines Creation d'Art

MEN'S SOLID 14K GOLD BRACELET WATCHES

Bracelet watches
of this style are
worth at the wholesale level
(dealer to dealer)
about 5% to 10% over salvage value.

Left:
1909
Solid 14K yellow gold,
Florentine finished case
and bracelet
$250.

Center left:
1922
Solid 14K yellow gold,
Bright polished case
and bracelet
$295.

Center right:
1912
Solid 14K yellow gold,
Florentine finished case
and bracelet
$275.

Right:
1907
Solid 14K yellow gold,
Florentine finished case and
bright polished bracelet
$325.

THE WORLD'S MOST HONORED WATCH

Winner of Innumerable Prizes in Government Observatory Accuracy Contests

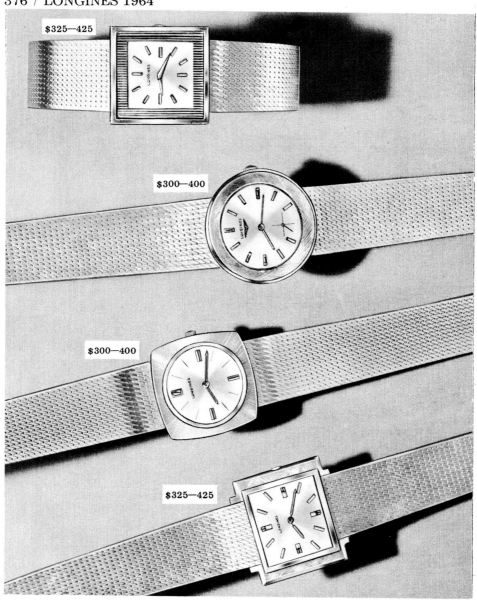

$325—425

$300—400

$300—400

$325—425

Longines Creation d'Art

MEN'S SOLID 14K GOLD BRACELET WATCHES

Left:
1920
Solid 14K yellow or
white gold,
florentine finished
case and bracelet
$325.

Center left:
1905
Solid 14K yellow gold,
shimmering radial diamond cut
finished case with bright
polished bracelet
$325.

Center right:
1904
Solid 14K yellow gold,
bracelet watch
florentine
reflector
$325.

Right:
1911
Solid 14K yellow gold,
bright polished
case and
bracelet
$325.

$500—600

$500—600

$450—550

$450—550

Longines Creation d'Art

MEN'S SOLID 14K AND 18K GOLD DIAMOND-SET BRACELET WATCHES

Left:
1910
Solid 18K yellow
or white gold,
florentine finished
case and bracelet,
set with 13 diamonds
$495.

Center left:
1921
Solid 14K white gold,
florentine finished
case and bracelet,
set with 22 diamonds
$495.

Center right:
1919
Solid 18K white gold,
florentine finished bracelet,
case set with 42 diamonds
$795.

Right:
1900
Solid 14K white gold,
florentine finished
and bright polished case,
set with 40 diamonds
$575.

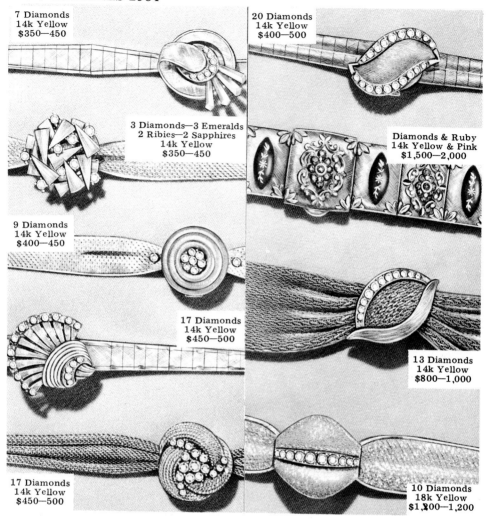

7 Diamonds
14k Yellow
$350—450

20 Diamonds
14k Yellow
$400—500

3 Diamonds—3 Emeralds
2 Ribies—2 Sapphires
14k Yellow
$350—450

Diamonds & Ruby
14k Yellow & Pink
$1,500—2,000

9 Diamonds
14k Yellow
$400—450

17 Diamonds
14k Yellow
$450—500

13 Diamonds
14k Yellow
$800—1,000

17 Diamonds
14k Yellow
$450—500

10 Diamonds
18k Yellow
$1,200—1,200

Longines Creation d'Art

LADIES' SOLID 14K YELLOW GOLD DIAMOND-SET COVER-LID BRACELET WATCHES

Ladys bracelet watches have a
wholesale value of 5% to 10% over
salvage value at wholesale
(dealer to dealer)
unless they are one of the top names like
Patek Philippe, Vacheron Constantin,
Rolex or Cartier.

* *All values are given for the head only unless the band is included in the description.*
* *Read page 12 before using this book to value your wrist watch.*
* *Values are given for a mint watch with original dial, movement and case.*

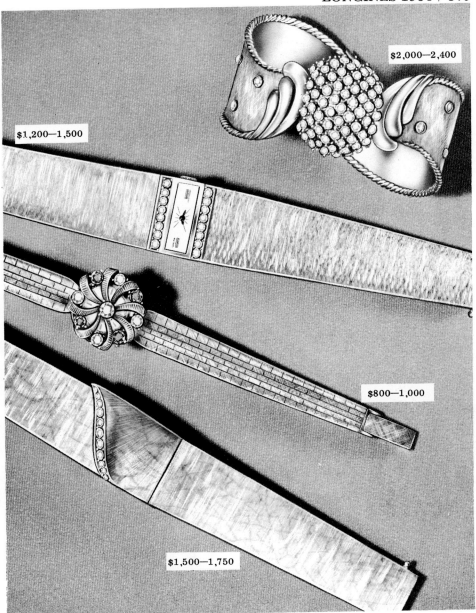

$2,000—2,400

$1,200—1,500

$800—1,000

$1,500—1,750

Longines Creation d'Art

LADIES' SOLID 18K GOLD DIAMOND-SET BRACELET WATCHES

Left:
173
Solid 18K yellow gold
cover-lid bracelet watch,
set with 11 diamonds
$1750.

Center left:
445
Solid 18K yellow gold
cover-lid bracelet watch,
set with 5 diamonds
and 4 sapphires

Center right:
235
Solid 18K white gold
bracelet watch,
set with 16 diamonds
$2000.

Right:
303
Solid 18K yellow
gold bangle bracelet
cover-lid watch,
set with 77 diamonds

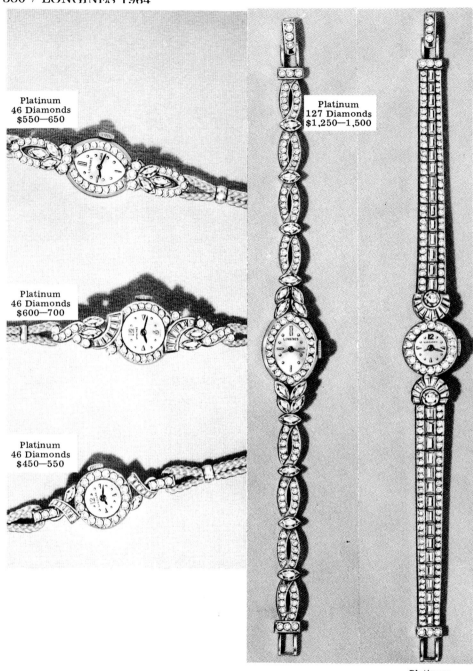

Platinum
46 Diamonds
$550—650

Platinum
46 Diamonds
$600—700

Platinum
46 Diamonds
$450—550

Platinum
127 Diamonds
$1,250—1,500

Platinum
209 Diamonds
$2,000—2,400

Longines Creation d'Art

LADIES' PLATINUM DIAMOND-SET WATCHES

LUSINA WATCH, PAMM FRÈRES - GENÈVE

... mais aux âmes bien nées,

La valeur n'attend pas le nombre des années.

Cette sentence classique du grand Corneille s'applique tout particulièrement à cette maison genevoise, qui a rapidement fait son chemin dans la voie de la précision, de l'élégance et de la nouveauté.

Voici quelques-uns de ses modèles les plus remarqués.

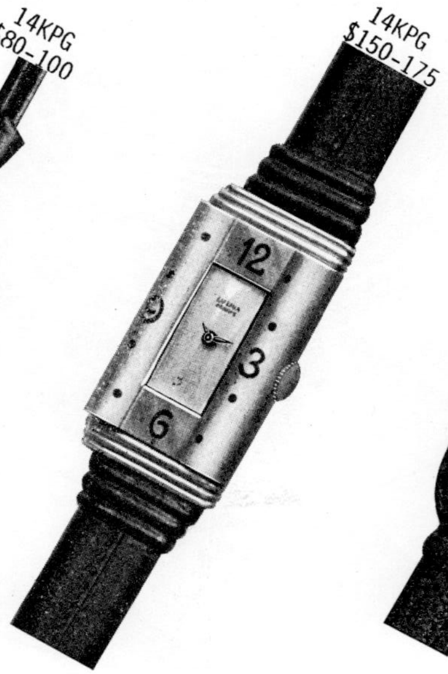

14KPG
$125-150

14KPG
$150-175

14KPG
$80-100

14KPG
$125-150

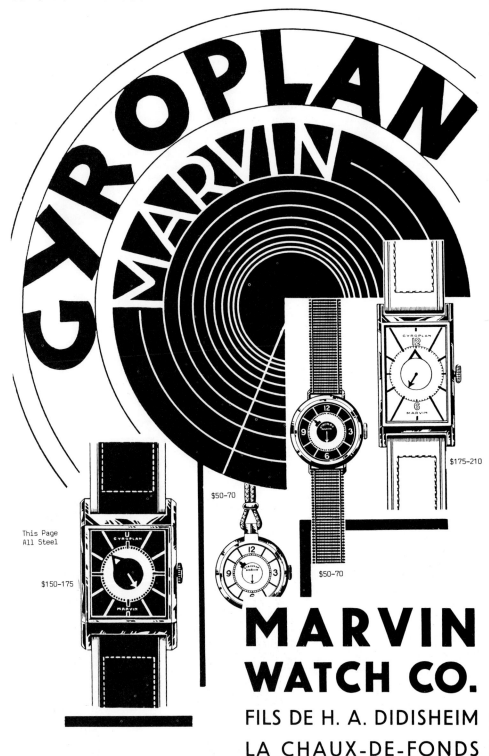

GYROPLAN

MARVIN

This Page
All Steel

$150–175

$50–70

$50–70

$50–70

$175–210

MARVIN
WATCH CO.
FILS DE H. A. DIDISHEIM
LA CHAUX-DE-FONDS

Le premier chronographe étanche

On peut considérer que le problème de l'étanchéité appliquée aux montres-bracelets simples est aujourd'hui résolu, sans pour cela vouloir dire que toutes les montres soi-disant étanches le sont en réalité.

Depuis quelques années, par contre on cherchait à réaliser le chronographe étanche, parce que pour ce genre de montres la protection absolue du mouvement contre l'humidité, les infiltrations de sable et de poussière est d'autant plus nécessaire qu'elles sont surtout portées par des sportifs. C'étaient les poussoirs qui paraissaient opposer des obstacles insurmontables à l'étanchéité absolue. La maison Mido S.A. de Bienne a pourtant trouvé une solution à ce problème-là par la création de son chronographe Multichrono, qu'elle présente comme parfaitement étanche. Malheureusement, il ne nous est pas possible de donner aujourd'hui des détails sur la façon dont les difficultés techniques mentionnées plus haut ont été surmontées, mais étant donnée la compétence acquise par la maison Mido dans le domaine de la montre étanche, cette solution doit présenter un intérêt technique considérable, et nous nous réservons d'y revenir.

En dehors de l'étanchéité, ce chronographe a l'avantage d'être protégé contre les chocs, antimagnétique et naturellement inoxydable. Il peut s'obtenir avec cadran à chronographe pour tous les usages. Il répond certainement à une nécessité, non seulement pour les sportifs et les arbitres obligés de contrôler l'heure aux fractions de seconde près par tous les temps, mais encore pour les médecins, les dentistes, les ingénieurs et les chimistes, obligés soit de se laver souvent les mains, soit de travailler dans l'humidité. C'est sans aucun doute un article qui sera hautement apprécié de toutes les personnes appartenant à cette catégorie, ainsi que, cela va sans dire, de tous les sportifs.

Steel
$225–270

Steel
$225–270

Steel
$225–270

Fabrique des Montres **MILDIA S. A.**

La Chaux-de-Fonds (Suisse)

GF $3-5

636 — 5 ³/₄'''

Steel $10-15

526 — 10 ¹/₂''' — étanche — ⌀ 33 mm.

GF $3-5

643 — 5 ¹/₄'''

GF $3-5

635 — 5 ³/₄'''

GF $3-5

638 — 5 ¹/₄'''

GF $3-5

633 — 5 ³/₄'''

Steel $10-15

228 — 10 ¹/₂''' — ⌀ 32 mm.

GF $3-5

639 — 5 ¹/₄'''

GF $15-20

528 — ⁸/₉''' — étanche

High Grade Bracelet Watches and Watch Bracelets

$15-25

506 Shown with Watch.

506 Each.............**5.00**
Watch Holder and Bracelet. Heavy rolled gold plate; Polished finish; extension and flexible bracelet, obtainable for sizes "10-0" "5-0" and "0."

$3.5

505 Each...........**.60**
Leather Watch Bracelet. Made to fit any Ladies' watch; choice of colors, black, gray or brown suede.

$20-30

$20-30

504 Each..........**.30**
Leather Watch Bracelet. Made to fit any Ladies' watch; choice of colors, black, gray or brown.

14.50

2112 Each.............**14.50**
"0". Size, 7 Jewel Elgin Movem. Heavy nickel case; leather strap brac.

$20-25

2107 Each.............**13.00**
11 Ligne, 7 Jewel Swiss Movement. White enameled dial; real gunmetal case; black leather strap bracelet.
2108 Each.............**15.00**
As above. Sterling silver case.

$15-20 $30-35

2109 Each.............**8.00**
"0". Size, 7 Jewel Swiss Movement. White dial; real gunmetal case; black leather strap bracelet.

$10-20

2127 Each.............**4.70**
10 Ligne Swiss Movement. White dial; real gunmetal case; leather strap bracelet.

$10-20

MILITARY WRIST WATCH STRAPS

Same as illustration next above, but with plain Buckle.
½ inch Strap.   ⅝ inch Strap.

		Each			**Each**
No. 014/63.	Nickel Buckle..	$1.20	No. 014/67.	Nickel Buckle..	$1.20
No. 014/64.	Silver Buckle..	1.90	No. 014/68.	Silver Buckle..	1.90
No. 614/65.	G. F. Buckle...	1.60	No. 014/69.	G. F. Buckle...	1.60
No. 014/66.	14k Gold Buckle	8.50	No. 014/70.	14k Gold Buckle	8.50

No. 014/14. With Cloth Pad ....Each, $0.40
No. 014/15. With Pigskin Pad..........................Each, $0.36

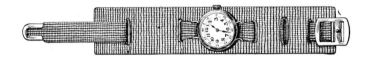

No. 014/3. Nickel Buckle...................................Each, $0.50

Watch Holder and Protector.
Genuine cowhide strap fitted with a glass protector. This is destined to be one of the most popular cup straps on the market. Colors—black and tan.

For Watch without Lugs.
No. 006/3. 3/0 Size ....Per Dozen, $11.00
No. 006/5. 0 Size ....Per Dozen, 11.00
No. 006/7. 6 Size ....Per Dozen, 11.00

For Watch with Side Lugs.
No. 005/3. 3/0 Size ....Per Dozen, $12.00
No. 005/5. 0 Size ....Per Dozen, 12.00
No. 005/7. 6 Size ....Per Dozen, 12.00

Camouflage Wrist Watch Strap.

Made with a leather cover that eliminates glare from case and luminous dial. Space inside cover can be used for photographs of loved ones at home. Can be used for watch with or without lugs. Tan color only.

No. 007/3. 3/0 Size ....Per Dozen, $12.00
No. 007/5. 0 Size ....Per Dozen, 12.00
No. 007/7. 6 Size ....Per Dozen, 12.00

WATCH GLASS PROTECTORS

Showing effect on Square Watch. Showing effect on Watch. Note Visibility of Dial.

THE DUO WATCH GLASS PROTECTOR.

No. 016/1.	For 10 Ligne Watch, Nickel Plated	Per Dozen,	$3.00
No. 016/2.	For 11 Ligne Watch, Nickel Plated	Per Dozen,	3.00
No. 016/3.	For Small 3/0 Size Watch, Nickel Plated	Per Dozen,	3.00
No. 016/4.	For Regular 3/0 Size Watch, Nickel Plated	Per Doz,	3.00
No. 016/5.	For Regular 0s Watch, Nickel Plated	Per Dozen,	3.00
No. 016/6.	For Large 0s Watch, Nickel Plated	Per Dozen,	3.00
No. 016/7.	For 6s Watch, Nickel Plated	Per Dozen,	3.00

All above sizes can also be furnished in Gun Metal.

WATCH GLASS PROTECTOR WITH LUGS. Nickel Plated.

This style furnished in both wide and narrow Lugs.

Wide Lugs, Per Dozen

No. 016/20.	3/0 Size	$2.50
No. 016/21.	0 Size	2.50
No. 016/22.	6 Size	2.50

Gold Filled. Narrow Lugs,

No. 016/32.	3/0 Size	$18.00
No. 016/33.	0 Size	18.00
No. 016/34.	6 Size	18.00

Narrow Lugs. Per Dozen

No. 016/15.	5/0 Size	$2.50
No. 016/16.	3/0 Size	2.50
No. 016/17.	0 Size	2.50
No. 016/18.	6 size	2.50

WATCH GLASS PROTECTOR.

Snap over Bezel of Case
Nickel Plated.

No. 016/50.	3/0 Size	Per Dozen,	$2.50
No. 016/51.	0 Size	Per Dozen,	2.50
No. 016/52.	6 Size	Per Dozen,	2.50

All Protectors $10-15 Each

WATCH GLASS PROTECTOR FOR SQUARE CASE.

Nickel Plated. Narrow or Wide Lugs.

Narrow Lugs.

No. 016/29. 0 Size .....Per Dozen, $2.50

Wide Lugs.

No. 016/30. 0 Size .....Per Dozen, $2.50

Gold Filled. Narrow Lugs.

No. 016/31. 0 Size.........Per Dozen, $18.00

KHAKI MILITARY WRIST WATCH STRAPS

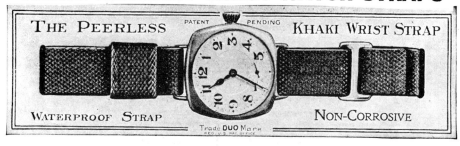

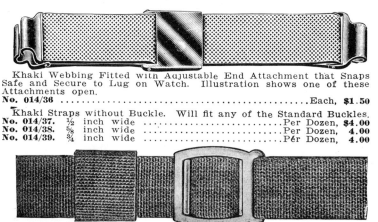

Khaki Webbing Fitted with Adjustable End Attachment that Snaps Safe and Secure to Lug on Watch. Illustration shows one of these Attachments open.

No. 014/36 .... Each, $1.50

Khaki Straps without Buckle. Will fit any of the Standard Buckles.

No. 014/37. ½ inch wide .... Per Dozen, $4.00
No. 014/38. ⅝ inch wide .... Per Dozen, 4.00
No. 014/39. ¾ inch wide .... Per Dozen, 4.00

Buckle on this Strap is easily adjusted yet perfectly secure.

½ inch Strap.   ⅝ inch Strap.

	Each		Each
No. 014/51. Nickel Buckle..	$1.20	No. 014/53. Nickel Buckle..	$1.20
No. 014/52. Silver Buckle..	1.90	No. 014/54. Silver Buckle..	1.20

Wrist Watch Strap
N. A-B Co.
WATER-PROOF FINISH

Khaki Webbing with Safe Serviceable Buckle.

½ inch Strap.   ⅝ inch Strap.

	Each		Each
No. 014/24. Nickel Buckle..	$1.10	No. 014/28. Nickel Buckle..	$1.10
No. 014/25. Silver Buckle..	1.70	No. 014/29. Silver Buckle..	1.70
No. 014/26. G. F. Buckle...	1.70	No. 014/30. G. F. Buckle...	1.70
No. 014/27. 14k Gold Buckle	9.00	No. 014/31. 14k Gold Buckle	9.50
No. 014/32. ¾ inch Strap, Nickel Buckle.............Each	1.10		
No. 014/33. ¾ inch Strap, Silver Buckle.............Each	2.00		
No. 014/34. ¾ inch Strap, G. F. Buckle.............Each	1.70		
No. 014/35. ¾ inch Strap, 14k Gold Filled Buckle.........Each	11.00		

This Strap is made to go **under** the Watch, preventing the full metal back of watch from coming in direct contact with skin of wrist. This same buckle used on the other two straps shown above.

½ inch Strap.   ⅝ inch Strap.

	Each		Each
No. 011/40. Nickel Buckle..	$1.10	No. 011/42. Nickel Buckle..	$1.10
No. 011/41. Silver Buckle..	1.80	No. 011/43. Silver Buckle..	1.80

KHAKI MILITARY WRIST WATCH STRAPS

Showing the "Strong Hold" ready to be worn.
Showing inside and front view of buckle, also the arrangement for attachng strap.

THE "STRONGHOLD."

We direct particular attention to the smooth, rounded edges and corners of buckle.

½ inch Strap.   ⅝ inch Strap.

		Each			Each
No. 014/71.	Nickel Buckle..	$1.10	No. 014/75.	Nickel Buckle..	$1.10
No. 014/72.	Silver Buckle..	1.70	No. 014/76.	Silver Buckle..	1.90
No. 014/73.	G. F. Buckle...	1.70	No. 014/77.	G. F. Buckle...	1.90
No. 014/74.	14k Gold Buckle	9.80	No. 014/78.	14k Gold Buckle.	10.20

No. 014/12. Khaki Strap with Nickel Buckle and End Piece; ½ inch Strap ....Each, **$0.36**

No. 014/2. Nickel Buckle ....Each, **$0.70**

Buckle on this Strap is of the "Purse Ball" style—A Sure Grip. A very effective number for the boys in uniform and the civilian.

½ inch Strap.   ⅝ inch Strap.

		Each			Each
No. 014/55.	Nickel Buckle..	$1.20	No. 014/59.	Nickel Buckle..	$1.20
No. 014/56.	Silver Buckle..	1.90	No. 014/60.	Silver Buckle..	1.90
No. 014/57.	G. F. Buckle...	1.60	No. 014/61.	G. F. Buckle...	1.60
No. 014/58.	14k Gold Buckle	8.50	No. 014/62.	14k Gold Buckle	8.50

Military Wrist Watches

HAMPDEN MILITARY WRIST WATCH
Plain or Luminous Dials.

$30-45

Movement is Hampden 7 and 15 jewels, expansion balance with meantime screws, Breguet hairspring, plain or luminous dials, fitted in military model nickel cases, dull finish with extra fine quality Kitchener strap.

No. H1 7J. Plain dial.. **$24.38**

No. H2 7J. Luminous dial **32.25**

No. H3 15J. Luminous dial **42.15**

$10-15

WALTHAM MILITARY WRIST WATCH
New square shaped case. Specially constructed for military men.

$150-175

WALTHAM, 7 JEWEL MOVEMENT
STERLING SILVER CASE
Sterling silver cushion shape case, thin and flat with first quality pig skin strap, silver buckle fitted complete with 7 jewel Waltham movement.

No. 4070 7 jewel Waltham, complete..**$41.90**

Movement is the Lancet, extra quality, 7 jewel lever escapement, stem wind, pendant set, bridge model, richly damaskeened with exposed winding wheels; all parts interchangeable and materials available in case of breakage. Fully warranted to give satisfaction. Fitted in Nickel case.

The strap is latest style Kitchener, extra wide, and can be had either pig skin or black. This strap is being used extensively amongst the European Armies and is most appropriate for the soldier.

No. 4068 Nickel case, luminous
Radium dial **$21.85**

No. 4069 Nickel case, white
dial **15.85**

Military Wrist Watches

$10-20

$10-20

$10-20

Appearance by daylight   **Appearance in the dark**

Wristlet Watches with New York Standard Movement. Luminous dial. Figures and hands are redium treated and stand out brightly in the dark.
No. **4071** Price complete, with N. Y. Standard movement and strap **$19.80**

O Size, 7 jewel N. Y. Standard, nickel case, fine leather strap.
No. **4072** Complete **$15.25**
   Same style watch with American movement named Ideal.
   O Size, American make, jeweled movement, nickel case, with fine leather strap.
No. **4073** Complete **$12.90**

$75-100

$10-20

TONNEAU STYLE GUN METAL BRACELET WATCH

With Full, Round Dial.

Fine gun metal, full open face case, fitted with 7-jewel Swiss cylinder movement. Black leather wrist strap.

No. **4078** **$8.80**

LEATHER STRAP WRIST WATCH

Just the thing for outdoor wear, small size watch attached to leather strap. The movement is Swiss, highly finished throughout, regular stem wind and set, with cylinder escapement. The straps can be had in either black leather or pig skin.
No. **4079** Gun metal case, complete with strap..**$7.95**
No. **4080** Nickel case, complete with strap...... **7.95**

STRAP WATCHES AND SWISS CYLINDER CONVERTIBLE WATCHES

$10-20

Patria "Luminous" Complete.
No. 3716. $20.00
Patria 15 Jewel Swiss Lever Movement, with Luminous Dial and Hands, Complete in Round Nickel Case and Kitchener Leather Strap.

$10-20

Nurse's Sweep Second Watch.
No. 3718. $32.20
15 Jewel Swiss Lever Movement with Luminous Dial and Luminous Hour, Minute and Sweep Second Hands, Complete in Round Silver Case and Leather Strap.

$125-150

Lancet Armored Military Watch.
No. 3715. $21.00
Lancet 7 Jewel Lever Movement with Luminous Dial and Hands, Complete in Round Nickel Case with Armored Bezel and Khaki Strap.

$350-400

Lancet Armored Military Watch.
No. 3717. $32.80
Lancet 15 Jewel Swiss Lever Movements with Luminous Dials and Hands, Complete in Square Silver Case with Armored Bezel and Khaki Strap.

LUMINOUS DIAL MILITARY WATCHES

$65-80

Enamel Dial
$10-15

Lancet Square Military Watch.
No. 3720. $32.00

Lancet 15 Jewel, Swiss Lever Movement with Luminous Dial and Hands. Complete in Square Silver Case and Hand Sewed Leather Strap.

Wizard Cylinder Military Watch.
No. 3719. $9.70

Swiss Cylinder, Wizard Movement with Luminous Dials and Hands. Complete in Round Nickel Case and Kitchener Leather Strap.

$20-30

New Haven "Luminous" Watch.
No. 3724. $6.90

6 Size New Haven Nickel Watch with Luminous Dial and Hands Fitted in Leather Wristlet. Watch can be removed and worn without strap.

Enamel Dial
$10-15

No. 3714. $16.00 with Luminous Dial and Hands, 7 Jewel, Swiss Lever Movement with Luminous Dial and Hands, Complete in Round Nickel Case with Kitchener Leather Strap.

$125-150

3/0 Size, Elgin Gold Filled.
No. 3668. 15 Jewel, Complete......**$43.00**
No. 3669. 7 Jewel, Complete..... 34.90
Elgin Movements with Luminous Dials and Hands, Complete in Square Gold Filled Case and Hand Sewed Leather Strap with Gold Filled Buckle.

$175-200

3/0 Size, Elgin Silver.
No. 3666. 15 Jewel, Complete......**$42.60**
No. 3667. 7 Jewel, Complete..... 34.50
Elgin Movements with Luminous Dials and Hands, Complete in Octagon Silver, Case and Hand Sewed Leather Strap with Silver Buckle.

$150-175

3/0 Size, Elgin Silver.
No. 3664. 15 Jewel, Complete......**$42.60**
No. 3665. 7 Jewel, Complete..... 34.50
Elgin Movements with Luminous Dials and Hands, Complete in Square Silver Case with Swinging Loops and Hand Sewed Leather Strap with Silver Buckle.

$45-60

3/0 Size, Elgin Gold Filled.
No. 3674. 15 Jewel.....**$36.30**
Complete..... 28.00
No. 3675. 7 Jewel .....
Complete.....
Elgin Movements with Luminous Dials and Hands in Round Gold Filled Case, with Kitchener Leather Strap.

$115-130

All Have Glass
Enamel Dials

3/0 Size Elgin Silver.
No. 3676. 15 Jewel, Complete.....**$43.90**
No. 3677. 7 Jewel, Complete..... 36.60
3/0 Size, Waltham Silver.
No. 3678. 15 Jewel, Complete.....**$49.00**
No. 3679. 7 Jewel, Complete..... 39.90
Movements with Luminous Dials and Hands in Square Silver Case with Hand Sewed Leather Strap, with Compass and Silver Buckle.

LUMINOUS DIAL MILITARY WATCHES

$75-100

3/0 Size, Elgin Nickel.
No. 3670. 15 Jewel, Complete......**$35.20**
No. 3671. 7 Jewel, Complete..... 27.00
3/0 Size, Waltham Nickel.
No. 3672. 15 Jewel, Complete.....**$39.40**
No. 3673. 7 Jewel, Complete..... 30.50
Movements with Luminous Dials and Hands in Round Nickel Cases with Swinging Loops and Hand Sewed Leather Strap.

LUMINOUS DIAL MILITARY WATCHES

$100-125

$110-135

$150-175

O Size, Ferrero 15 Jewel.
No. 3655. $155.00
O Size, 15 Jewel Ferrero Swiss Lever Movement with Luminous Dial and Hands, Complete in 14k Square Case with Engraved Bezel and Edge and Pigskin Leather Strap With 14k Buckle. The Ferrero is a high grade movement and guaranteed to give satisfaction.

O Size, Ferrero 15 Jewel.
No. 3656. $155.00
O Size, 15 Jewel Ferrero Swiss Lever Movement with Luminous Dial and Hands, Complete in 14k Tonneau Shaped Case with Engraved Bezel and Edge and Pigskin Leather Strap with 14k Buckle. The Ferrero is a high grade movement and guaranteed to give satisfaction.

O Size, Ferrero 15 Jewel.
No. 3657. $155.00
O Size, 15 Jewel Ferrero Swiss Lever Movement with Luminous Dial and Hands, Complete in 14k Hexagon Case with Engraved Bezel and Edge and Pigskin Leather Strap with 14k Buckle. The Ferrero is a high grade movement and guaranteed to give satisfaction.

$200-225

$175-200

$200-225

3/0 Size, Waltham 14k Gold.
No. 3658. 15 Jewel, Complete........$82.00
No. 3659. 7 Jewel, Complete.........73.00
Waltham Movements with Luminous Dials and Hands, Complete in 14k Cushion Shape, 14k Gold Case and Pigskin Strap with 14k Buckle.

3/0 Size, Elgin 14k Gold.
No. 3660. 15 Jewel ...$74.40
No. 3661. 7 Jewel 66.10
Elgin Movements with Luminous Dials, Complete in 14k Round Gold Case and Khaki Strap with 14k Gold Buckle.

3/0 Size, Elgin 14k Gold.
No. 3662. 15 Jewel, Complete........$77
No. 3663. 7 Jewel, Complete........ 69
Elgin Movements with Luminous Dials and Hands, Complete in 14k Cushion Shape, 14k Gold Case and Pigskin Strap and 14k Gold Buckle.

SWISS LUMINOUS DIAL MILITARY WATCHES

$10-20

$15-25

$15-25

No. 3712. Lancet Nickel.
7 Jewel......$17.40
Complete.
Lancet Lever Swiss Movment with Luminous Dial and Hands, Complete in Round Nickel Cases with Kitchener Leather Straps.

No. 3711. Admiral Nickel.
7 Jewel......$16.10
Complete.
Admiral Lever Swiss Movement with Luminous Dial and Hands, Complete in Round Nickel Cases with Kitchener Leather Straps.

No. 3710. 7 Jewel......$20.70
Complete.
Cyma Reliable Lever Swiss Movement with Luminous Dial and Hands, Complete in Round Nickel Cases with Kitchener Leather Straps.

$75-85

No. 3708. Cyma Silver.
15 Jewel......$35.20
Complete.

No. 3709. 7 Jewel......31.20
Complete.
Cyma, Reliable Lever Swiss Movement with Luminous Dial and Hands, Complete in Square Silver Cases with Heavy Leather Straps and Silver Buckles.

CROWN SILVER

$50-60

3/0 Size, Waltham Nickel.
No. 3690.　15 Jewel, Complete......**$37.00**
No. 3691.　7 Jewel, Complete......**28.10**
　　　Waltham Movements with Luminous
Dials and Hands, Complete in Square
Nickel Case with Kitchener Leather Strap.

$75-95

3/0 Size, Waltham Silver.
No. 3698.　15 Jewel, Complete......**$39.90**
No. 3699.　7 Jewel, Complete......**31.10**
　　Waltham Movements with Luminous
Dials and Hands, Complete in Round
Silver Cases with Kitchener Straps.

$90-110

CROWN SILVER

3/0 Size Elgin Silver.
No. 3680.　15 Jewel, Complete......**$35.90**
No. 3681.　7 Jewel, Complete......**27.60**
　　Elgin Movements with Luminous Dials and
Hands, Complete in Round Silver Case with
Kitchener Leather Strap.

MILITARY WATCHES

S $110-125
GF $60-70

3/0 Size, Elgin Silver and Gold Filled.
No. 3694.　15 Jewel Silver, Complete........**$42.80**
No. 3695.　7 Jewel Silver, Complete........**34.50**
No. 3696.　15 Jewel Gold Filled, Complete........**43.70**
No. 3697.　7 Jewel Gold Filled, Complete........**35.40**
　　Elgin Movements with Luminous Dials and Hands,
Complete in Square Cases with Heavy Hand Sewed
Leather Straps.

$45-55

3/0 Size, Elgin Nickel.
No. 3686.　15 Jewel, Complete......**$33.30**
No. 3687.　7 Jewel, Complete......**25.40**
　　Elgin Movements with Luminous Dials
and Hands, Complete in Square Nickel
Case with Khaki Strap.

$50-60

3/0 Size, Elgin Nickel.
No. 3692.　15 Jewel, Complete...**$32.80**
No. 3693.　7 Jewel, Complete...**24.90**
　　Elgin Movements with Luminous
Dials and Hands, Complete in Square
Nickel Cases with Kitchener Leather
Straps.

MILITARY WRIST WATCHES

3/0 Size   1918   **3/0 Size**

N $95-115
S $150-175

N $75-95
S $125-150

"TONNEAU"
14K. GOLD, D. S. BACK

No. 3265-N	Nickel Case, 15 J.,	$30.70
3265-S	Silver Case, 15 J.,	33.20
3261-N	Nickel Case, 7 J.,	22.90
3261-S	Silver Case, 7 J.,	25.40

Full Figured Luminous Dials and Hands,
$4.70 Extra

"CADET"
14K. GOLD, D. S. BACK

No. 3165-N	Nickel Case, 15 J.,	$27.60
3165-S	Silver Case, 15 J.,	29.80
3161-N	Nickel Case, 7 J.,	19.90
3161-S	Silver Case, 7 J.,	22.30

Full Figured Luminous Dials and Hands,
$4.70 Extra

1919

N $50-70
S $90-110

CADET
(New)

Non-breakable crystal with Patented
Bezel. Finest Web Khaki Strap with
Special Detachable Patented Fastener
Gold Double Stock Engine-Turned
Back.

No. 3465-S	Silver Case, 15 J.,	$38.70
3465-N	Nickel Case, 15 J.,	36.20
3461-S	Silver Case, 7 J.,	30.30
3461-N	Nickel Case, 7 J.,	27.80

(Not ready for delivery before August, 1918)

N $50-70
S $90-110

CADET
BEST QUALITY STRAPS
Gold Double Stock Engine-Turned
Back.

No. 3165-S	Silver Case, 15 J.,	$35.20
3165-N	Nickel Case, 15 J.,	32.70
3161-S	Silver Case, 7 J.,	27.00
3161-N	Nickel Case, 7 J.,	24.50

ELGIN MILITARY WATCHES

With Plain or Luminous Dials

N $40-60

With Plain Dial

N $40-60

ELGIN Military Watches have 3/O-size, 7-jewel movements and are equipped with double-roller escapements. They are especially adapted to hard outdoor use.

Complete in sturdy, compact case of special design. Strong, mannish looking, silvered dial with heavy figures and hands. Heavy cowboy-style strap of battleship gray, perforated for ventilation.

Price: With plain dial and hands $13.40
Extra for luminous hands and dots $2.70
Extra for luminous hands and figures $4.20

Sportsmen, motorists, golfers, athletes and army and navy men instantly appreciate the features which make this the handy "extra watch" for outdoor service.

Luminous Dial
(Night View)

Luminous Dial
(Day View)

ELGIN NATIONAL WATCH CO., ELGIN, U.S.A.

The Hamilton Wrist Watch for Men

Glass Enamel Dial
Cushion Silver $250-275
Round Silver $200-225

No. 981

Illustrating Luminous Dial and Khaki Strap

An accurate, durable timekeeper, constructed to stand the hard service to which a wrist watch is subjected. Especially designed for Army and Navy Officers, Aviators, Automobile Drivers, Civil Engineers, Foresters, and others who realize the advantage of a wrist watch in their occupations.

This watch was tremendously popular with the American Expeditionary Force and the United States Navy, and we have never been able to meet the demand for it.

No. 981. 0-size, nickel, ¾ plate movement, 17 fine jewels in settings, Breguet hairspring, double roller escapement, compensation balance, adjusted. Cased in either round or cushion shape silver case.

		Luminous Dial
Sterling silver, round case	$37.00	$43.00
Sterling silver, cushion shape	40.00	46.00

$65-85

$25-40

$75-95

$50-70

5468W.............$32.00
0 size, sterling silver, cushion-shape case, leather strap, fitted with 15 jewel Swiss movement, lever escapement, luminous dials and hands.

Prices in "THE RED BOOK" 1919 are subject to change without notice owing to conditions resulting from the European war.

5467W.............$25.00
0 size, nickel, square cushion-shape case, khaki strap, fitted with 15 jewel Swiss movement, lever escapement, luminous figures and hands.

5466W.............$21.00
0 Size, Nickel Octagon Case. Khaki strap, fitted with 7 jewel Swiss movement, lever escapement, luminous figures and hands.

5464W 0 Size, Nickel Case..$19.00
Leather strap, fitted with 7 jewel Lancet movement, with luminous dial and hands.
5465W.............$30.00
0 Size, Sterling Silver Case. With leather strap, fitted with 15 jewel Swiss movement, lever escapement, luminous dial and hands.

Luminous Military Watches

Illustrating a Few or the Many Designs Which We Are Able to Secure

6 size nickel case, with leather strap, fitted as follows:

5458W 7 J. N.Y.S, plain dial..$.....
5459W 7 J. N.Y.S, lumin. dial..$.....
5460W 7 Jewel Columbia Movement, plain dial...$.....
5461W 7 Jewel Columbia Movement, luminous dial..$.....

Prices on Application

5463W.......$.....
0 size, nickel case, leather strap, fitted with 7 jewel New York Standard movement, with luminous dials and hands.

Price on Application

3/0 size 20-year square, plain polished case, leather strap, fitted as follows:

5454W 7 J. Elgin, plain dial..$25.60
5455W 7 J. Elgin, luminous dial.$29.80
3/0 size sterling silver plain polished case, leather strap, fitted as follows:
5456W 7 J. Elgin, plain dial..$25.80
5457W 7 J. Elgin, luminous dial.$29.80

For 15 Jewel Elgin add $7.70, list, to the above prices.

3/0 size 20-year fancy engraved case. leather strap, fitted as follows:
5450W 7 J. Elgin, plain dial...$25.60
5451W 7 J. Elgin, luminous dial.$29.80
3/0 size sterling silver oxidized, plain case, leather strap, fitted as follows:
5452W 7 J. Elgin, plain dial.. $25.60
5453W 7 J. Elgin, luminous dial.$29.80

We cannot guarantee delivery or prices on these watches. We will furnish you as long as we are able to obtain them or the nearest we have in stock the time the order is received. There is a tremendous demand for these, so that we are not able to secure enough to fill our orders.

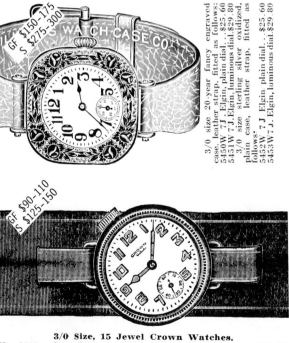

5462W.......................$24.00
0 size, nickel, square cushion-shape case, leather strap, fitted with 15 jewel Swiss lever movement, luminous figures and hands.

3/0 Size, 15 Jewel Crown Watches.

No. 3700.   Complete in Gold Filled Cases.......**$26.80**
No. 3701.   Complete in Silver Cases............**$25.80**

Every Man of Distinction Will Wear an "Elgin" Strap Watch

Sturdy and Mannish. Convenient. Accurate and Reliable. Convenient and Handy all the Year. Right on your Arm—Time right "Off the Bat."

Illustrations reduced size

"Foch"

"PERSHING" STYLE

Cushion shape; heavy pigs strap.
No. M6036   Sterling silver, each........ $42
No. M6037   Gold filled, each... 44

GF $110-125
S $170-190

"KITCHENER" STYLE

Square shape; wide pigskin strap, double.
No. M6030   Nickel, each.... $33.50
No. M6031   Sterling silver, each........ 39.00
No. M6032   Gold filled, each........ 40.25

N $100-125
GF $125-150
S $200-225

"FOCH" STYLE

Round shape as per illustration. Khaki or pigskin strap.
No. M6033   Nickel, each.................... $30.75
No. M6034   Sterling Silver, each.......... 38.75
No. M6035   Gold Filled, each.............. 36.50

N $75-100
GF $100-125
S $150-175

Handy in winter, when gloves and overcoat make fumbling in your pocket clumsy and unsafe. Handy in summer, when you wear no vest and half the time no coat. Genuine black dial full-luminous Elgins, in your choice of three styles of case and strap herein illustrated. All three styles have genuine Elgin movements —American through and through. Specially constructed for hard outdoor use. Wear one a week and you'd feel lost without.

Ferrero
Sterling 38mm Swiss-15J
Luminous Dial & Hands
"O" Size Oval Tormeau
1920's Metal Dial
Head $150-175

Rolex
Sterling 33mm-"O" Size-15J
Swiss Case Dial & Movement
Signed, Hinged Case
Luminous Hands Metal Dial
Head $600-700

Bulova
Sterling Tank 34mm-17J
Case Dial & Movement Marked
Hinged Case-Rare!-Ca 1920's
Luminous Hands & Numbers
Head $100-125

J.W. Benson
Sterling Covered Wirstwatch-17J
Push Button to Open-Swiss Movment
Wire Lugs-Dial Marked-35mm Very Rare
Head $350-400

Tavanes
Nickel Numbered Case-Luminous Hands
U.S.A. Signal Corps Military Dial
Wire Lugs-Procelain Dial
Head $125-150

Cyma
Swiss Compass Watch
Sterling 48mm Swiss Movement-Rare
Hinged Lugs-Luminous Dial & Hands
Head $550-650

Longines
Sterling 34mm-17J Three Adj.
Case Movement & Dial Marked
Wire Lugs-Porcelain Dial-Ca 1900's
Head $275-325

Swiss Watch
Sterling 39x26mm Tank Watch-15J
Swiss Movment-Wire Lugs
Head $200-225

Hamilton
Sterling-1940's-17J
Case Dial & Movement Marked
Head $275-325

Goering
Unusual Sterling 39mm-15J Two Adj.
Movement Case & Dial Signed
Second Hand at the Nine
Head $100-125

Hamilton
U.S. Navy Bureau of Ships
Divers Watch-31mm-Hack Feature-Ca 1940's
Small Carved Crown & Marked Back
Head $350-400

Elgin
U.S. Navy Bureau of Ships
Divers Watch-Hack Feature-32mm
Carved Case & Large Crown
Dial & Case Marked-Ca 1940's
Head $350-400

Elgin
U.S.A. Airforce Pocket Watch
Sterling, Airforce Insignia-15J
Inside Hinged Case-Probably had a fog
Glass Enamel Dial
Head $100-125

Seeland
Duo Dial-Swiss Unadjusted-17J
Head $125-175

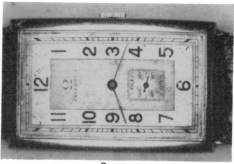

Omega
Tank Sterling-47x29mm
Case Dial & Movement All Signed
Extremely Rare-Wire Lugs
Head $1,000-2,000

Helbros
Brevet Military Dial
Luminous Hand & Numbers
Head $75-100

Waltham
Silveroid Case-Waltham Movement
Extremely Rare Detachable Cover
Ca 1940's Head $400-450

Tracy
Sterling Large 38mm-6J Two Adj.
Wire Lugs-CYMA-Swiss-Tournneau
Elongated Numbered Dial-Hinged Case
Head $200-225

LeCoultre
Automatic with Power Window
Military Dial-Inscribed Property of
U.S. Air Force with Serial Numbers
Very Unusual Head $200-225

Bulova
Army Issue Sterling Top-32mm
Hack Feature
Head $75-100

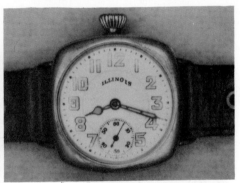

Illinois
Sterling Cushion Case-30x30mm-15J
Luminous Numbers & Hands-Fahy's Case
Head $150-175

LeCoultre
Sterling Case-32mm-15J Three Adj.
Wire Lugs-Swiss-Early 1900's
Head $225-250

Elgin
A-11 Military Issue-24 Hour Dial-18J
Head $150-175

Waltham
Military Issue-Nickel Case-17J
Original Army Band-Integrated Cage
Nickel Wire Lugs-Luminous Dial & Hands
Head $400-450

Swiss
Sterling Push Button Open Military Cover
Hinged Lug-Swiss Movement
CA Early 1900's Head $550-600

Gruen
Sterling Gruen-Round 29mm-15J Three Adj.
Movement Marked Gruen Guild
Case Marked ID Sterling
Head $125-150

A SPECIAL THANKS TO:
Richard Cohen
Philadelphia, PA
for photographs of his military
collection on page 404-409

Elgin
Cushion Case-Elgin Movement-31mm
Wadsworth Case-Luminous Numbers & Hands
Head $50-75

Waltham
Sterling Integrated Cage Military Watch
Waltham Movement-Fahy's Case-Wire Lugs
Early 1900's Head $550-600

Swiss with English Hallmarks
Sterling Round-35mm-Movement Unmarked
Push Button Opens Lid to Reveal Dial
Black Enamel Numbers on Top Cover
Head $200-225

Swiss
Sterling Highly Unusual
Movement Unmarked-Sterling Integrated
Cover with Opening For Each Number
Luminous Hands
Head $350-400

Waltham
Sterling Case & Hinged Lugs-32mm-15J
Case Dial & Movement Signed
Porcelain Dial-Early 1900's
Head $175-200

Brevett
Sterling Oval Shape-39mm-15J
Swiss Movement-Case Market
Wire Lugs-Porcelain Dial
Head $125-150

WALTHAM WRIST WATCH, 6/0 SIZE, 9-JEWEL, MODEL 10609
AND 6/0 SIZE, 17-JEWEL, MODEL 10617

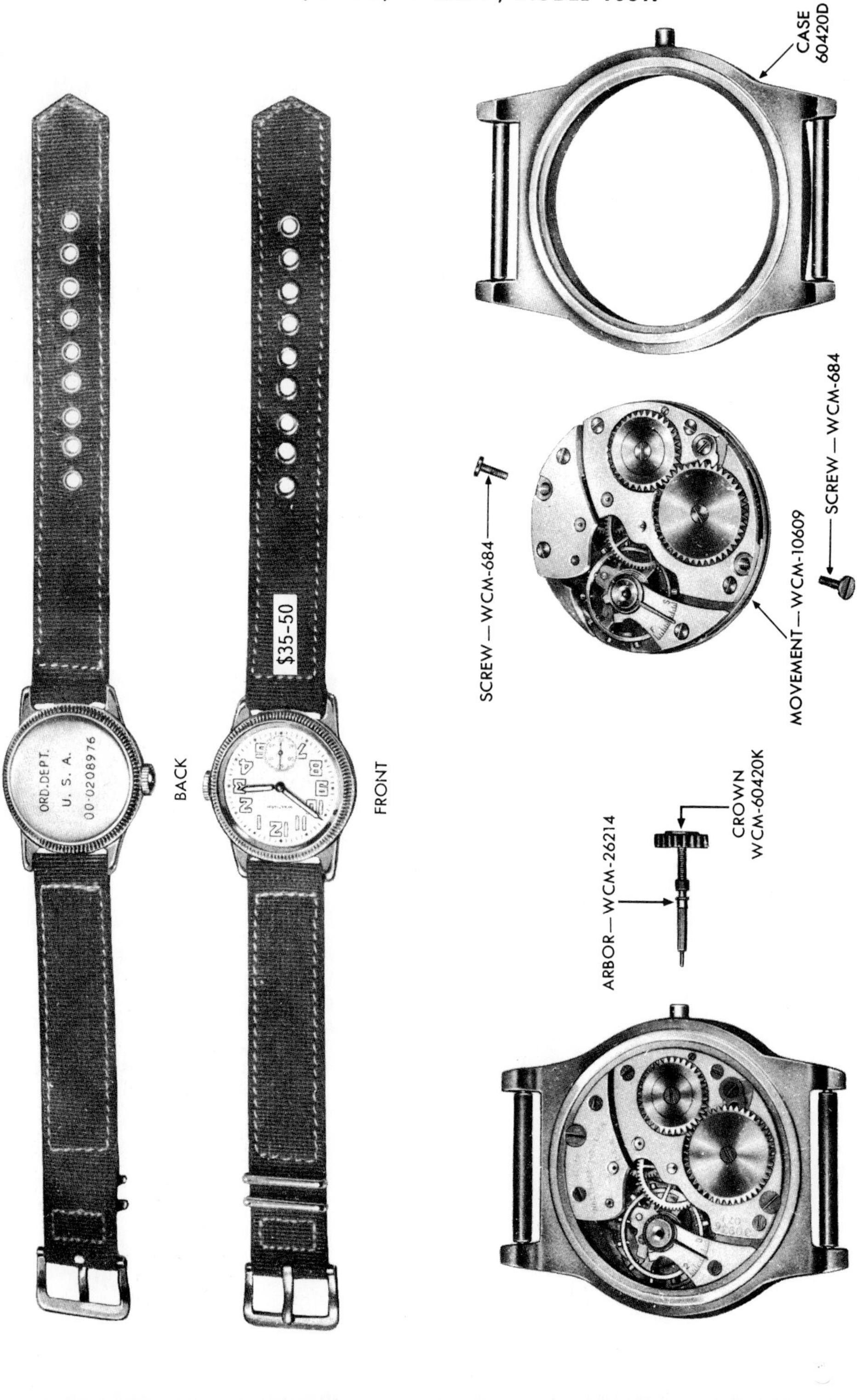

CASE 60420D

ORD. DEPT. U. S. A. 00-0208976

BACK

$35-50

FRONT

SCREW—WCM-684

SCREW—WCM-684

MOVEMENT—WCM-10609

ARBOR—WCM-26214

CROWN WCM-60420K

ELGIN WRIST WATCH, 8/0 SIZE, 7- OR 15-JEWEL

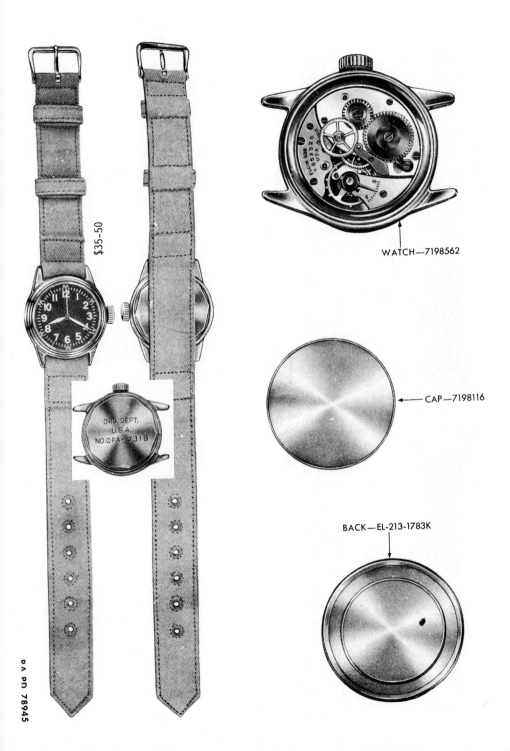

$35-50

WATCH—7198562

CAP—7198116

BACK—EL-213-1783K

Elgin Wrist Watches — 7- and 15-jewel, 8/0 Size

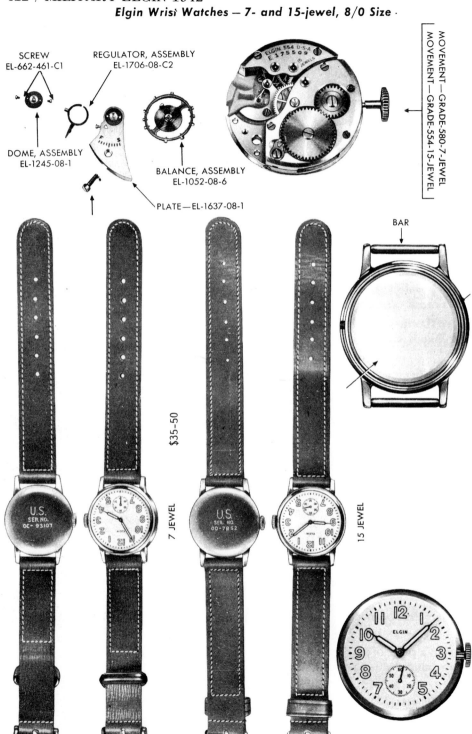

SCREW
EL-662-461-C1

REGULATOR, ASSEMBLY
EL-1706-08-C2

DOME, ASSEMBLY
EL-1245-08-1

BALANCE, ASSEMBLY
EL-1052-08-6

PLATE—EL-1637-08-1

MOVEMENT—GRADE-580-7-JEWEL
MOVEMENT—GRADE-554-15-JEWEL

BAR

$35–50

7 JEWEL

15 JEWEL

U.S.
SER. NO.
0C- 93107

U.S.
SER. NO.
0D-7852

HAMILTON WRIST WATCH, 6/0 SIZE, 17-JEWEL, MODEL 987A

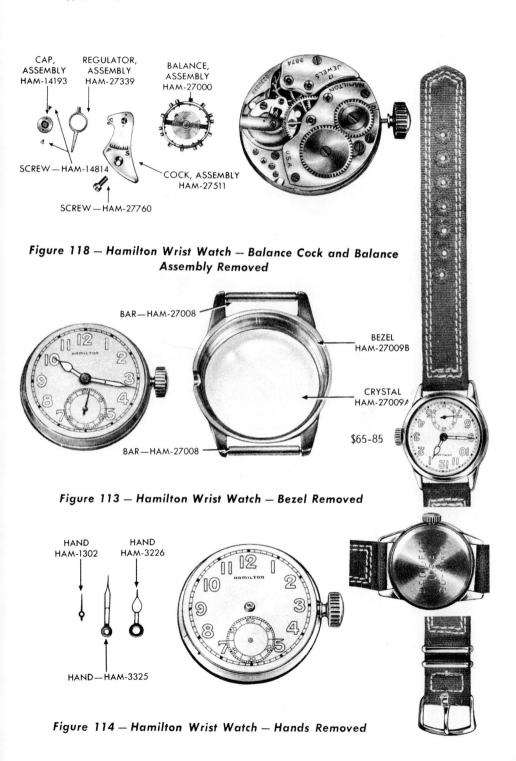

CAP,
ASSEMBLY
HAM-14193

REGULATOR,
ASSEMBLY
HAM-27339

BALANCE,
ASSEMBLY
HAM-27000

SCREW — HAM-14814

COCK, ASSEMBLY
HAM-27511

SCREW — HAM-27760

Figure 118 — Hamilton Wrist Watch — Balance Cock and Balance Assembly Removed

BAR—HAM-27008

BEZEL
HAM-27009B

CRYSTAL
HAM-27009A

$65-85

BAR—HAM-27008

Figure 113 — Hamilton Wrist Watch — Bezel Removed

HAND
HAM-1302

HAND
HAM-3226

HAND—HAM-3325

Figure 114 — Hamilton Wrist Watch — Hands Removed

BULOVA WRIST WATCH, MODEL 10 AK, 10½ LIGNE SIZE, 15-JEWEL, WATERPROOF CASE

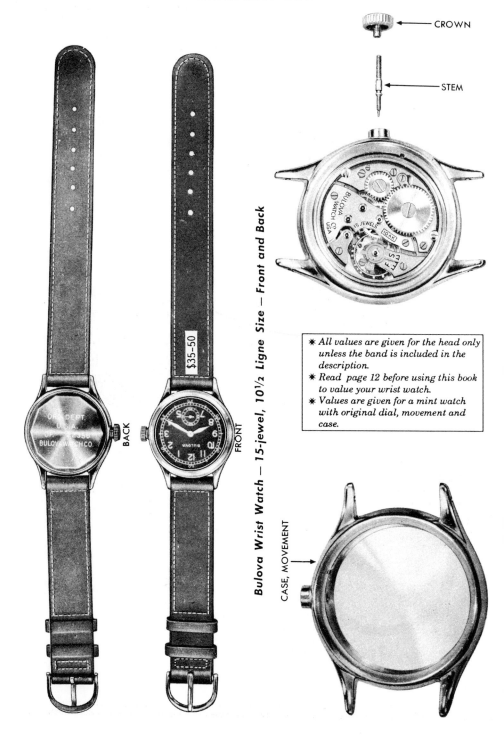

CROWN

STEM

$35-50

BACK

FRONT

CASE, MOVEMENT

Bulova Wrist Watch — 15-jewel, 10½ Ligne Size — Front and Back

* All values are given for the head only unless the band is included in the description.
* Read page 12 before using this book to value your wrist watch.
* Values are given for a mint watch with original dial, movement and case.

ELGIN PRECISION INSTRUMENTS LIKE THESE

AIRPLANE CLOCK

FIELD SERVICE WATCH

AVIATION NAVIGATION WATCH

ELGIN RAILROAD WATCH

CHRONOMETRIC TACHOMETER

CHRONOMETRIC TACHOMETER

MARINE CORPS SERVICE WATCH

CENSORED FOR NAVY BUREAU OF AERONAUTICS

CENSORED FOR U. S. AIR FORCES

ELGIN TIMER

ELAPSED TIME AIRPLANE CLOCK

These are some of the fine precision instruments

ARE PART OF YOUR WAR CONTRIBUTION ...

Fewer watches for you mean more for our fighting men

ELGIN SERVICE WATCH

ELGIN SERVICE WATCH

CENSORED
FOR
U. S. AIR FORCES

CENSORED
FOR
NAVY BUREAU
OF AERONAUTICS

AIRPLANE COMPASS

FIELD SERVICE WATCH

WATCH FOR THE
BRITISH ARMY

GROUND SPEED
NAVIGATION WATCH

CENSORED
FOR
AIR FORCES
AND NAVY BUREAU
OF AERONAUTICS

MASTER NAVIGATION WATCH

CENSORED
FOR
ALL ARMED SERVICES

Elgin is supplying to the armed forces

"E" *Makes It Unanimous!*

LONG ago America placed its O.K. on Hamilton's peacetime products.

Now the Army and Navy have added their "E" for the excellent quality and satisfactory quantity of Hamilton's wartime products.

That makes it unanimous!

The things Hamilton learned by making fine watches exclusively for fifty years, came in mighty handy when Uncle Sam asked Hamilton to take on the job of making *super*-fine timepieces for the armed forces.

The things Hamilton learned by designing, developing and producing the famous Hamilton marine chronometer and many other accurate war timepieces, have set new standards of accuracy for Hamilton's post-war watches.

That's why after the war—as before the war—Hamilton will be the watch you'll proudly show, when your customer says "Show me America's *Fine* Watch!" Hamilton Watch Company, Lancaster, Pennsylvania.

Hamilton

Makers Of The Watch Of Railroad Accuracy
NOW MAKING ACCURATE WAR TIMEPIECES

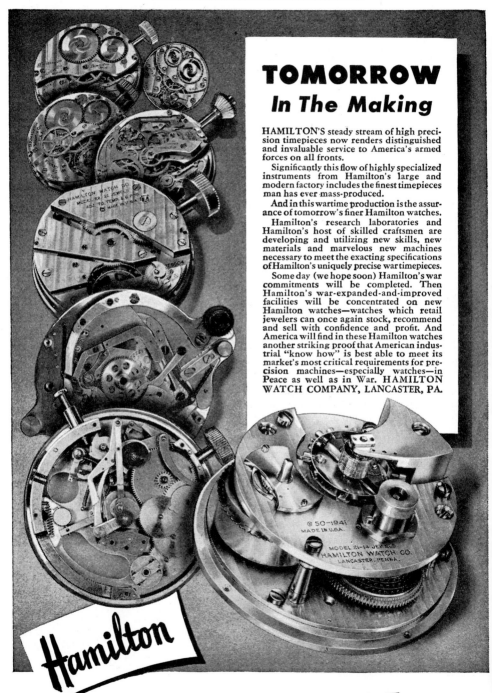

TOMORROW
In The Making

HAMILTON'S steady stream of high precision timepieces now renders distinguished and invaluable service to America's armed forces on all fronts.

Significantly this flow of highly specialized instruments from Hamilton's large and modern factory includes the finest timepieces man has ever mass-produced.

And in this wartime production is the assurance of tomorrow's finer Hamilton watches.

Hamilton's research laboratories and Hamilton's host of skilled craftsmen are developing and utilizing new skills, new materials and marvelous new machines necessary to meet the exacting specifications of Hamilton's uniquely precise war timepieces.

Some day (we hope soon) Hamilton's war commitments will be completed. Then Hamilton's war-expanded-and-improved facilities will be concentrated on new Hamilton watches—watches which retail jewelers can once again stock, recommend and sell with confidence and profit. And America will find in these Hamilton watches another striking proof that American industrial "know how" is best able to meet its market's most critical requirements for precision machines—especially watches—in Peace as well as in War. HAMILTON WATCH COMPANY, LANCASTER, PA.

Hamilton

Makers of the Watch of Railroad Accuracy—NOW MAKING ACCURATE   WAR TIMEPIECES

During the war, Hamilton's entire facilities were devoted to the manufacture of Marine Chronometers and other highly specialized timepieces for navigational purposes, in addition to time fuses, hang-fire recorders, map measures, and many other miscellaneous precision products.

The Hamilton MARINE CHRONOMETER

Quality in quantity. Old time watchmakers said it couldn't be done—but we did it! For nearly two hundred years fine Marine Chronometers used for navigation were largely made abroad by hand by skilled old craftsmen. But when war came to America, the U. S. Navy couldn't wait! They needed thousands of chronometers and other precise navigational instruments in a hurry! So Hamilton defied tradition, developed modern production equipment to operate to finer dimensions than had ever before been achieved. Result: more and finer Marine Chronometers than anyone had ever produced before. And in a hurry!

Moeris
38mm—CA 1960
Triple calendar—Moonphase
2 Dial chronograph—Flat pusher
Steel $350-400

Mimo—Digital—Jump Hour
21x36mm—CA 1930's—17 Jewels
18KYG $1,500-1,800

Mistral
31x31mm—CA 1920's—15 Jewels
Wire lugs
18KYG $200-240

Mimorex—Doubleface
12x30mm—CA 1931—Reversible
Lady's Chromium Case $400—500?

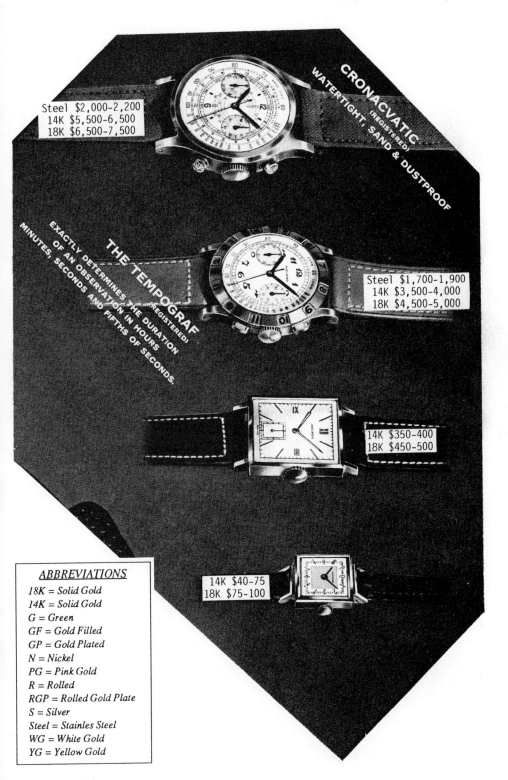

CRONACVATIC (REGISTERED)
WATERTIGHT, SAND & DUSTPROOF

Steel $2,000-2,200
14K $5,500-6,500
18K $6,500-7,500

THE TEMPOGRAF (REGISTERED)
EXACTLY DETERMINES THE DURATION OF AN OBSERVATION IN HOURS, MINUTES, SECONDS AND FIFTHS OF SECONDS.

Steel $1,700-1,900
14K $3,500-4,000
18K $4,500-5,000

14K $350-400
18K $450-500

14K $40-75
18K $75-100

ABBREVIATIONS

18K = Solid Gold
14K = Solid Gold
G = Green
GF = Gold Filled
GP = Gold Plated
N = Nickel
PG = Pink Gold
R = Rolled
RGP = Rolled Gold Plate
S = Silver
Steel = Stainles Steel
WG = White Gold
YG = Yellow Gold

Self-winding CALENDAR WATCHES
~ WATER RESISTANT

Steel $250-300
S & G $350-400
14KYG $800-1,000

Steel $300-350
S & G $350-450
14KYG $800-1,000

Steel $50-70
Steel & G $75-90
14KYG $150-200

MOVADO

	A	B	C
Stainless steel	$110.	100.	95.
Steel and 14K gold	140.	125.	125.
14K gold	240.	230.	230.

17 jewels   Fed. Tax Incl.

A. calendomatic
B. calendolux
C. calendoplan

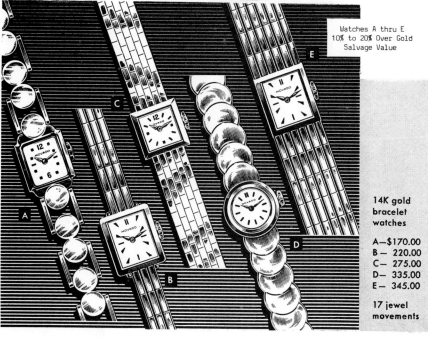

Watches A thru E
10% to 20% Over Gold
Salvage Value

**14K gold
bracelet
watches**

A—$170.00
B — 220.00
C — 275.00
D— 335.00
E — 345.00

**17 jewel
movements**

Quality In
Classic Cord Designs

14K Gold watches in a variety of fashions to please your fancy.

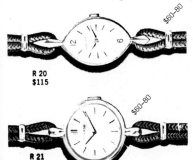

$60-80

R 20
$115

R 21
$85

$60-80

$60-80

R 17
$145

$60-80

R 18
$135

$60-80

*R 19
$125

*R 15
$250

R 16
$195

Fashion "Originals"— Every One

Distinctive bracelet designs in 14K Gold are in the forefront of today's mode:—all the "chic" of Paris.

10% to 20% Over Gold Salvage

Quality In
Casual Models

Movado mermaids—water-resistant sub-sea miniatures, and tailored functional designs in casual strap watches.

$60-80

R 22
Water-resistant miniature, 14K Gold, $140

$60-80

*R 24
14K Gold
$145

$60-80

R 25
14K Gold
$95

$60-80

R 26
14K Gold
$110

14KYG $60-80
14KYGF $25-35
Steel $20-30

R 23
Water-resistant miniature, 14K Gold, $140; 14K Gold filled, $95; St. Steel, $95; in self-winding Queenmatic - St. Steel from $115.

The Nobility Of
The New Movado
Kingmatic "S"

This royal family of self-winding watches features a completely new movement — the most advanced, the most dependable made.

14KYG $100–120
Steel $35–45

◄ R 28
Sub-Sea, Water-Resistant. 17 Jewels. St. Steel. $100

14KYG $100–120
Steel $35–45

14KYG $125–150
Steel $50–70

R 29
Sub-Sea, Water-Resistant, Uni-case, 28 Jewels, 14K Gold. $185 ►

THE NEW
Silhouettes
THIN AS A WHISPER

◄ R 34
The Watchmaker's Watch. Sub-Sea, Water-Resistant, Unicase.
14K Gold $140.
14K Gold filled 85.
St. Steel   79.50

14KYG $125–150

14KYG $100–120
14KYGF $45–55
Steel $35–45

R 35
The Diplomat.
14K Gold $150 ►

Automatic Watches

Slimmer, trimmer: —micro-miniaturization makes it possible to rival the sleekness of a dress "silhouette" watch, while improving accuracy and dependability.

◀ R 30
14K Gold, 28 Jewels
$175
14K Gold filled,
17 Jewels $110

14KYG $100–120
14KYGF $40–50

R 31 ▶
**Kingmatic
Calendar,
Sub-Sea,**
Water-Resistant,
with date-
setting mech-
anism operated
from the crown.
28 jewels.
14K Gold $245
St. Steel from
$125

14KYG $100–120
Steel $40–50

14KYG $100–120
Steel $35–45

◀ **R 36
The Viscount.**
14K Gold $175
Also available
with self-winding
movement $210

14KYG $100–120

18KYG
$125–150

**R 37
The Aristocrat.
Super-silhouette.
18K Gold $250**

FOR CHAMPAGNE OCCASIONS

A distinguished series of ultra-thin dress watches.

Steel $1,500-2,000
14KYG $5,000-6,000

R 38
The Chronograph. Stop watch and superb timepiece combined.
Sub-Sea, water-resistant.
14K Gold $285   St. Steel $145

Nice Watch
38mm—CA 1950's
2 Dial—Chronograph—Square pushers
Bezel chapter ring
18KYG $550-600

Nice Watch
38mm—CA 1950's
2 Dial—Chronograph—Square pushers
18KYG $350-400

Ollendorff "Odin". Luminous hands & numerals, subsidiary seconds. 15J or 17J movement. Tonneau case. ca 1927. 14K . $125—150
Gold-filled . . . . 25— 30

Octo "Skymaster". Antimated rocket circles the dial every 40 seconds. Raised gold figures showing earth, moon and sun. Center seconds. Automatic movement. Stainless steel round case. ca 1963 . . . . $100-125

Ollendorf "Oldorf". Luminous hands & numerals, subsidiary seconds. 15J movement. Cushion case. ca 1927. 14K gold . . . $85—100
14K gold-filled . . . . 20— 25

1952

Ollendorff "Ostend". Luminous hands & numerals, subsidiary seconds. 17J & 15J movement. Molded rectangular case, embossed bezel. ca 1927. 14K gold . . . . . . $110—135
14K Gold-filled . . . . 25— 30

$35-50

Ollendorff "Ivan". Radium silvered dial, luminous hands & numerals, subsidiary seconds. 15J movement. 14K gold-filled, square case with faceted corners. ca 1927 . . . . $20—25

OLMA AUTOMATIC

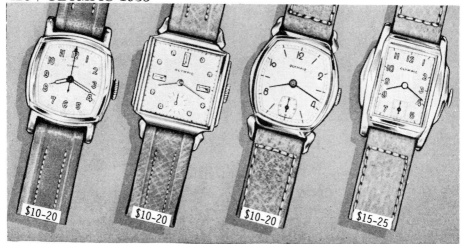

MS65799S
Attractive cushion style, 10K yellow R.G.P. case, steel back, 17 jewel movement, sweep second hand, leather strap
LIST **$33.00**

MS55794R
Masculine design, 10K yellow rolled gold plate case, steel back, fine strap, 17 jewel Olympic movement with rich looking rhinestone dial, gift box.
LIST **$37.00**

MS55796
Sturdy and distinctive cushion style, 10K yellow rolled gold plate case, steel back, 17 jewel Olympic movement, fine leather strap, gift box.
LIST **$31.00**

MS55890
A handsome plain model in 10K yellow rolled gold plate case, steel back, 7 jewel Olympic movement, fine strap, gift box.
LIST **$21.70**

MS65539
Distinguished looking model, 14K yellow gold case, heavy crystal, 17 jewel movement, leather strap, gold buckle.
LIST **$94.00**

MS65556
Same with 10K yellow goldfilled case.
LIST **$42.50**

MS65558
A handsome plain tailored model in 10K goldfilled case with fine leather strap, 17 jewel Olympic movement, gift box.
LIST **$45.00**

EC55594
Streamlined beautiful modern style, 10K yellow rolled gold plate case, steel back, dome crystal, smart matched 10K goldfilled basketweave expansion bracelet, 17 jewel Olympic movement, gift box.
LIST **$40.50**

EC55599A
Smart plain long cushion style, 10K yellow rolled gold case—steel back, matching 10K goldfilled link expansion bracelet, 17 jewel Olympic movement, gift box.
LIST **$40.00**

**Men's Diamond-Set
Watches**

left **D6782G**
14K yellow solid gold
set with 30 diamonds on
bezel. 14K bracelet
matches 14K florentined
finished dial.

D6782
Same watch with white
dial.

right **D6757WD**
14K white solid gold
bracelet watch with
12 brilliant diamonds
set on dial.

$350–400

$350–400

**Men's Diamond-Set
Watches**

left **D6752**
46 glittering diamonds
frame the 14K solid white
or yellow gold case.
Dial echoes the woven
mesh pattern of the
matching bracelet.

right **D6758**
45 sparkling diamonds
describe a perfect circle
around the 14K solid
white gold case. With
matching mesh bracelet.

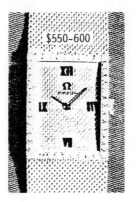

$550–600

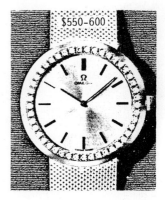

$550–600

**Man's Diamond-Set
Watch**

left **D6800**
54 sparkling diamonds
set on the bezel trace a
rectangular shape in this
dramatic 14K white solid
gold watch with striking
black dial.

right **D6765X**
A black suede dial is
outlined in 40 diamonds
for this 14K solid white
gold dress watch.

D6765
Same watch with white
dial.

$125–150

$100–125

**Men's Diamond-Set
Watches**

left **D6765**

40 brilliant diamonds
rim the case of this
elegantly simple 14K
solid white gold watch.
Easy-to-read markers
accent the classic dial.

right **D6672DR**

36 diamonds follow the
march of time around the
dial. A brilliant array, in
a case of 14K solid
white gold.

$300–325

$275–300

**Men's Diamond-Set
Watches**

left **D6764**

40 magnificent diamonds
blazon this 14K solid
white gold watch with
masculine herring-bone
patterned bracelet.

right **D6782**

30 glittering diamonds
frame this classic 14K
solid gold cushion shape
watch with matching
mesh bracelet.

$550–650

$500–600

**Men's Diamond-Set
Watches**

left **D6752**

46 glittering diamonds
frame the 14K solid white
gold case. Dial echoes
the woven mesh pattern
of the matching bracelet.

right **D6758**

45 sparkling diamonds
describe a perfect circle
around the 14K solid
white gold case. With
matching mesh bracelet.

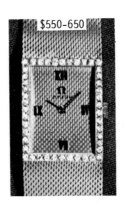

$550–650

$550–650

$250-275

**Men's Diamond-Set
Seamaster De Villes**

right top **LL6769D**

20 diamonds dominate
the dial of this 14K solid
white or yellow
gold Seamaster De Ville.
Self-winding, water-
resistant case.

$150-175

**Man's Diamond-Set
Watch**

D6767D

20 sparkling diamonds
mark time handsomely
on the dial of this 14K
solid white or yellow
gold watch.

$125-150

**Men's Diamond-Set
Watches**

left top **D6725D**

8 fiery diamonds
illuminate the 8 hour
markers of this 14K solid
gold cushion-shaped
watch.

$125-150

left bottom **D6766D**

8 sparkling diamonds
take the place of hour
markers in this smartly
styled 14K solid white or
yellow gold square case.

right **D6787**

24 diamonds, set at
intervals, circle this
round 14K solid white
gold case.

$125-150

$115-130

**Men's Diamond-Set
Watches**

left **D6768D**

12 gleaming diamonds
accent the 12, 3, 6 and
9 hour markers. Classic
14K solid white or yellow
gold case.

right **D6650D**

8 diamonds punctuate
time within a florentined
case of 14K solid white
or yellow gold that's
correct for every dress
occasion.

$100-125

**Men's 14K Gold
Dress Watches**

left **D6726**

Florentined tonneau-
shaped case of 14K
solid gold. Polished oval
frame dramatizes the
classic Roman numeral
dial. Matching textured
mesh bracelet.

right **D6772**

14K solid gold bracelet
watch. Unusual tonneau-
shaped case with oval
dial-opening.

$350–450

$350–450

**Men's 14K Gold
Dress Watches**

left **D6751**

14K yellow or white solid
gold bracelet watch in a
distinctive florentined pattern.
The dial repeats the texture
of the bracelet, providing
a luxurious "flow" from
end to end.

center **D6773X**

Men's 14K yellow solid
gold dress watch.
Complemented by green
enamel dial.

D6773

Same watch with silver
dial.

right **D6805**

Florentined finish
14K solid gold yellow
or white dress watch.
Matching dial with
Roman numerals.

$450–500

$350–450

$450–500

$350-450

$350-450

Men's 14K Gold Dress Watches

left **D6761**
The classic case is 14K solid gold complemented by a matching, tapered mesh bracelet.

right top **D6771**
Traditional round case in 14K solid gold with today's look in combination stick-and-roman numerals set in a gilt dial. Matching fine mesh bracelet.

right bottom **D6757**
Large, easy-to-read dial set in a 14K solid white or yellow gold case with matching mesh bracelet.

$350-450

$350-450

Men's 14K Gold Dress Watches

left **D6778**
Traditional rectangular styling in 14K solid gold watch with matching mesh bracelet.

right **D6779**
Classic square design of this 14K solid gold watch is complemented by a matching mesh bracelet.

$350-450

Men's 14K Gold Dress Watches

left top **D6709**
14K white solid gold strap watch with Roman figure dial.

left bottom **D6793**
The classic look in a 14K solid gold watch — rectangular case and Roman numerals.

right **D6791**
Smart cushion shape and gilt dial in a handsome 14K solid gold dress watch.

$100-125

$125-150

$100-125

**Men's 14K Gold
Dress Watches**

left **P6638**
14K solid white or yellow
gold watch in traditional
round dial with sweep
second hand.

right top **D6672**
14K solid white or yellow
gold watch with modern
stick markers. perfect
for dress-up occasions.

right bottom **D6672N**
Same watch with Roman
numerals.

$125-150

$100-125

$100-125

**Man's Self-Winding
Constellation
Chronometer**

left **9174**
18K solid gold
Constellation Chro-
nometer. Automatic with
day/date telling dial and
water-resistant case.

$400-500

**Man's Self-Winding
Constellation
Chronometer**

9192

18K solid gold
Constellation
Chronometer with day-
date calendar, sweep
second hand, in a self-
winding water-resistant
case with matching 18K
gold bracelet.

6187
Same watch in stainless
steel.

Steel $100-125
18K $1,500-1,700

Steel $150-175
G Top $200-225

Men's Self-Winding Constellation Chronometers

left **6176G**

Constellation Chronometer in 14K solid gold top, stainless steel back water-resistant case, with matching gold-filled bracelet. Day-date calendar.

6175G
Same watch in stainless steel.

right **6175**

Constellation Chronometer in water-resistant stainless steel with day-date calendar.

6176
Same watch in 14K solid gold top and stainless steel back case.

9167
Same watch in 18K solid gold with strap.

18K $550-650

Steel $150-175
14K Top $200-225
18K $450-500

Man's Self-Winding Seamaster Chronometer

left **9164**

Seamaster Chronometer with 18K solid gold water-resistant case, matching 18K solid gold bracelet. Date-telling calendar.

Man's Self-Winding Constellation Chronometer

right **9183**

Constellation Chronometer with 14K solid gold water-resistant case, matching 14K solid gold bracelet. Day-date calendar.

14K $750-850

Men's Self-Winding Seamasters

left top **B6744**
Seamaster in 14K solid gold with distinctive circle-in-the-square water-resistant case with etched radial lines and matching bracelet.

left bottom **B6763**
Seamaster in 14K solid gold with round dial set in a tonneau-shaped water-resistant case. Matching bracelet.

right **KM6731**
14K solid gold Seamaster in a water-resistant case with a heavy mesh matching bracelet. Date-telling calendar.

$350-400

$375-425

$400-450

Men's Self-Winding Seamasters

left **6160F**
Seamaster in 14K solid gold top, stainless steel back case with gold-filled bracelet. Day-date telling calendar. Water-resistant.

6159F
Same watch in stainless steel.

right **6160**
Seamaster in 14K solid gold top, stainless steel back case. Day-date telling calendar. Water-resistant.

6159
Same watch in stainless steel.

Steel $50-75
G Top $125-150

Steel $40-65
G Top $120-140

Men's Self-Winding Seamaster DeVilles

left **6097R**
Intermediate size Seamaster DeVille in a stainless steel, water-resistant case, with matching bracelet.

right top **B6671**
Intermediate size Seamaster DeVille in 14K solid gold. Water-resistant.

B6320
Same watch in gold-filled top, stainless steel back case with matching bracelet.

6097
Same watch in stainless steel.

right bottom **B6318**
Intermediate size Seamaster DeVille in 14K gold-filled, water-resistant case.

Steel $40-50

Steel $40-50
14K $150-175

$50-75

Men's Self-Winding Seamaster DeVilles

left **KM6775**
Seamaster DeVille in 14K solid gold with matching herring-bone patterned bracelet. Date-telling calendar. Water-resistant.

right **KM6774**
Seamaster DeVille in 14K solid gold with matching basket-weave bracelet. Date-telling calendar. Water-resistant.

14K $350-450

14K $350-450

14K $350-450

Man's Self-Winding Seamaster DeVilles

left **KM6759**
Seamaster DeVille in 14K solid gold with matching bracelet. Date-telling calendar. Water-resistant.

The Dynamic Watch Series

The unique oval-shaped case of the Dynamic watch is designed to fit comfortably on the wrist. All Dynamic watches are made with a sturdy stainless steel, water-resistant case, and a recessed winding crown to complement the unusual oval shape. Dials are available in a wide range of colors and combinations, and you can develop a strap wardrobe, choosing from many strap colors, all air-vented for cool-wearing comfort. Another feature of the Dynamic watch is the method in which the strap is attached to the case. It rests in a groove in the back of the watch case, and is held in position by a screw-in steel ring. A special key is provided for the changing of straps, and this strap fitting gives the Dynamic a streamlined, modern look. Stainless steel bracelets are also available, and many Dynamics are self-winding and have date-telling calendars.

left **6165B**
Self-winding Dynamic with matching stainless steel bracelet and date-telling calendar.

right top **6165**
Same watch with strap.

right bottom **6168**
Manual-wind Dynamic with strap. No calendar.

$25-35

$20-25

$20-25

Men's Self-Winding Watches

right **KM6312H**
Date-telling calendar watch in gold-filled top, stainless steel back case, water-resistant with matching bracelet.
KM6312
Same watch with strap.

left top **KM6303**
Date-telling Seamaster in a gold-filled, water-resistant case.

left bottom **6183**
Date-telling calendar watch in yellow top, stainless steel back, water-resistant case.

6195
Same watch in stainless steel.

$20-25

$20-25

$25-30

Men's Self-Winding Watches

left **LU6304H**
Classic round styling in gold-filled top, stainless steel back water-resistant case. Matching bracelet.
LU6304
Same watch with strap.

right **6105H**
Smart round design in stainless steel. water-resistant case. With matching bracelet.
6105
Same watch with strap.

$30-35

$25-30

Model #6126

$250-300

A – Large Second Hand
B – Second Dial
C – Minute Counter
D – Hour Counter
E – Button for Starting and Stopping
    Large Second Hand and pointers on
    Dials C & D
F – Winding Crown
G – Button for Returning Large Second
    Hand and pointers on Dials C & D to
    Zero
H – Tachymeter Scale

$100-150

Model #6182

$250–300

Speedmaster Professional Chronograph

left top **6126**

The watch worn by Gemini and Apollo Astronauts on their epoch-making walks in outer space and on the moon surface. Standard issue with N.A.S.A. 4-dial 2 push-button chronograph stop-watch, with tachymeter dial. Water-resistant, stainless steel heavy duty case. 3 small dials register elapsed intervals up to 12 hours. 30 minutes and 60 seconds. Large dial with full sweep-second hand tells regular time of day. Luminous markers. Manual wind. Adjustable bracelet.

Speedmaster Mark II

left bottom **6182**

Up-dated version of the "watch that went to the moon." New, cushion-shaped stainless steel case design and matching bracelet. Tachymeter scale set under crystal.

Flightmaster — Pilot's Watch

right **6185**

The Flightmaster Chronograph was designed for airline and sport pilots. With a tempered mineral glass crystal, the movement is sealed into its water-resistant position (tested at 6 atmospheres). Features include: 4 dials, 2 push-buttons, 2 technical winding crowns, revolving elapsed-time bezel set under glass. stop watch properties. 3 small dials register elapsed intervals up to 12 hours, 30 minutes, and indicate whether it's A.M. or P.M. Large dial with sweep second hand tells regular time of day. Special colored hand enables you to tell at a glance the time in two different time zones. Manual wind. With matching stainless steel bracelet.

$100–150

$100–125

$125-150

right **6001**
Electronic Chronometer
with stainless steel
water-resistant case.
Date-telling dial.
6001B
Same watch with steel
bracelet.

left top **6000F**
Electronic Chronometer
with 14K top, stainless
steel back case. Water-
resistant with date-telling
dial. Set off by gold-filled
bracelet.
6000
Same watch with strap.
6198F
Same watch in stainless
steel with stainless steel
bracelet.
6198
Same watch in stainless
steel with strap.

left bottom **6002**
An Electric Chro-
nometer with the look of a
precision instrument.
Stainless steel water
resistant case and
bracelet. Date-telling dial.

$15-20

$20-25

9188
2-button, 4-dial Omega
Speedmaster wrist
computer. Measures
elapsed intervals of
hours, minutes and
seconds. 18K solid gold,
engraved case with
matching bracelet.

Steel $300-350
18K $2,000-2,200

**Self-Winding
Seamaster "300"**

left top **6127**
Professional skindiver's
watch. Water-resistant,
stainless steel case
with rotating click-set
time indicator for
elapsed time. Large
luminous hour markers
and sweep second hand.
Matching stainless steel
adjustable bracelet.

**Self-Winding
Seamaster "120"**

left bottom **6135L**
Professional skindiver's
watch with date-telling
calendar. Water-
resistant, stainless steel
case with rotating
indicator for elapsed time.
Large luminous hour
markers and sweep
second hand. Matching
stainless steel adjustable
bracelet.
6135
Same watch with strap.

**Self-Winding
Seamaster "300"**

right **6149**
Same watch as 6127
with date-telling calendar.

**Seamaster
4-Dial Chronographs**

left **9148**
18K solid gold water-
resistant case and
matching 18K solid gold
bracelet. 4-dial, 2-push
button chronograph stop
watch. 3 small dials
register elapsed intervals
of 12 hours, 30 minutes
and 60 seconds. Large
dial with sweep second
hand tells time of day.
Tachymeter scale
measures speed per
hour or production rates.

right **9196**
Same watch with strap.

left bottom **6186**
Water-resistant, stainless
steel 4-dial, 2-push button
chronograph. Moveable
24 hour scale set under
crystal. Matching
stainless steel bracelet.

$30-35

$35-40

$35-40

$800-1,000

$500-600

$100-150

Seamaster "120" Divers Watches

left **6154**
Professional divers watch in stainless steel, water-resistant case. With rotating time-indicator and luminous hands and hour markers.

right top **5042B**
Intermediate size of the professional divers watch in stainless steel case with matching bracelet. Date-telling calendar. self-winding, with rotating time indicator. Luminous hands and hour markers.

right bottom **5035E**
Same watch without calendar.

$30–35

$35–40

$30–40

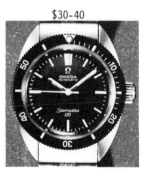

Seamaster Chronostop Wrist Stop-Watch

left **6155**
Red sweep-second hand can be stopped to measure short intervals. Tachymeter scale. Water-resistant, stainless steel case. Adjustable clasp strap.

Seamaster Chronostop Diver's Watch

right **6156**
Measures short intervals of elapsed time in 5th's of a second. Stem on left operates rotating time-lapse scale. Water-resistant, stainless steel case. Red sweep-second can be stopped to register short intervals. Adjustable clasp strap.

$60–70

$70–75

$50-75

$50-75

Chronostop Top-Of-The-Wrist Stop Watches

left **6141**
Measures elapsed time to ⅕ of a second. Brushed stainless steel, water-resistant case. Red stop hand. Assorted dial colors with ⅕ second trackers. Adjustable clasp strap.

right **6141B**
Same watch with stainless steel bracelet.

$100-125

Chronostop Under-The-Wrist Stop Watch

6141UB
Same as above, but designed to be worn under the wrist. Dial is turned so that the 12 o'clock hour marker is at 3 o'clock position for easy and direct reading when wrist is turned. In stainless steel, water-resistant case and matching bracelet.

Seamaster 4-dial Chronographs

left **6148B**
4-dial, 2 push-button chronograph stop watch. 3 small dials register elapsed time intervals for periods up to 12 hours, 30 minutes and 60 seconds. Large dial with sweep second hand tells regular time of day. Tachymeter scale measures speed per hour or production rates. Stainless steel, water-resistant case with matching bracelet.
6148
Same watch with strap.

right top **6180**
4-dial, 2 push-button chronograph stop watch. Performs same functions as 6148B shown at left. In yellow top, stainless steel back water-resistant case.
6179
Same watch in stainless steel case.

Seamaster 3-dial Chronograph

right bottom **6178**
3-dial, 2 push-button chronograph stop watch. Performs same function as 4-dial chronographs except for 12-hour time intervals. In stainless steel, water-resistant case.

Steel $200-250
GF $250-300

Steel $75-100
GF $100-125

Steel $175-225
GF $225-275

OPTIMA - GRENCHEN

MONTRES-BRACELETS ET DE POCHE EN TOUS GENRES

$10-15

$15-20

$15-20

$5-10

$5-10

All Priced
As Steel

$50-60

$10-15

$15-25

$10-20

$15-20

OPTIMA WATCHES

35W1 ....$23.75
With Expansion Band.
35W2 ....$19.75
With Leather Strap.

35W3 ....$23.75
With Expansion Band.
35W4 ....$19.75
With Leather Strap.

35W5 ....$23.75
With Expansion Band.
35W6 ....$19.75
With Leather Strap.

35W7 ....$23.75
With Expansion Band.
35W8 ....$19.75
With Leather Strap.

35W9 ....$23.75
With Expansion Band.
35W10 ....$19.75
With Leather Strap.

35W11 ....$23.75
With Expansion Band.
35W12 ....$19.75
With Leather Strap.

MASONIC DIAL WATCH

35W13 ....$25.00
A very unusual 17 jewel watch for
Masons. Has Masonic working tools in
place of numerals. Yellow R.G.P. stainless steel back case. High domed crystal.
Genuine leather strap. Attractively
boxed.

35W14. 17 Jewels.....$31.00
White rolled gold plate
case with high domed
crystal. Grey finished dial
set with eleven simulated
white stones. Grey leather
strap. Gift box.

Steel $5-10
14KYGF $5-10

Steel $100-120
14KYG $500-600

Steel $5-10
14KYGF $10-20

Steel $5-10
14KYGF $5-10

PATEK, PHILIPPE & C?
GENÈVE

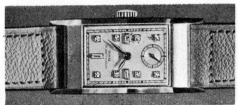

Patek Philippe-1937
20x43mm-Diamond Dial
Platinum Head $6,000-7,000

Patek Philippe-1936
Ladies
18KYG Head $1,000-1,100
18KPG Head $1,100-1,200

Patek Philippe-1936
Ring
18KYG $2,000-2,200

Patek Philippe-1936
Divers
18KYG Head $20,000-22,000
18KYG Head $18,000-20,000

Patek Philippe-1936
Ladies Diamond
Platinum Head $4,000-5,000

Patek Philippe-1936
Ladies
18KYG Head $800-1,000
18KPG Head $900-1,100

Patek Philippe-Ref. 241
18KYG Head $1,100-1,200

Patek Philippe-1938
18KPG Head $5,000-5,500
18KPG Head $5,000-6,000
18K TuTone Head $7,500-8,000

Patek Philippe-Ref. 240
1938-Calatrava
Steel Head $3,000-3,500
18KYG Head $3,500-4,000

Patek Philippe-1938
18KYG Head $9,000-10,000
18KPG Head $10,000-11,000

Patek Philippe-1942
Diamonds
18KWG Head $1,000-1,200

Patek Philippe-1938
18KYG Head $1,000-1,100
18KPG Head $1,100-1,200

Patek Philippe-1938
18KYG Head $1,200-1,300
18KPG Head $1,400-1,500

Patek Philippe-1942
18KYG Head $7,000-8,000
18KPG Head $8,000-9,000
18KP&WG Head $11,000-12,000

PATEK PHILIPPE

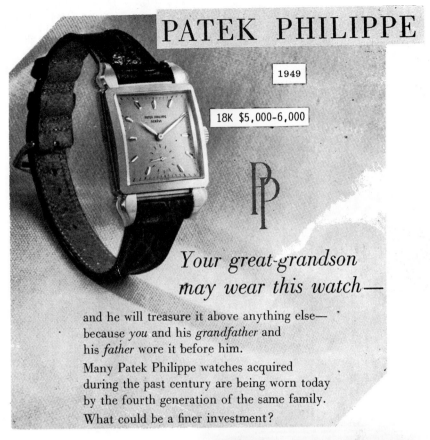

1949

18K $5,000-6,000

Your great-grandson may wear this watch—

and he will treasure it above anything else—
because *you* and his *grandfather* and
his *father* wore it before him.

Many Patek Philippe watches acquired
during the past century are being worn today
by the fourth generation of the same family.
What could be a finer investment?

Enamel Dial
Waterproof
18KYG $4,000-5,000
18KPG $4,500-5,500

1954

The story of this timepiece with its
thirty jewels and its 18 Kt. gold double
action rotor weight, is so fascinating that
we would welcome the opportunity of
sending you a descriptive booklet.

Patek Philippe-1940
18KPG Head $3,500-4,000

Patek Philippe
1956-31x35mm
18KYG Head $3,000-3,500

Patek Philippe-1941-Strap
18KYG Head $4,500-5,000

Patek Philippe
1956-45x32mm
18KYG Head $8,000-9,000
18KPG Head $9,000-10,000
18KWG Head $10,000-11,000

ABBREVIATIONS
18K = Solid Gold
14K = Solid Gold
G = Green
GF = Gold Filled
GP = Gold Plated
N = Nickel
PG = Pink Gold
R = Rolled
RGP = Rolled Gold Plate
S = Silver
Steel = Stainles Steel
WG = White Gold
YG = Yellow Gold

A SPECIAL THANKS TO:
Bob, Jean & Jennifer Webb
St. Charles, MO
for the use of their wrist
watch research.

MANUFACTURE DES MONTRES &
CHRONOGRAPHES **PIERCE** S.A.
BIENNE (SUISSE)   USINES A MOUTIER

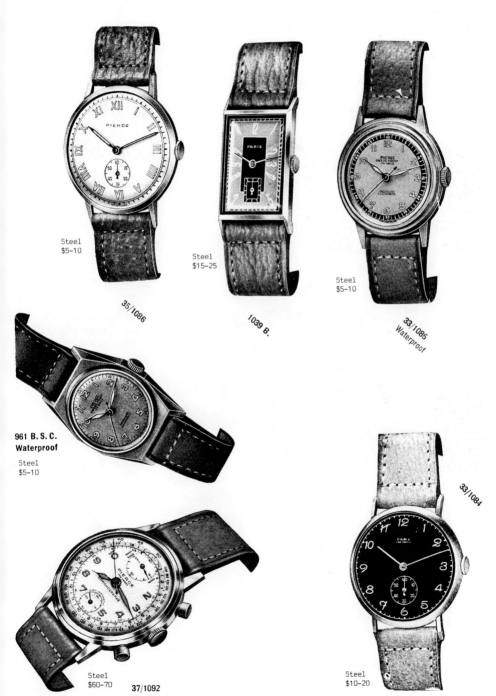

Steel
$5–10

35/1086

Steel
$15–25

1039 B.

Steel
$5–10

33/1085
Waterproof

961 B.S.C.
Waterproof

Steel
$5–10

33/1084

Steel
$60–70   **37/1092**

Steel
$10–20

Record Watch C° S.A.

GENÈVE-TRAMELAN Tous modèles
de montres de qualité

1932

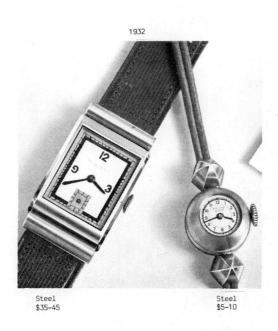

Steel
$35–45

Steel
$5–10

Steel
$25–35

Steel
$30–40

Steel
$5–10

$5–10

1940

Steel $20-30
14KYGF $25-35
14KYG $100-120
18KYG $120-145

Steel $20-30
14KYGF $25-35
14KYG $100-120
18KYGT $120-145

Steel $20-30
14KYGF $25-35
14KYG $100-120
18KYG $120-145

RECORD GENÈVE

Automatic + Datofix + Reserve-power indicator

Another outstanding Record achievement. Always in the forefront, the Record Watch Co. succeeded to combine the two preceding features in one movement, a truly exceptional accomplishment of technical conception and skill.

Automatic + Reserve-power indicator

The new Automatic Record will continue to work smoothly whilst you sleep. The reserve-power indicator, an ingenious mechanism, assures you that, whether on your wrist or lying on your table, it will go on ticking late into the next day.

Automatic + Datofix

Wear the new Automatic Record... and you actually carry your calendar on your wrist. No more confusion, no more searching of the date. Wherever your are, the moment you need it: just a glance at the dial and you have the exact day of the month.

The AUTOMATIC RECORD wristwatch 9³/₄" — 174 with ROTOR, 21 jewels, shock-proof, antimagnetic, waterproof, obtainable in all metals, whether in its elemental construction or comprising the above complementary features, is a masterpiece of the Swiss Watch Industry

RECORD WATCH Co. S. A.

GENÈVE 1, RUE CÉARD

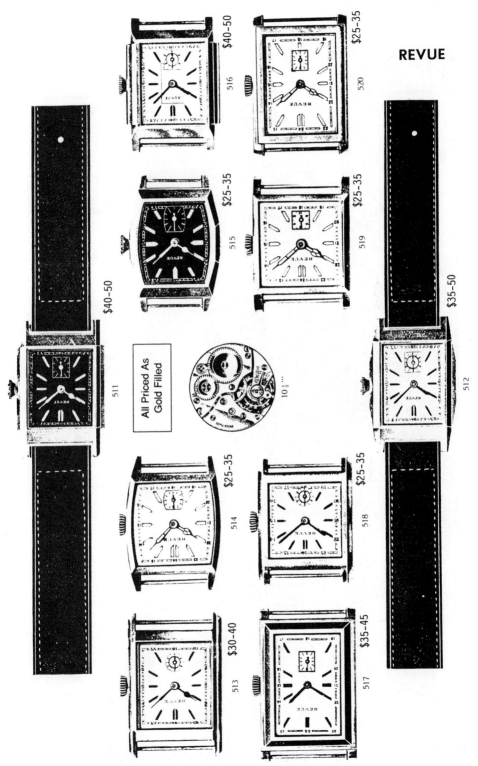

REVUE

All Priced As
Gold Filled

511 $40-50
512 $35-50
513 $30-40
514 $25-35
515 $25-35
516 $40-50
517 $35-45
518 $25-35
519 $25-35
520 $25-35

REVUE

All Priced As
Gold Filled

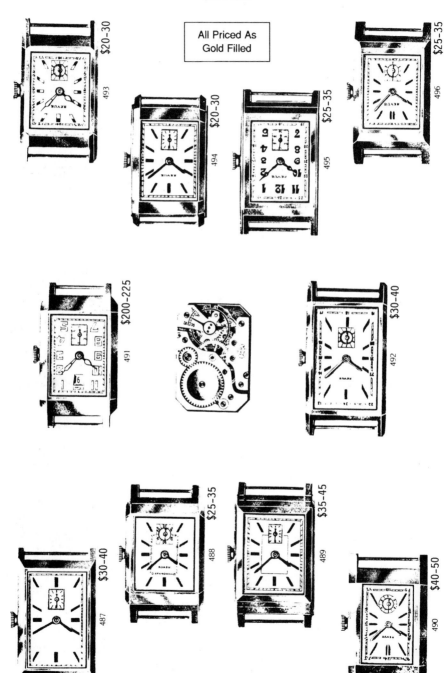

$20-30 493

$20-30 494

$25-35 495

$25-35 496

$200-225 491

$30-40 492

$30-40 487

$25-35 488

$35-45 489

$40-50 490

REVUE

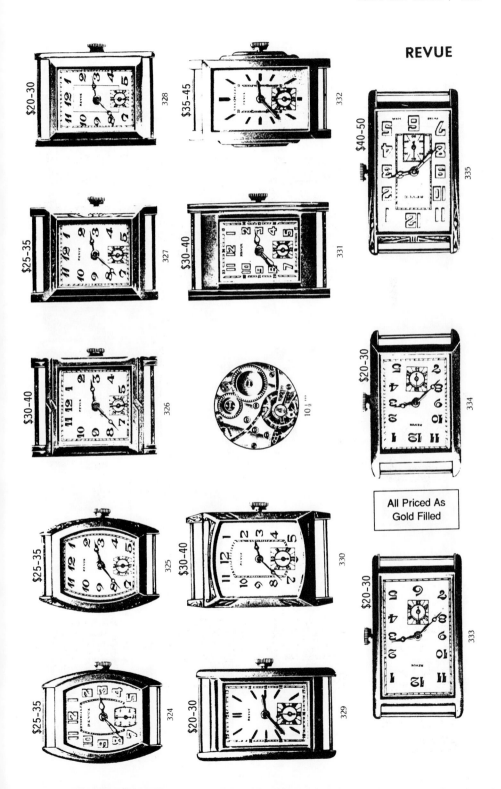

$20-30   328

$35-45   332

$40-50   335

$25-35   327

$30-40   331

$30-40   326

$20-30   334

All Priced As
Gold Filled

$25-35   325

$30-40   330

$25-35   324

$20-30   329

$20-30   333

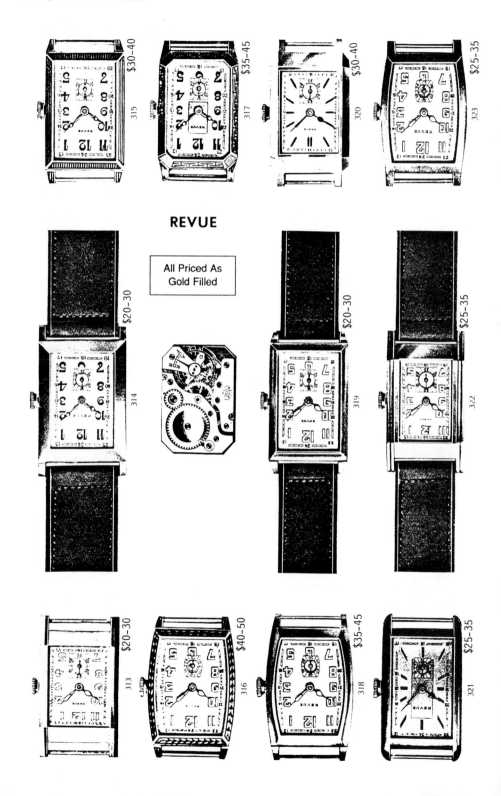

REVUE

All Priced As
Gold Filled

$30-40   315

$35-45   317

$30-40   320

$25-35   323

$20-30   314

$20-30   319

$25-35   322

$20-30   313

$40-50   316

$35-45   318

$25-35   321

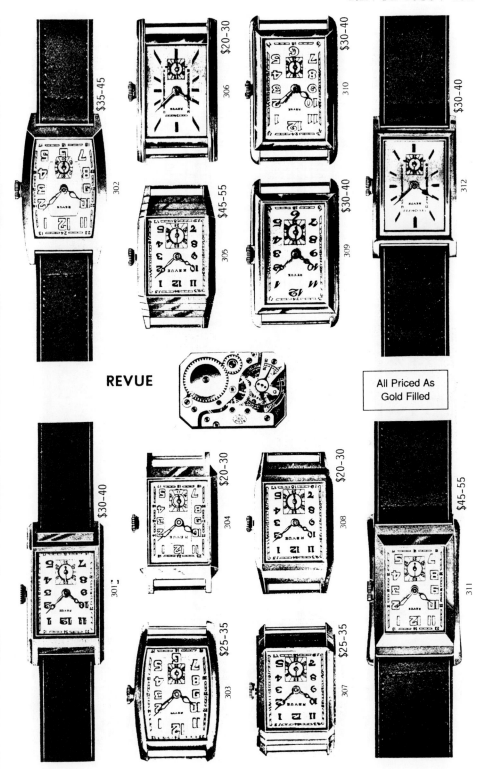

$35-45

306    $20-30

310    $30-40

$30-40

302

305    $45-55

309    $30-40

312

REVUE

All Priced As
Gold Filled

$30-40

304    $20-30

308    $20-30

$45-55

301

303    $25-35

307    $25-35

311

REVUE

$25-35

506

$20-25

510

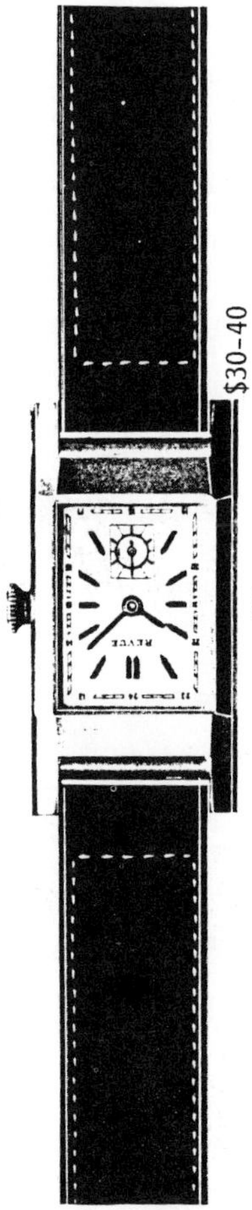

$30-40

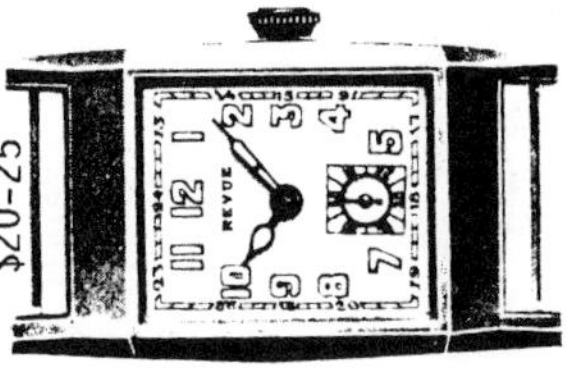

$20-25

509

503

8 ¾'''

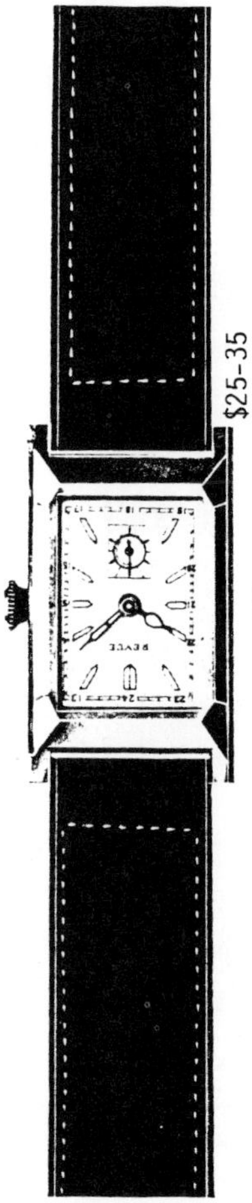

$25-35

505

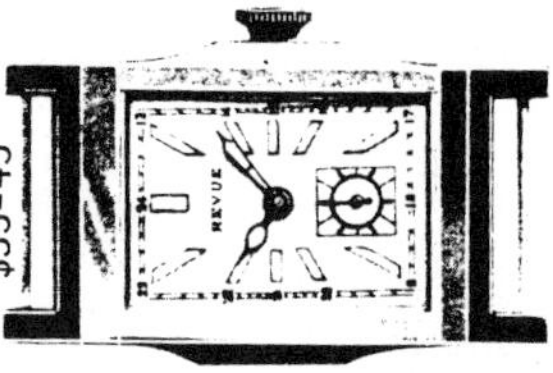

$35-45

508

$30-40

507

All Priced As
Gold Filled

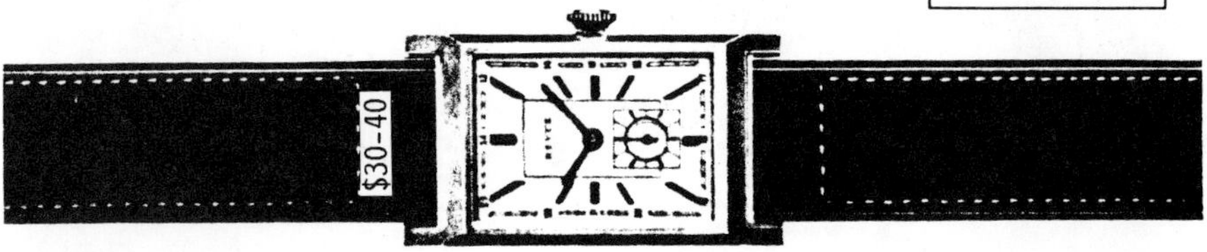

$30-40

504

REVUE

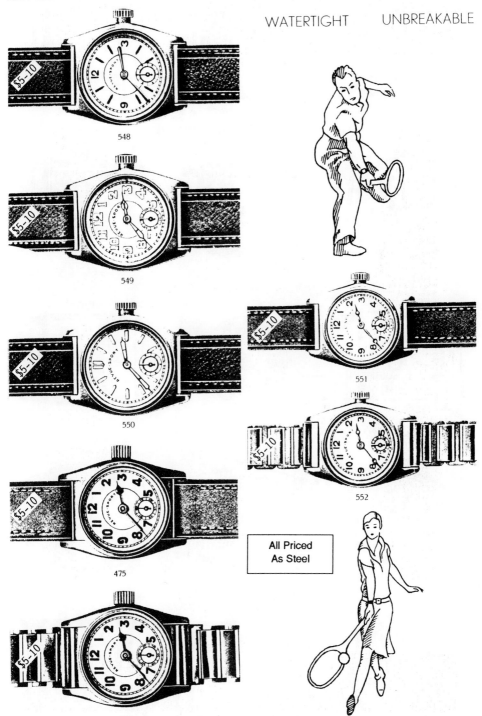

WATERTIGHT   UNBREAKABLE

548

549

550

551

552

475

All Priced
As Steel

476

REVUE

340 — $20-30

344 — $40-50

349 — $20-30

339 — $10-15

343 — $10-15

348 — $20-30

338 — $15-20

All Priced As Gold Filled

10 ½'''

347 — $15-20

337 — $10-15

342 — $25-35

346 — $15-20

336 — $10-15

341 — $20-30

345 — $20-30

14KYG
$135-150

14KYG
$175-210

14KYG
$60-80

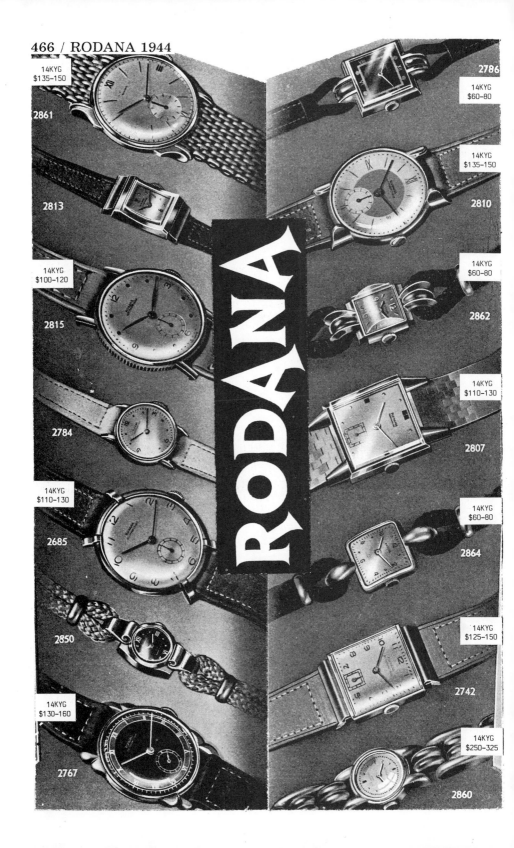

2861 — 14KYG $135–150

2813

2815 — 14KYG $100–120

2784

2685 — 14KYG $110–130

2850

2767 — 14KYG $130–160

2786 — 14KYG $60–80

2810 — 14KYG $135–150

2862 — 14KYG $60–80

2807 — 14KYG $110–130

2864 — 14KYG $60–80

2742 — 14KYG $125–150

2860 — 14KYG $250–325

Rodania "Alarm". Waterproof. Luminous hands & markers. 11½, 17J movement. Round case. ca 1957. Rolled gold plate top, steel back .... $35—45
Stainless steel .... 30—40

Rodania "Gold Top". Center seconds. 9¼''', 17J, self-winding movement. Square 14K gold top case with steel back. ca 1957. . . . . $40—60

Rodania "Chrome Calendar". Center seconds, day & month windows with outer date ring. 11½''', 17J movement. Round chrome case with steel back. ca 1957 .... $30—50

Rolls (Hatot's Patent)
Automatic—38mm—CA 1930—11 Jewels
Hidden Crown Setting
18K Polished Yellow Gold $1,200-1,500

Rolls-Automatic
40mm—CA 1930—17 Jewels
Hinged cover—Hidden setting
Lady's silver $400—600

Rodania. Waterproof. 9¼''', 17J, self-winding movement. Molded square, rolled gold plate case with steel back. ca 1957 ..... $10—20

Rodania. Subsidiary seconds. 11½''', 17J movement. Rolled gold plated, molded tonneau case. ca 1957 .... $6—18

Rose—Swiss
39mm—CA 1920—15 Jewels—Luminous
Glass enamel dial—Wire lugs
2 Dial one button chronograph
Silver Hinged Case $450—550?

ROLEX
The Presentation Watch

The Rolex Prince is a brilliant example of Rolex leadership.

Through its ingenious and patented construction it has obtained the highest rating ever to be received by a wristwatch at Kew Observatory.

Fitted to an elegant Geneva-made case and supplied with a Government Certificate, there is no finer presentation watch.

14K solid white or green gold with Government Certificate of timekeeping, **$100.00**
14K gold filled, white or green, without certificate, **$50.00**

14KWGF $2,500–2,800
14KGGF $2,500–2,800
Steel $2,800–3,000
Silver $3,000–3,300
Steel & Gilt $3,000–3,300
9K $3,200–3,500
Steel & YG $3,500–4,000
Steel & PG $4,000–4,500
9K TuTone $5,500–6,000
18K $5,500–6,000
18K TuTone $7,000–8,500
Platinum $8,000–9,000

The **ROLEX PRINCE**

$250–300

R-2500—14K Solid White Gold, **$50.00**
Gold filled, 30.00

$700–800

R-2400—14K Solid White Gold,
4 Sapphires, 6 Diamonds **$65.00**

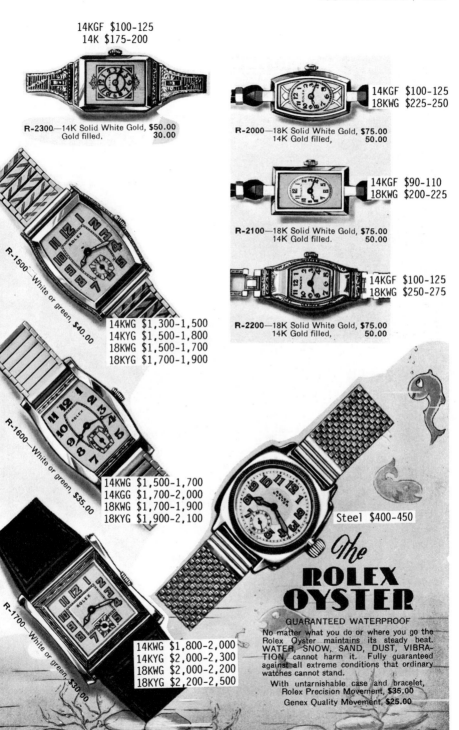

14KGF $100-125
14K $175-200

R-2300—14K Solid White Gold, $50.00
Gold filled. 30.00

14KGF $100-125
18KWG $225-250

R-2000—18K Solid White Gold, $75.00
14K Gold filled, 50.00

14KGF $90-110
18KWG $200-225

R-2100—18K Solid White Gold, $75.00
14K Gold filled. 50.00

14KGF $100-125
18KWG $250-275

R-2200—18K Solid White Gold, $75.00
14K Gold filled, 50.00

R-1500—White or green, $40.00

14KWG $1,300-1,500
14KYG $1,500-1,800
18KWG $1,500-1,700
18KYG $1,700-1,900

R-1600—White or green, $35.00

14KWG $1,500-1,700
14KGG $1,700-2,000
18KWG $1,700-1,900
18KYG $1,900-2,100

Steel $400-450

R-1700—White or green, $30.00

14KWG $1,800-2,000
14KYG $2,000-2,300
18KWG $2,000-2,200
18KYG $2,200-2,500

The
ROLEX OYSTER
GUARANTEED WATERPROOF

No matter what you do or where you go the
Rolex Oyster maintains its steady beat.
WATER, SNOW, SAND, DUST, VIBRA-
TION, cannot harm it. Fully guaranteed
against all extreme conditions that ordinary
watches cannot stand.

With untarnishable case and bracelet,
Rolex Precision Movement, $35.00
Genex Quality Movement, $25.00

Rolex Sporting Prince

Leather $3,000-3,500
9K $4,000-4,500
18K $5,000-5,500

The various advantages
found singly in other watches
are combined in this new
model:—

1. Precision Chronometer.
2. Unusually robust and yet
very neat.
3. Very clear "New Patented" dial for precise reading.
4. Pocket-, sporting-, desk-,
satchel-, travelling-watch,
all in one.
5. Shockproof.

The world's best wristwatch
with **Swiss Official Timing Certificate** is now
available as a sporting watch
for really rough wear. By
its ingenious construction,
the watch being suspended
from **"invisible springs"**
within a frame — no shock
can do it any harm.

S $6,000-6,500
9K $8,000-9,000
14K $9,500-10,500
18K $11,000-12,000
TuTone $12,500-13,500
Platinum $14,000-15,000

Rolex Oyster

Steel $400-450
Yellow & Steel $700-800
Pink & Steel $800-1,000
9KYG $800-1,000
9KPG $1,000-1,100
14KYG $1,500-1,800
14KPG $1,800-2,000
18KYG $1,800-2,000
18KPG $2,000-2,200

Guaranteed **waterproof,
dust proof,**
not affected
by the heat
nor by the cold.

The Rolex Prince

with hours moving
automatically

1. The only wristwatch showing at a glance and with-
out any calculation the
exact hour, minutes
and **seconds.**
2. Swiss Official Timing Certificate supplied with each
Prince.
3. The mechanism operating
the automatic figures is
simplicity itself and cannot
get out of order.

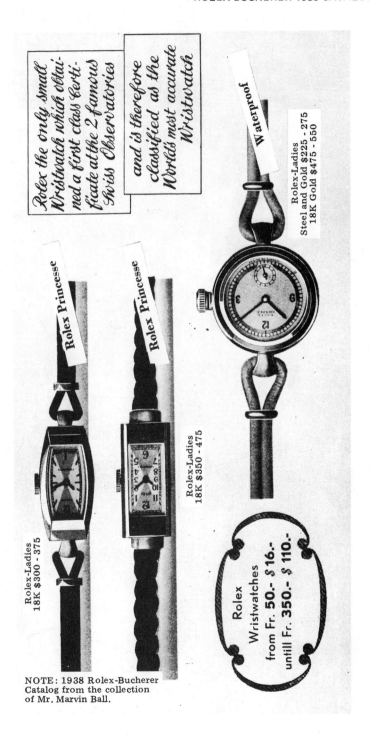

Rolex the only small Wristwatch which obtained a first class Certificate at the 2 famous Swiss Observatories

and is therefore classified as the World's most accurate Wristwatch

Waterproof

Rolex-Ladies
Steel and Gold $225 - 275
18K Gold $475 - 550

Rolex Princesse

Rolex Princesse

Rolex-Ladies
18K $350 - 475

Rolex-Ladies
18K $300 - 375

Rolex
Wristwatches
from Fr. 50.- $ 16.-
until Fr. 350.- $ 110.-

NOTE: 1938 Rolex-Bucherer
Catalog from the collection
of Mr. Marvin Ball.

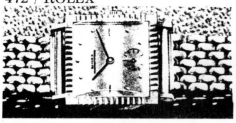

Rolex-1941
14KYG Head $1,200-1,400
14KPG Head $1,300-1,400
18KYG Head $1,500-1,800
18K Bracelet $300-350

Rolex-No. 4257
Hunting-1942
Diamonds & Sapphires
18KYG Head $1,000-1,200
18KPG Head $1,100-1,300

Rolex-No. 3869
1942-Oyster
Steel Head $350-400
Steel & Gold Bezel Head $450-500
Steel & Gold Top $550-600
9KYG Head $550-600
9KPG Head $600-650
14KYG Head $1,000-1,200
14KPG Head $1,100-1,300
18KYG Head $1,400-1,500
18KPG Head $1,500-1,600

Rolex-Ladies
15x15mm-Ca 1941
18KPG Watch & Bracelet $400-500

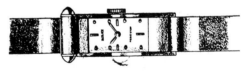

Rolex-Ladies
12x32mm-Ca 1939
18KPG Watch & Bracelet $650-750

Rolex-No. 4134
Smooth Case
14KYG Head $800-900
14KPG Head $900-1,000
18KYG Head $1,200-1,400
18KPG Head $1,300-1,500

Rolex-Ladies
13x45mm-Ca 1939
Diamonds & Rubies
Platinum Head $800-1,000

ROLEX

The Masterpiece of
Watch Craftsmanship

Rolex Watch Company, Inc.
580 Fifth Avenue, New York

(*A chronometer is more than just a watch. It is an instrument measuring the time in accordance with precise limits and definite rules laid down officially.)

3134-2
GF $500-550
Steel $600-650
Steel & Yellow $800-900
Steel & Pink $900-1,000
YG Top $1,400-1,500
PG Top $1,600-1,800
9K $1,800-2,000
10K $1,800-2,000
14KYG $2,500-2,700
14KPG $2,800-3,000
18KYG $3,300-3,600
18KPG $3,500-3,800

3361-1
14KYG $7,000-8,000
14KPG $8,000-9,000
18KYG $11,000-13,000
18KPG $14,000-16,000

3121-4
YGF $450-550
Steel $690-750

3754
14KYG $1,100-1,300
14KPG $1,200-1,400
18KYG $1,300-1,500
18KPG $1,400-1,600

3684
14KYG $900-1,000
14KPG $1,000-1,100
18KYG $1,100-1,300
18KPG $1,200-1,400

3121-4

3361-1

3134-2

3684

3754

With Bracelet
Steel $300-350
Steel & Gold $450-550
14K $1,500-1,700
18K $1,800-2,000

President
18K $3,000-3,300

President
18K $2,000-2,500

You are invited to write for fully illustrated catalogue to :—

"Thos. RUSSELL & Son"
Watch Co., Ltd.
12 Church Street, Liverpool.
65 Holborn Viaduct, London, E.C.1

YGF
$60-80

YGF
$40-50

YGF
$40-50

YGF
$30-40

YGF
$30-40

YGF
$200-280

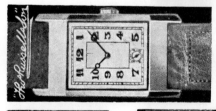

YGF
$50-75

YGF
$50-70

YGF
$50-70

YGF
$50-70

YGF
$50-70

Sabina
36mm—CA 1950's—21 Jewels
Two dial chronograph—Flat pusher
18K Polished Yellow Gold $350-450

Mans
18KYG $150-175
Steel $45-55

Sabina
36mm—CA 1950's—21 Jewels
Two dial chronograph—Flat pusher
18K Polished Yellow Gold $350-450

Diamond
Platinum
$200-250

18KYG
$75-95

18KYG
$950-1,100
Steel
$375-450

*Détenteurs de la
Coupe Chronométrique
au Concours National de
l'Observatoire de Besançon
(pour 1932-33)*

Glass Enamel
14KYG $1,250-1,500
Steel $325-400

Seeland "Invictus". Tu-tone dial, subsidiary
seconds. 17J movement. 10K rolled gold plate,
square case, hinged lugs. ca 1940 . . . . $55-65

Seiger & Son, M. "Happiness". Horseshoe, platinum, white, green or rose gold case, set with diamonds & sapphires. ca 1923 .$125—175

Solrex. Ladies. Gold finished or silvered dial. 10½''', 7J or 15J movement. Round, gold-filled case. ca 1918 . . . .$10—20

Seth Thomas. Raised gold figure dial, subsidiary seconds, 10½''' movement. 10K gold-filled, massive molded square case & lugs. ca 1955. . . . .$20—30

MANUFACTURE D'HORLOGERIE
Silvana S. A.
TRAMELAN

Steel $30-40

Steel $10-20

Steel $10-20

Steel $10-20

Sinn
35mm—CA 1950's.
Triple date—Moonphase
Two dial chronograph—Round pusher
14K Polished Yellow Gold $900—1,100

Solrex. Ladies. Gold finished or silvered round dial. 8¾''', 15J movement. Gold-filled, diamond shaped case. ca 1918 . . . .$10—20

SILVANA S. A.

MANUFACTURE D'HORLOGERIE

TRAMELAN (SUISSE)

Ladies
$5-20

Mens
$5-15

11311

7027

4811

4820

4510

5003

5710

5005

4828

4828 C.

10106

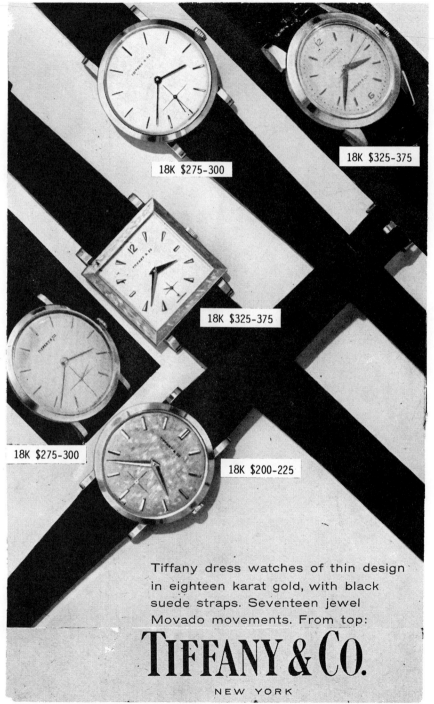

18K $275-300

18K $325-375

18K $325-375

18K $275-300

18K $200-225

Tiffany dress watches of thin design
in eighteen karat gold, with black
suede straps. Seventeen jewel
Movado movements. From top:

TIFFANY & CO.

NEW YORK

Tissot

LA MONTRE ANTIMAGNÉTIQUE DE QUALITÉ
PRÉSENTE QUELQUES MODÈLES ÉTANCHES

Steel
$10-20

U 7056 cal. 21,7 — bracelet homme,
étanche, acier inoxydable

14KYGF
$5-10

Steel
$10-20

U 6172 cal. 21,7 — bracelet homme,
étanche, acier inoxydable

Steel
$10-20

U 6069 cal. 27 — bracelet homme,
étanche, acier inoxydable

14KYGF
$30-40

Steel
$5-10

U 5203 cal. 11,7 — bracelet dame,
étanche, acier inoxydable

Steel
$125-150

Z 6156 cal. 28,9 — chronographe
étanche 2 poussoirs, acier inoxydable

Steel
$125-150

Z 6155 cal. 33,3 — chronographe
étanche 2 poussoirs, acier inoxydable

Sideral Chronograph

left **T0754**
Sideral 3-dial chronograph with rotating bezel. Measures elapsed time of 60 seconds and 30 minutes. Water-resistant fiberglass case.

right **T4702**
Sideral self-winding calendar watch in fiberglass case with stainless steel top. Water-resistant. Matching steel bracelet with interwoven fabric insets.

T4702Y
Same watch in yellow top, with strap.

$15-20 $10-15

Sideral Electronic Watches

left **T0711**
Sideral Electronic water-resistant calendar watch. Fiberglass case with stainless steel top and deluxe steel bracelet.

right **T0700**
Sideral Electronic water-resistant calendar watch. Fiberglass case with stainless steel top and air-vented strap.

$5-10 $5-10

Sideral Watches

left **T4731**
Sideral self-winding diver's calendar watch in fiberglass case with stainless steel top. Water-resistant. Air-vented strap.

right **T4700A**
Sideral self-winding calendar watch in fiberglass case with stainless steel top. Water-resistant. Racing strap. Full Arabic dial.

$15-20 $5-10

Sideral Watches

left **T4752**
Intermediate size Sideral
self-winding calendar
watch in water-resistant
fiberglass case with
stainless steel top.
Tapered strap. Beige dial.

right **T4751**
Intermediate size Sideral
self-winding calendar
watch in water-resistant
fiberglass case with
stainless steel top.
Tapered strap. Blue dial.

$5-10

$5-10

Sideral Watches

left **T4700**
Sideral self-winding
calendar watch in
fiberglass case with
stainless steel top.
Water-resistant. Air-
vented strap.

right **T4700A**
Sideral self-winding
calendar watch in
fiberglass case with
stainless steel top.
Water-resistant case.
Air-vented strap.

$5-10

$5-10

Sideral Watch

left **T4701**
Sideral self-winding
calendar watch in
fiberglass case with
stainless steel top.
Water-resistant. Air-
vented strap.

$5-10

Multi-Purpose Watches

left **3311**
Special function watch in white top, stainless steel back water-resistant case. Easy-to-snap-on changeable colored bezels include: elapsed time scale, world time scale, tachymeter scale, pulsation scale, decimal scale.

right **3312**
Same watch in yellow top, stainless steel back case.

Fashion Watches

left **3313**
The fashion look with colored dials in white top, stainless steel back, water-resistant case. Easy-to-snap-on changeable colored bezels in gray, green, violet, yellow, coral.

right **3314**
Same watch in yellow top, stainless steel back case.

Fashion Dress Watches

left **3329**
Dress-up fashion watch in yellow top, stainless steel back water-resistant case.

right **3328**
Same watch with different dial color.

$10-15

$25-30

$5-10

$5-10

$5-10

$5-10

$5-10

Fashion Dress Watch

left **3350**
Dress-up fashion watch in yellow top, stainless steel back water-resistant case. With roman numerals and sweep second hand.
3350G
Same watch with gilt dial.

$10-15

Men's Self-Winding Watches

left **3384**
Cushion shaped automatic calendar watch. Yellow top, stainless steel back case. Integral bracelet.
3385
Same watch in stainless steel.

$20-25

Men's Technical Watches

left **3333**
T-12 Seastar, 2-push button, 4-dial chronograph. Large dial tells regular time. Small dials register elapsed time intervals of 12 hours, 30 minutes and 60 seconds. Stainless steel water-resistant case and matching bracelet, with sweep second hand and tachymeter scale.

$15-20

right top **3335**
T-12 Seastar Electronic. Electronically operated battery powered watch in stainless steel water-resistant case with matching bracelet and Visodate calendar. Rotating elapsed time indicator set under the crystal for added protection. Sweep second hand.

$15-20

right bottom **3331**
T-12 Seastar self-winding water-resistant watch in stainless steel with matching bracelet. Day/date-telling calendar with sweep second hand and rotating elapsed time indicator set under the crystal for added protection.

$10-15

$10-15

Men's Self-Winding Watches

left top **T3805**
Self-winding calendar watch, round dial in cushion-shaped, yellow top, stainless steel back water-resistant case. Racing strap.

left bottom **T3806**
Self-winding calendar watch, round dial in cushion-shaped, yellow top, stainless steel back water-resistant case. Racing strap.

right **3347**
Seastar "7" self-winding water-resistant watch with Visodate calendar in distinctive round shape with radial lines on the bezel. In yellow top, stainless steel back case.

3348
Same watch in stainless steel.

$10-15

$10-15

Men's Self-Winding Watches

left **3306M**
PR-516 self-winding Seastar. Unusual dial with "step down" dimensional hour-markers. Day/date telling features. Sturdy, brushed yellow top, stainless steel back water-resistant case. With matching bracelet.
3305M
Same watch in brushed stainless steel with matching bracelet.

3306
Same watch in brushed yellow top, stainless steel back water-resistant case with Grand Tourismo strap.
3305
Same watch in brushed stainless steel with Grand Tourismo strap.

3306GT
Same watch in brushed yellow top, stainless steel back water-resistant case and matching Grand Tourismo bracelet.
3305GT
Same watch in brushed stainless steel with matching bracelet.

Men's Self-Winding Watches

3282M
PR-516 self-winding Seastar Visodate calendar watch in brushed yellow top, stainless steel back water-resistant case. With matching bracelet.
3282
Same watch with Grand Tourismo strap.

3281GT
Same watch in brushed stainless steel with matching Grand Tourismo bracelet.
3281
Same watch with Grand Tourismo strap.

$10-15

Men's Self-Winding Watches

left **3287B**
Seastar "7" self-winding watch with Visodate calendar in yellow top, stainless steel back water-resistant case. With matching bracelet.
3286B
Same watch in stainless steel with matching bracelet.

right **3285B**
Seastar "7" self-winding watch in yellow top, stainless steel back water-resistant case. With matching bracelet.
3284B
Same watch in stainless steel with matching bracelet.

$10-15

$10-15

Men's Self-Winding Watches

left **3324M**
Self-winding Seastar day/date calendar watch in stainless steel water-resistant case. With matching bracelet.

3324
Same watch in stainless steel case and Grand Tourismo strap.

$10-15

Men's Electronic Watches

left **3315**
PR-516 Seastar Electronic. Electronically operated, battery powered watch with Visodate calendar in stainless steel. With GT racing strap.

right **3345S**
PR-516 Electronic date/telling watch. In stainless steel water-resistant case.

3345P
With stainless steel mesh bracelet.

3345
With strap.
3346
In yellow top, stainless steel back case with strap.

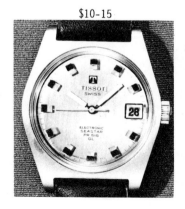

$10-15

$10-15

$10-15

$15-20

Men's Technical Watches

left **3332**

T-12 Seastar Navigator water-resistant watch, self-winding with Visodate calendar, sweep second hand and rotating 24-hour scale set under the crystal for added protection. In stainless steel with matching bracelet.

right **3334**

T-12 "Sonorous" wrist alarm. Water-resistant stainless steel case with matching bracelet. Rotating elapsed time scale set under the crystal for added protection. Sweep second hand.

Men's Technical Watches

left **3299**

T-12 Seastar 24-hour dial navigator world-time watch. Self-winding, stainless steel, water-resistant. Two-tone date-telling dial divides A.M. and P.M. Tells world time* for each of the 24 time zones. Sweep second hand.
*For example, 1800 is equal to 6 P.M., 2200 is equal to 10 P.M.

right top **3295**

T-12 Seastar 2 push-button, 4-dial chronograph. Large dial tells regular time. Small dials register elapsed time intervals of 12 hours, 30 minutes and 60 seconds. Stainless steel water-resistant case with sweep second hand and tachymeter scale. Luminous dot hour markers.

right bottom **3298**

T-12 Seastar diver's watch. Self-winding, Visodate date-telling calendar. Heavy duty, stainless steel water-resistant case. Bold, luminous hour markers with sweep second hand. Elapsed time indicator operates inside the crystal providing extra protection.

$30-35

$20-25

$10-15

$30-35

Man's Chronograph
left 3339B
PR-516, 2-push button, 4-dial chronograph. Water-resistant stainless steel watch with matching bracelet. Large dial tells regular time. Small dials register elapsed time intervals of 12 hours. 30 minutes and 60 seconds as well as right hand dial showing blue triangle to mark 5-minute "rally" alert before yacht race or other sporting events. With sweep second hand.
3339
Same watch with strap.
3338M
Same watch in yellow top, stainless steel back with matching bracelet.
3338
Same watch in yellow top, stainless steel back with strap.

Man's Navigator Watch
right top 3340
PR-516 24-hour self-winding Navigator watch in stainless steel. With movable 24-hour A.M. — P.M. dial shown on 2-color bezel. With Visodate calendar, water-resistant and sweep second hand.
3340B
Same watch with bracelet.
3341
Same watch with strap in yellow top, stainless steel back case.
3341M
Same watch with bracelet in yellow top, stainless steel back case.

Man's Skin Diver Watch
right bottom 3342
PR-516 skin diver self-winding watch in stainless steel with water-resistant case and sea-strap. Day/date-telling calendar, sweep second hand and rotating elapsed-time indicator.
3342B
Same watch with bracelet.
3355
Same watch with strap and "date-only" calendar.
3355B
Same watch with bracelet and "date-only" calendar.

$15-20

$10-15

Men's Wrist Alarm Watches

3297
Seastar "Sonorous" wrist alarm in yellow top, stainless steel back water-resistant case. Wakes ... reminds ... alerts with easy-to-use push-button. Sweep second hand.
3293
Same watch in stainless steel.

3293GT
Same watch in stainless steel with matching Grand Tourismo bracelet.

$10-15

$20-25

Men's Chronographs

left **3291GT**

PR-516 Seastar Chronograph with 4 dials and two push-buttons in a yellow top, stainless steel back water-resistant case. Large dial tells regular time. Small dials register elapsed time intervals of 12 hours, 30 minutes and 60 seconds. Tachymeter scale and sweep second hand. With matching GT bracelet.

3291
Same watch with strap.

right **3300**

PR-516 Chronograph with 3 dials and 2 push-buttons in a stainless steel water-resistant case. Large dial tells regular time. Small dials register elapsed time intervals of 30 minutes and 60 seconds. Right hand dial has blue triangle to mark 5 minute "rally" alert before yacht race or other sporting events. Sweep second hand and bold, luminous hour markers.

3300GT
Same watch with Grand Tourismo bracelet.

$20-25

$10-15

Men's Skin Diver Watches

left **3296**

PR-516 Seastar self-winding diver's watch in stainless steel water-resistant case. Visodate calendar dial with rotating indicator tells elapsed time. Bold, luminous hour markers with sweep second hand.

$10-15

Man's Skin Diver Watch

left **1045**

PR-516 Intermediate size Seastar diver's watch in stainless steel water-resistant case. Visodate calendar dial with rotating time indicator for elapsed time. Easy-to-read luminous hour markers and sweep second hand.

Tissot

$10-15

$5-10

$20-25

All Priced
As Steel

$25-30

$15-20

TOUCHON WATCHES

SINCE 1866, it has been the proud privilege of better jewelers throughout America to offer Touchon Watches to a discriminating clientele. The highest standards of watch perfection are represented by Touchon. Movements and cases are finished by hand with the most minute care, assuring the highest degree of accuracy and timekeeping and the most striking individuality of style. ¶ Touchon Watches are the choice of those seeking the exceptional in timekeeping; their value increases with the years as their accuracy becomes indispensable.

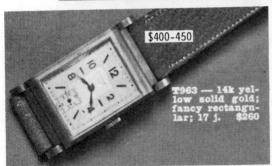

$400-450

T963 — 14k yellow solid gold; fancy rectangular; 17 j. $260

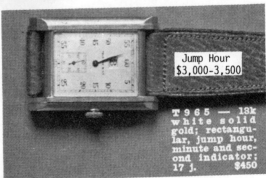

Jump Hour
$3,000-3,500

T965 — 18k white solid gold; rectangular, jump hour, minute and second indicator; 17 j. $450

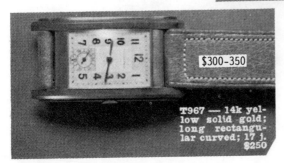

$300-350

T967 — 14k yellow solid gold; long rectangular curved; 17 j. $250

TOUCHON

T961 — 14k yellow solid gold; oval, knife edge bezel, fancy end, gilt dial; 17 j. $270

Ladies
$200-250

T959 — 14k yellow solid gold; rectangular knife edge bezel, fancy end, pink dial; 17 j. $250

$800-1,000

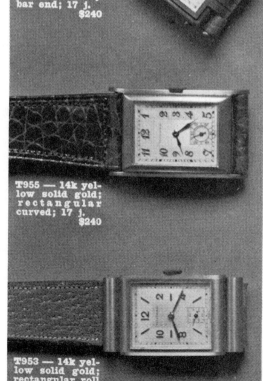

T957 — 14k yellow solid gold; rectangular curved, fancy bar end; 17 j. $240

$500-550

T955 — 14k yellow solid gold; rectangular curved; 17 j. $240

$350-400

T953 — 14k yellow solid gold; rectangular roll end; 17 j. $280

$350-400

TOUCHON

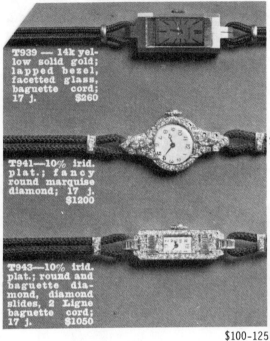

$75-100

T939 — 14k yellow solid gold; lapped bezel, facetted glass, baguette cord; 17 j. $260

$150-175

T941—10% irid. plat.; fancy round marquise diamond; 17 j. $1200

$225-250

T943—10% irid. plat.; round and baguette diamond, diamond slides, 2 Ligne baguette cord; 17 j. $1050

$550-600

$100-125

T951 — 14k yellow solid gold; cushion, fancy ends; 17 j.; strap. $225

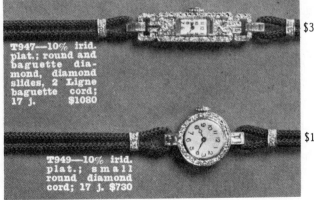

$350-400

T947—10% irid. plat.; round and baguette diamond, diamond slides, 2 Ligne baguette cord; 17 j. $1080

$125-150

T949—10% irid. plat.; small round diamond cord; 17 j. $730

T945—10% irid. plat.; fancy diamond flexible bracelet; 17 j. $1680

ULYSSE NARDIN, Locle et Genève, 7 Grands Prix

18K $150-175

18K $500-550

Platinum & Diamonds
$300-350

Platinum & Diamonds
$700-800

18K $550-650

Glass Enamel
18K $4,000-4,500

No 269

Chronographe-compteur
bracelet 15 '''

Glass Enamel
$3,500-4,000

No 271

Chronographe-compteur
bracelet 13 '''

Ulysse Nardin-1940
Steel Head $175-200
14KYG Head $350-400
18KYG Head $400-450

Ulysse Nardin-1940
8-Diamonds
18KWG Head $100-125

Ulysse Nardin-1940
Steel Head $200-225
18KYG Head $500-550

Ulysse Nardin-1939
18KPG Head $275-300

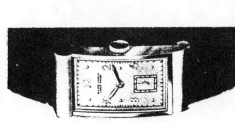

Ulysse Nardin-1939
Asymetrical
18KPG Head $700-800

Ulysse Nardin-Strap
18x30mm-Ca 1939
Hidden Lugs
18KYG Head $650-750

18K $125-150

18K $350-400

18K $100-125

18K $150-175

18K $225-250

18K $300-325

18K $225-250

18K $225-250

ULYSSE NARDIN S. A. - LE LOCLE

EXECUTI

Ulysse Nardin "Navigator Automatic". 14K gold applied dial. 21J, sweep second movement. 14K yellow gold round case. ca 1963. . . . . $120—145

Ulysse Nardin "Executive". 14K gold applied dial. 17J, sweep second movement. 18K yellow gold round case. ca 1963. . . . . . $140—165

ASSIC

Ulysse Nardin "Astrojet Automatic". 14K gold applied dial. 21J, sweep second movement. 14K yellow gold round case. ca 1963 . . $120—145

Ulysse Nardin "Classic". 14K gold applied dial, subsidiary seconds. 17J movement. Gold-filled round case. ca 1963 . . . .$35—55

Ulysse Nardin "Professor". 14K gold applied dial, subsidiary seconds. 17J movement. 14K yellow gold round case. ca 1963 . . $110—135

Ulysse Nardin "Olympic". 14K gold applied dial. 17J, sweep second movement. Gold-filled round case. ca 1963 . . . .$40—60

cadran télémétrique indique les distances
sur base de la vitesse du son.

es divisions tachymétriques donnent les vitesses
kilométriques horaires.

Le pulsomètre donne le nombre exact de
pulsations à la minute.

our la première fois se trouve réalisé, sous
n volume restreint, un chronographe de très
rande précision, muni d'un double poussoir
de trotteuse et servant à la fois de
CHRONOMÈTRE - TÉLÉMÈTRE
TACHYMÈTRE ou PULSOMÈTRE
COMPTEUR.

1935
Steel $500-700
18KYG $1,200-1,500

La qualité du mouvement et la présentatio
irréprochable des boîtes en font un cadea
parfait pour le sportif, l'ingénieur, l'officier,
le médecin....

La trotteuse, dont les tours sont enregistré
jusqu'à 45 minutes par le compteur, mesur
le temps au 1/5 de seconde.

Le double poussoir permet de déduire
les temps d'arrêt survenant en
cours de chronométrage.

UNIVERSAL GENÈVE

ESTABLISHED 1894

14KYG
$100–120

"There's more to beauty
than meets the eye."
Watches of *personality* and
character reflect the care,
skill and pride of craftsmanship
which have made Universal
Genève Watches world-famous
for great beauty—
and consistent accuracy.

14KYG
$225–275

18KYG $800–1,000
Steel $300–350

18KYG
$65–75

18KYG
$65–75

18KYG
$65–75

18KYG
$65–75

Compax
Steel $350-400
Gold Filled $250-300
Steel Bracelet $15-25

Space-Compax
w/Bracelet
Steel $250-275
Waterproof
Rotating Bezel

A= Stop-Start
B= Zero Return

Tri-Compax
Steel $800-1,000
14K $5,000-5,500
18K $5,500-6,000

Aero-Compax
Steel $650-700
Steel Bracelet $15-25
Rotating Bezel

Vacheron Constantin

V. C. 430 — 18k yellow solid gold; fancy dial; 18 j. $320 $3,700-4,000

V. C. 416 — 18k yellow solid gold; curved, fancy dial; 17 j. $230 $3,000-3,300

$1,800-2,000

V. C. 418 — 18k yellow solid gold; thin bezel, black dial; 17 j. $280

$2,700-3,000

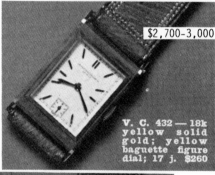

V. C. 432 — 18k yellow solid gold; yellow baguette figure dial; 17 j. $260

$6,000-6,500

V. C. 414— 10% irid. platinum; thin bezel; round and baguette diamond figure dial; 18 j. $850

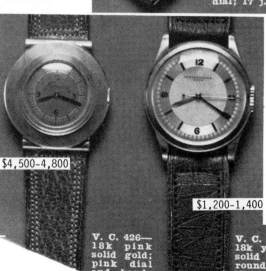

$4,500-4,800

$1,200-1,400

V. C. 426— 18k pink solid gold; pink dial and hands match; $350

V. C. 428— 18k yellow solid gold; round bass. 17 j. sweep. $350

V. C. 420 — 18k pink solid gold; thin bezel, fancy dial; 17 j. $280

$2,700-3,000

$3,700-4,000

V. C. 424— 18k yellow solid gold; round scalloped loop, fancy dial; 17 j. $300

V. C. 406 — 18k pink solid gold; square CC, fancy dial; 17 j. $300

$4,000-4,500

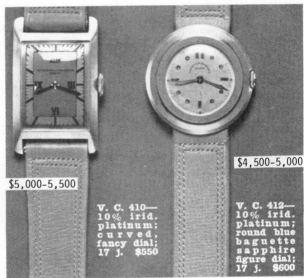

$5,000-5,500

$4,500-5,000

V. C. 410— 10% irid. platinum; curved, fancy dial; 17 j. $550

V. C. 412— 10% irid. platinum; round blue baguette sapphire figure dial; 17 j. $600

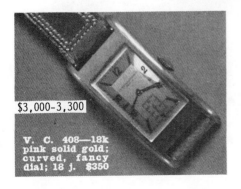

$3,000-3,300

V. C. 408—18k pink solid gold; curved, fancy dial; 18 j. $350

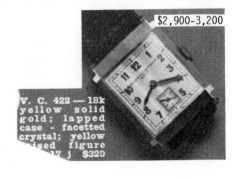

$2,900-3,200

V. C. 422 — 18k yellow solid gold; lapped case - facetted crystal; yellow raised figure ... 17 j. $320

VACHERON & CONSTANTIN

$4,000-4,500

V.C. 492
18K yellow gold
17 j. **$350**

$3,000-3,300

V.C. 490
18K yellow gold,
black dial, 17 j.
$320

$3,500-3,800

V.C. 488
18K pink gold, pink
dial 17 j. **$280**

No. 4072—13"
chronograph, 21j,
18K yellow gold
or staybrite steel.

Steel $14,000-16,000
18KYG $18,000-20,000

No. 4100—18K
yellow or pink
gold, 17j.

18KYG $3,200-3,500
18KPG $3,300-3,600

No. 4035
—18K yel-
low or pink
gold, 17j.

18KYG $2,000-2,200
18KPG $2,100-2,300

18KYG
$1,200-1,400

No. 501—18K
yellow gold, 17j.

18KYG $3,500-3,800
18KPG $3,700-4,000

No. 4088—18K
yellow or pink

18KYG
$22,000-25,000

No. 4083—18K yel-
low gold, 13" chrono-
graph, 21j.

$2,500-2,700

V.C. 466
18K yellow gold
17 j. $280

$4,000-4,400

V.C. 464
18K yellow gold,
facetted crystal,
black dial 17 j.
$370

$3,800-4,200

V.C. 462
18K yellow gold
17 j. $280

$1,300-1,600

V.C. 484
18K yellow gold
18 j. Sweep $350

$1,500-1,700

V.C. 468
18K pink gold,
pink dial 17 j.
$260

$7,000-8,000

V.C. 478
10% Irid. Platinum
Onyx Figures 17 j.
$650

$3,000-3,300

V.C. 478
18K yellow gold
17 j. $290

$3,300-3,600

V.C. 482
K yellow gold
j. $310

$2,900-3,200

V.C. 480
18K yellow gold
17 j. $310

Asymetrical
$7,000-8,000

V.C. 456
18K pink gold,
pink dial 18 j.
$450

$4,000-4,500

V.C. 458
18K yellow gold,
facetted crystal
17 j. $330

$3,500-3,800

V.C. 470
18K yellow gold,
chocolate dial 17 j.
$310

$3,500-3,800

V.C. 450
18K pink gold,
chocolate dial 18 j.
$320

$3,500-4,000

V.C. 452
18K yellow gold
17 j. $300

Asymetrical
$7,000-8,000

V.C. 454
18K yellow gold
18 j. $420

$2,500-2,800

V.C. 476
18K yellow gold
17 j. $280

Asymetrical
$6,000-6,500

V.C. 460
18K pink gold,
pink dial 17 j.
$400

$4,000-4,400

V.C. 474
18K yellow gold
18 j. $330

$850-750

V. C. 206—18k yellow solid gold; lap case, fancy dial; baguette cord; 16 j. $320

$750-850

V.C. 258 18K yellow gold 17 j. $260

$800-900

V.C. 262 18K pink gold, pink dial 18 j. $340

$700-800

V.C. 264 18K yellow gold 18 j. $270

$1,200-1,500

V. C. 103—Fine 10% irid. platinum; fancy flexible bracelet diamond watch; 17 j. $3600

$700-800

V. C. 404— 18k pink solid gold; pink dial— ladies strap; 17 j. $350

$1,100-1,200

V.C. 260 18K pink gold, pink dial 18 j. $360

$650-750

V. C. 202 — 18k yellow solid gold; baguette cord; 17 j. $270

$1,200-1,400

V.C. 214 18K yellow gold, black dial 18 j. $350

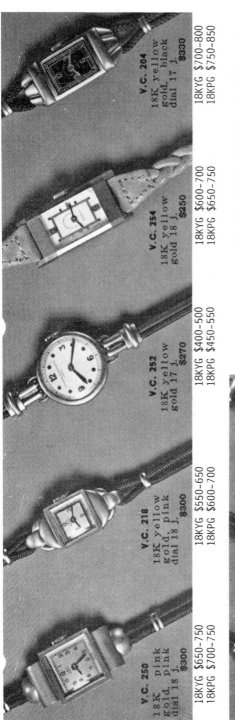

V.C. 204
18K yellow gold, black dial 17 j. **$330**
18KYG $700-800
18KPG $750-850

V.C. 254
18K yellow gold 18 j. **$250**
18KYG $600-700
18KPG $650-750

V.C. 252
18K yellow gold 17 j. **$270**
18KYG $400-500
18KPG $450-550

V.C. 218
18K yellow gold, pink dial 18 j. **$300**
18KYG $550-650
18KPG $600-700

V.C. 250
18K pink gold, pink dial 18 j. **$300**
18KYG $650-750
18KPG $700-750

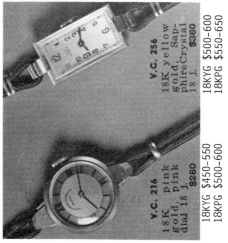

V.C. 256
18K yellow gold, SapphireCrystal 18 j. **$360**
18KYG $500-600
18KPG $550-650

V.C. 216
18K pink gold, pink dial 18 j. **$260**
18KYG $450-550
18KPG $500-600

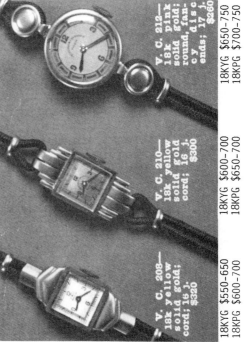

V. C. 212—
18k solid gold; round, fancy disc ends; 17 j. **$260**
18KYG $650-750
18KPG $700-750

V. C. 210—
18k yellow solid gold cord; 16 j. **$300**
18KYG $600-700
18KPG $650-700

V. C. 208—
18k yellow solid gold; cord; 16 j. **$320**
18KYG $550-650
18KPG $600-700

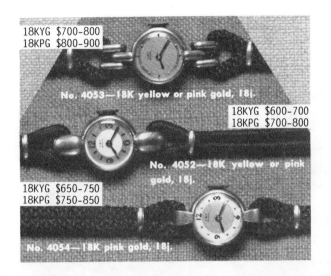

18KYG $700-800
18KPG $800-900

No. 4053—18K yellow or pink gold, 18j.

18KYG $600-700
18KPG $700-800

No. 4052—18K yellow or pink gold, 18j.

18KYG $650-750
18KPG $750-850

No. 4054—18K pink gold, 18j.

18KYG $1,300-1,400
18KPG $1,400-1,500

V. C. 101—Fine
10% irid. plati-
num; fancy flex-
ible bracelet;
diamond watch;
17 j. $3240

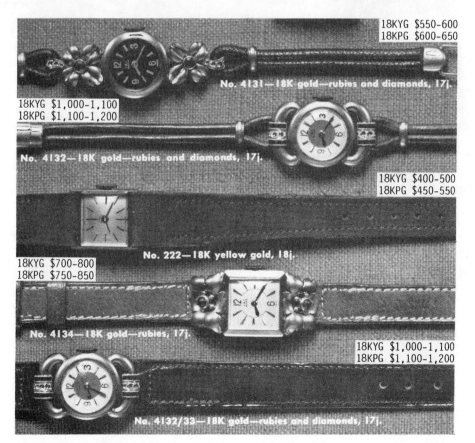

18KYG $550-600
18KPG $600-650

No. 4131—18K gold—rubies and diamonds, 17j.

18KYG $1,000-1,100
18KPG $1,100-1,200

No. 4132—18K gold—rubies and diamonds, 17j.

18KYG $400-500
18KPG $450-550

No. 222—18K yellow gold, 18j.

18KYG $700-800
18KPG $750-850

No. 4134—18K gold—rubies, 17j.

18KYG $1,000-1,100
18KPG $1,100-1,200

No. 4132/33—18K gold—rubies and diamonds, 17j.

18KYG $2,700-3,000
18KPG $2,800-3,100

18KPG $1,100-1,300

18KYG $2,500-2,700

No. 4036—18K
pink or yellow
gold, 17j.

No. 3596—
18K pink
gold, 17j.

18KYG $4,000-4,500
18KPG $4,500-5,000

18KYG $3,200-3,500
18KPG $3,400-3,700

No. 525—18K
yellow gold, 18j.

No. 536—18K
yellow or pink
gold, 18j.

18KYG $1,800-2,100
18KPG $2,000-2,300

No. 4129—18K
yellow or pink
gold, 17j.

18KYG $3,000-3,300
18KPG $3,200-3,500

No. 4018
—18K yel-
low or pink
gold, 17j.

18KYG $2,900-3,200
18KPG $3,000-3,300

No. 4019—18K
yellow gold, 17j.

No. 4040—18K
yellow or pink
gold, 17j.

18KYG $14,000-15,000
No. 3681—18K
yellow gold, 17j.

18KYG $1,200-1,400
18KPG $1,300-1,500

No. 503—
18K yellow
or pink
gold, 17j.

No. 493—
18K yellow
gold

Hinged Lugs
18KYG $4,000-4,500

18KYG $2,800-3,000
18KPG $2,900-3,200

18KYG $1,800-2,100
18KPG $2,000-2,200

No. 514—18K
yellow or pink
gold, 17j.

No. 546—18K
yellow or pink
gold, 17j.

18KYG $2,200-2,400

No. 4070
—18K yel-
low gold,
17j.

No. 508—18K
yellow gold, 17j.

18KYG $3,000-3,300

18KYG $2,200-2,400
18KPG $2,300-2,500

18KYG $1,800-2,100
18KPG $1,900-2,200

No. 4097—18K
yellow or pink
gold, 17j.

Asymetrical
18KYG $10,000-12,000

No. 516—18K
yellow or pink
gold, 17j.

No. 472—18K
yellow gold, 17j.

VACHERON & CONSTANTIN
GENÈVE

3737
Asymetrical
18KYG $7,000-8,000
18KPG $8,000-9,000

Platinum & Diamonds
$500-600

2943.

3608
18KYG $450-500
18KPG $500-550

3737 and 3608. Modern watches.

3686
18KYG $2,200-2,500
18KPG $2,500-2,800

3586
18KYG $400-450
18KPG $450-500
Platinum & Diamonds
$500-600

3686. Fine classical gold watches. 3586

VACHERON & CONSTANTIN

3827-Ladies
18KYG $650-700
18KPG $700-750

3806
18KYG $3,000-3,500
18KPG $3,500-4,000

3827. Lady's gold watch with figures marked in rubies, sapphires or onyx.

3806. An Elegant watch bracelet.

3595
18KYG $1,500-1,800
18KPG $1,600-1,900

3596
18KYG $1,200-1,500
18KPG $1,300-1,600

3595. Fine watches in gold or   *3596*
steel.

3682
18KYG $3,000-3,500
18KPG $3,500-3,800

3722-Ladies
18KYG $600-650
18KPG $650-700

3682. Latest creation in gold watches.

3722. Gold watch with rubies.

VACHERON & CONSTANTIN

3794
Hinged Lugs
18KYG $4,000-4,500
18KPG $4,500-5,000

3782-Ladies
18KYG $400-450
18KPG $450-500

3794 and 3782. Fancy watches.

3504
18KYG $1,200-1,400
18KPG $1,300-1,500

3564
Split Second
18KYG Est.
$80,000-100,000

3504. Watch with centre seconds hand.

3564. Split second chronograph with tachometer, pulsometer, telemeter, etc.

3762-Ladies
Platinum $800-850

3762. Platinum and diamond watch with
black leather bracelet.

18KYG $2,200-2,300
18KPG $2,400-2,700

18KYG $2,500-2,800
18KPG $2,700-3,000

18KYG $2,800-3,100
18KPG $3,000-3,300

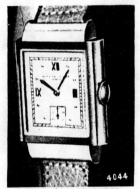

18KYG $3,000-3,300
18KPG $3,200-3,500

18KYG $2,000-2,200
18KPG $2,200-2,400

18KYG $550-650
18KPG $600-700

18KYG $1,800-2,000
18KPG $2,000-2,200

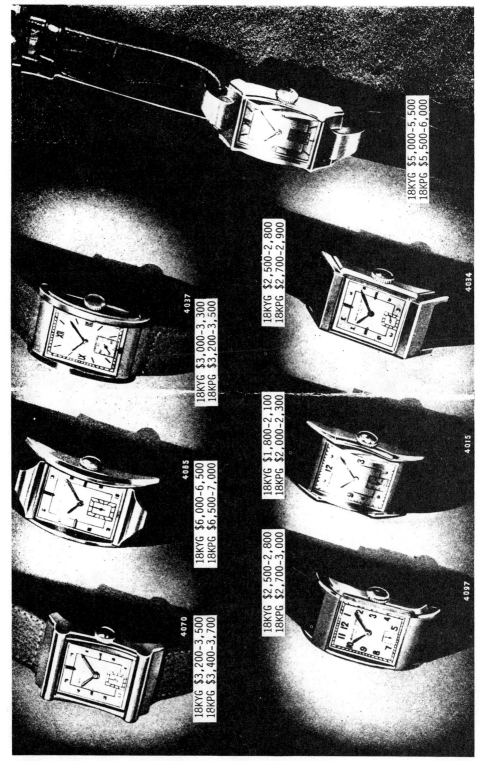

18KYG $5,000-5,500
18KPG $5,500-6,000

4034

18KYG $2,500-2,800
18KPG $2,700-2,900

4037

18KYG $3,000-3,300
18KPG $3,200-3,500

4085

18KYG $6,000-6,500
18KPG $6,500-7,000

4015

18KYG $1,800-2,100
18KPG $2,000-2,300

4097

18KYG $2,500-2,800
18KPG $2,700-3,000

4070

18KYG $3,200-3,500
18KPG $3,400-3,700

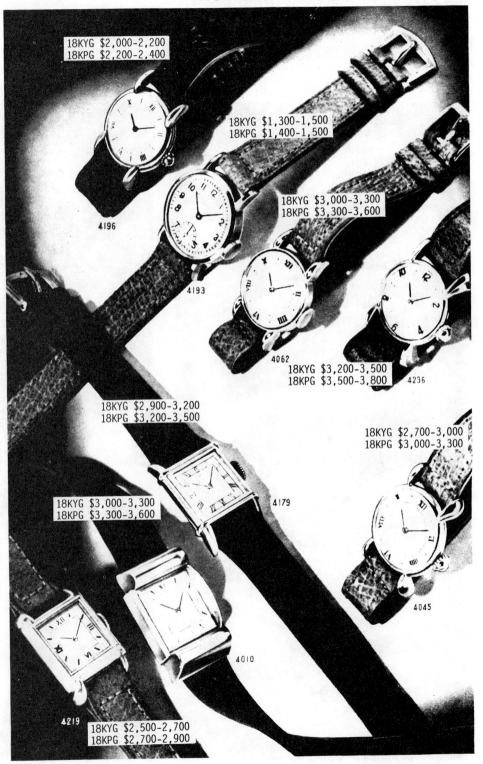

18KYG $2,000-2,200
18KPG $2,200-2,400

18KYG $1,300-1,500
18KPG $1,400-1,500

18KYG $3,000-3,300
18KPG $3,300-3,600

4196

4193

18KYG $3,200-3,500
18KPG $3,500-3,800

4062

4236

18KYG $2,900-3,200
18KPG $3,200-3,500

18KYG $2,700-3,000
18KPG $3,000-3,300

18KYG $3,000-3,300
18KPG $3,300-3,600

4179

4045

4010

4219

18KYG $2,500-2,700
18KPG $2,700-2,900

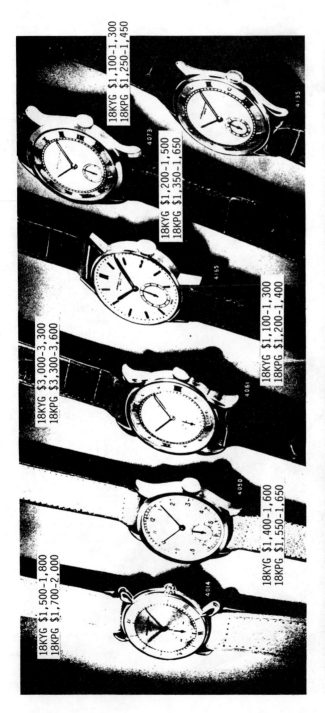

18KYG $1,100-1,300
18KPG $1,250-1,450

18KYG $1,200-1,500
18KPG $1,350-1,650

18KYG $3,000-3,300
18KPG $3,300-3,600

18KYG $1,100-1,300
18KPG $1,200-1,400

18KYG $1,400-1,600
18KPG $1,550-1,650

18KYG $1,500-1,800
18KPG $1,700-2,000

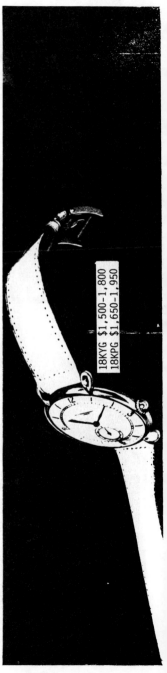

18KYG $1,500-1,800
18KPG $1,650-1,950

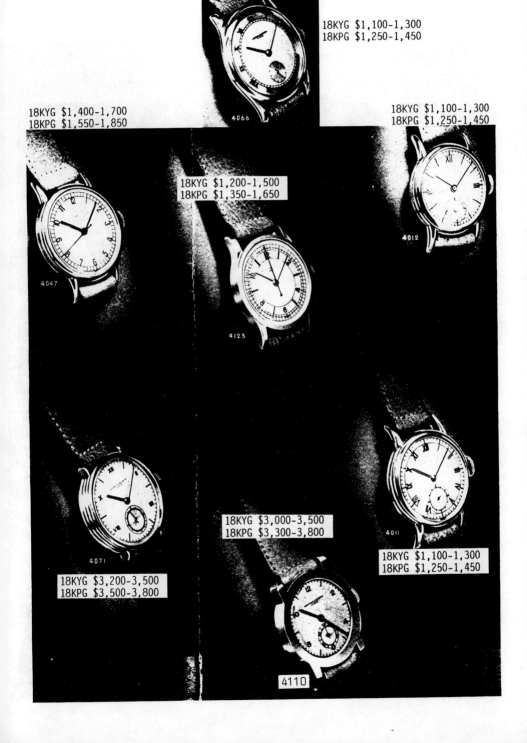

18KYG $1,100-1,300
18KPG $1,250-1,450

4066

18KYG $1,400-1,700
18KPG $1,550-1,850

18KYG $1,100-1,300
18KPG $1,250-1,450

18KYG $1,200-1,500
18KPG $1,350-1,650

4012

4047

4125

18KYG $3,000-3,500
18KPG $3,300-3,800

4071

18KYG $3,200-3,500
18KPG $3,500-3,800

4011

18KYG $1,100-1,300
18KPG $1,250-1,450

4110

18KYG $15,000-17,000
18KPG $16,500-18,500

18KYG $16,000-18,000
18KPG $17,500-19,500

4072

4178

18KYG $4,500-5,000
18KPG $5,000-5,500
4240

4261

Repeater
18KYG $100,000-125,000
18KPG $125,000-150,000

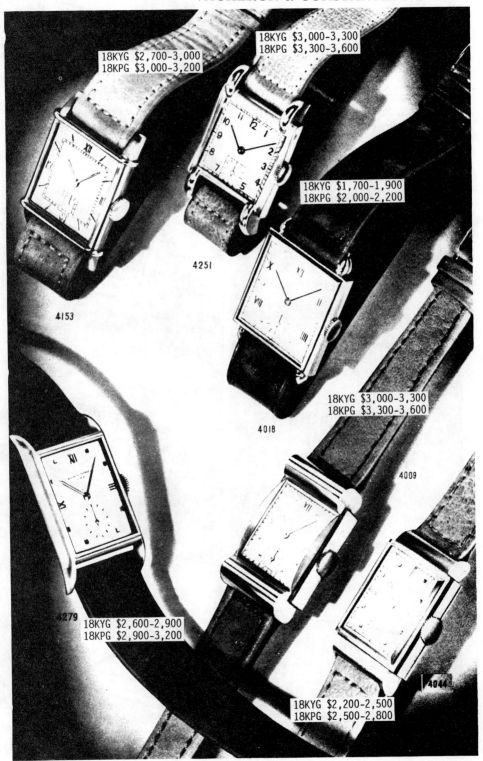

18KYG $2,700-3,000
18KPG $3,000-3,200

18KYG $3,000-3,300
18KPG $3,300-3,600

18KYG $1,700-1,900
18KPG $2,000-2,200

4251

4153

4018

18KYG $3,000-3,300
18KPG $3,300-3,600

4009

4279

18KYG $2,600-2,900
18KPG $2,900-3,200

4044

18KYG $2,200-2,500
18KPG $2,500-2,800

A SPECIAL THANKS TO:
Luther & Vivian Grinder
Naples, FL
for the use of their wrist
watch research.

4001
18KYG $2,300-2,600
18KPG $2,500-2,800

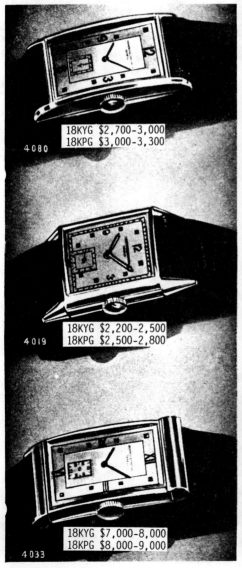

4080
18KYG $2,700-3,000
18KPG $3,000-3,300

4113
18KYG $2,700-3,000
18KPG $3,000-3,300

4019
18KYG $2,200-2,500
18KPG $2,500-2,800

4109
18KYG $2,000-2,200
18KPG $2,200-2,400

4033
18KYG $7,000-8,000
18KPG $8,000-9,000

4002
18KYG $2,100-2,300
18KPG $2,300-2,600

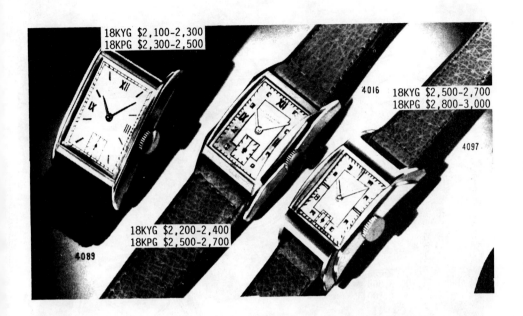

18KYG $2,100-2,300
18KPG $2,300-2,500

4016

18KYG $2,500-2,700
18KPG $2,800-3,000

4097

18KYG $2,200-2,400
18KPG $2,500-2,700

4089

18KYG $3,200-3,500
18KPG $3,500-3,800

18KYG $4,000-4,500
18KPG $4,500-5,000

4753

18KYG $4,500-5,000
18KPG $5,500-6,000

4203

18KYG $2,700-3,000
18KPG $3,000-3,300

18KYG $2,600-2,900
18KPG $2,900-3,200

18KYG $3,000-3,300
18KPG $3,300-3,600

4334

4333

18KYG $3,500-3,800
18KPG $3,800-4,100

4322

4321

4324

18KYG $2,700-3,000
18KPG $3,000-3,300

4323

18KYG $3,000-3,300
18KPG $3,300-3,600

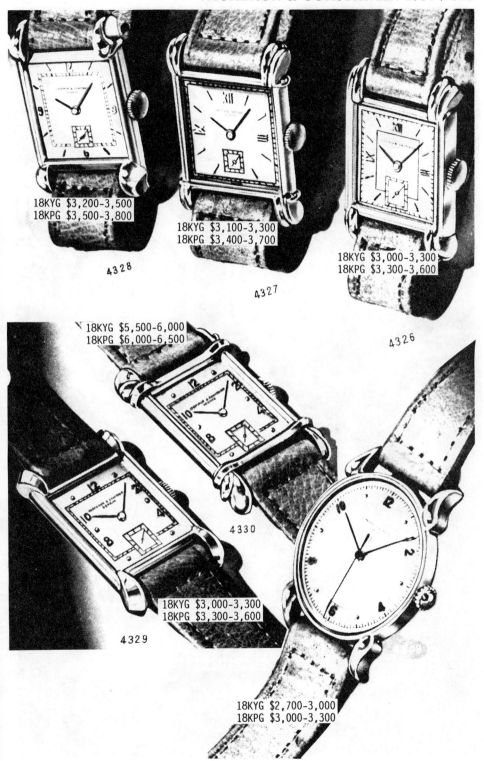

18KYG $3,200-3,500
18KPG $3,500-3,800

4328

18KYG $3,100-3,300
18KPG $3,400-3,700

4327

18KYG $3,000-3,300
18KPG $3,300-3,600

4326

18KYG $5,500-6,000
18KPG $6,000-6,500

4330

18KYG $3,000-3,300
18KPG $3,300-3,600

4329

18KYG $2,700-3,000
18KPG $3,000-3,300

18KYG $2,300-2,600
18KPG $2,600-2,900

4061

18KYG $1,000-1,200
18KPG $1,250-1,350

4165

18KYG $1,100-1,300
18KPG $1,200-1,400

4217

18KYG $1,700-2,000
18KPG $1,850-2,150

4218

4190

18KYG $1,100-1,300
18KPG $1,200-1,400

Van Cleef and Arpels
Bracelet—17x33mm—CA 1950's—17 Jewels
18K Polished Yellow Gold $600–860

Vialux, retailed by **Asprey**. Curvex, white matte dial, round movement. 18K gold, 39mm. rectangular case, curved corners. ca 1925.
. . . . $500–650

Vomard-V2000
Backwind & set
Swiss Analog-Steel
Head $100-150

VULCAIN

Steel $100-125
14KYGF $125-150

Ca 1952

Cricket-Alarm
Steel $75-100
14KGF $100-125
14KYG $350-400
18KPG $400-450

AMERICAN WALTHAM WATCH CO., WALTHAM, MASS. 1885–1923
WALTHAM WATCH CO., WALTHAM, MASS. 1923–1957

Waltham (we will use for short), first listed ladies convertible bracelet wrist watches in their 1912 Catalog. In this complete, product line catalog, was offered the Jewel Series "Ruby", 17 jewel, 6/0 size movement, in five round cases in combinations of case metals with bracelets or straps. A note explains that those combinations could also be obtained in 0 size by writing for prices.

A 1921 product catalog in the library of Roland Thomas "Rod" Minter, issued from The Waltham Watch Company Limited, Montreal, Canada (stating: Factories in Montreal and Canada), listed six styles of 3/0 size, 7 and 15 jewel, ladies convertible bracelet and ribbon watches; 12 varieties of 6/0 size, 7 and 15 jewel, ladies round convertible (disappearing eye) bracelet watches; 11 varieties of 10 ligne, 15 jewel, ladies detachable bracelet watches in round, cushion, square, decagon & octagon, plain and engraved bezel cases in both solid and gold-filled; and, last but not least, a man's "Cadet Model" tonneau case with a 7 or 15 jewel, 3/0 size round movement in a silver case with leather strap.

The 1922 product catalog continued to list most of the past models, with the addition of a man's strap watch in 6/0 size "Sapphire", 15 jewel round movement in a 14K solid green gold cushion case. All of the above listed watches were cased, timed & boxed at the factory.

Prior to 1912, Waltham sold to the trade both cased and uncased pocket watch movements, and the demand increased for wrist watch size movement, and, of course, they supplied them until the end of production to anyone who wanted to buy them without cases. (All of the American companies and most European companies did this as a regular business practice).

The 1928 product catalog offered six, 7¼ ligne rectangular ribbon wrist watches; nine, 6/0 size strap wrist watches; six, 10 ligne strap wrist watches; and six, 7¼ ligne strap wrist watches. From then on, the line continued to expand with literally hundreds of case styles until 1957, the end of U.S. production. Since then, the Waltham name has been used on imported wrist and pocket watches (usually Swiss).

Waltham "Ladies Convertible Bracelet and Strap". Glass enamel or gilded metal or silver dial. 17J, "Ruby", 6/0 size nickel round movement. Round case. By unfastening the bracelet from the convertible wrist watch (top illustration), it can be worn either as a chatelaine, a charm or a locket, or in the pocket. All Waltham wrist watches made at this time wind at 12 and the crown is protected by a patent bow. Cased, timed & boxed at the factory. They were also supplied in 0 size, with the values a little more. ca 1912.
14K solid gold. $50–75
20 Yr. gold-filled 10–20

**AMERICAN WALTHAM
WATCH COMPANY**
Waltham, Mass.
1859—1957

NAME CHANGES

Howard, Davis & Dennison
Roxbury, Mass.
Sept. 1850 Adopted Name
American Horologe Co., Roxbury, Mass.
1851 Name Change (For 6 months)
The Warren Mfg. Co., Roxbury, Mass.
1851—1853 Name Change
Boston Watch Co.
Roxbury, Mass. & Waltham, Mass.
Sept. 1853—May 1857
New Company formed
Tracy Baker and Company
Waltham, Mass.
1857 Reorganized as
Appleton Tracy and Co., Waltham, Mass.
1857—1859 Name Change
American Watch Company
Waltham, Mass.
1859—1885 Name Change
American Waltham Watch Co.
Waltham, Mass.
1859—1923 Name Change
Waltham Watch Co., Waltham, Mass.
1923—1957 End of Production

Serial No.	Date
9,000,000	1899
10,000,000	1901
12,000,000	1903
13,000,000	1904
14,000,000	1905
15,000,000	1907
17,000,000	1908
18,000,000	1910
19,000,000	1913
20,000,000	1914
21,000,000	1917
22,000,000	1918
23,000,000	1919
24,000,000	1921
26,000,000	1927
27,000,000	1929
28,000,000	1934
29,000,000	1936
30,000,000	1939
31,000,000	1942
32,000,000	1945
33,600,000	1951
33,830,300	1953
35,000,000	1957

EA 105 American Waltham Watch Co.
0 Size—Hunting—Nickel
Model 1900 & 1907—Pendant Set—¾ Plate

EA 106 American Waltham Watch Co.
0 Size—Open Face—Nickel
Model 1900 & 1907—Pendant Set—¾ Plate

EA 107 American Waltham Watch Co.
0 Size—Hunting—Nickel
Model 1891—Pendant Set—¾ Plate

EA 108 American Waltham Watch Co.
6/0 Size—Hunting—Nickel
Model 1898 & 1912—Pendant Set—¾ Plate

EA 109 American Waltham Watch Co.
6/0 Size—Open Face—Nickel
Model 1898 & 1912—Pendant Set—¾ Plate

EA 112 American Waltham Watch Co.
00 Size—Hunting—Nickel
Model 1891*—Pendant Set—"OM" Model

1948
WALTHAM WRIST AND BRACELET WATCH MOVEMENTS

6/0s 1945 Calendar

6/0s 1945 Regular

6/0s 1945 Center
Second (Sweep)

6/0s 1898 — Htg.

670 Model

6/0s 1912 O.F.

870 R Model

675 Model

10 Ligne

7½ Ligne
Round

870 Model

5¼ L Rectangular
(Enlarged)

450 Model

400 Model

7¼ L Rect. Cut Cor.

750 B Model

650 Model

678 Model

750 Model

EA 113   American Waltham Watch Co.

*Wrist watch movements smaller than 3/0
size are not collected unless they are in a
nice case. Some of the Waltham small size
are illustrated above and have a value of
$1.00 to $15.00, depending on the buyer.*

3/0 size nickel chrome plated, fancy shaped strap case, with genuine leather strap and chrome plated buckle. Can be had with the following movements.

R3776 7 jewel Waltham, etched dial.
Each, $27.00

R3777 17 jewel Waltham. **Each, 38.00**

3/0 size nickel chrome plated, fancy shaped strap case, with genuine leather strap and chrome plated buckle. Can be had with the following movements.

R3770 7 jewel Waltham, etched dial.
Each, $25.00

No. 65   Style No. 2   Price $89.40
15-Jewel, 10-Ligne Movement, 14K White, Green or Yellow Gold, Plain or Oxidized Case and Buckle, Curved Back, Radium or Etched Dial.

No. 75   Price $103.08
LADIES' SPORT STYLE No. 3
17-Jewel, 7¼-Ligne Movement, 14K White en or Yellow Gold Case and Buckle, Plain Bezel aved Center, Curved Back, Etched Dial.
No. 65 STYLE No. 3   Price $89.40
15-Jewel, 7¼-Ligne Movement, 14K White en or Yellow Gold Case and Buckle, Plain Bezel raved Center, Curved Back, Etched Dial.
No. 50 STYLE No. 3   Price $68.76
15-Jewel, 7¼-Ligne Movement, 14K Filled White. Green or Yellow Gold Case and Buckle, Plain ., Engraved Center, Curved Back, Etched Dial.
No. 40 STYLE No. 3   Price $54.96
7-Jewel, 7¼-Ligne Movement, 14K White, Green or Yellow Gold Case and Buckle, Plain R Engraved Center, Curved Back, Etched Dial.

No. 50   Style No. 1   Price $67.20
15-Jewel, 10-Ligne Movement, 14K Filled White. or Green Gold, Oxidized Case and Buckle, Extended Center, Curved Back, Radium Dial.
No. 45   Style No. 1   Price $61.80
15-Jewel, 10-Ligne Movement, 14K Filled White, or Green Gold, Oxidized Case and Buckle, Extended Center, Curved Back, Etched Dial.
No. 4250   Style No. 1   Price $57.00
7-Jewel, 10-Ligne Movement, 14K Filled White, or Green Gold, Ox.dized Case and Buckle, Extended Center, Curved Back, Radium Dial.
No. 3750   Style No. 1   Price $51.60
7-Jewel, 10-Ligne Movement, 14K Filled White, or Green Gold, Oxidized Case and Buckle Extended Center, Curved Back, Etched Dial.

WITTNAUER

The
JON
HALL
WATCH

United
Artists
Star

$45-50

Yellow rolled gold
plate; 15 j. $32.50

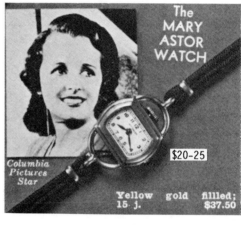

The
MARY
ASTOR
WATCH

Columbia
Pictures
Star

$20-25

Yellow gold filled;
15 j. $37.50

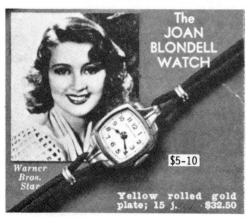

The
JOAN
BLONDELL
WATCH

Warner
Bros.
Star

$5-10

Yellow rolled gold
plate; 15 j. $32.50

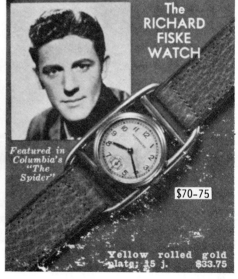

The
RICHARD
FISKE
WATCH

Featured in
Columbia's
"The
Spider"

$70-75

Yellow rolled gold
plate; 15 j. $33.75

Watches of the Stars

For over 72 years Wittnauer Watches have been known as "the popular priced watch with the fine movement," and have been worn with pride in the most select society. Associated with Longines Watches for 72 years — Wittnauer Watches, though moderately priced, have always been sold to patrons of better jewelers and are a product of:

The ANNE SHIRLEY WATCH

$5-10

Featured in Columbia's "Girl's School"

Yellow rolled gold plate; 15 j. $33.75

The ROBERT PAIGE WATCH

Featured in Columbia's "The Lady Objects"

$60-70

Yellow rolled gold plate; 15 j. $30

The ERROL FLYNN WATCH

Warner Bros. Star

$20-25

Yellow rolled gold plate; 15 j. $30

The ELLA LOGAN WATCH

United Artists Star

$5-10

Yellow rolled gold plate; 15 j. $29.50

LONGINES-WITTNAUER WATCH CO., Inc.

The Wittnauer Movement, celebrated since 1866, is unique among popular priced watches in being made by a single group of watchmakers entirely under one roof.

Only fine watches enjoy this distinction, which is vitally important in its effect on standardization and running qualities in a timepiece.

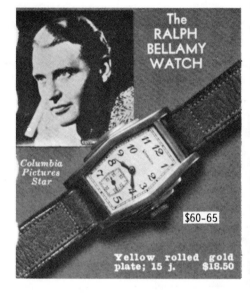

The
RALPH
BELLAMY
WATCH

Columbia
Pictures
Star

$60-65

Yellow rolled gold plate; 15 j. $18.50

The
CHARLES
STARRET
WATCH

Columbia
Pictures
Star

$50-55

Yellow rolled gold plate; 15 j. $24.75

The
ANITA
LOUISE
WATCH

Warner
Bros.
Star

$5-10

Yellow rolled gold plate; 15 j. $25

* All values are given for the head only unless the band is included in the description.
* Read page 12 before using this book to value your wrist watch.
* Values are given for a mint watch with original dial, movement and case.

The
ANN
MILLER
WATCH

Featured in Columbia's "You Can't Take It With You"

$5-10

Yellow rolled gold plate; 15 j. $29.75

The
RICHARD
ARLEN
WATCH

Columbia Pictures Star

$50-55

Yellow rolled gold plate; 15 j. $27.50

The
OLIVIA
de HAVILLAND
WATCH

Warner Bros. Star

$50-60

Yellow 14k solid gold; 15 j. $39.50

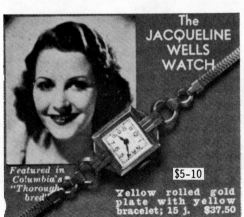

The
JACQUELINE
WELLS
WATCH

Featured in Columbia's "Thoroughbred"

$5-10

Yellow rolled gold plate with yellow bracelet; 15 j. $37.50

The
GEORGE
BRENT
WATCH

Columbia Pictures Star

$45-50

Yellow rolled gold plate; 15 j. $25

$200-225

208T WITTNAUER TELEMETER
½ second telemeter dial, stainless steel, 17J.

$150-175

210T WITTNAUER CHRONOGRAPH
½ second, 30-minute register, timeout feature, stainless steel, 17J.

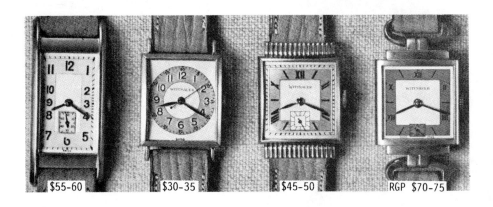

$55-60 $30-35 $45-50   RGP $70-75

$65-70 $55-60 $50-55 $50-55

WITTNAUER MAINLINER SERIES

MAINLINER DISPATCHER	MAINLINER PILOT	MAINLINER CAPTAIN	MAINLINER COMMANDER
natural rolled gold plate, non-corrosive steel back, 15j.	natural rolled gold plate, non-corrosive steel back, 15j.	natural rolled gold plate, non-corrosive steel back, 15j.	natural rolled gold plate, non-corrosive steel back, 15j, matching link bracelet.

$45-50 $50-55 $55-60

YALE F	HARVARD M	STANFORD B
7 j. yellow rolled gold plate **$19.50**	15 j. yellow rolled gold plate **$22.50**	15 j. yellow rolled gold plate **$24.75**

$50-55 $15-20 $55-60

CHARLES STARRET	HARVARD H	STANFORD C
15 j. yellow rolled gold plate **$24.75**	15 j. yellow rolled gold plate **$24.75**	15 j. yellow rolled gold plate **$27.50**

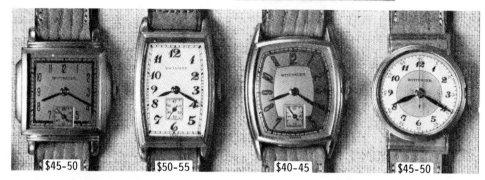

$40-45

RGP $70-95

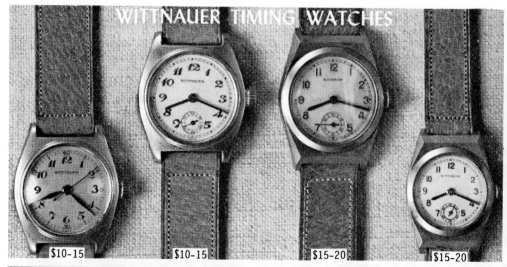

WORLD A SWEEP	WORLD A	WORLD B	WORLD D
ort or doctors' atch, sweep second, moisture-proof, stain- less steel, 7j.	moisture-proof sport design, stainless steel, 7j.	stainless steel sport watch, moisture-proof, 15j.	small size stainless steel sport watch, moisture-proof, 15j.

$175-200

217T WITTNAUER CHRONOGRAPH
½ second, 30-minute and 12-hour register, timeout feature, stainless steel, 17J.

$150-175

$200-225

CHRONOGRAPH
17 jewel stainless steel **$80.00**

CHRONOGRAPH
17 jewel stainless steel **$75.00**

$45-50

$60-65

$50-55

$45-50

HARTWICK
distinctively designed, natural rolled gold plate, 15j.

BUCKNELL
handsome rectangular style, new set-in end pieces, natural rolled gold plate, 17j.

$55-60

$50-55

HARVARD H
small round style, pink rolled gold plate, 15j.

PARSONS
new spherical dial and crystal, natural rolled gold plate, 15j.

$15-20

HARVARD I

$35-40

ELMHURST C

WITTNAUER

$55-60	$50-55	$35-40
RUTGERS D	**VANDERBILT E**	**WEST POINT**
15 j. yellow rolled gold plate **$29.75**	15 j. yellow rolled gold plate **$29.75**	17 j. pink rolled gold plate **$29.75**

$50-55	$55-60	$55-60
JAMES DUNN	**VANDERBILT D**	**STANFORD D**
17 j. yellow rolled gold plate **$32.50**	15 j. yellow rolled gold plate **$33.75**	15 j. yellow rolled gold plate **$33.75**

ANNAPOLIS	**JOHN CARROL**
17 j. pink rolled gold plate **$27.50**	15 j. yellow rolled gold plate **$29.75**

$60-65

$50-55

* All values are given for the head only unless the band is included in the description.
* Read page 12 before using this book to value your wrist watch.
* Values are given for a mint watch with original dial, movement and case.

Wittnauer Technical and Timing

FOR SPORTS, SCIENCE AND INDUSTRY

Watches

$40—60

$150—200

$100—150

Left:

Chronograph 228T
A reliable time-out
two-button chronograph
with 30-minute register,
telemeter-tachymeter scales,
day and night reading dial.
All-Proof®,
stainless steel, strap
$75.

Center:

Chronograph 235T
A reliable time-out two-button
chronograph with 30-minute register,
telemeter-tachymeter scales, 12-hour
independent register and luminous
dial. A complete flight-calculating
instrument for pilots and navigators.
All-Proof®, stainless steel, strap
$100.

Right:

Globemaster
A watch with a rotating ring
around the dial
showing the time in
all world time zones.
All-Proof®, stainless steel, strap
$49.95

with bracelet
$55.

Wittnauer Trophy and Viscount

MEN'S CALENDAR WATCHES

Left:
Trophy C302
Calendar watch,
gold-filled top
with steel back,
strap
$29.95
―――――――――
with matching bracelet
$39.95

Center left:
Trophy C305
Calendar watch,
All-Proof®,
florentine finished dial,
stainless steel, strap
$35.95
―――――――――
with matching bracelet
$39.95

Center right:
Viscount A102
Calendar watch,
All-Proof®,
stainless steel,
strap
$45.95
―――――――――
with matching bracelet
$49.95

Right:
Viscount C301
Calendar watch, All-Proof®,
sweep-second,
rolled gold plate top
with steel back,
matching bracelet
$49.95
―――――――――
with strap
$45.95

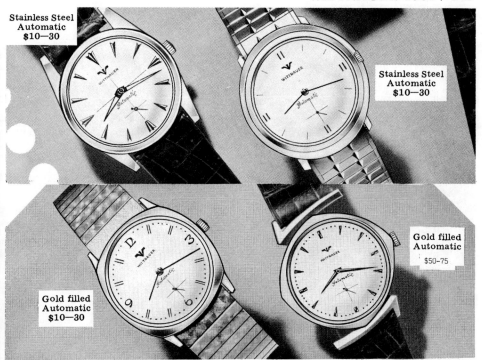

Stainless Steel
Automatic
$10—30

Stainless Steel
Automatic
$10—30

Gold filled
Automatic
$50-75

Gold filled
Automatic
$10—30

Wittnauer Sportsmaster

MEN'S AUTOMATIC ALL-PROOF® WATCHES

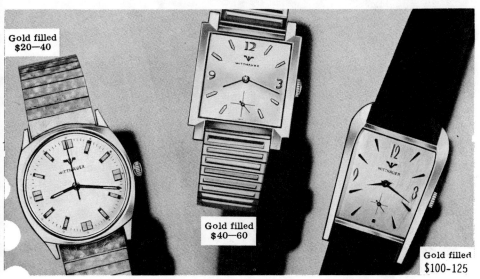

Gold filled
$20—40

Gold filled
$40—60

Gold filled
$100-125

Wittnauer Ambassador and Statesman

MEN'S GOLD-FILLED DRESS WATCHES

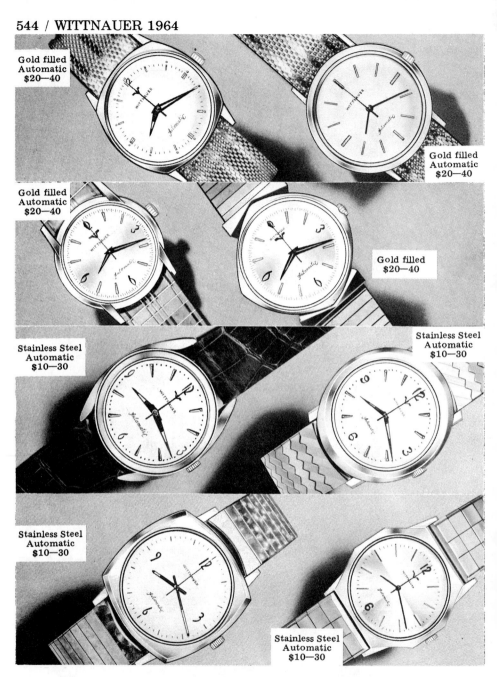

Gold filled
Automatic
$20—40

Gold filled
Automatic
$20—40

Gold filled
Automatic
$20—40

Gold filled
$20—40

Stainless Steel
Automatic
$10—30

Stainless Steel
Automatic
$10—30

Stainless Steel
Automatic
$10—30

Stainless Steel
Automatic
$10—30

Wittnauer Execu-Matic and Astro-Matic

MEN'S AUTOMATIC ALL-PROOF® WATCHES

$20—40

$20—40

$10—30

$10—30

Wittnauer Execu-Matic and Exposition

MEN'S AUTOMATIC ALL-PROOF® CALENDAR WATCHES

Left:
Execu-matic B203
Self-winding, calendar,
All-Proof®, sweep-second,
stainless steel,
strap
$55.

with matching bracelet
$59.95

Center left:
Execu-matic C301
Self-winding, calendar,
All-Proof®, sweep-second,
stainless steel,
with matching bracelet
$69.50

with strap
$55.

Center right:
Execu-matic F601
Self-winding, calendar,
All-Proof®, sweep-second,
gold-filled top, steel back,
alligator strap
$59.95

with matching bracelet
$71.50

Right:
Exposition MI
Self-winding, calendar,
All-Proof®, sweep-second,
gold-filled,
with matching bracelet
$71.50

DISTINGUISHED COMPANION WATCH TO THE WORLD HONORED LONGINES

Wittnauer Has Always Been a Leader in Styling and Design.

Wittnauer Diamond Aristocrat

MEN'S DIAMOND DIAL WATCHES

Left:	*Center left:*	*Center right:*	*Right:*
Diamond Aristocrat 3B Dial set with 3 diamonds, yellow or white gold-filled, dress strap $79.50	Diamond Aristocrat 3C Dial set with 3 diamonds, yellow or white gold-filled, dress strap $79.50	Diamond Aristocrat 4C Dial set with 4 diamonds, yellow or white gold-filled, dress strap $89.50	Diamond Aristocrat 4D Dial set with 4 diamonds, yellow or white gold-filled, with matching bracelet $99.50
with matching bracelet $89.50	with matching bracelet $89.50	with matching bracelet $99.50	with dress strap $89.50

DISTINGUISHED COMPANION WATCH TO THE WORLD HONORED LONGINES

Every Wittnauer Watch Is Jeweler Finished ... Each Is Custom Designed.

Wyler
WATERPROOF

$100-125

$3-5

$5-10

$15-20

$15-20

$20-25

$50-55

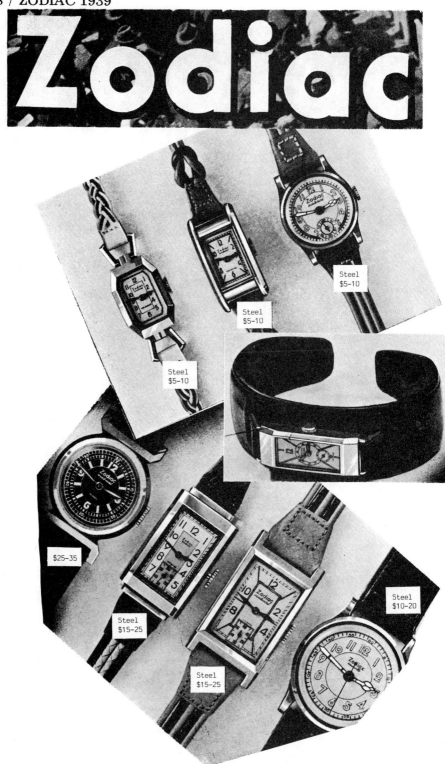

Steel
$5-10

Steel
$5-10

Steel
$5-10

$25-35

Steel
$15-25

Steel
$15-25

Steel
$10-20

INDEX TO VINTAGE AMERICAN & EUROPEAN
WRIST WATCH GUIDES BOOKS 1, 2, 3, 4 & 87

This index shows the illustrated contents of the five (5) Wrist Watch Price Guide Books that were published in 1984, 1987, 1988 & 1989.

Name   = Name of the Watch
Number = Number of illustrated wrist watches
Book   = Wrist Watch Book 1,2,3,4, or 1987 Update to Book 1
Page   = Page where the section starts or an individual watch appears

INDEX TO VINTAGE AMERICAN & EUROPEAN
WRIST WATCH GUIDES BOOKS 1, 2, 3, 4 & 87

INDEX TO VINTAGE AMERICAN & EUROPEAN
WRIST WATCH GUIDES BOOKS 1, 2, 3, 4 & 87

INDEX TO VINTAGE AMERICAN & EUROPEAN
WRIST WATCH GUIDES BOOKS 1, 2, 3, 4 & 87

* This total of 13,972 reflects the
  number of different wrist watches
  identified and valued in the five
  (5) books.

This index shows the illustrated contents of the five (5) Wrist Watch Price Guide
Books that were published in 1984, 1987, 1988 & 1989.

This index shows the illustrated contents of the five (5) Wrist Watch Price Guide Books that were published in 1984, 1987, 1988 & 1989.

SUBJECT INDEX TO VINTAGE AMERICAN & EUROPEAN
WRIST WATCH GUIDES BOOKS 1, 2, 3, 4 & 87 UPDATE

This index shows the illustrated contents of the five (5) Wrist Watch Price Guide Books that were published in 1984, 1987, 1988 & 1989.

MAJOR WORLD AUCTION HOUSES

Auction houses play an important role in the wrist watch market. Prices realized at these auctions have a definite effect on values worldwide. Wrist watches have become an important auction item during the past three years.

The auction houses listed here have numerous auctions (2 to 8) per year. They are attended by many dealers and collectors all over the world, and the results are anxiously awaited by many others.

All of the auction houses issue beautiful catalogs (sometimes in color), on a subscription or an individual auction basis. For subscription information and auction dates, write to the addresses listed below.

SOTHEBY PARKE BERNET & CO.
980 Madison Avenue
New York, NY 10021
Telephone (212) 472-3400

Sotheby's Subscription Dept.
P.O. Box 4020
Woburn, MA 01801
Telephone (617) 229-2282

CHRISTIE, MANSON & WOOD LTD.
502 Park Avenue
New York, NY 10022
Telephone (212) 546-1000
Facsimile (212) 980-8163

Christie's Subscription Dept.
21-24 44th Avenue
Long Island City, NY 11101

MULLER & JOSEPH
Bismarckstr. 109
D-4050 Moenchengladbachi
WEST GERMANY
Telephone (011) 49-216-181422
TeleFax (011) 49-2166-25316

UTO AUKTIONEN
Falkenstrasse 12 Beim Opern Haus
CH-8008 Zurich
SWITZERLAND
Telephone (01) 25-25-888

HABSBURG, FELDMAN INC.
Osvaldo Patrizzi
202, route du Grand-Lancy
1213 Onex Geneve
SWITZERLAND
Telephone (022) 57-25-30

Habsburg, Feldman Inc.
36 East 75 Street
New York, NY 10021
Telephone (212) 570-4040
Contact: Claudia Strauss

DR. HELMUT CROTT
Pontstrasse 21-Postfach 146
D-5100 Aachen, WEST GERMANY
Telephone (011)49-241-36900

PHILLIPS, SON AND NEALE
406 E. 79th Street
New York, NY 10021
Telephone (212) 570-4830

Me HERVE' CHAYETTE
12, rue Rossini
75009 Paris, FRANCE
Telephone 770-38-89

KLAUS NIEDHEIDT
Niederdonker Strasse 34
4000 Dusseldorf 11
WEST GERMANY
Telephone (0211) 594401

TABLE OF WATCH SIZES

1 ligne = 2.2559 mm.   1 inch = 25.40005mm.

American Sizes	Fractions of an Inch	Decimal Inches	Millimeters	Swiss Ligne
36/0	0	0.0	0.0	0
26/0	10/30	0.3333	8.46	3–3/4
20/0	16/30	0.533	12.73	6
18/0	18/30	0.600	14.41	6–3/4
16/0	20/30	0.666	16.10	7–1/2
14/0	22/30	0.733	17.78	8–1/4
12/0	24/30	0.800	19.47	9
10/0	26/30	0.8666	21.17	9–3/4
8/0	28/30	0.933	22.86	10–1/2
6/0	1–0	1.000	24.55	11–1/4
4/0	1–2/30	1.066	26.25	12
2/0	1–4/30	1.133	27.94	12–3/4
0	1–5/30	1.166	29.63	13–1/7
2	1–7/30	1.233	31.33	13–9/10
4	1–9/30	1.300	33.02	14–2/3
6	1–11/30	1.366	34.71	15–2/5
8	1–13/30	1.433	36.41	16–1/8
10	1–15/30	1.500	38.10	16–9/10
12	1–17/30	1.566	39.79	17–2/3
14	1–19/30	1.633	41.49	18–2/5
16	1–21/30	1.700	43.18	19–1/7
18	1–23/30	1.766	44.87	19–9/10
20	1–25/30	1.833	46.57	20–2/3

Sizes of Watches: The American sizes are based on 30ths of an inch. The Europeans use the ligne which is equal to .089 inches or 2.255 millimeters. In every case, the diameter is measured across the outside or largest part of the lower plate of the watch, right under the dial. In oval or other odd shaped movements, the size is measured across the smaller axis.

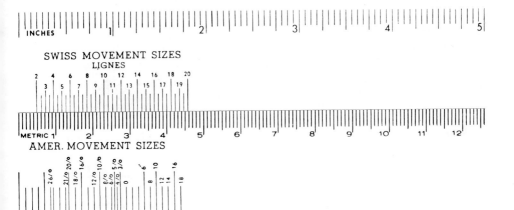

BEGINNING TO END

IDENTIFICATION AND PRICE GUIDE
TO 400,000,000 AMERICAN WATCHES

by
Roy Ehrhardt and William "Bill" Meggers

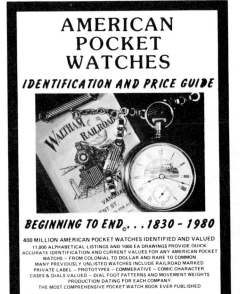

AMERICAN POCKET AND WRIST WATCH BALANCE STAFF INTERCHANGEABILITY LIST

by George E. Townsend

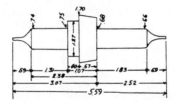

A "MUST HAVE" BOOK FOR
THE WATCHMAKER & COLLECTOR

Over 925 Staff Measurements Including
Manny Trauring's New Balance Staff System

(BS-00-0)

FOR A COPY OF THIS BOOK
SEND $10.00
PLUS 75 CENTS POSTAGE TO

HEART OF AMERICA PRESS
10101 BLUE RIDGE
KANSAS CITY, MISSOURI, 64134

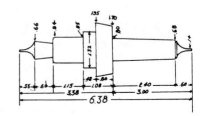

POCKET WATCH BOOKS FROM HEART OF AMERICA PRESS

AMERICAN WATCHES - BEGINNING TO END, ID AND PRICE GUIDE.
Meggers and Ehrhardt 1987, Revolutionizes American Watch Collecting - Identification and prices for 2 million American Pocket Watches, 464 6 x 9 pages, 2 lbs............................$15.00
VINTAGE AMERICAN & EUROPEAN WRIST WATCH PRICE GUIDE
Ehrhardt and Planes, 1984, 336 6 x 9 pages, 2 lbs...$15.00
VINTAGE WRIST WATCH UPDATE 1987
Additional illustrations and prices 60 5 x 8 pages, 6oz...$10.00
VINTAGE AMERICAN & EUROPEAN WRIST WATCH PRICE GUIDE BOOK 2
Ehrhardt & Demesy, 1988, 448 5 x 8, 2 lbs..$25.00
VINTAGE AMERICAN & EUROPEAN WRIST WATCH PRICE GUIDE BOOK 3
Ehrhardt & Mycko 1989 224 6 x 9 Pages, 1 lb..............NEW...$25.00
VINTAGE AMERICAN & EUROPEAN WRIST WATCH PRICE GUIDE BOOK 4
Ehrhardt & Demesy 1969 624 6 x 9 Pages, 2 lbs.........NEW..$25.00
WRIST WATCH PACKAGE: VINTAGE AMERICAN & EUROPEAN WRIST WATCH
PRICE GUIDE BOOKS 1, 2, 3, 4, & 1987. Price update to Book 1 Regular $100.00...............$80.00

AMERICAN POCKET WATCH ENCYCLOPEPIA & PRICE GUIDE. Volume 1
Ehrhardt, 1982, 216 8½x11 pages. 1 lb. 10 oz. June 1982 .... $25.00
ILLINOIS, Volume 2, Ehrhardt & Meggers, 432 8½x11 pages, 2½ lbs. 1985 .... $50.00

AMERICAN POCKET WATCH IDENTIFICATION & PRICE GUIDE, BOOK 2.
Ehrhardt, 1974 **(Prices revised in 1980)** 192, 8½x11 pages. 1 lb. 10 oz. $15.00
FOREIGN & AMERICAN POCKET WATCH IDENTIFICATION & PRICE GUIDE, BOOK 3.
Ehrhardt, 1976, 172 8½x11 pages, 1 lb. 8 oz... **Out Of Print**
1976 POCKET WATCH PRICE INDICATOR. Ehrhardt, 1975, 64 8½x11 pages, 14 oz. .... $ 5.00
1977 POCKET WATCH PRICE INDICATOR. Ehrhardt, 1976, 110 8½x11 pages, 1 lb............. $ 7.00
1978 POCKET WATCH PRICE INDICATOR. Ehrhardt, 1978, 110 8½x11 pages. 1 lb. 2 oz. $10.00
1979 POCKET WATCH PRICE INDICATOR. Ehrhardt, 1979, 110, 8½x11 pages, 1 lb. 2 oz...... $10.00
1980 POCKET WATCH PRICE INDICATOR. Ehrhardt, 1980, 110, 8½x11 pages, 1 lb. 2 oz....... $12.00

AMERICAN POCKET WATCH COMPANIES. (Pocket book with 50 inventory pages).
Ehrhardt, 1979, 96 3½x5½ pages, 2 oz.. $ 3.00
MASTER INDEX TO 13 WATCH BOOKS. (Books published before 1980).
Ehrhardt, 1979, 16 8½x11 pages, 6 oz.. $ 4.00
ELGIN POCKET WATCH IDENTIFICATION & PRICE GUIDE.
Ehrhardt, 1976, 120 8½x11 pages, 1 lb. 2 oz.. $10.00
WALTHAM POCKET WATCH IDENTIFICATION & PRICE GUIDE.
Ehrhardt, 1976, 172 8½x11 pages, 1 lb. 4 oz.. $10.00
HAMILTON POCKET WATCH IDENTIFICATION & PRICE GUIDE.
Ehrhardt, 1976, **(Revised 1981)** 53 8½x11 pages, 1 lb. 4 oz................................ $10.00
ROCKFORD GRADE & SERIAL NUMBERS WITH PRODUCTION FIGURES.
Ehrhardt, 1976, 44 8½x11 pages, 12 oz... $10.00
TRADEMARKS. Ehrhardt, 1976, 128 8½x11 pages, 1 lb. 2 oz. .... **Out Of Print**
THE PRICELESS POSSESSIONS OF A FEW. A brief history of the Gruen Watch Company, their 50th Anniversary Watch, and contemporary watches: Edward Howard - Premier Maximus - C. H. Hurlburd - Lord Elgin - Hamilton Masterpiece. Eugene T. Fuller.
1974, 64 perfect bound pages. 10 oz. .... **Out Of Print**

EVERYTHING YOU WANTED TO KNOW ABOUT AMERICAN WATHCES & DIDN'T KNOW WHO TO ASK.
Col. George E. Townsend, 1971. **(With 1983 Price Guide by Roy Ehrhardt).**
88 6x9 pages, 8 oz... **Out Of Print**
AMERICAN RAILROAD WATCHES. Col. George E. Townsend, 1977.
(With 1983 Price Guide by Roy Ehrhardt). 44 6x9 pages, 8 oz. .... $ 8.00
THE WATCH THAT MADE THE DOLLAR FAMOUS. Col. George E. Townsend, 1974.
(With 1983 Price Guide by Ralph Whitmer). 45 6x9 pages, 8 oz......................... $ 8.00
SET OF 3 PRICE GUIDES TO TOWNSEND BOOKS (for books bought before 1983).........$ 9.00

POCKET WATCH BOOKS

E. HOWARD & CO. WATCHES 1858-1903. The last word on Howard watches: Identification-Production-Price Guide, Col. George E. Townsend, Author. **(With Price Guide by Roy Ehrhardt).** 1983. This manuscript was ready for publication when Col. Townsend died. The Price Guide was written by Roy Ehrhardt. 48 8½x11 paperback, 6 oz.. **$ 8.00**

AMERICAN POCKET & WRIST WATCH BALANCE STAFF INTERCHANGEABILITY LIST. Col. George E. Townsend, 1986, 925 Staff Measurements 8½x11 pages, 1 lb. **$10.00**

CLOCK BOOKS

CLOCK IDENTIFICATION & PRICE GUIDE, BOOK 1. Ehrhardt & Rabeneck, 1977. **(Prices revised in 1979).** 198 8½x11 pages, 1 lb. 12 oz. **$15.00**

CLOCK IDENTIFICATION & PRICE GUIDE, BOOK 2. Ehrhardt & Rabeneck, 1979. 192 8½x11 perfect bound pages, 1 lb. 8 oz. **$15.00**

CLOCK INDENTIFICATION & PRICE GUIDE, BOOK 3. Ehrhardt & Rabeneck, 1983. 203 8½x11 perfect bound pages, 1 lb. 8 oz. **$15.00**

(All three clock books contain different clocks. You need all three to have a complete library.)

F. KROEBER CLOCK CO. IDENTIFICATION & PRICE GUIDE. Ehrhardt & Rabeneck, 1983. 36 8½x11 pages, 8 oz. .... **$ 8.00**

VIOLIN BOOKS

VIOLIN IDENTIFICATION & PRICE GUIDE, BOOK 1. Ehrhardt & Atchley, 1977. 192 8½x11 pages, 1lb. 10 oz. **$25.00**

VIOLIN IDENTIFICATION & PRICE GUIDE, BOOK 2. Ehrhardt & Atchley, 1978. 206 8½x11 pages, 1 lb. 10 oz. **$25.00**

MISCELLANEOUS BOOKS

AMERICAN COLLECTOR DOLLS PRICE GUIDE BOOK 1. S. Ehrhardt & D. Westbrook, 1975. 128 8½x11 pages, 1 lb. 2 oz. .... **$ 9.00**

AMERICAN CUT GLASS PRICE GUIDE. (Revised 1977). Alpha Ehrhardt 120 8½x11 pages, 1 lb. 2 oz. .... **$ 7.00**

POCKET KNIFE BOOK 1 & 2 PRICE GUIDE. (Revised 1977). J. Ferrell & R. Ehrhardt. 128 8½x11 pages, 1 lb. 2 oz. .... **$ 7.00**

The books listed on these two pages are sold on a satisfaction guarantee. If you are not sure about the books you want, send a self-addressed, stamped envelope and we will send you detailed brochures on all of the publications. For orders in the U. S. send the price of the book plus $2.00 UPS (United Parcel Service) for the first book and 50 cents for each additional. C.O.D. $3.25 Extra.

Foreign countries—Check with your post office for rate, uour choice, Air or Sea Mail, Book Rate. Book and carton weights listed.

Foreign Postage Sea Mail (2 lbs. $4.00 US)
Foreign Postage Air Mail (2 lbs. $10.00 US)
Canada & Mexico (2 lbs. Land $3.75)
United States of North America (2 lbs. $2.00)
Send your Check or Money Order (US Funds)
C.O.D. $3.25 Extra

Send orders to:
HEART OF AMERICA PRESS
10101 Blue Ridge Blvd.
Kansas City, MO 64134
(816) 761-0080

We sell reliable information

AN INVITATION FROM ROY EHRHARDT

TEMPUS VITAM REGIT

THE NATIONAL ASSOCIATION OF WATCH AND CLOCK COLLECTORS, INC.
BOX 33, 514 POPLAR STREET, COLUMBIA, PA 17512

This non-profit, scientific and educational corporation was founded in 1943 to bring together people who are interested in timekeeping in any form or phase. More than 33,000 members now enjoy its benefits. The Headquarters, Museum and Library are located in the Borough of Columbia on the eastern bank of the Susquehanna River within historic Lancaster County, Pennsylvania, where a continuing heritage of clock and watch-making spans two and one-quarter centuries.

Some of the tangible benefits of membership are the Association's publications. The bi-monthly **Bulletin** is the world's leading publication devoted to timekeeping. It contains papers written by members on technical and historic aspects of horology. Through its "Answer Box" column it also provides the member with an opportunity to direct his "knotty" horological problems to a panel of fifty volunteer authorities from around the world, many of whom are authors of definitive works in their respective areas of interest. Reviews help the collector keep abreast with the ever growing number of horological publications. Activities of the more than 100 Chapters located around the world are also included as are listings of stolen items. The **Mart,** also bi-monthly, is an informal medium in which members may list items that they wish to buy, trade, or sell. Like the **Bulletin,** its circulation exceeds 33,000. Other publications include the **Roster of Members,** a listing of books available through the Association's Lending Library, and occasional papers meriting separate publication.

Another benefit of membership is the use of the Nation's largest collection of books devoted to timekeeping. A number of the titles are duplicated in the Lending Library and may be borrowed through the mail for merely the cost of postage and, on occasion, insurance. The Library is under the supervision of a professional librarian who will also help a member in his research. A visitor can study the various horological periodicals of many sister horological associations around the world. The serious researcher may also examine rare and early works concerning horology. The Nation's only computerized Horological Data Bank is at the member's disposal as are thousands of American patents dealing with timekeeping.

Free admission to the NAWCC Museum in Columbia for both the member and his immediate family is yet another benefit. The Museum offers a rare opportunity to examine a collection of watches, clocks, tools, and other related items which range from the primitive to the modern. The "how and why" of timekeeping is emphasized throughout whether the display be of early non-mechanical timepieces or of the highly sophisticated "Atomic Clock." Movements of wood, iron, and brass are displayed for study. Many of the items exhibited are becoming increasingly rare and beyond the reach of many private collectors. Two special exhibitions are mounted each year: a three-month winter exhibition and a six-month summer exhibition. Items included in the special exhibitions are drawn from the collections of members, friends, and other museums.

Membership in the National Association also makes one eligible for membership in one or more of the more than 100 Chapters located in the United States, Australia, Canada, England, and Japan. It also makes one eligible to register for the regularly scheduled regional and national meetings each year. Chapter, regional, and national meetings usually consist of seminars, exhibits, and an opportunity to improve the member's own collection through trading, buying, or selling to other members. Finally, membership can enable a person to form lasting friendships with some of the finest people in the world: timekeeper enthusiasts!

It is easy to become a member of the NAWCC, Inc. Send the following information with your check or money order to the above address.

Name_____

(please print clearly)   **Dues**

Street_____ U.S. $25.00

City_____ State_____ZIP_____

Occupation_____Telephone( )_____

Have you ever been a member? YES____NO____ If "Yes," please give number _____

Sponsor_____*Roy Ehrhardt*_____ **NAWCC No.** ____*23096*____

Street_*P.O. Box 9808*____ City_*K. C.*___State_*MO*_ZIP _*64134*_

BOOKS

JEWELERS' CIRCULAR-KEYSTONE, NOVEMBER 1984

Versatile handbook

Vintage American & European Wrist Watch Price Guide, by Sherry Ehrhardt and Peter Planes. 333 pages. 1900 illustrations. 1984. soft cover. (Jewelers' Book Club CF-031)

Inspecting this book carefully, one observes that it has been put together very nicely. Almost 2000 wrist watches are illustrated in alphabetical order according to name brand. The index is in the front, as is a six-page glossary. A few introductory pages explain how the au-

thors arrived at the stated values. Another few pages illustrate and explain all types of chronographs.

Until three or four years ago, few, if any, wrist watches were pictured or offered in auction catalogs. Today, such catalogs from all over the world feature many pages of them.

True, wrist watches do not fetch the high prices commanded by more ancient, heavier pocket watches with multiple services and tour de force execution. However, the wrist watch lends itself to countless variations in shape, construction and miniaturization.

Some very ordinary wrist watches of the early 1930s have a current value of only $2 or $3. But some early self-winding types bring a premium, as do gold ones with heavy gold bracelets, not to mention those super-exotic status brands, embellished with diamond-studded cases and bracelets in the four- and five-figure price range.

Wrist watches with moon phases invariably create spirited bidding at auctions. So do perpetual calendar, minute-repeating and skeletonized types.

The book includes early electronics, the tuning-forked Accutrons and Pulsar, the first solid state watch, each pictured with the offers it might bring at an auction or watch mart sale. Eight-day, comic strip character, jump-hour, navigational, chronometer, mystery, yachting, alarm, military and railroad-approved watches also are pictured and priced, together with those with reserve power indicators and universal time dials.

Most of the illustrations are from original sales and advertising art. Many lesser-known wrist watches are missing, but these are minor items which probably have not yet shown up for sale or been observed by the authors.

The book is featured as a price guide, but its encyclopedic coverage makes it also a versatile handbook.—Henry B. Fried, JC-K horological editor; Jewelers' Book Club Judge.

ISBN 0-913902-51-9 $15.00

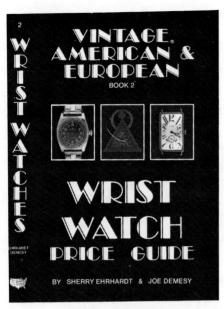

Auctioneer
Dr. Helmut Crott

P.O. BOX 146 — PONTSTR. 21
D-5100 AACHEN — WEST GERMANY
TEL. 011-49-(0241)-37606

EXPERTS ON HIGH GRADE OR IMPORTANT
EUROPEAN CLOCKS, WRIST OR POCKET WATCHES
GERMANY IS THE PLACE TO SELL THEM

WHEN YOU HAVE AN IMPORTANT
EUROPEAN WATCH OR CLOCK
TO SELL OR CONSIGN GET IN TOUCH WITH ME.

Representative for
**UNITED STATES, ENGLAND,
CANADA, WEST GERMANY**
Dr. Helmut Crott, Auctioneer
P.O. Box 146 - Pontstr. 21
D-5100 Aachen - West Germany
Tel. 011-49-241-36900

*SEE ME IN PERSON AT
ALL THE MAJOR NAWCC REGIONAL
SHOWS AND AUCTIONS IN THE
UNITED STATES, LONDON,
HONG KONG, AND GENEVA*
OR
I WILL COME TO YOUR CITY BY APPOINTMENT

Representative for
BELGIUM
Frau E. Hock-Fuhrer
Ave. Rogier 10
B-4000 Liege
Tel. (32) (41) 23 08 23

BUYING — SELLING — TRADING — APPRAISAL
BROKERS — AUCTION
FUTURE AUCTION DATES AND
CATALOGS ARE AVAILABLE
BY PHONE OR POST

Representative for
HONG KONG
Herr Manfred Schoeni
G/F 8 Staunton Street
Hong Kong
Tel. 5-255225

Representative for
SINGAPORE
Volker von Knobloch
Eurasaf Pte Ltd.
9 Battery Road 14-03
Straits Trading Building
Singapur 0104
Telex: 21830 - Tel: 2225026

Representative for
SWITZERLAND
Frau E. Meier-Solfrain
Dufourstr. 34
CH-8702 Zollikon-Zurich
Tel. (41) (1) 391 2424

Representative for
ITALY
Frau N. Marotta
Via Camerona 6
I-28065 Cerano/Novara
Tel. (39) (321) 72 65 32

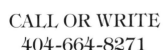

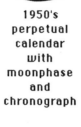

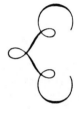

Steve Campbell

CANADA'S LARGEST VINTAGE WATCH DEALER

WANTED

YOUR FINE EUROPEAN AND AMERICAN
WRIST OR POCKET WATCHES
FOR MY RETAIL MARKET

LeCoultre
Jules Jurgensen
Concord
Adolph Lange
Pigaet
Patek Phillippe
Audemars Piguet
Cartier
Rolex Prince (Doctors)
Vacheron-Constantine

Chronographs
Moon Phase Calendar
Bubble Backs
Jump Hour
Split Seconds
Repeaters
Doctors Duo-Dial
Eatons ¼ Century Club

ALSO BUYING
Vintage and
Contemporary

Coins
Jewelery
Automobiles
Musical Instruments

Anything Nice or Unusual in
Gold, Platinum or Diamonds

CHARLESTON CLOCKS & WATCHES
102 Lakeshore Road East
Toronto, Canada LG5 IE3
Office: 416-274-0913
Home: 416-274-6683

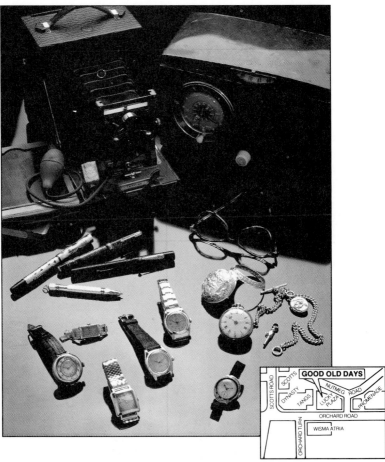

IT'S TIME!

PURCHASING FINE, HIGH QUALITY
WRISTWATCHES:

**PATEK PHILIPPE,
CARTIER, ROLEX,
VACHERON & CONSTANTIN,
AUDEMARS PIGUET,
GUBELIN, IWC,
MOVADO, LECOULTRE.**

MOONPHASE, CALENDAR,
CHRONOGRAPH, REPEATING
FUNCTIONS ESPECIALLY DESIRABLE.

**WE OFFER EXTREMELY
HIGH PRICES AND SPEEDY
PAYMENT.**

Burt Finger
817/382-3417

IT'S TIME!

207 W. HICKORY
SUITE 107
DENTON, TX 76201

**CALL US LAST.
TOLL-FREE
1-800-284-4042**

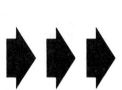

RON STARNES ENTERPRISES

BUY - SELL - TRADE

Wrist Watches,
Pocket Watches,
Diamonds, Jewelery.
Antique and Classic Cars

CALL FOR FAIR PRICES
& HONEST DEALINGS

By Appointment Only

918-663-7326   Tulsa, OK

WANTED:

Patek Phillippe - Rolex
- Vacheron Constantine -

Buying Complete Watches,
movements, cases, & bands.

CALL FOR ESTIMATE

DAVID B. SEARLES II
Rare Watches

University Place, Harvard Square
124 Mt. Auburn Street, Suite 200
Cambridge, MA 02138
By Appointment only 1-617-576-5810

I am actively buying and selling both
pocket and wrist watches of all types:

Patek Philippe
Vacheron and Constantin
Audemars Piguet
Rolex
Cartier
Moonphase Calendar
Repeaters
Rare Escapements
Technical Watches
Fine Enamels
Early American
Railroad Watches
Jules Jurgensen
Adolf Lange

Please contact me at any time should you
wish to sell or purchase, or should you need
evaluation of single pieces or entire
collections.

EVERYBODY'S GOING TO CLOCK AUCTIONS by Col. Glen La Rue

Specializing in:
Clocks
Antiques in General
Coins
Aladdin Lamps
Tools
Furniture
Glass
Collector's Items
Horses

All Types of Sales:
Estate Auctions
Dispersal Sales
Stock Reductions
Bankruptcy Sales
Retirement Sales
Moving Sales
Collections Sold
Real Estate
Farm Machinery

Large Mailing Lists — Extensive Following — Good Reputation

Save Yourself the Work & Worry — We Handle All Details — 20 Years Experience

Let Us Sell Your Prized Possessions!

La Rue Auction Service
Col. Glen La Rue, Auctioneer
Sweet Springs, MO 65351
816-335-4538

"I do my homework so that I know what I'm selling."

Equipped to handle anything — any time — anywhere!

Vintage Wrist Watches
Bought and Sold
Frederick E. Mayer

NAWCC # 087082

Specializing in
Fine Timepieces
Also Interested In Purchasing
Estate Jewelry - Diamonds
& Coin Collections

P.O. Box 17049
Pittsburgh, PA 15235
Mobile Phone
412-551-3457

412-241-3600 or 412-621-4455
Professional & Confidential

Atlanta Connection

To

HEART OF AMERICA PRESS

Sherry Ehrhardt-La Noue

Selling and Preparing

ADVERTISING

in the

NEXT EDITION

of

Vintage Wrist Watch Price Guide

CALL OR WRITE   **404/664-8271**

8825 Roswell Road
Suite 496
Atlanta, Georgia 30350

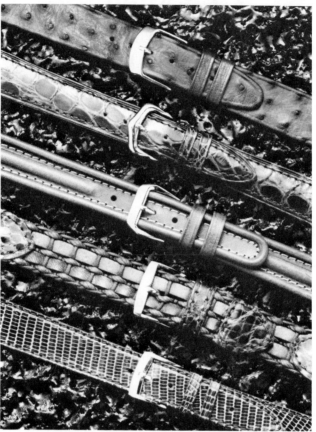

The largest collection of vintage timepieces in America

Collector's Catalog: $10/annual subscription. (Four issues per year)

AARON FABER GALLERY

666 FIFTH AVENUE (ENT. ON 53RD ST.) NEW YORK, NY 10019   212-586-8411

BUYING: MEN'S VINTAGE WRISTWATCHES
Call (214) 245-1096

I will top any legitimate offer you receive
on any of these makes and types:

PATEK Philippe	Movado	EWC	Hamilton	Jump Hours
Vacheron & Constantin	Tiffany	Universal Geneve	Gruen	Reversos
Cartier	Breitling	Record	Chronographs	Duo-Dials
Rolex	Longines	I.W.C.	Curvexes	Triple-Calendars
Le Coultre	Gubelin	Gallet	Moonphases	Military Watches
				World-Time Zone

Any unusual gold-filled wrist watches
Any oversized watches
Patek/Vacheron Pocket Watches/Automaton Erotica Pockets

CALL - SHIP OR WRITE TODAY

We will pay 5%-10% more than anybody for High Grade, Complicated or Unusual Wristwatches.

ESPECIALLY WANTED LIST:

	PAYING
LeCoultre Memovox GF/s. Steel	$125 - $225
LeCoultre Memovox 14K - 18K (Waterproof)	$800 - $1300
LeCoultre Futurematics GF/14K	$125 - $550
Lord Elgin Direct Reading GF	$175 - $250
Any Movado Chronographs	CALL
Breitling Navitimers GF/SS	$425 - $550
Rolex Stainless Steel Daytona Cosmographs	$1700 - $2100
Gruen Curvexes 50MM GF	$500 yo
Gruen Duo Dial Jump Hour in Steel	$3000
Any Steel - 14K - 18K World-Time Zone	CALL
Any Unusual Illinois	Ship with best price
Accumulation of Movements, Dials, Cases	Ship any amount

TO SELL YOUR WRIST WATCHES/COINS:
CALL: (214) 245-1096
Monday - Saturday
10:00 A.M. - 6 P.M.

SHIP Your watches to:
DON MEYER VINTAGE
TIMEPIECES WORLDWIDE
1818 N. I-35 E. Suite 100
Carrollton, TX 75006

Pack securely and ship via: Federal Express, Express Mail (Post Office), UPS next day air, registered or insured mail. Include your name, address and phone # and we'll call you upon receipt (if necessary) to finalize a price. (97% of all our offers are accepted.)

PAYMENT: Check, Cash or Bank Wire YOUR CHOICE!
ALL SHIPMENTS ARE PROCESSED AND PAID FOR THE SAME DAY AS RECEIVED.

Reference: Deposit Guaranty Bank, Rowlett (214) 475-3232
JOYCE CUMMINGS (Assistant Vice President/Sales Mgr)
* * * SEND A SASE FOR OUR BI-MONTHLY ILLUSTRATED PRICE LIST * * *